THE AEROBICS PROGRAM FOR TOTAL WELL-BEING

Other books by Kenneth H. Cooper, M.D.

AEROBICS

THE NEW AEROBICS

AEROBICS FOR WOMEN
(with Mildred Cooper)

THE AEROBICS WAY

THE AEROBICS PROGRAM FOR TOTAL WELL-BEING

EXERCISE • DIET • EMOTIONAL BALANCE

KENNETH H. COOPER, M.D., M.P.H.

BANTAM BOOKS

TORONTO · NEW YORK · LONDON · SYDNEY · AUCKLAND

DEDICATION

This book is dedicated to my Brazilian friend and colleague, Claudio Coutinho, who will be remembered not only as one of the great soccer coaches of all time, but as the one who, more than any other person, was responsible for introducing aerobics to the world.

THE AEROBICS PROGRAM FOR TOTAL WELL-BEING
A Bantam Book / published by arrangement with
M. Evans & Co., Inc.

PRINTING HISTORY

M. Evans edition published November 1982
A Selection of The Literary Guild of America
"Super Foods for Super Health" from chapters 5 and 9 serialized in Glamour, November 1982; "Aerobic Update" from chapters 6 and 9 serialized in Runner's World, January and February 1983; "Four Steps to Starting an Exercise Program" appeared in Vogue, October 1982.

The Calorie Equivalents for Popular Foods and Beverages list in the Appendix contains material from Food Values of Portions Commonly Used, Thirteenth Edition, revised by Jean A. T. Pennington, and Helen Nichols Church. Copyright © 1980 by Helen Nichols Church, B.S., and Jean A. T. Pennington, Ph.D., R.D. Reprinted by permission of Harper & Row, Publishers, Inc.

The Fat-Cholesterol Chart in the Appendix is reprinted with permission from the American Heart Association Cookbook, New Expanded Edition. Copyright © 1975 American Heart Association, Inc. Published by David McKay Company, Inc.

The list of Sports Medicine Clinics in the Appendix is reprinted with permission from Running & Fitness, a publication of the American Running & Fitness Association. Copyright © 1982 American Running & Fitness Association.

Bantam edition / September 1983

Library of Congress Cataloging in Publication Data

Cooper, Kenneth H.
  The aerobics program for total well-being.
  Bibliography: p. 310
  Includes index.
  1. Aerobic exercises. 2. Physical fitness.
I. Title.
RA781.15.C657 1982   613.7' 1   82-16361

ISBN 0-553-34018-2

Published simultaneously in the United States and Canada

Bantam Books are published by Bantam Books, Inc. Its trademark, consisting of the words "Bantam Books" and the portrayal of a rooster, is Registered in U.S. Patent and Trademark Office and in other countries. Marca Registrada. Bantam Books, Inc., 666 Fifth Avenue, New York, New York 10103.

PRINTED IN THE UNITED STATES OF AMERICA

B   0   9   8   7   6   5   4

CONTENTS

PREFACE

As readers of previous aerobics books know, the major emphasis always has been one of increasing physical activity. Yet, as we have become more knowledgeable in this field, it is obvious that total well-being is dependent upon much more than just regular exercise. At one time, I felt that a good program could compensate for poor health habits and was guilty of saying that exercise can overcome many if not all of the deleterious effects of diet. If a person was smoking and carrying a few extra pounds, I was not overly concerned, as long as he or she exercised regularly—and I still am convinced that exercise helps normalize bad health habits. Yet, it was brought to my attention in far too many cases, that overweight people and those who smoke developed severe progressive arteriosclerosis and heart disease, even though they were running regularly. In these cases, exercise probably delayed the disease process and may have helped in prolonging their lives, but it was not totally protective. To my knowledge, there is still nothing known to man that is completely protective against coronary heart disease—medicine, surgery, or even marathon running.

Another principle emphasized throughout this book is one of moderation. The old concept that "if something is good, more of it is better" is seriously questioned whether it be fastidious dieting or ultramarathoning. The statement "if you are running more than 3 miles, 5 times per week, you are running for something other than fitness" will surprise many previous readers of the aerobics books. Yet, during the past 10 years, it has been possible to identify thresholds of physical activity beyond which there is a beneficial change in the cardiovascular system as well as the level of activity at which there are detrimental effects. I predict that the scientific data used to document these thresholds will be too impressive to be ignored.

We have only scratched the surface in the fields of health maintenance and preventive medicine, and as more embrace these concepts, both the quality and quantity of life will substantially improve. It has been said that when a person dies, he dies not so much of the particular disease as of his entire life. With proper motivation, education, and implementation, that can be changed. However, all that I can do in this book is help in the education and motivation; you the reader must be responsible for the implementation.

To complete this plan for total well-being, I would be grossly negligent if I did not emphasize the most important component, that is spiritual well-being. "For bodily exercise profiteth little: but godliness is profitable unto all things, having promise of the life that now is, and of that which is to come" [1 Timothy 4:8 Authorized (King James) Version].

Even though there is no way I can guarantee that anyone who follows the principles outlined in this book will live one day longer, I can assure them that the lives that they will live will be happier, healthier, and more productive. If those goals are achieved, my purpose in writing *The Aerobics Program for Total Well-Being* will have been accomplished.

Kenneth H. Cooper, M.D.
DALLAS, TEXAS

ACKNOWLEDGMENTS

If it were not for the assistance, support, and encouragement of many people, this book could not have been written. To adequately acknowledge all of those who in some way contributed, would require all of the pages of this book. Yet, a few were invaluable, including Bill Proctor who assisted extensively in the preparation of the manuscript, as did Mrs. Laurana Allen in the typing. Many of the staff of the Aerobics Center made major contributions, including Ms. Georgia Kostas, Cooper Clinic Nutritionist; Mr. Mike Smith, Director of Computer Services for the Institute for Aerobics Research; and my able assistant, Mr. Harold Burkhalter. Ms. Kostas worked extensively on the preparation of the diets and the information in the nutrition chapters, and Mr. Smith helped in the updating of the aerobics point charts as well as the point derivation equations. The editorial advice of Herb Katz was of immense value, as was the understanding and patience of George de Kay. Last, but certainly not least, was the faithful support and encouragement of my wife Millie and the understanding of our two wonderful children, Berkley and Tyler.

PART ONE

THE BALANCE PRINCIPLE

1

What Is Total Well-Being?

One of the great principles of the universe is the principle of balance. If the earth were a few miles closer to the sun, it would be an inferno. If it were a few miles farther away, it would be a desolate, frigid desert. But in its present location, balanced at an ideal distance from the sun, our planet is in a perfect position to sustain an exciting proliferation of life forms.

The atoms that are the basic building blocks of all matter on earth are another example of this perfect balance. The nucleus of the atom is made up of neutrons and protons, an incredibly harmonious organization. Yet, it is through the splitting of one of these atoms that the cataclysmic eruptions of nuclear power take place. To function properly, every part of our world, no matter how miniscule, must be in a state of complete equilibrium.

And so it is with our bodies.

The human body is just another part of the universe that is meant to be in perfect balance. We have been constructed in such a way that we need just so much exercise, no more and no less. We need just so much food of certain types. And we need just the right amount of sleep and relief from the tensions and stresses of daily life.

If a person goes too far in either direction—too little *or* too much exercise, food, or rest—then his or her entire physical and psychological system gets out of kilter. And where there is a lack of balance, there is also a lack of personal well-being.

By the same token, on the positive side, where there is balance, there is a sense of well-being. And where there is perfect balance, there is what I call *total well-being.*

I have been exploring this principle in great detail recently in my research at the Aerobics Center in Dallas, Texas. And my growing conviction about the overwhelming importance of this principle of total well-being through balanced living is what has prompted me to write this book.

Even as my other books on aerobic exercise have been selling in the millions, and while many countries have been implementing the concepts in those books, our physicians and medical researchers at the Aerobics Center have continued their explorations of the frontiers of preventive medicine. We have studied and worked with thousands of patients and are now ready to present our latest findings to you in this book.

And let me say this right at the outset: I believe that our most recent conclusions about what it takes to be in a perfect state of physical balance, or a state of total well-being, are more important for your present and future happiness than anything I've ever written before. In short, I'm convinced that if you embark on a personal quest to achieve total well-being—a quest which will be outlined in detail in this book—you'll begin to enjoy an exciting array of personal benefits that you may have assumed could never possibly be yours.

Just to give you a taste of what can happen in your life, here are some of the benefits of total well-being that data from our research have shown us can be yours for the asking:

- More personal energy;
- More enjoyable and active leisure time;
- Greater ability to handle domestic and job-related stress;
- Less depression, less hypochondria, and less "free-floating" anxiety;
- Fewer physical complaints;
- More efficient digestion and fewer problems with constipation;
- A better self-image and more self-confidence;
- A more attractive, streamlined body, including more effective personal weight control;
- Bones of greater strength;
- Slowing of the aging process;
- Easier pregnancy and childbirth;
- More restful sleep;
- Better concentration at work, and greater perseverance in all daily tasks;
- Fewer aches and pains, including back pains.

This list could go on and on, but I think you get the point. In short, the achievement of total well-being can completely transform your life and make you a happier, more productive person.

But now, in more specific terms, what's the formula for reaching this state of total well-being?

Our extensive research at the Aerobics Center has convinced me that there are three basic human needs that must be satisfied if you hope to achieve the overall balance that is a necessary prerequisite for total well-being. As the word "balance" implies, these needs must be met in a way that will keep your body and mind in harmonious equilibrium. I've referred briefly to these needs before, but now let me mention them again in a little more detail because they comprise the backbone of what I'll be saying throughout the book.

BASIC NEED #1: AEROBIC EXERCISE

The term "aerobic" means "living in air" or "utilizing oxygen." But this word hasn't always been understood particularly well.

For example, shortly after my first book was published, I was asked to speak on the subject of aerobic exercise, or "aerobics." Unfortunately, though, the reporter who wrote up the announcement about the lecture in the local newspaper wasn't familiar with exercise concepts. So when I arrived, I learned that he had said, in effect, "Be sure to come and hear Dr. Kenneth Cooper talk about aerobics, the bacteria that utilize oxygen."

Needless to say, that is not my definition of aerobics.

Aerobic exercises refer to those activities that require oxygen for prolonged periods and place such demands on the body that it is required to improve its capacity to handle oxygen. As a result of aerobic exercise, there are beneficial changes that occur in the lungs, the heart, and the vascular system. More specifically, regular exercise of this type enhances the ability of the body to move air into and out of the lungs; the total blood volume increases; and the blood becomes better equipped to transport oxygen.

Aerobic exercises usually involve endurance activities which don't require excessive speed. In fact, when recommending various kinds of aerobic exercise, I always stress that it's better to use long, slow distances (or "L.S.D.") than it is to rely on short, fast bursts of energy.

But at the heart of any effective aerobic exercise program is the basic principle of balance. For example, most people should achieve a balance in terms of the distances they cover during any exercise period. Recent research has shown that unless a person is training for marathons or other competitive events, it's best to limit running to around 12 to 15 miles per week. More than that will greatly increase the incidence of joint and bone injuries and other ailments; on the other hand, less mileage will fail to achieve the desired improvement in the body.

If you run more than 15 miles per week, you are running for something other than fitness and the emotional balance, good health, and good looks that accompany it. You may be running to prepare for competition or to prove something to yourself if you go for long mileage, but you're not running for basic fitness!

One of the most startling examples of the importance of getting out of your seat and getting *some* exercise, no matter how ill-suited to exercise you think you are, involved one of my women patients. She came into my office with terrible back pains—so terrible that she could not walk farther than 75 to 100 yards before the pains forced her to stop.

As you might expect, all her activities and social outings were severely limited because of her disability.

I'll admit that at first, I advised surgery as the best approach to her problem, which was the result of pressure on a nerve from a lumbar disc. But she refused surgery; and after watching what exercise had done for some of our patients at the Aerobics Center, she decided to cast aside her sedentary ways and elected to try exercise herself.

On her own, she experimented with walking on a treadmill, and soon discovered that she could walk without pain when the treadmill belt was tilted up to a certain incline. The more she walked over a period of several weeks, the less pain she experienced. Soon, she found she could lower the incline on the treadmill more and more, until finally she was walking on a flat surface—and without any pain for the first time in months.

Next, she started some slow jogging with her walking routine, and eventually began jogging continuously from 3, to 5, to 10 miles at each outing. As this book goes to press, this 46-year-old woman has run nine marathons, with her best time being 3:03 hours—a great time for a woman or man of any age!

In this woman's case, then, we have a person who had developed problems with her back, probably as a secondary reaction to the combined problem of poor muscular tone and an old injury. She didn't have any dietary or other problems, but her physical system was out of balance because of her failure or inability to engage in sufficient muscular activity. But when her body regained its balance, she was freed to undertake all sorts of physical activities that had been denied her before. The balance achieved by exercise enabled her to reach a state of total well-being for the first time in years.

In my opinion, this principle of balance through physical activity simply reflects what the human body was originally intended to do. Think back on what you know about early men and women (and people living in traditional societies today). Physically, they were quite active, with the hunters in the band often running miles to track down game and the tribe members at the campsite gathering wood, picking berries, and otherwise constantly moving about.

Also, tales abound of the feats of the American Indians, who might run hundreds of miles, with little time for rest, to deliver messages from one tribe to another. We might assume that they were unbalanced toward too much exercise, just as we sometimes tend to be unbalanced in the other direction. But their bodies were conditioned to operate at maximum performance over the long haul—for days at a time—and to achieve physical heights that seem almost superhuman when compared with our own meager powers of strength and endurance.

Granted, we have made great "progress" in terms of science and technology. And some would also argue that we've come a long way in developing more civilized political and social systems. But in the area of physical endurance and personal energy, I think we've fallen light years behind our forebears.

In our time, despite the upsurge in concern about the well-being and appearance of our bodies, *most* people are employed in sedentary office jobs. They walk from the parking lot or bus stop to the office, and from their desk to the water cooler or company cafeteria. Except for occasional bursts of tennis or golf on the weekends, that's about the extent of their physical activity. And this lack of physical activity very likely puts a relatively low ceiling on their potential in the other pursuits of life. That, of course, was the problem with my patient until she decided to do something about it.

But as I've indicated, I don't believe our bodies were constructed for such a lack of exercise, and the latest medical research supports my belief. We know now that exercise helps a person develop stronger bones, a more positive mental attitude, better circulation, and greater protection against heart disease. So it seems to me that once we begin to recapture some of the physical activity of primitive people—activity which our bodies and minds desperately need in order to function properly—we'll be well on the road to achieving total well-being.

BASIC NEED #2: A POSITIVE EATING PLAN (P.E.P.)

I should say right here that I have nothing against the word "diet." But because the idea of a diet has sometimes been associated with a short-term crash program to achieve weight loss, our nutritionist has developed a concept at the Aerobics Center called the Positive Eating Plan, or P.E.P. Our P.E.P. approach stresses the development of eating habits that are designed to last for a lifetime, and that's a goal I'd like you to work toward in your own life.

As with aerobic exercise, the fundamental principle that lies behind good eating habits is balance. If you find, after reading this book, that you need to lose some weight, you don't have to cut out every one of your favorite foods or go on some lopsided fad diet. Instead, we'll show you ways to keep a tasty balance in your daily menus even as you reduce the calories you consume.

One rather dramatic example of what can happen if a person's diet and weight are out of balance involved a 48-year-old businessman. He had been running distances of 3 to 6 miles, several times a week, for at least 8 years, and he was extremely regular about his exercise program.

As might be expected, his high level of fitness showed up on the various exams we gave him: On the treadmill stress test, for example, he always scored in the excellent to superior categories for a man his age.

As a matter of fact, he was in such good shape that after the last stress test we gave him, he ran several long-distance races, and in October, 1980 he completed the New York City Marathon. In addition to this rigorous running regimen, he also did stationary cycling for 45-minute sessions, one to two times a week.

But despite this devotion to aerobic exercise, he ignored some key factors that were necessary to keep his body in good balance. For one thing, he ignored his weight, which stayed consistently 15 to 20 pounds above what we had determined to be his ideal weight. He just ate more or less what he wanted, believing that exercise could overcome many, if not all, of the deleterious effects of diet. Consequently, he was not concerned about the quality of his food or the "spare tire" he carried around his middle.

Also, he made the mistake of thinking he didn't need to undergo regular medical exams. I've always insisted that to maintain and monitor the body's balance, it's necessary to make regular visits to see a trained, objective observer—a specialist in preventive medicine. But he did not agree. He told me, "I couldn't have heart disease and run the way I run." So he allowed nearly 7 years to elapse between his physicals.

And for this lack of balance in his life, he paid the price by losing the well-being that he was so certain was firmly within his grasp. He suffered a severe heart attack while overseas, but fortunately received immediate, effective medical treatment and survived. His recovery has been slow but progressive and it is hoped that he will not require bypass surgery.

So in this case, regular running simply wasn't enough to ensure total well-being. If his weight, diet, and regularity of physical examinations had only been in proper balance, he would likely still be as healthy today as he seemed to be on his first visit to our clinic.

Finally, another extremely important area of balance as far as your food is concerned, involves cholesterol, the waxy substance in body tissues that has been associated with hardening of the arteries and serious heart disease. Cholesterol is an essential substance in our systems, and we certainly wouldn't want to try to do away with it entirely. But our research at the Aerobics Center and at related laboratories and clinics demonstrates, once again, that with cholesterol as with anything else, balance is the key to good health.

We now have good reason to believe that it's not the total amount of cholesterol in your body that is the health hazard, but rather the *lack of a proper balance* between two different types of cholesterol—the so-called "good cholesterol," high-density lipoprotein, or HDL, and "bad cholesterol," low-density lipoprotein, or LDL. (We'll be using these terms, HDL and LDL, frequently throughout the book. You will want to memorize them, not only for your future reading, but in order to be able to discuss your cholesterol levels intelligently with your doctor.) As we'll see later, a person's diet can be a key factor in striking the proper balance with the body's cholesterol.

BASIC NEED #3: EMOTIONAL EQUILIBRIUM

With the stresses and strains of modern life, increasing numbers of people are expressing a need to find the way to lasting inner peace, freedom from anxiety, and the solution to other emotional problems. Everybody desperately wants to feel relaxed and happy about life, and to possess the extra reserves of energy that often accompany this sort of emotional equilibrium. But there is a constant tendency for minds and emotions under pressure to get out of balance—perhaps to swing like a psychological pendulum toward excessive concern for some personal problem, or to fall victim to unusual fatigue or lack of energy.

Periodically, most of us lose our emotional equilibrium, with the result that our energy levels drop and our drive to achieve and excel begins to flag. When that happens, the solution to the emotional problems may lie in something as simple as a need for more rest or sleep. Or the answer may lie in one of the first two "basic needs for balance"— aerobic exercise or a positive eating plan.

For example, people often ask me, "How much sleep should I get each day?" And I have to say that although the ideal amount varies from individual to individual, most studies indicate that the average person needs somewhere between the traditional 7 and 8 hours a night.

If you get much more sleep than that—say up to 10 hours a night— you'll probably find you feel sluggish and fuzzy-headed during the day. Also, medical research shows that your risk of having a heart attack will increase with too much sleep because your body needs a certain minimum of wakeful activity to stay healthy.

Similarly, if you get too little sleep, which for the average person might be as little as 3 to 4 hours per night, your risk of getting heart disease may increase. And as for the more immediate effects of sleepless nights, most of us have had the experience where we got too little sleep for 2 or 3 days in a row. In that case, you tend to feel like death warmed over, without even a bare minimum of energy to do anything effectively or joyfully.

One of the most powerful testimonies to the importance of rest came from the founder of Methodism, John Wesley, who was in fine, vigorous health at age 85. In his *Journal* he attributed his remarkable well-being at such an advanced age in part to "my never having lost a night's sleep, sick or well, at land or at sea, since I was born. . . ."

On the other hand, a lack of proper rest isn't always the culprit that leads to emotional imbalance. Many times, an irritable disposition or a lack of desire to pursue work or social activities at an energetic pace may be the result of too much or too little food—an eating plan which is excessive or unbalanced in the sense that it does not provide the body with the nutrients essential to keep it operating on all cylinders.

And some emotional problems may be traced to a lack of proper balance in exercise. Here's an illustration of what I'm talking about.

Many people complain of an inability to concentrate on a job for any length of time. Or they may feel they are missing sufficient self-discipline to do that extra bit of work that transforms a merely good result into one that is truly excellent.

Those who have begun to run, swim, or otherwise engage in endurance activities for about 30 minutes at a time, are rediscovering certain primordial principles of perseverance that help them overcome this lack of concentration or discipline. It seems they are not only increasing the raw power of their bodies but are also tapping broader physical and psychological resources that spill over into their other pursuits as well.

For example, people have told me that after they become fit enough to run 3 miles without breathing hard, somehow it seems easier to stick with a project at work that requires a few extra hours of effort to achieve excellence. Or perhaps they once believed they were completely unathletic, but by committing themselves to an aerobic program, they can now swim a mile without stopping. And somehow, as they achieve their physical goal and find that they *are* athletic, they are also more ready to believe that they can achieve success in their marriages or careers as well.

Emotional equilibrium, then, can often be achieved through balanced exercise, diet, and rest, and we'll see many other examples of psychological benefits in the ensuing pages. But in the meantime, remember: Whether you're awake and in the midst of an invigorating run or a good meal—or asleep and merely dreaming about such activity—it's always important to keep the principle of balance in mind. Balance is the master key for opening the door to total well-being in your life.

So total well-being is a condition that arises from an overall state of physical and emotional equilibrium in one's life. It is *not*, as I see it, a substitute for certain of the important things you may be seeking. It's not a substitute for a challenging job; it's not a substitute for a meaningful marriage; and it's not a substitute for religious faith.

But total well-being *can* provide the physical and emotional base for finding and savoring these other goals: For example, it will undoubtedly enrich a career or a deep spiritual commitment, especially as you get more involved in these endeavors and as the time and energy demands they place on you become greater.

I suspect that a principle of total well-being, which is deeply rooted in the basic balances of nature, is as deeply imbedded in our humanity as any other universal law or instinct.

What's more, I believe we have some startling natural powers within us which can propel us toward total well-being, if we'll only learn how to take advantage of them.

Now, to illustrate in a more concrete way how some of these principles can transform one individual from a state of inner disruption and imbalance into a condition of overall equilibrium and well-being, let me turn to the trials and tribulations of a patient I know rather well—a fellow by the name of Kenneth H. Cooper, M.D.

2

The Development of a Dream

've given lip service to the importance of a balanced life for as long as I can remember. Even as a grade-schooler in Oklahoma, I often heard teachers and other adults in authority praise the "well-rounded" student who could do everything, including athletics, rather well.

As far as my own little body was concerned, I didn't have the foggiest notion of what the word "balance" meant. Ironically, the more deeply I got involved in sports as a youngster, the more ignorant I seemed to become.

To illustrate what I'm talking about, let's go back a few decades, to the mid- to late-1940s when I was a high school student in Oklahoma City. As a ninth-grader, I began to get interested in track and many other sports. In fact, to some people it seemed that I almost "overdosed" on athletics at that early age—though, as we'll see, that wasn't the cause of the unbalanced life I eventually came to lead.

For example, I got involved in football, basketball, and cross-country. Also, I went out for the various medium-distance track events, such as the half-mile and mile runs. My father got so concerned about my extensive participation in high school athletics that he became afraid I would develop a weak "athletic heart" if I continued at the pace I was going. So he insisted that I at least quit football.

As it happened, it was an excellent idea that I quit football—but not because of the myth of the "athletic heart" that worried many parents in those days. The main thing I probably avoided by dropping football was the proverbial knee and other joint and bone injuries that often plague football players throughout their adult lives.

But mythology and misconceptions have always been a part of athletics. As a result, it took me a long time to sort through the folklore and begin to discover the core of truth about the relationship between fitness and general health.

For example, there's the question of how an athlete should go about getting in condition to run the medium-distance races like the half-mile and mile. Let me illustrate from my own experiences some of the bad advice many people get.

With very little coaching, I did rather well in both track and basketball in high school. Oddly enough, I stumbled onto the current concept of L.S.D., or long slow distance, all by myself when I was a senior. In those days, since I didn't have a full-time coach guiding me, I had to come up with many of my own training concepts.

As a cornerstone of my personal fitness regimen, I decided it just made sense that if I was going to run a good mile, I would have to run a lot of miles to get prepared for it. So I often ran 50 to 60 miles per week as part of my training, with some extra preliminary spring training, before the regular season, thrown in for good measure. As a result of my conditioning program, I made the all-state basketball team as a senior in 1949; won the 1-mile-run state championship by covering the distance in 4:31.9; and qualified for the state finals in the half-mile by running the distance in 2:01.4.

After these achievements, I was literally overwhelmed with offers of athletic scholarships to college. I finally chose the University of Oklahoma, where I enrolled in a premedical program on a track scholarship, and my involvement in sports continued unabated. During my college years, I continued to improve my running times: For example, I was able to bring my mile time down to 4:18; my half-mile down to 1:56; and my 2-mile cross-country time down to 9:45.

But now I was getting a great deal more direction from coaches—and that's where some of my later misconceptions about exercise began. Since I was a very serious intercollegiate athlete and had the opportunity to think about the long-range impact of exercise on my health as I sat in various premed courses, you'd think I would have been developing some understanding of athletic training techniques. But actually, I didn't understand a thing.

Like many young athletes in those days, I had been conditioned by my college coaches to accept certain training principles as ultimate truth—even though, as I later learned, they were about as far from the truth as you could get. In fact, if I had known then what I know now, I might have run much faster in college and also could have laid a solid groundwork for total well-being in my adult life.

Let me explain this point in a little more detail: You see, when I was a college runner, there was a belief in athletic circles that medium-distance runners should concentrate on doing sprints, not long-distance training. Most coaches seemed to feel that the first sub-4-minute-miler would be the man who could run the 100-yard dash in less than 9.4 seconds.

So in college, my coaches made me drop the L.S.D. workouts I had pursued as a self-coached high school athlete and concentrate primarily on the sprints. In other words, the idea of building what we now call an "aerobic base," with a lot of long-distance work to give the runner that added bit of endurance, was unknown. Present-day training techniques for the mile, where the athlete runs at least 100 miles a week to prepare for competition, would have been laughed off the track in the early 1950s.

Coaches in those days limited our distances to 20 miles a week because they felt any more running would "take the spring out of our legs." Also, we weren't allowed to run year-round because the coaches feared we would "burn out." So there might be enforced layoffs for as long as 6 weeks between the fall cross-country races and the indoor track season. During the summer months, we were advised not to run at all, but to rest up so that we could perform better when we went back into training. But we now know, to the contrary, that you have to run *continuously* for 8 to 10 years before you can expect to reach national or even regional championship caliber.

One of the reasons for the limitations that earlier coaches placed on workouts by their athletes was that they noticed a "flattening-out effect" in their performance. Over a certain period of training, the runner's times would improve, but then they would start to flatten out. And a fear arose that continuing to run during this "flattened-out" stage might cause burn-out. As a result, the argument went, it was best to cut down on your mileage at this point.

But we now know that this flattening-out phase occurs regularly and is what is called a "plateau effect." If the person continues with the exercise program and runs *past* the plateaus he or she reaches, performance will most likely begin to improve again and the runner can reach new heights and better times.

I now feel that if I had used our current training techniques when I was in college, I could have dropped my mile down to below 4:10 and maybe even below 4:05. But that's all water under the bridge. The important thing for me now—and also for you—is the principles that my early experiences illustrate. And it's also important to understand the negative impact that a lack of knowledge and understanding about your body can have on your total well-being.

I never achieved what I had hoped to achieve in track competition in college, and that left me tremendously frustrated with my athletic efforts when I finally left college and entered medical school. I had been running only to beat certain times and to place well or win certain track meets. The idea that exercise might have had the potential to keep me healthier and give me total well-being throughout my adult life didn't enter my mind.

So I plunged into my medical studies at the University of Oklahoma. And through a combination of (1) stressful, heavy study; (2) minimal sleep; (3) a sedentary life-style characterized by little or no exercise; and (4) too much food, I allowed my body to deteriorate gradually, but thoroughly.

Physically, I was in a state of almost total imbalance. As a result, even though I had recently been an intercollegiate athlete and was still in my early twenties, my body—along with my sense of well-being—was starting to fall apart.

By the time I had completed 4 years of medical school and a year of my internship, I had ballooned from my normal weight of 170 pounds to 205 pounds. My blood pressure had also been increasing steadily during that period, and at times verged on what would be classified as hypertension. The complete extent of my poor condition finally came out after I entered the Army as a flight surgeon, with the intention of making the military my career.

I was stationed at Fort Sill, Oklahoma and I met my wife, Millie, there. Our marriage, and especially her cooking, didn't help bolster my declining physical condition. I hit my all-time high of 210 pounds shortly after we were married, and I estimate now, even though I didn't go through the tests we now have available, that I had reached about 30 percent body fat.

During this same period, I became thoroughly frustrated with military life and more than once commented to Millie that I was "dying of mental stagnation." My base practice was boringly routine, with long hours of taking care of sore throats and runny noses. Unfortunately, I wasn't engaged in a regular exercise program to help relieve the stress I was feeling at work. My energy level was so low sometimes that I felt I had aged well beyond my years.

The experience that made the greatest impact on me—and succeeded in changing my life—involved a water-skiing outing, the first one I had been on in years. As a teenager, I had water-skied extensively and would have been classified as an advanced or expert skier. Because I had no idea that any serious changes had occurred over the years in my physical condition or skiing ability, I did just what I had always been accustomed to do: I put on a slalom ski, told the driver to accelerate immediately to almost 30 miles per hour, and prepared to have a great time, just like in the old days.

But I was in for a surprise.

Within 3 to 4 minutes, I was totally exhausted, and I suddenly began to feel nauseated and weak. I told the boat driver to stop and get me back to land as quickly as possible. For the next 30 minutes, as I lay in nauseous agony on the shore, my head was spinning and I honestly couldn't put a series of logical thoughts together.

As I reflect back on that experience, I'm not absolutely certain what caused the problem. But I strongly suspect that I had suffered some type of cardiac arrhythmia (an irregularity of the heartbeat). You wouldn't classify this as a true heart attack, because the term "heart attack" customarily means an obstruction of the coronary artery with damaged tissue beyond it in the heart itself. Yet people can *die* of arrhythmias, and when that happens, by anyone's definition they become heart attacks.

Most disturbing of all, at the time this incident occurred, I was only 28 years old.

As you might imagine, after this disastrous water-skiing episode, I began to pay closer attention to what was happening to my own body. Here I was, a full-fledged physician, trying to cure the ills of others, and my own body was deteriorating before my very eyes. It was truly a case of "physician, heal thyself"—and that was exactly what I set out to do.

As I examined my own overweight and deconditioned body—and compared my situation with that of others I had been examining as a doctor—I decided that there must be some connection between heart disease on the one hand, and inactivity, obesity, and poor eating habits on the other. So I began to devote all my efforts to finding out what this connection was.

It was at this point, in 1960, that the dream that has controlled my life for the past two decades really began to take shape. Before that water-skiing incident, I had been an enthusiastic amateur athlete and had been exposed to copious amounts of sports training theory and medical knowledge. But I was completely ignorant of the balanced way of life that can give a person total well-being and a resulting long, happy, and energetic life.

In a very real sense, the serious physical problem I faced triggered a conversion experience—one which I believe "turned me around" so that I could see for the first time in my life the downward, life-threatening path that I and many of my fellow human beings were traveling. Suddenly, I was motivated as I had never been motivated before, to understand specifically what action a person could take to feel better in the present and lead a healthier, more energetic life in the future.

Of course, there was a very personal element in this conversion because I knew I was headed for serious health trouble if I didn't do something very quickly. But there's another side to this conversion, too. You see, I believed then, as I believe now, that everything in my life happens for a broader purpose. So I not only saw my own life being threatened; I also sensed that God was trying to tell me something that He wanted me to communicate to others. As a result, I began to look for a deeper, more wide-ranging meaning in that water-skiing incident. And slowly but surely I found that meaning as a dream began to develop in greater and greater detail in my mind.

To put it simply, my great dream was this: I began to feel that my purpose in life should be to become a preventive medicine specialist and to share my findings in practical, life-enhancing ways with as many people as possible. Exactly how all this was going to take place, I didn't know. But I did know that somehow this dream was going to become reality.

The formulation of my dream took a giant leap forward in 1960, one year after my physical calamity, when I was given the opportunity to transfer directly from the Army to the Air Force and start a training program at the School of Aerospace Medicine in San Antonio, Texas. For the next year, I was an instructor on the staff of the aviation physiology division. In that position, I taught such topics as what changes occur in the body when a person rises too rapidly to the surface from deep underwater, or when pressures change abruptly in high altitude flying.

But the most important thing that happened to me was that I had the chance to meet and work with Dr. Bruno Balke, the great pioneer in exercise physiology. Among other things, he was the guiding light behind the use of the treadmill stress test to determine an individual's level of cardiovascular fitness. That man, perhaps more than any other, changed my life. Under his direct guidance, I embarked on an exercise and diet program and got my weight down from 210 pounds to my current level of 165 to 170 pounds. Also, instead of my estimated all-time high of 30 percent body fat, my obesity level fell to an athletic 14 percent.

This transformation didn't occur overnight because, remember, I had allowed 8 years to elapse between the time I ran competitively in college and the time I started back in on a regular exercise program. I had done nothing physically during that period except gain weight, study, and occasionally try to play some basketball or touch football.

But under Dr. Balke, I got serious about getting in shape again. I began to run regularly, and before long had worked up to regular runs of 5, 7, and as much as 8 miles. Also, I altered my eating habits in my efforts to get my weight down.

My own personal involvement in physical fitness as well as the important things I was learning about exercise as a primary tool of preventive medicine prompted me to enroll at the Harvard School of Public Health for a Master's degree in public health. While attending Harvard, I got deeply involved in work at their exercise physiology laboratory, and in the course of this research I had the privilege of working with several top marathoners.

In fact, I got so interested in the marathon as a sport that I ran in the Boston Marathon myself in 1962 and 1963. The first year, I ran the distance in 3:54 and placed 101st. The next year, after training much harder, I ran the distance in 3:20 and placed 98th.

Of course, these times were not exactly of championship caliber, especially not at today's levels of competition: If I had run my best time in the 1981 race, for example, I would have placed about number 7,500 in the field! But just the fact that I was running the marathon at all showed how far I had come in affirming the significance of distance running as an important form of fitness in my own life. Finally, my body was approaching the state of balance that it was intended to have.

My increasing involvement in ground-breaking fitness programs and preventive medicine research was almost like an intellectual marathon in itself. One exciting field of inquiry always seemed to lead to another that held even more promise for enhancing the health and well-being of the average man and woman in the street.

Because of my deep interest in the research I was pursuing at Harvard, I sought and obtained the permission of the Air Force to continue my graduate studies for an extra year. My research focused on maximum oxygen consumption during exercise, and my basic concept of aerobics training came out of this work.

When I finally returned to full-time duty with the Air Force, I was made Director of the Aerospace Medical Laboratory, Clinical, at Lackland Air Force Base in San Antonio, Texas, and in that capacity I continued my research into the connection between physical fitness and health. Of course, it took time to identify the basic principles of proper exercise and physical fitness, and then to learn to apply them in such a way that the nonathlete could make them a regular part of his or her life. But I knew the path I had chosen would involve a long-distance lifetime of research and application; so I didn't hesitate to take the time.

During this period, I also kept up with my own personal conditioning program, sometimes to the derision of my colleagues. But despite the snide remarks, I kept running regularly, and I soon found there were other "nuts" on the base who liked to join me in a noontime run of 2 to 3 miles. The numbers soon swelled to fifteen or twenty men and an occasional woman, who became known as "Cooper's Poopers."

Some of the comments we heard from our more sedentary colleagues went like this:

- "You're crazy to be running in the hot Texas sun at your age!" (I was an ancient 34 years old at the time.)
- "You're going to have a heart attack if you keep this up!"
- "I'd rather die after a good meal than on a running track!"

And so on. But we continued to run, and gradually, the criticisms faded as people began to see that exercise could enhance, rather than detract from a person's well-being and general health.

Before long, I was asked to work as a consultant to the Lackland military training school, which supervises the basic training of all Air

Force recruits. During this assignment, I was able to formulate ways to raise the general level of conditioning of these young people and also to establish the now famous 12-minute running test to determine a person's general level of fitness (see Chapter 8).

In addition, I began to conduct field studies on young second and first lieutenants, and this research led to some interesting correlations between levels of fitness and levels of performance in academic courses. The correlation was almost perfect in showing that those who scored the highest on the 12-minute fitness test I had devised also made the best grades academically.

Why should there be a connection between aerobic fitness and brain power?

Perhaps the more efficient circulation of blood that exercise produces in all parts of the human body, including the brain, enhances mental acuity. Or maybe the greater sense of relaxation and freedom from stress that accompanies aerobic activity frees the mind to operate more effectively. We're still trying to pinpoint the exact reason why aerobic exercise and mental ability go together. But whatever the reason, we do know that *exercise is an important factor in total mental well-being.*

Because of my work on these studies and fitness programs, I gradually came to be identified as the "Air Force expert in physical conditioning." So when the "Age of the Astronaut" came upon us, I was assigned to develop the conditioning and training program for the U.S.A.F. astronauts to use prior to blast-off. As a result, we came up with the *aerobic point system*, which has been the basis of several of my previous publications and will also be described in the fitness section of this book.

The main idea of this system is that in order to stay in good shape and move toward the goal of total well-being, a person must earn a certain number of points each week by doing a certain amount of aerobic exercise. After extensive research, we settled on a system of points that could be earned by a person who was engaged in various types of aerobic exercise during a given number of minutes. For example, an individual who runs 3 miles in 24 to 30 minutes would receive 14 points, while a person who runs 2 miles in the same time period would receive 5 points.

After establishing this program, I worked as a consultant to NASA as they developed more sophisticated exercise programs and equipment for the astronauts. And also, I was directed to develop a conditioning program for the entire Air Force. Over one 6-month period, I had 27,000 people involved in our aerobics testing program, including 15,000 exercisers and 12,000 controls.

Before long, top officials in the military had pronounced our program a success, and the Air Force issued a guide which implemented our findings and replaced the Royal Canadian "5 Bx" Air Force exercises. Soon afterward, the U.S. Navy accepted the aerobics program, along with the Canadian Armed Forces, and dozens of other foreign organizations.

But despite this series of successes, all was not well between me and the military. My first book, *Aerobics*, had been published and became a bestseller in 1968, and many of my problems with the Air Force got worse at that point.

The main difficulty seemed to center on different philosophies of medicine. In the late 1960s, both inside and outside the military, there was little interest in stressing preventive medicine. The most important forms of medical help were thought to involve treatment of existing injuries and ailments, not the prevention of those that might occur at some uncertain point in the future. So many of my ideas and suggestions, couched as they were in terms of preventive medicine, seemed less and less acceptable to my military superiors. Consequently, I found myself getting more and more frustrated.

Finally, things came to a head when I submitted a lengthy proposal for setting up a triservice physical conditioning and rehabilitation center. This was part of that dream that had been developing inside me of a far-reaching preventive medical program to enable the average person to experience greater well-being and a longer, more productive life.

My concept was rather simple and nowadays wouldn't seem very radical: I believed that it would be cheaper and more effective to establish a center to prevent disease than to treat it. Also, I thought it would be more efficient to rehabilitate those service people with physical problems rather than to retire them. But the concept was rejected with little comment, and pressure was placed on me to abandon my experimental work with physical fitness and assume command of a military hospital.

I realized at this point that there was no future for me in the Air Force. So despite the fact that I was a lieutenant colonel, with only a few years to go to retirement, I turned in my resignation and moved, lock, stock, and treadmill, to Dallas.

Now, on its face, this was a crazy thing to do. Millie was pregnant at the time with our second child, and I had no prospects or contacts for setting up an independent medical practice in Dallas. We had enough money to get along on for a while. But despite the success of my books, I had very little capital that I could use to finance a really big project. And I *had* a big project—a fantastic dream—in mind.

As I've indicated, my big idea, which had been evolving for years, ever since my water-skiing fiasco, was to establish a preventive medical center for the general public. With a proper clinic and exercise facility, I could put into effect all the ideas and research findings I had been developing during the last few years. And I would have a solid base from which to travel and speak to others about the merits of a scientifically balanced exercise and diet program which could lead to total well-being.

This was a professional dream which, for me, also involved a huge step of faith. After considerable prayer and thought, I really believed God was leading me to quit the military, go to Dallas, and set up a completely new kind of "medical shop" there. But I must say, it took all the faith I had to survive the welcome I received just after I arrived.

The first problem was getting some patients. I thought the success of my books indicated that the American people were ready to plunge enthusiastically into preventive medicine programs. So I was quite optimistic when I established a practice with one other physician, Dr. Joe Arends, a former Navy flight surgeon, and a secretary, in a small three-room office in the northern part of Dallas. I sent out my cards and announcements, put my name in the telephone book, and sat back confidently to wait for the patients to flock in.

But no one came. For days we waited, but still no patients. Finally, my first patient came in, a man from a Dallas suburb. I recall him distinctly—mainly because he never paid his bill.

So things got off to a slow, rather discouraging start for me in Dallas. And they quickly went from bad to worse when we started running into resistance from some other physicians and their supporters. At that time in the early 1970s, limiting a practice to preventive medicine just wasn't an accepted form of medicine in Dallas, any more than it had been in the Air Force. As a matter of fact, I had the only treadmill for use in stress testing in the entire city. In those days, apparently nobody else felt that there was any validity in taking an electrocardiogram (EKG) under exercise conditions.

There was so much criticism of my approach in my first years in Dallas that I'm sure if one of my patients had died during a stress test, I would have been run out of town. Fortunately, though, our methods of using the treadmill have, from the very beginning, involved so many safeguards that we haven't had a death in the entire 11-year existence of the Aerobics Center. And during that period, we've performed more than 43,000 maximum performance treadmill stress tests on more than 22,000 people.

There were times during that period when I felt so low that I seriously considered returning to the military. But whenever I would really start feeling "down," those were the times I began to depend more and more upon running to control stress and frustration. It was better than any tranquilizer!

But most important, there were always a few staunch supporters to lift my spirits and help me start driving toward my ultimate goal with renewed energy. Even though I didn't realize it at the time, these key people were extremely important in helping me keep my stress at a manageable level. In fact, they were essential to helping me maintain any semblance of psychological well-being during this trying period.

If you've ever tried to buck considerable resistance in putting one of your big dreams into effect, you know what I'm talking about. It's very hard to keep your equilibrium without the support of a handful of people who love and respect you—people who will listen to you blow off steam when things get especially frustrating and who will give you honest advice when you start losing perspective.

First of all, there was my wife, Millie. She was always at my side, encouraging me when I began to have doubts. And most important of all, she contributed her prayers when it seemed only God could resolve some problem.

Another key person at this crucial point in the development of my dream was Dr. Milford Rouse, a past president of the American Medical Association, who often acted as my personal cheerleader and public relations man. He could see the future of the aerobic center concept I was promoting, and he wanted it established in Dallas. But also, he knew the uphill fight I was facing getting accepted by the medical establishment and raising sufficient funds to get my center off the ground. So he provided a great deal of moral support and also gave his professional endorsement when I ran into difficulties.

In general, physicians are not known for their business acumen, and certainly I am no exception. Many times during those early years, I needed solid advice and found it in the person of Fred Meyer, executive vice president of the Tyler Corporation. Fred not only became my business consultant and adviser but also my closest friend.

Finally, there was Joe McKinney, the chairman of the Tyler Corporation in Dallas. Joe was especially unusual because he was willing to put his money behind his enthusiasm. He got quite excited about the aerobic approach to well-being soon after I met him, while I was still in the military. As a result, he offered to help me financially in any way he could—and I found I really *needed* his help as we reached the stage of actually erecting some sort of facility.

To realize my dream of a significant preventive health center, I needed land; and land in Dallas, even in the early 1970s, didn't come cheap. After some intense looking, I found a tract in northern Dallas that seemed ideal. The problem was that the woman who owned it, Mrs. Clarice Nichols, insisted on selling her entire 22 acres, while I could only afford about 8½ acres.

At first, Mrs. Nichols wouldn't budge from her resolve to sell the entire tract as a package. She felt her deceased husband had put too much effort into developing the tract, and she thought she would be dishonoring his memory if she broke it up into parcels. My realtor talked to her for a while about our plans, and then suggested that maybe we could buy the smaller tract outright and take out an option on the remainder of the 22 acres.

She immediately said, "No." But then, almost like a bolt out of the blue, she stopped and asked, "Is this Dr. Cooper who wants to buy this land the same man who wrote the book on exercise?"

My realtor said, "Yes."

And Mrs. Nichols replied, "For him, I'll do it."

I didn't find out the whole story until several years later. It seems that she had heard Millie and me speak at a Christian lay conference in Colorado Springs, and she resolved at that point that if ever she had the opportunity to help us in our work, she would. Now, that's what I call answered prayer.

But getting Mrs. Nichols' agreement was only the first step. We also needed more than a million dollars to buy the small parcel of land that she had offered us out of her total tract, but bank after bank turned me down when I asked for loans. And this is where Joe McKinney came in. I finally went to him to describe the problems I was facing. And he, in effect, gave me a blank check to buy the land and get the Aerobics Center off the ground.

A number of problems popped up after we bought the land. For one thing, we had to get support from the local residents and approval from the zoning commission to erect a medical center on the property. And after we had built our facility and established a reputation both in Dallas and on the national scene, we faced a devastating fire that almost put us out of business.

But in general, it's all been smooth sledding since those difficult early days. Preventive medicine of the kind we practice at the Aerobics Center has become generally accepted throughout the United States— and that includes the Dallas medical establishment as well. I've mentioned that I had the first treadmill in Dallas that was used to conduct stress tests. It's perhaps symbolic of how times change that now there are over 100!

In 1977, we reached our membership capacity of 2,300 men and women at the Aerobics Activity Center, where our ongoing, controlled exercise programs are conducted. We've maintained that capacity membership ever since, and at times we have had a waiting list of as many as 600 people wanting to join. Professional athletes, corporate executives, and celebrities like TV broadcaster Roger Staubach, former star quarterback of the Dallas Cowboys, exercise side by side with any other members who happen to drop by for a workout. There are outdoor tracks that wind through landscaped gardens past trees and ponds; a heated swimming pool; handball and racketball courts; and a variety of other facilities.

Most important of all, the Aerobics Center has become the research facility that I had always hoped for, and has provided us with solid guidelines to help people in all walks of life achieve a healthy and energetic existence. And the international attention that our work at the Center has attracted has enabled me to spread the gospel of total well-being all over the world through lectures and seminars.

So a large part of my original dream has been realized. And the implications of this dream-become-reality become more and more staggering as the evidence of the importance of aerobic fitness pours in.

For example, beginning in the late 1960s, after my book, *Aerobics*, and a book entitled *Jogging* by Harris and Bowerman were published, some dramatic changes occurred in the state of health of individual Americans. In terms of hard statistics, here's what I'm talking about:

Between 1968 and 1977, we saw a 23 percent decrease in deaths from heart attacks; a 36 percent decrease in deaths from strokes; and a 48 percent decrease in deaths from hypertensive disease. In addition, between 1971 and 1979 there was a 2.7-year increase in the longevity of the American people, which almost tripled the increase in life span during any previous decade.

What is the cause of all this progress in individual health?

Several factors have been mentioned by medical experts: (1) Fewer people are smoking; (2) more people are aware of the importance of monitoring their blood pressure; (3) more are minimizing cholesterol in their diets; and (4) more are becoming attuned to signs of stress in their lives and learning to deal better with the pressures of everyday living.

But the last reason—and in my opinion the single most important factor—is the increased commitment of Americans to aerobic exercise. The number of adults who exercised regularly in the United States went up dramatically, from about 25 percent prior to 1968 to 47 percent in 1977. And in a trend that bodes well for the future, a 1979 Gallup Poll revealed that more than 50 percent of all American teenagers are engaged in some type of regular aerobic exercise.

So a large part of my original dream of making Americans more aware of the importance of aerobic-based preventive medicine is in the process of being realized. And knowing that in some way I've contributed to the awareness among Americans about the ways they can improve their health and well-being is certainly personally satisfying.

But much more remains to be said, and done, and dreamed into reality—especially as far as *you* are concerned. Now that you know something about me and my personal adventures with good health, let me invite you to join me for some further exploration of how proper balance can result in total well-being in your own life.

PART TWO

THE FOOD FACTOR IN TOTAL WELL-BEING

3

The Basic Principles of Balance in your Diet

The next time you're in the middle of a crowd of people—especially at a party in the evening with some of your friends—take a close look at the individuals around you. If you're like me, you'll probably find yourself selecting a few outstanding people here and there, and placing them apart in a very special, almost elite kind of group.

The main characteristic that hits you about this group is their alertness. Their faces are animated and their complexions clear and full of "good color." They may seem a little restless or their bodies a little taut, but that's because they're so involved in the conversations and events going on around them. Also, you'll notice they are for the most part relatively slim people, without double chins and with bodies that seem quite firm and down to "fighting weight."

Like some of their less attractive neighbors, the people in the elite category may be argumentative. But the big difference is that they don't get irrational about it. They like verbal combat, but they're sensitive enough to know when a discussion has slipped from entertaining intellectual sparring to destructive emotional street fighting. They are people who are eager to participate, but not to disrupt.

Above all, this special group of people have seemingly boundless energy. And if there's some sort of "party after the party," they'll be the ones who are in the best condition to continue the festivities at a fast pace.

What's the reason for the striking difference between the attractive, compelling individuals and their less vibrant companions at the party?

Probably the most likely explanation for those projecting the most vibrant image is that they are physically and emotionally in a state of near perfect balance. First of all, I would predict that most of those who project the best image at the typical social gatherings you attend do take some sort of regular exercise. In fact, many are likely to be joggers who put in 15 miles or so a week on their neighborhood sidewalks. Also, I doubt that any of them are burning the candle at both ends and not getting enough sleep. They may well be under tremendous stress from their jobs or from family problems, but they've learned how to manage the stress associated with high achievement and an extremely active life-style. As a result, they have the energy reserves that enable them to avoid just collapsing at an evening get-together, or taking out their irritation on someone who happens to engage them in conversation.

But most likely, there's more to it than just exercise, rest, and stress management. In fact, even though most people might expect me to come down harder on a lack of aerobic exercise than anything else, I would lay odds that the *major* difference between the most attractive, energetic group of people and those who are the "second-stringers" in appearance and vitality is that the first group is more conscious of diet and weight than the second.

But this is just common sense, when you think about it. You can't erect *any* sort of substantial structure, human or otherwise, without paying close attention to the foundation on which it is laid. We all know, for example, that every great building or bridge must have a solid base if it's to keep standing and serve its main purpose over the years.

In a similar way, your diet is the foundation upon which your total physical and emotional well-being is based. It's the firm base which enables everything else to reach a state of equilibrium. Without proper eating habits, all the exercise, rest, or physical exams in the world won't do you much good in your efforts to develop a healthy body. In fact, without proper nutrition, you may not even have the energy to participate in a regular exercise program.

You see, good nutrition is the first key to the high level of physical conditioning that is necessary to find total well-being. And without a good physical conditioning, it's very hard for most people to achieve their maximum performance in intellectual, psychological, and spiritual pursuits.

So I've concluded that the delicate physical balance that leads to total well-being *must* begin with the food we eat. As a result, the research division at the Aerobics Center has formulated *eight basic principles for establishing a healthy balance in your eating habits.* To summarize briefly, these principles include:

1.   Strike a 50-20-30 percentage balance among the three main food types. To keep your energy at peak levels, your daily intake of calories should be distributed so that about 50 percent come from complex carbohydrates, 20 percent from protein, and 30 percent from fats.

2.   Follow another percentage formula—the "25-50-25 rule"—to lose weight by controlling the amount of food you consume at each meal. The percentages refer to eating 25 percent of your daily calories at breakfast, 50 percent at lunch, and 25 percent at supper. In other words, eat regularly and distribute your calories throughout the day, but reduce the customary heavy evening meal. Also, even for those who don't have to lose weight, it's a good idea to use a modification of this formula to ensure that you'll be able to *maintain* your best weight. In this regard, I recommend that you still eat most of your calories before supper, with

a 25-30-45 percentage approach (25 percent of your calories at breakfast, 30 percent at lunch, and 45 percent at dinner).

3.   Do your aerobic exercise at the *end* of the day, just before the evening meal, to depress the appetite and thus enhance weight loss and maintain your ideal weight. Weight loss resulting from a combination of caloric restriction and exercise primarily reduces fat, whereas dietary restriction without exercise results in considerable loss of muscle mass.

4.   Develop a healthy fear of obesity, which may be a more mysterious killer than many people today suspect.

5.   Avoid an imbalance in your eating in the direction of consuming too few calories. This mistake can be deadly, especially for those who engage in very strenuous and prolonged aerobic exercise.

6.   Know the scientific formula for determining your ideal weight.

7.   Learn the formula for determining the number of calories you need to take in each day to maintain your ideal weight.

8.   If you're overweight, establish a P.E.P. (Positive Eating Plan) diet to get yourself off the "roller-coaster effect" of constant weight gain and weight loss.

These principles seem to reflect something very fundamental to good human health. In a sense, they represent a return to the natural diets of our distant, primitive ancestors that can enable our bodies to function at maximum levels of performance.

If you understand and follow these eight principles of dietary balance, I'm convinced that you'll find your energy levels increasing, your mental faculties growing keener, and your physical strength surging forward. Now, here are some of the details:

PRINCIPLE ONE: FOR MAXIMUM PERSONAL ENERGY, YOU SHOULD STRIKE A 50-20-30 PERCENT BALANCE AMONG THE THREE MAIN FOOD TYPES

At the Aerobics Center, we recommend that the calories you consume each day be distributed so that approximately 50 percent of them come from complex carbohydrates, 20 percent from protein sources, and 30 percent from fat. Whether you want to lose weight or maintain your present poundage, this 50-20-30 percent distribution of the three food types is the most fundamental principle for establishing the proper equilibrium in your personal program.

Why is it so important to establish such an equilibrium?

One of the major reasons is to enable you to keep a high energy level. You may sometimes find yourself looking at extremely active, achievement-oriented people and thinking,"I wish I had that kind of energy!" You may even decide, "Well, some people have a naturally high level of energy and some don't—and I'm just one of those who doesn't!"

But if you allow yourself to think in these terms, you may be making the biggest mistake of your life. Your energy level is much more under your control than you may realize. And, in addition to exercise, one of the major ways to increase your level of energy is to pay close attention to what you eat.

You see, food is fuel, human fuel. And your body, including your brain, contains the motors and computers that enable you to do your job and engage in meaningful human relationships at the highest levels of efficiency and sensitivity. But if you don't eat a balanced diet, with the correct distribution of calories among the three main food groups to sustain your average daily activity level, your energy reserves will be relatively low. And you may well experience frequent fatigue in your daily business and social dealings.

Even if you don't feel tired *all* the time and you have enough inner horsepower to make it to suppertime, you may still find that you run out of steam after the evening meal. As a result, you just don't have the energy to give high-quality time to your family or friends in the evenings. Also, grabbing a nonnutritious snack, or skipping a meal entirely when you're on the run, may cause you to become irritable about minor problems and can reduce your ability to concentrate on a task for any length of time.

Now, the way I look at it, poor eating patterns like these are just not conducive to total well-being. If you're going to feel good, why not feel good *all* the time—past supper and well into the wee hours, if need be? Why not build up inner reserves that will enable you to enjoy yourself and take full advantage of *every* business and social situation, no matter when or how often they occur during the day?

And as I've already said, it won't do to make excuses, such as, "I'm just not an energetic person." Or, "I'm just not as young as I used to be." No matter who you are, you *can* be an energetic person if you'll just resolve to pay better attention to your body—and that means starting with the fuel you put into that body.

Now, let's examine in a little more detail how a proper balance of the three main nutrient groups can enhance your energy level.

First of all, as I've said, 50 percent of the foods you consume each day should come from what we call the complex carbohydrate group. We recommend that everyone emphasize these foods the most because, as a group, they provide us with the most efficient and quickly available energy. Also, they give us many minerals and vitamins that are important for good health, and they supply the fiber which is essential for good digestion and which has some effect on reducing the incidence of cancer of the colon.

Most complex carbohydrates are also high in water content and thus provide our body's most crucial nutrient. The combination of water and fiber in these foods gives us food volume which allows us to feel "full" so we don't overeat. Yet the number of calories is relatively low.

As a real plus for weight watchers, here are some ideas for food choices that can give you a lot (in quantity) for relatively little (in calories): A small orange or apple contains only 50 calories, a vegetable has 25, and a small potato or slice of bread has 70 calories. Compare these low-calorie foods with a high-protein 8-ounce steak (800 calories) or a sugar-rich candy bar (200 calories). You can see from these examples that complex carbohydrates are a true bargain, calorie-wise, for weight watchers.

To summarize, then, the complex carbohydrates include foods such as fresh fruits, fruit juices, fresh vegetables, beans, peas, lentils, potatoes, corn, pasta, bread made from whole-grain flour, and cereals such as oatmeal made from whole oats, brown rice, and bran. You should always choose whole-grain products over white flour products because the whole-grain foods contain more nutrients and fiber.

The second group of foods that are important to help you keep up your energy levels and maintain generally good health are those that supply you with protein. Protein foods may not give you energy as quickly as complex carbohydrates, but they provide much-needed energy reserves that come into play once the energy in the complex carbohydrates "burns out."

These protein foods should comprise about 20 percent of your daily calorie intake. They include protein-rich dishes like fish, poultry, veal, lean beef, lamb, pork, cheese, milk, yogurt, eggs, peanut butter, and dried peas and beans (legumes).

I would recommend that you stick to very lean cuts of beef, lamb, and pork when you do eat these foods, and also, select low-fat cheeses, milk, and yogurt. In most cases, it's best to emphasize fish, poultry, and veal as the three primary sources of protein because they are so much lower in fat than beef or pork.

To be more specific, I would suggest that for the healthiest diet you consider eating fish, poultry, or veal at least ten times a week, and limit yourself to the leaner cuts of beef, lamb, and pork three to five times a week.

Finally, in your daily diet fats should comprise about 30 percent of what you eat. The main problem here is not that you eat insufficient fats, but being sure that you *limit* your fat intake to 30 percent.

There are several big problems with a fatty diet. Fats are a relatively inefficient source of energy, and often they add too much low-density lipoprotein (LDL) to your system. Also, fats load you up with extra calories you don't need. A high-fat diet also may be associated with a greater incidence of cancer of the colon, breast, pancreas, prostate, ovaries, and rectum.

In animal experiments, reducing fat content from 20 percent to 10 percent by weight of the diet, inhibited tumor formation. Such studies suggest that reducing the fat content of the diet might improve the outlook for breast cancer patients by blunting the spread of cancer. So it seems appropriate to recommend that total fat intake be reduced from the usual 40 to 30 percent of available calories, and that you increase your consumption of fresh fruits and vegetables and fiber-containing foods. As you're choosing among these recommended dishes, by the way, try to avoid picking any highly salted foods. And as an added benefit, if you follow these suggestions and preserve a balanced diet with adequate vitamins, you'll be much more likely to maintain an ideal body weight.

The best way to keep your fats down to a minimum is to avoid fried foods, sauces, gravies, rich desserts, cold cuts, hot dogs, and excessively large meat portions. Also, it's a good idea to limit the quantities of margarine, mayonnaise, and salad dressings you consume. Finally, one of the reasons we suggest holding the protein-rich foods you eat to 6 or 8 ounces a day is that by so doing, you automatically limit the amount of fat that you take in through such foods.

Remember this, too: It's important for you to consider both fat quantity *and* quality. Fats from vegetable sources (as in corn oil, tub margarines, mayonnaise, salad dressings, nuts, and seeds) are preferable to animal fats (as in butter, cream, whole-milk dairy products, shortening, meat fat and bacon).

Now, to put all this in more usable terms, let's look at three sets of sample menus, over a 7-day period. These suggested eating plans are based on diets of 1,000, 1,500, and 2,200 calories per day, but you may want to adjust these calorie amounts depending on your personal needs (see Principle Seven later in this chapter).

The six food groups we use at the Aerobics Center in planning menus include (1) fruits; (2) vegetables; (3) meat and meat substitutes; (4) milk or milk products; (5) breads and cereals; and (6) fats. These six, if distributed properly, will give you the 50-20-30 percentages you need of complex carbohydrates, protein, and fats, respectively.

But before we get into the specifics of the menus, let me mention a few guidelines you should keep in mind:

First of all, the three calorie levels have been chosen either to help you lose weight, or to help you maintain your best weight as a woman or man. The 1,000-calorie diet is the bare minimum number of calories that a female should eat if she wants to lose weight. The minimum for men who want to lose weight at the fastest safe rate would be a 1,200-calorie diet, which would involve eating the same dishes as the 1,000-calorie diet, but adding two starchy foods and one fruit daily to make up the extra 200 calories.

The 1,500-calorie diet provides the average minimum daily requirements for a female who wants to maintain her present weight. Or to be more precise, a female aged 23–50 would normally consume 1,600–2,400 calories a day, and a female aged 51–75 would eat 1,400–2,200.

The average minimum calorie requirements for a man who wants to keep a stable weight would be 2,200 calories. Or in more specific terms, a male aged 23–50 would require 2,300–3,100 calories, and a male aged 51–75 would need 2,000–2,800.

In all the following menus, these principles and guidelines should be applied:

- For beverages, choose a calorie-free drink, such as water, a diet drink, or tea. You should limit all caffeine-containing beverages (e.g., cola drinks, coffee, tea) to 2–3 servings daily.
- Tub margarine is recommended throughout because it is generally higher in polyunsaturated fats than is stick margarine. This helps balance the saturated fat in your system.
- "Tossed salad" refers to any combination of vegetables you prefer. The salads should be *varied*. This means variety in color, texture, and food type—and especially combinations that make a salad more appealing and nutritious. For example, you might mix: different types of lettuce (the darker the lettuce, the more iron and vitamin A), watercress, raw spinach, red cabbage, yellow squash, carrots, tomato, cucumber, zucchini, celery, radishes, bean sprouts, broccoli, cauliflower, green peppers, onions.
- Choose skim milk, fortified with vitamins A and D.
- Choose polyunsaturated vegetable oils for dressings (e.g., safflower, sunflower, corn). Avoid coconut oil, palm kernel oil. Limit olive oil, peanut oil.
- Choose lean beef choices (tenderloin, chuck, rump cuts). Skin poultry.

- Limit eggs to three per week.
- Vegetables should be eaten raw or steamed, baked, or broiled. Do not overcook, as this reduces vitamin and mineral content.
- Soups should be homemade without commercial bouillon. You can also use a low-sodium commercial product.

Finally, you'll notice there are certain letters and symbols I've used in these menus. Here is the coding system, which I think will help you understand much more clearly how these eating plans work:

(#) = calorie content
P = protein source
F = fat source
C = complex carbohydrate source

The calorie values are taken from *Bowes & Church's Food Values of Portions Commonly Used,* thirteenth edition, by Jean Pennington and Helen Church (J.B. Lippincott Company, 1980). The values listed in this source may vary somewhat from those in government tables, which were formulated at an earlier date.

In general, the protein sources include meats, fish, poultry, cheese, and peanut butter. The fat sources include margarine, mayonnaise, oil, and salad dressing. And the complex carbohydrates are included in fruit, vegetables, grain products (e.g., bread, cereal, crackers, oatmeal, pasta, rice), and starchy foods (e.g., potatoes, popcorn, corn). Good sources of both protein and complex carbohydrates include milk, yogurt, beans, and lentils.

The following symbols are also used in the menus:

* = vitamin C source
** = vitamin A source
*** = vitamin A and C
† = cholesterol and saturated fat source

Note: All menus average 200–300 milligrams of cholesterol daily, even with the inclusion of lean meat, veal, and low-fat cheese in the specified quantities. Also, although many foods are *good* sources of vitamins *A* and *C*, we have marked only the *excellent* sources of vitamins and other nutrients. For example, we've only marked the vitamin A sources that include 20–25 percent of the recommended daily allowance (RDA) per serving, and the vitamin C sources that have more than 30 percent of the RDA per serving.

Now, here are the three menus:

1,000-CALORIE MENUS (WEIGHT LOSS DIET)

(*Note:* This diet is based on women's caloric needs. For safe weight loss, men should add two starchy foods and one fruit daily for an extra 200 calories. The average daily meal composition is 50 percent complex carbohydrates, 20 percent protein, and 30 percent fat. The approximate calorie distributions are 25 percent for breakfast, 50 percent for lunch, and 25 percent for supper, as follows the 25-50-25 principle for optional weight loss. *Important:* This plan is low in calcium, in that it includes 300–500 milligrams of calcium a day (the RDA is 800 milligrams). So if this diet is followed for more than 3 months, you should take a calcium supplement of 400–500 milligrams a day.)

Day #1

breakfast:

* ½ cup unsweetened orange juice (40) (C)
† 1 poached egg (80) (P)
1 slice wholewheat toast (70) (C)
1 tsp tub margarine (35) (F)
(total calories: 225)

lunch:

1 cup vegetable soup (70)
tuna sandwich:
      2 slices wholewheat bread (140) (C)
      ½ cup water-packed tuna (120) (P)
      1 tsp mayonnaise (35) (F), lemon juice, pickle (F)
* 1 cup skim milk (80) (P, C)
1 small apple (50) (C)
(total calories: 495)

supper:

2 oz broiled, skinless chicken (120) (P)
* 1 small baked potato (70) (C), with
      1 tsp tub margarine (35) (F)
** ½ cup fresh carrots (20) (C)
½ cup fresh green beans (20) (C)
1 cup tossed lettuce/tomato/cucumber salad (20) (C) with
      herbed vinegar dressing
(total calories: 285)
(Day's Total: 1005)

Day #2

breakfast:

*** ¼ cantaloupe (45) (C), topped with
    ¼ cup low-fat cottage cheese (50) (P)
½ wholewheat English muffin (70) (C)
1 tsp tub margarine (35) (F)
½ cup skim milk (40) (P, C)
(total calories: 240)

lunch:

turkey sandwich:
    2 slices wholewheat bread (140) (C)
    2 oz turkey (120) (P), 1 tsp mayonnaise (35) (F), lettuce and
    tomato
** 1 small raw carrot, in sticks (20) (C)
1 medium pear (50) (C)
milkshake: 1 cup skim milk (80) (P, C), ¼ banana (20) (C), ** 1 fresh
    peach or 2 unsweetened canned halves (40) (C), blended together
(total calories: 505)

supper:

2 oz baked or broiled sole (110) (P), with lemon
1 small ear of corn (70) (C), with 1 tsp tub margarine (35) (F)
½ cup steamed broccoli (20) (C), with lemon
1 cup tossed vegetable salad (20) (C), lemon/vinegar dressing
(total calories: 255)
(Day's Total: 1,000)

Day #3

breakfast:

½ small banana (40) (C)
¾ cup dry wholewheat cereal, e.g., mini-shredded wheat (135) (C)
1 cup skim milk (80) (P,C)
(total calories: 255)

lunch:

1 cup lentil soup (165)(P,C)
½ cup low-fat cottage cheese (100) (P), atop 1 cup fresh fruit salad, including citrus fruit (80) (C)
1 slice wholewheat toast (70) (C), with 1 tsp tub margarine (35) (F)
*** 1 tomato, in wedges (20) (C)
** 1 cup spinach salad (30) (C), with herbal vinegar dressing
(total calories: 500)

supper:

2 oz broiled veal chop (120) (P)
½ cup spaghetti (90) (C), topped with 1 tbs Parmesan cheese (25) (P)
½ cup zucchini (8) (C)
½ cup cauliflower (12) (C)
sliced cucumbers, with mint, dill, vinegar
(total calories: 255)
(Day's Total: 1,010)

Day #4

breakfast:

* ½ grapefruit (40) (C)
½ cup hot oatmeal (75) (C), with cinnamon if desired and 1 tsp tub margarine (35) (F)
1 cup skim milk (80) (P, C)
(total calories: 230)

snack:

† 1 oz low-fat cheese (e.g., Mozzarella, farmer's) (80) (P)
3 wholewheat crackers (40) (C)
(total calories: 120)

lunch:

2 oz roasted chicken (120) (P)
½ cup wild rice (110) (C)
½ cup green beans (20) (C)

** ½ cup carrot-raisin salad: ½ cup shredded carrots (30) (C), 1 tbs
     raisins (20) (C), 1 tsp diet mayonnaise (15) (F) or 1 tbs
     unsweetened apple juice (15) (C)
1 small baked apple, with cinnamon (50) (C)
(total calories: 365)

snack:

1 nectarine (40) (C)

supper:

† 2 oz lean roast beef (120) (P)
* 1 small baked potato (70) (C) with 2 tsp diet margarine (30) (F)
1 cup yellow squash (15) (C)
1 cup tossed salad (20) (C), with 1 tbs herbed tomato juice dressing
(total calories: 255)
(Day's Total: 1,010)

Day #5

breakfast:

* ¾ cup fresh strawberries (40) (C)
1 slice wholewheat toast (70) (C)
1 tbs nonhydrogenated peanut butter (100) (P)
½ cup skim milk (40) (P, C)
(total calories: 250)

lunch:

*** 1 cup tomato soup (75) (C)
"cheese pocket":
    † 1 oz low-fat cheese, e.g., Mozzarella (80) (P), melted in 1
        wholewheat pita (pocket) bread (140) (C) with lettuce,
        tomato, onion, mushrooms and 1 tsp tub margarine (35) (F)
relish tray and yogurt dip:
    1 cup sliced cauliflower, broccoli, green pepper, celery, carrots,
        etc. (25) (C)

¼ cup low-fat plain yogurt (40) (P, C) as dip, seasoned with ½
tsp dry onion flakes or ½ tsp ranch dressing mix
** 1 cup watermelon pieces (45) (C)
1 cup skim milk (80) (P, C)
(total calories: 520)

supper:

† 2 oz broiled London broil (flank steak) (120) (P)
½ cup noodles (85) (C), cooked in chicken broth
** ½ cup carrots (20) (C), with *** parsley
* ½ cup steamed cabbage (20) (C), with lemon
(total calories: 245)
(Day's Total: 1,015)

Day #6

breakfast:

* ½ cup unsweetened orange juice (40) (C)
1 wholewheat bagel (140) (C)
1 oz smoked turkey (60) (P)
(total calories: 240)

lunch:

hamburger:
1 wholewheat hamburger bun (140) (C)
† 2 oz lean ground beef (120) (P)
mustard, lettuce, tomato, onion, pickle with 1 tbs mayonnaise (35)
    (F)
½ cup ambrosia (½ cup mandarin orange and grapefruit sections)
    (40) (C) and 1 tbs coconut and nuts (60) (F)
1 cup skim milk (80) (P, C)
(total calories: 475)

snack:

** 1 medium peach (40) (C)

supper:

seafood creole:
>   2 oz mixed seafood (110) (P), cooked in ½ cup tomato sauce with
>   diced pepper, onion, celery (45) (C), served over ½ cup
>   plain rice (80) (C)

1 cup tossed salad (20) (C), with 1 tbs herbed vinegar dressing
(total calories: 255)
(Day's Total: 1,010)

Day #7

breakfast:

1 small banana (80) (C)
† cheese toast: 1 oz low-fat cheese (e.g., farmer's cheese) (80) (P),
    melted on 1 slice wholewheat bread (70) (C)
½ cup skim milk (40) (P, C)
(total calories: 270)

lunch:

Chinese stir-fry dinner:
>   2 oz sliced chicken (120) (P), and 1 cup mixed vegetables: sliced
>   broccoli, mushrooms, onions, snowpeas, celery, carrots,
>   bamboo shoots, water chestnuts, almonds (45) (C), cooked
>   in 2 tsp oil (70) (F), 2 tsp soy sauce, over ½ cup brown rice
>   (90) (C)
>   1 cup tossed salad (20) (C) with 1 tbs low-calorie dressing (20)
>   (F)

* Hawaiian salad: ¾ cup strawberries, banana, pineapple (60) (C)
½ cup skim milk (40) (P, C)
(total calories: 465)

snack:

2 small or 1 medium plum (45)

supper:

*** stuffed tomato: 1 tomato (20) (C), filled with ½ cup water-
    packed tuna or salmon (120) (P), 1 tsp mayonnaise (35) (F),

diced green pepper, celery, onion, parsley, seasonings
½ cucumber, sliced
4 wholewheat crackers (55) (C)
(total calories: 230)
(Day's Total: 1,010)

1,500-CALORIE MENUS (WEIGHT MAINTENANCE FOR AVERAGE WOMAN)

(Note: the average composition of the daily menus on this diet consists of 50 percent carbohydrates, 20 percent protein, and 30 percent fat. The approximate calorie distribution is 25 percent for breakfast, 30 percent for lunch, and 45 percent for supper. The calories for the snacks vary.)

Day #1

breakfast:

* ½ cup unsweetened orange juice (40) (C)
† 1 poached egg (80) (P)
2 slices wholewheat toast (140) (C)
      with 1 tsp tub margarine (35) (F)
1 cup skim milk (80) (P, C)
(total calories: 375)

lunch:

tuna sandwich:
      2 slices wholewheat bread (140) (C)
      ½ cup water-packed tuna (120) (P), with 2 tsp mayonnaise (70)
            (F), lemon juice, pickle, lettuce
* 1 cup coleslaw (25) (C), with lemon juice and vinegar
1 medium apple (80) (C)
(total calories: 435)

supper:

3 oz broiled, skinless chicken (180) (P)
1 small baked potato (70) (C), with 1 tsp tub margarine (35) (F)
2 wholewheat dinner rolls (2 inches across) (180) (C)

½ cup fresh carrots (20) (C)
½ cup fresh green beans (20) (C)
1 cup tossed lettuce/tomato/cucumber salad (20) (C), with 1 tsp oil
    (35) (F), vinegar (any amount)
½ cup fresh (or canned unsweetened) pineapple chunks (65) (C)
1 cup skim milk (80) (P, C)
(total calories: 705)
(Day's Total: 1,515)

Day #2

breakfast:

*** ¼ cantaloupe (45) (C), topped with ¼ cup low-fat cottage cheese
    (50) (P)
1 wholewheat English muffin (140) (C), with 1 tsp tub margarine (35)
    (F)
1 cup skim milk (80) (P, C)
(total calories: 350)

lunch:

turkey sandwich:
    2 slices wholewheat bread (140) (C)
    2 oz turkey (120) (P), 2 tsp mayonnaise (70) (F),
    lettuce, tomato
* 1 small raw carrot, in sticks (20) (C)
1 medium pear (50) (C)
20 seedless Thompson grapes (50) (C)
(total calories: 450)

supper:

3 oz baked sole (165) (P), cooked with ½ cup onions and mushrooms
    (20) (C), lemon
1 large ear of corn (130) (C), with 1 tsp tub margarine (35) (F)
2 wholewheat dinner rolls (2 inches across) (180) (C)
1 cup tossed vegetable salad (20) (C), with lemon/vinegar dressing
milkshake: 1 cup skim milk (80) (P, C), ½ banana (40) (C), 1 fresh
    peach or 2 unsweetened halves (40) (C), blended together
(total calories: 710)
(Day's Total: 1,510)

Day #3

breakfast:

½ small banana (40) (C)
¾ cup dry wholewheat cereal, e.g., mini-shredded wheat (1 or 2
    biscuits) (135) (C), with ¼ tsp cinnamon, if desired
1 cup skim milk (80) (P, C)
1 slice wholewheat toast (70) (C), with 1 tsp tub margarine (35) (F)
(total calories: 360)

lunch:

** 1 cup vegetable soup (70) (C)
½ cup low-fat cottage cheese (100) (P), atop *** 1 cup fresh fruit
    salad, including citrus fruit (80) (C)
1 wholewheat muffin (2 inches across) (100) (C), with 1 tsp margarine
    (35) (F)
*** 1 tomato, in wedges (20) (C)
sliced cucumbers, with mint, dill, vinegar, 1 tsp oil (35) (F)
(total calories: 440)

supper:

3 oz broiled veal chop (210) (P)
½ cup spaghetti (90) (C), topped with 3 tbs Parmesan cheese (75) (P)
1 slice wholewheat garlic bread (70) (C), with 1 tsp tub margarine
    (35) (F)
½ cup zucchini (8) (C)
½ cup cauliflower (12) (C)
** 1 cup spinach salad (30) (C), with 2 tsp Italian dressing (45) (F)
** 1 fresh nectarine (45) (C)
1 cup skim milk (80) (P, C)
(total calories: 700)
(Day's Total: 1,500)

Day #4

breakfast:

* ½ grapefruit (40) (C)
1 cup hot oatmeal, with cinnamon if desired (150) (C) and with 1 tsp
    tub margarine (35) (F)
1 cup skim milk (80) (P, C)
(total calories: 305)

snack:

† 1 oz low-fat cheese (e.g., Mozzarella, farmer's) (80) (P)
3 wholewheat crackers (40) (C)
(total calories: 120)

lunch:

2 oz roasted chicken (120) (P)
½ cup wild rice (110) (C)
½ cup green peas (55) (C)
** ½ cup carrot-raisin salad: ½ cup shredded carrots (30) (C), 2 tbs
    raisins (40) (C), 1 tsp mayonnaise (35) (F)
2 small or 1 medium plum (45) (C)
(total calories: 435)

supper:

† 3 oz lean roast beef (180) (P)
* 1 medium baked potato (100) (C), with 1 tsp tub margarine (35) (F)
1 wholewheat roll (2 inches across) (90) (C), with 1 tsp tub margarine
    (35) (F)
1 cup yellow squash (15) (C)
** ½ cup spinach with lemon, vinegar (20) (C)
1 cup tossed salad (20) (C), with 1 tbs French dressing (65) (F)
1 cup skim milk (80) (P, C)
(total calories: 640)
(Day's Total: 1,500)

Day #5

breakfast:

1 small baked apple, with cinnamon (50) (C)
2 slices wholewheat toast (140) (C), with 1 tbs nonhydrogenated
    peanut butter (100) (P)
1 cup skim milk (80) (P, C)
(total calories: 370)

lunch:

"cheese pocket":
    † 2 oz low-fat cheese, e.g., Mozzarella (160) (P), melted in 1
        wholewheat pita (pocket) bread (140) (C), with lettuce,
        tomato, onions, mushrooms
relish tray and yogurt dip:
    *** 1 cup sliced cauliflower, broccoli, green pepper, celery,
        carrot, etc. (25) (C)
    ½ cup low-fat yogurt (80) (P, C), as dip, seasoned with 1 tsp dry
        onion flakes or 1 tsp ranch dressing mix
(total calories: 405)

snack:

* ¾ cup fresh or frozen unsweetened strawberries (40) (C)
1 small slice (1½-inch wedge) angel food cake (70) (C)
(total calories: 110)

supper:

† 3 oz broiled London broil (flank steak) (180) (P)
½ cup noodles (85) (C), with 1 tsp tub margarine (35) (F)
** ½ cup carrots (20) (C), with *** parsley
* ½ cup steamed cabbage (20) (C), with lemon
1 cup tossed salad (20) (C), with 1 tbs Italian dressing (65) (F)
** 1 cup watermelon (45) (C)
(total calories: 470)

snack:

1 cup skim milk (80) (P, C)
2 graham cracker squares (70) (C)
(total calories: 150)
(Day's Total: 1,505)

Day #6

breakfast:

½ cup apple juice (hot or cold) (60) (C)
1 wholewheat bagel (140) (C), with 1 tsp tub margarine (35) (F)
1 oz smoked turkey (60) (P)
1 cup skim milk (80) (P, C)
(total calories: 375)

lunch:

*** 1 cup minestrone soup (115) (C)
hamburger:
    1 wholewheat hamburger bun (140) (C), † 2 oz lean ground beef
       (120) (P), mustard, lettuce, tomato, onion, pickle
    ** 1 medium peach (40) (C)
    (total calories: 415)

snack:

3 cups air-popped popcorn (popped without fat or salt) (90) (C)

supper:

seafood creole:
    3 oz mixed seafood (165) (P), cooked in ½ cup tomato sauce with
       diced pepper, onion, celery (45) (C), served over 1 cup rice
       (160) (C)
½ cup green beans (20) (C), with lemon juice
1 cup tossed salad (20) (C), with 1 tsp oil (35) (F), vinegar
* ½ cup ambrosia (½ cup mandarin orange and grapefruit sections)
    (40) (C), with 1 tbs coconut and nuts (60) (F)
1 cup skim milk (80) (P, C)
(total calories: 625)
(Day's Total: 1,505)

Day #7

breakfast:

1 medium banana (80) (C)
cheese toast:

† 1 oz low-fat cheese, e.g., farmer's cheese (80) (P) melted on 2
    slices wholewheat bread (140) (C)
1 cup skim milk (80) (P, C)
(total calories: 380)

lunch:

1 cup vegetable bean soup (130) (C)
*** stuffed tomato:
    1 tomato (20) (C), filled with ½ cup water-packed tuna or
        salmon (120) (P), 2 tsp mayonnaise (70) (F), diced green
        pepper, celery, onion, parsley, seasonings
6 wholewheat crackers (80) (C)
(total calories: 420)

supper:

Chinese stir-fry dinner:
    3 oz sliced chicken (180) (P) and *** 1½ cups mixed vegetables:
        sliced broccoli, mushrooms, onions, snowpeas, celery,
        carrots, bamboo shoots, water chestnuts, almonds (75) (C),
        cooked in 1 tbs oil (105), 1 tbs soy sauce, over 1 cup brown
        rice (180) (C)
Hawaiian salad:
    ¾ cup strawberries, banana, pineapple (60) (C), topped with ½
        cup low-fat plain yogurt (80) (P, C), and 1 tbs grapenuts
        (25) (C)
(total calories: 705)
Day's Total: 1,505)

2,200-CALORIE MENUS (WEIGHT MAINTENANCE FOR MEN)

(Note: The daily average menu composition for this diet is 50 percent
complex carbohydrates, 20 percent protein, and 30 percent fat. The
approximate daily calorie distribution is 25 percent of the calories at
breakfast, 30 percent at lunch, and 45 percent at supper. Calorie values
of snacks vary.)

Day #1

breakfast:

* 1 cup unsweetened orange juice (80) (C)
1 poached egg (80) (P)
1 slice wholewheat toast (70) (C), with 1 tsp tub margarine (35) (C)
1 cup shredded wheat cereal (180) (C), with 1 cup skim milk (80) (P,
    C), and ½ banana (40) (C)
(total calories: 565)

lunch:

tuna sandwich:
    2 slices wholewheat bread (140) (C), ¾ cup water-packed tuna
        (180) (P), with 2 tsp mayonnaise (70) (F), lemon juice,
        pickle, lettuce
* 1 cup coleslaw (25) (C) made with 1 tsp mayonnaise (35) (F),
    lemon, vinegar
1 medium apple (80) (C)
4 graham crackers (140) (C)
(total calories: 670)

supper:

4 oz broiled, skinless chicken (240) (P)
* 1 large baked potato (130) (C), with 2 tsp tub margarine (70) (F)
2 wholewheat dinner rolls (2 inches across) (180) (C)
** 1 cup fresh carrots (40) (C)
1 cup fresh green beans (40) (C)
1 cup tossed lettuce/tomato/cucumber salad (20) (C), with 1 tsp oil
    (35) (F) and vinegar
1 cup fresh or unsweetened pineapple chunks (130) (C)
1 cup skim milk (80) (P, C)
(total calories: 965)
(Day's Total: 2,200)

Day #2

breakfast:

*** ¼ cantaloupe (45) (C), topped with ½ cup low-fat cottage cheese
(100) (P)
2 wholewheat English muffins (280) (C), with 2 tsp tub margarine
(70) (F)
1 cup skim milk (80) (P, C)
(total calories: 575)

lunch:

turkey sandwich:
2 slices wholewheat bread (140) (C), 3 oz turkey (180) (P), 2 tsp
mayonnaise (70) (F), lettuce, tomato
** 1 small raw carrot, in sticks (20) (C)
½ cup three-bean salad (150) (P, C)
1 medium pear (50) (C)
(total calories: 610)

snack:

3 cups air-popped popcorn, popped without fat or salt (90) (C)

supper:

3 oz baked sole (165) (P), cooked with ½ cup onions and mushrooms
(20) (C)
1 large ear of corn (130) (C), with 1 tsp tub margarine (35) (F)
1 cup green peas (110) (C)
1 cup tossed vegetable salad (20) (C), with 1 tsp oil (35) (F), and
vinegar
2 wholewheat dinner rolls (2 inches across) (180) (C), with 2 tsp tub
margarine (70) (F)
milkshake: blend together: 1 cup skim milk (80) (P, C), 1 fresh peach
or 2 canned unsweetened halves (40) (C), ½ banana (40) (C)
(total calories: 925)
(Day's Total: 2,200)

Day #3

breakfast:

½ small banana (40) (C)
¾ cup grapenuts (330) (C), with ½ tsp cinnamon, if desired
1 cup skim milk (80) (P, C)
1 slice wholewheat toast (70) (C), with 1 tsp tub margarine (35) (F)
(total calories: 555)

lunch:

1 cup lentil soup (160) (P, C)
½ cup low-fat cottage cheese (100) (P), atop * 1 cup fresh fruit salad,
     including citrus fruit (80) (C)
2 wholewheat muffins (2 inches across) (200) (C), with 2 tsp tub
     margarine (70) (F)
*** 1 tomato, in wedges (20) (C)
sliced cucumbers, with 1 tsp oil (35) (F), mint, dill, vinegar
(total calories: 665)

supper:

3 oz broiled veal chop (210) (P)
1 cup spaghetti (180) (C), topped with 3 tbs Parmesan cheese (75) (P)
2 slices wholewheat garlic bread (140) (C), with 2 tsp tub margarine
     (70) (F)
1 cup zucchini (15) (C)
1 cup cauliflower (25) (C)
** 1 cup spinach salad (30) (C), with 1 tbs Italian dressing (65) (F)
** 1 fresh nectarine (40) (C)
20 seedless Thompson grapes (50) (C)
1 cup skim milk (80) (P, C)
(total calories: 980)
(Day's Total: 2,200)

Day #4

breakfast:

* ½ grapefruit (40) (C)
2 cups hot oatmeal (300) (C), with cinnamon if desired, and 2 tsp tub
    margarine (70) (F)
1 cup skim milk (80) (P)
(total calories: 490)

snack:

† 1 oz low-fat cheese (e.g., Mozzarella, farmer's cheese) (80) (P)
6 wholewheat crackers (80) (C)
(total calories: 160)

lunch:

3 oz roasted chicken (180) (P)
1 cup wild rice (220) (C)
1 cup green peas (110) (C)
** 1 cup carrot-raisin salad: 1 cup shredded carrots (60) (C), 2 tbs
    raisins (40) (C), 1 tsp mayonnaise (35) (F)
2 small or 1 medium plum (45) (C)
(total calories: 690)

supper:

† 4 oz lean roast beef (240) (P)
* 1 large baked potato (130) (C), with 1 tsp tub margarine (35) (F)
2 wholewheat rolls (2 inches across) (180) (C), with 2 tsp tub
    margarine (70) (F)
1 cup yellow squash (15) (C)
** 1 cup spinach in lemon, vinegar (40) (C)
1 cup tossed salad (20) (C), with 1 tbs French dressing (65) (F)
1 cup skim milk (80) (P, C)
(total calories: 875)
(Day's Total: 2,215)

Day #5

breakfast:

* ½ cup unsweetened orange juice (40) (C)
1 medium baked apple, with cinnamon (80) (C)
2 slices wholewheat toast (140) (C), with 2 tbs nonhydrogenated
    peanut butter (200) (P)
1 cup skim milk (80) (P, C)
(total calories: 540)

lunch:

"cheese pocket":
    † 3 oz low-fat cheese, e.g., Mozzarella (240) (P), melted in 1
        wholewheat pita (pocket) bread (140) (C), with lettuce,
        tomato, onions, mushrooms
relish tray and dip:
    1 cup sliced cauliflower, broccoli, green pepper, celery, carrots
    ½ cup low-fat yogurt (80) (P, C), as dip, seasoned with 1 tsp dry
        onion flakes or 1 tsp ranch dressing mix
1 banana (80) (C)
(total calories: 560)

snack:

* ¾ cup fresh or unsweetened strawberries (40) (C)
1 small slice (1½-inch wedge) angel food cake (70) (C)
(total calories: 110)

supper:

4 oz broiled London broil (flank steak) (240) (P)
1 cup noodles (170) (C), with 2 tsp tub margarine (70) (F)
3 bread sticks (120) (C)
** ½ cup carrots, with *** parsley (20) (C)
* ½ cup steamed cabbage, with lemon (20) (C)
1 cup tossed salad (20) (C), with 1 tbs Italian dressing (65) (F)
** 1 cup watermelon (45) (C)
(total calories: 770)

snack:

1 cup skim milk (80) (P, C)
4 graham crackers (140) (C)
(total calories: 220)
(Day's Total: 2,200)

Day #6

breakfast:

½ cup apple juice (hot or cold) (60) (C)
2 wholewheat bagels (280) (C), with 2 tsp tub margarine (70) (F)
1 oz smoked turkey (60) (P)
1 cup skim milk (80) (P, C)
(total calories: 550)

lunch:

*** 1 cup minestrone soup (115) (C)
4 wholewheat crackers (60) (C)
hamburger:
    1 wholewheat hamburger bun (140) (C), † 3 oz lean ground beef
        (180) (P), mustard, lettuce, tomato, onion, pickle
* ½ cup potato salad: ½ cup potato cubes (70) (C), with 2 tsp
    mayonnaise (70) (F), celery, onion, seasonings
** 1 medium peach (40) (C)
(total calories: 675)

snack:

3 cups air-popped popcorn without fat or salt (90) (C)

supper:

seafood creole:
    4 oz mixed seafood (220) (P), cooked in *** ½ cup tomato sauce,
        diced green pepper, onion, celery (45) (C), served over 1
        cup rice (160) (C)
1 cup green beans (20) (C), with lemon juice
1 cup tossed salad (20) (C), with 1 tsp oil (35) (F), vinegar
1 wholewheat muffin (2 inches across) (100) (C)
* 1 cup ambrosia (1 cup mandarin orange and grapefruit sections)
    (80) (C) and 2 tbs coconut and nuts (120) (F)
1 cup skim milk (80) (P, C)
(total calories: 880)
(Day's Total: 2,195)

Day #7

breakfast:

½ cup unsweetened orange juice (40) (C)
1 banana (80) (C)
2 cheese toasts: 4 slices wholewheat bread (280) (C), with melted 2 oz
        † low-fat cheese, e.g., farmer's cheese (160) (P)
(total calories: 560)

lunch:

1 cup vegetable-bean soup (130) (P, C)
6 wholewheat crackers (80) (C)
stuffed tomato:
        1 tomato (20) (C), filled with ¾ cup water-packed tuna or
                salmon (180) (P), 1 tbs mayonnaise (105) (F), diced green
                pepper, onion, celery, parsley, seasonings, etc. (C)
1 medium apple (80) (C)
1 cup skim milk (80) (P, C)
(total calories: 675)

supper:

Chinese stir-fry dinner:
        3 oz sliced chicken (180) (P), and 1½ cups mixed vegetables:
                sliced broccoli, mushrooms, onions, snowpeas, celery,
                carrots, bamboo shoots, water chestnuts, almonds (75) (C)
                cooked in 1 tbs soy sauce, 1 tbs oil (105) (F), poured over 1
                cup brown rice (180) (C)
2 wholewheat rolls (2 inches across) (180) (C), with 2 tsp tub
        margarine (70) (F)
Hawaiian salad:
        ¾ cup strawberries, banana, pineapple (60) (C), topped with ½
                cup low-fat plain yogurt (80) (P, C), and 1 tbs grapenuts
                (25) (C)
(total calories: 955)
(Day's Total: 2,190)

So these specific menus represent some practical examples of the
50-20-30 percentage formula that should control the distribution of the
calories among the foods that you consume each day. But there's another
important percentage formula that concerns the number of total calories
you should consume at *each meal* during the day. And that brings us to

the second basic principle of balanced eating, which is intended for those who want to lose weight or who have a great deal of trouble maintaining their ideal weight once they reach it.

PRINCIPLE TWO: FOLLOW THE 25-50-25 RULE TO DETERMINE THE AMOUNT OF FOOD YOU SHOULD EAT AT EACH MEAL TO ACHIEVE WEIGHT LOSS

I am convinced that if you consume the largest proportion of your calories *before* 1:00 P.M., you will have less of a problem controlling your weight than if you consume the same number of calories *after* 1:00 P.M. The reason for this isn't entirely clear. Perhaps if you take in most of your food early in the day, you can process it more readily because your body remains relatively active during most of the digestive process. But whatever the reason, I'm sufficiently convinced of the validity of this principle that I recommend that if you want to lose weight, you should try to eat at least 25 percent of the daily calories at breakfast and 50 percent at lunch, with only 25 percent on the table at supper.

In a recent study at the Aerobics Center, one group of overweight women followed a 1,200-calorie daily diet and ate 25 percent of those calories at breakfast, 50 percent at lunch, and 25 percent at supper. Even at this relatively generous calorie level, they maintained an average weight loss of 1 to 2 pounds per week.

Even if you don't want to lose weight right now, the older you get the more likely you are to develop some sort of weight problem. So I would suggest that everyone try to weight his or her caloric consumption somewhat more heavily in favor of the morning and early afternoon hours.

For example, if you want to be sure you'll maintain your present weight for the foreseeable future, you might eat 25 percent of your calories for breakfast, 30 percent for lunch, and 45 percent for the evening meal. In this way, you'll be taking in more than half of your daily calories by the early afternoon, and your chances of maintaining your present weight will be greatly improved.

PRINCIPLE THREE: ENGAGE IN AEROBIC EXERCISE PRIOR TO A MEAL, AND PREFERABLY THE EVENING MEAL

Research we are doing suggests that the timing of your exercise may have an effect on the control of fat and weight. In other words, if you exercise vigorously just before the evening meal—that is, no earlier than 2 hours prior to the meal—you'll be more likely to lose a larger percentage of body fat than if you exercise at other times during the day.

What's the reason for this principle which seems to be emerging in our research?

As with the 25-50-25 rule, we really don't have all the answers. But it is known that vigorous exercise tends to depress the appetite for a couple of hours after the activity, and so it may be that those who work out in the late afternoon just tend to eat less than they would otherwise. Also, it's known that the body metabolism tends to increase during the day, and then starts to slow down as nighttime approaches. As a result, you tend to burn less calories in the evening than earlier in the day. So if you exercise late in the afternoon, you may be increasing the pace of your metabolism, and simultaneously increasing the ability of your body to burn more calories in the evening.

Regardless of the time of the day that you work out, exercise in conjunction with a restrictive dietary program accelerates the loss of fat with minimal loss of muscle, whereas caloric restriction without exercise may burn up muscle. Ann Blankenship Ph.D./R.D., one of our staff nutritionists at the Aerobics Center, recently conducted a study documenting this fact. Thirty-eight overweight women were placed on 1,200-calorie-per-day diets. One group of 12 women followed the dietary restrictive program only, while the others exercised in conjunction with dieting. Fourteen exercised by walking and jogging for 30 minutes before breakfast, and 12 exercised for 30 minutes before the evening meal.

After 5 weeks, there was no significant difference in the amount of weight lost among the three groups (7.54 pounds for the control group; 8.35 pounds for the morning exercisers; and 8.08 pounds for the late-afternoon exercisers). Yet the percentage of body fat determined by underwater weighing showed that the control group who had not exercised had lost 3.14 pounds of muscle mass; the morning exercisers lost 1.67 pounds of muscle mass; and the late-afternoon exercisers actually *gained* 0.44 pounds of muscle mass!

As you consider these results, remember this very important fact: The key thing in any weight loss program is lowering your percentage of body fat, not just losing pounds. So this study tends to show that exercise prior to the evening meal, in conjunction with a dietary restrictive program, is an effective and beneficial way to lose body fat.

PRINCIPLE FOUR: DEVELOP A HEALTHY FEAR OF OBESITY

Carrying just five extra pounds around the middle or on the bottom may create a deadlier drag on the body than most people, including many physicians, now imagine. We already know definitely that being *grossly* overweight—say 30 or 40 pounds or more—can contribute to all sorts of life-threatening health problems, like coronary disease and cancer. But it may also well be that *any* amount of extra fat in some way acts as a trigger for much more serious diseases, or as a repository of deadly substances that we have little or no understanding of at our present stage of research.

As a matter of fact, certain research findings and case studies are now convincing me that obesity is one of the top three or four factors in causing coronary problems. Obesity may even be detrimental *alone*— that is, it may be unrelated to other coronary risk factors, such as hypertension. elevated cholesterol, triglycerides, and blood sugar. In other words, obesity seems to be an *independent* coronary risk factor. And if this conclusion is correct, we Americans have a truly monstrous problem to contend with.

To understand just how large a challenge we face, let's first look at a couple of rather startling facts. First of all, it has been estimated that at least 50 million Americans are, taken together, carrying in excess of *1 billion pounds* of extra weight. I hope that with a statistic like that, we don't sink beneath the surface of the earth!

Secondly, consider what happened in 1976 when the old Yankee Stadium in New York City was renovated. There was a loss of about 9,000 seats in the total seating capacity, and some people, concerned about the potential loss of revenues, wondered why. The answer apparently lay in the increased size of the modern American's posterior: The new seats were wider than the old seats by some 3 inches! And Yankee Stadium only presents the tip of the iceberg. Even airlines and movie theaters have installed larger seats for "growing" Americans.

But now, let's bring these figures down to a more personal level. One of the most dramatic and disturbing examples I've encountered of the life-threatening problems of obesity involved a patient and personal friend. As a dentist who was under some professional pressures, he first came to our clinic in 1972 after attending one of my seminars on aerobics and total well-being. At that time, he was 53 years of age; he was 6 feet 1 inch tall; and he weighed 204 pounds, with 25 percent body fat.

Except for his moderately elevated weight, everything else was quite normal. His blood pressure was well within limits; his cholesterol was in the normal range; and because he participated in a regular jogging program, his treadmill stress test scores were consistently within the excellent to superior categories. When we started identifying the ratio of total cholesterol to HDL in the late 1970s, his ratios were found to be within reasonably healthy limits—from about 4.5 to 5.0.

As you'll see in more detail in the following chapter, we believe that a man's total cholesterol to HDL cholesterol ratio should be less than 4.5 if possible, and should be corrected if it is above 5.0. Anything above 5.0 and certainly above 6.0 would indicate a steady build-up of fatty deposits in the blood vessels which could result in future coronary disease. The ratios for a woman, by the way, should generally be lower—always less than 4.0, and preferably less than 3.5.

But despite his apparently good health, my friend couldn't keep his weight down. We pegged his best body weight at 180 pounds, a level that would have put him at about 19 percent body fat (or the maximum fat that a healthy man should have). Anything above 19 percent involves a progressively greater risk of heart disease. But he was always 5 to 20 pounds overweight when he came in for his annual check-ups.

Now, 5 to 20 excess pounds may not seem that important: In fact, you yourself may be that much overweight. But for this patient, that additional weight was his Achilles' heel.

In the late 1970s his stress tests on our clinic treadmill began to indicate some sort of underlying coronary problem. Yet he didn't show any of the usual symptoms of heart disease and continued to run 15 to 20 miles a week with no apparent difficulty. So at the time, we felt that there was no need for a coronary arteriogram or bypass surgery—just that it was imperative that he stop eating so much and go on a strict weight reduction program.

But still, he failed to keep his weight down, and the results were disastrous. Nine years after he had first come to our clinic and had first been told to take off those extra pounds, he had a massive heart attack. His heart had to be shocked three times in the hospital just to restore the normal rhythm. Later, a pacemaker was placed in his heart to keep it functioning, and he remained almost an invalid for about 9 months. Finally, he died in the hospital of chronic congestive heart failure.

Now, I'm not saying that everybody—or even *almost* everybody—will face such a fate simply because of moderate obesity. But the evidence continues to mount that there is much more to a poor diet, which results in obesity, than meets the eye. You simply *can't* feel protected from coronary heart disease as long as you are overweight, even though all the other risk factors are normal. I'll confess that I don't completely understand why simply being overweight, when everything about a person's health seems all right, may be a key factor in an untimely death.

But as I indicated earlier, I'm becoming more and more convinced that obesity of *any* degree can be a major contributing factor to all sorts of health problems, including serious coronary disease.

Finally, in addition to being responsible for low energy levels, emotional problems related to a poor self-image, and heart trouble, too much body fat is directly connected to certain other life-threatening physical ailments. To give you an idea of the seriousness of the problems that you may be facing if you're carrying extra body fat, here are a few of the latest available findings:

- Recent studies indicate that certain types of fat distribution, such as fat that accumulates primarily above the waist, can be correlated with an increased risk of developing diabetes.
- The survival rate of women who have had a cancerous breast removed is higher for lighter than for heavier patients. In one study of the survival rates of women who had undergone a mastectomy to remove breast cancer, 62 percent of the women who weighed less than 140 pounds were still free of any recurrence of the disease 5 years later. In contrast, only 45 percent of the women in the study who weighed more than 140 pounds were still cancer-free.
- Another study has shown that women who are 40 percent or more above their ideal weight have an increased risk of cancer of the uterus, ovaries, gall bladder, and breast.
- The picture is similarly bleak for overweight men: Those who are 40 percent or more above their ideal weight show an increase in cancer of the colon, rectum, and prostate.
- If a person has high blood pressure—either the upper (systolic) or lower (diastolic) figure—the blood pressure usually will improve following weight loss. And if you control your blood pressure, you reduce your chances of suffering a stroke, which most commonly results from high blood pressure. Since an estimated 40 million Americans have high blood pressure, it's imperative that more people start cutting down on their excessive percentages of body fat.
- Obesity is included among the eleven major coronary risk factors listed recently by the American Heart Association. And as I've already indicated, our research at the Aerobics Center suggests that excessive body fat is fast becoming one of the most important factors to watch in predicting potential coronary problems.

So obesity is certainly a problem—indeed, it's the most serious problem we face as far as our diets are concerned. But strangely enough, in our overweight society there are also a number of cases of bad health or death, even among the affluent, from not getting enough food, or at least, not getting enough of the *right* food. Studies have shown that those who are the healthiest are those who (1) eat the most food (during three regular meals a day), *but* (2) *maintain a proper weight with exercise.*

PRINCIPLE FIVE: BE CAREFUL NOT TO STARVE YOUR BODY WITH TOO FEW CALORIES

This may seem strange advice since we in America have more of a problem with overweight than underweight people. But the tendency to consume too few calories *voluntarily*, with sometimes deadly results, is a growing concern on several fronts.

One of the most publicized forms of malnutrition among the well-to-do is anorexia nervosa, which usually affects young women. Perhaps you have encountered this problem in your own family or you know someone who has suffered from it. The young women in effect starve themselves by extremely restrictive dieting and, at times, self-induced vomiting. This is a problem which requires immediate, expert psychological care and certainly is cause for serious concern among other family members.

But there's another kind of inadequate nutrition which is not quite as well known, though in some ways it's even more insidious because it can slip up almost unnoticed on those who appear to be the most healthy among us. I'm talking about a condition called "nutritional arrhythmia," which may occur in hard-training athletes as a result of insufficient food.

Dr. Thomas J. Bassler, in a report in the *Journal of the American Medical Association*, discussed twelve top-flight, thin marathoners who recently had set new personal speed or mileage records—but who had all died, mostly during their sleep. At the time of death, they were at or near their lowest body weight as adults, and they were all severely restricting their diets so that they took in only minimal amounts of calories, fat, cholesterol, alcohol, or salt.

The exact cause of death of these runners is unknown, but the term "nutritional arrhythmia" has come into vogue to explain what happened to them. In other words, they starved their hearts by eating too little food to support the amount of exercise they were getting, and their hearts rebelled. Dr. Bassler concluded that joggers of average build who run average training mileage have less risk of death than those who vary greatly from the mean, as did these marathoners.

The moral to this story, once again, is balance. If you run or swim long distances or otherwise greatly increase your exercise, you also have to increase the food your body needs, or suffer the consequences. And in any case, for most people it's best to seek an exercise balance which is sufficient to keep the body in top shape but which doesn't involve going to the extremes of conditioning pursued by our top athletes.

PRINCIPLE SIX: KNOW THE FORMULA FOR DETERMINING YOUR IDEAL WEIGHT

The human physique is meant to have a proper balance between body fat on the one hand, and muscle mass and bone on the other. Unfortunately, as we've seen in Principles Four and Five, many people allow that state of equilibrium to disintegrate, usually so that there is far more body fat than we need, in proportion to the solid structures in our bodies.

At the Aerobics Center, we have a scientific method for determining a person's body fat balance: We measure the percentage of body fat through a combination of underwater weighing and measuring skinfold thicknesses at various parts of the body.

But for the average person, this measurement may be impossible or prohibitively expensive. So we've come up with a variation of the widely recognized "Mahoney Formula" to enable the average person to calculate his or her ideal weight.

The formula works like this:

Men should take their height in inches, multiply that figure by 4, and then subtract 128. Women should take their height in inches, multiply it by 3.5 and then subtract 108. These calculations will give men of medium bone structure a weight with roughly 15 to 19 percent body fat, and women of average build a weight with body fat in the 18 to 22 percent range.

We have set a maximum *athletic* body-fat weight for men at 15 percent and for women at 18 percent. But in no case should a man's body fat exceed 19 percent or a woman's 22 percent. Scientific research shows that an individual must establish a balance of fat-to-solid-mass at no more than these percentage ranges in order to be in the state of physical equilibrium that promotes the greatest well-being. Less body fat than this is common among highly conditioned athletes and is perfectly all right. But more body fat than these amounts will automatically increase the risk of coronary disease.

To use a concrete example, I am 6 feet 1 inch, or 73 inches tall. If you multiply 73 by 4, you end up with 292. Then subtract 128 from 292, and the answer is 164 pounds. For the past 20 years, my weight has fluctuated from about 164 to 170 pounds.

But you may say, "I have large bones—does this same formula work for me?"

The answer is yes, it does work, but it's necessary for large-boned people to *add 10 percent* to the figure they have determined as their best body weight. As a general rule of thumb, you can tell if your bone structure is large by measuring the circumference of your dominant wrist—i.e., the wrist supporting the hand with which you write. A man has large bone size if his wrist is greater than 7 inches. A woman has large bone size if her wrist size is greater than 6½ inches. Any measurements less than these would classify the person in either the medium or small-boned categories.

For example, when former Dallas Cowboys' quarterback Roger Staubach came in recently for a check-up, we determined that at his height of 6 feet 2½ inches (74½ inches), his weight if he were a medium-boned man should have been 170 pounds. But his wrist size is considerably larger than 7 inches, so we added 10 percent to his weight (or 17 pounds) to get 187 pounds for his ideal body weight.

As a matter of fact, underwater weighing methods have established Staubach's weight at 190 pounds, and his body-fat percentage is only 9 percent. This is an indication that despite the fact he is over the ideal weight for most men his size, he is carrying the extra few pounds on his body in muscle and bone, rather than fat. So for a highly conditioned athlete, the extra muscle may cause the total weight to be higher than our formula might predict. But for most of us, the ideal-weight formula works quite well.

One final note: Excessively low body fat can cause some abnormalities or irregularities. Women who reach a body-fat level under 15 percent may develop menstrual changes or irregularities. Even fertility experts are recognizing the percentage of body fat as a key factor in pregnancy.

PRINCIPLE SEVEN: KNOW THE FORMULA FOR THE NUMBER OF CALORIES YOU NEED EACH DAY TO MAINTAIN YOUR IDEAL WEIGHT

Just as there is a proper balance for fat in the body, so there is also a proper balance for the number of calories you should take in each day to maintain your best weight.

Now, I'm not a big advocate of calorie counting, because most people are just not going to take the time to figure out how many calories are contained in each helping on their plates. But at the same time, I think it's important to have some *general* idea of how many calories the foods you eat contain. So you might first make a short list of the foods you consume on a typical day, then figure out the total number of calories you're taking in on that typical day by using the calorie conversion charts in the Appendix at the back of this book.

The next step is to compare the number of calories you are eating with the number you *should* be eating, and make adjustments in your eating habits accordingly. The formula we use at the Aerobics Center to determine the number of calories you should be consuming each day is to take your ideal body weight, as determined under Principle Six, and multiply that number by 12 up to 40 years of age, and by 10 after that. This will give you the number of calories you need just to meet your very basic bodily requirements. For me, that would involve taking my ideal weight of 164 pounds and multiplying by 10 since I am over 40, to give me 1,640 calories per day.

But if you want to get maximum energy—without gaining any weight—it's necessary to add a few additional calories. For example, if you are involved exclusively in sedentary activities, such as office work without any outside exercise, you should multiply your ideal body weight by 15 or 13, according to whether you're under or over 40. So, if we assume that I'm a sedentary person, I would multiply my weight (164) times 13 and end up with 2,132 calories as the proper amount I should consume each day.

If you're involved in strenuous physical activity, I would suggest that you multiply your body weight by 20, regardless of age. Strenuous activity, as we define it, would involve either working at a job of manual labor for up to 8 hours a day, or exercising to the extent that you are burning at least 500 calories per day.

So, if you run 5 miles or more daily, you would multiply your weight by 20. For example, a man weighing 164 pounds should consume 3,280 calories, which is enough just to maintain ideal body weight. If you run 3 miles or less each day, I would suggest that you multiply your weight by 15 instead of 20 to get the number of calories you should consume daily.

As you can see, we're talking in terms of a delicate balance here as we discuss how much food and how many calories you should eat to maintain your weight. But even if your calorie balance is only slightly out of kilter, say in the direction of a hundred too many calories a day, you're heading for trouble at some point down the road.

Consuming 100 extra calories a day (10 potato chips) puts on 10 pounds per year. Or even worse, 200 calories more than you need each day will result in a weight gain of 1 pound every 18 days, or a total of almost 20 pounds per year!

By consuming too many calories, you're in effect putting too much total fuel into your system, with the result that the food is gradually, even imperceptibly, turning to fat. And before long, that imperceptible overabundance of calories is going to become quite obvious in the form of an unsightly and unhealthy roll around your middle. And believe me, well-being and overweight are simply not compatible.

It stands to reason that too many extra pounds will require you to put forth more effort to catch a bus, to walk from one appointment to the next, or to play some weekend games with your friends or family. Imagine how you would feel if each morning you strapped a 10- or 20-pound weight to your waist, then lugged it around with you until bedtime. It's more likely that your bedtime would come a little earlier than normal as the extra weight drained your energy reserves, wouldn't you say?

The same principle applies as far as your extra body fat is concerned. And that's why it's so crucial to determine the precise balance of calories to take into your system so that your human fuel is used for fuel, and not for fat.

PRINCIPLE EIGHT: IF YOU'RE CARRYING TOO MUCH FAT, GET STARTED ON YOUR OWN PERSONAL POSITIVE EATING PLAN (P.E.P.) FOR LOSING WEIGHT

It doesn't do a bit of good to go on a diet one month and then go off it the next. My experience has shown that if you need to lose a few pounds, control your cholesterol intake, or achieve some other important purpose, you're sure to fail unless you can be consistent.

I call this on-again, off-again dieting approach the "roller-coaster effect," because that's exactly what happens: The person's weight goes up and down as he or she goes off or on the diet. It's a sad fact that about 90 percent of all people who go on a weight-reduction program or other specialized diet eventually go off it—and before long they are tipping the scales right up there in the high poundage range where they were before they started the diet.

And to complicate this problem, after near-fasting dietary programs (500 calories a day or less), you may gain weight more rapidly even when you eat fewer calories than you did before.

In *The 200 Calorie Solution*, a recently published book by Martin Katahn from Vanderbilt University, the author has shown that after 3 weeks on a highly restrictive dietary program, the body readjusts its metabolism so as to maintain its weight at a lower caloric consumption.

For example, if a person requires 2,000 calories a day to maintain body weight and then goes on a 300–500 calorie per day diet for 3 weeks, his or her metabolism is readjusting to the reduced calories. By the third week, the readjusted metabolism can maintain the person's weight on only 1,000 calories per day. (If this didn't happen, he or she would die of starvation in about 2 weeks!)

So after losing the desired weight, the dieter will typically start back eating about 1,500 calories a day but then will be shocked to find that, even at this low level, he or she is gaining a pound per week— even though fewer calories are being consumed than when the dieter originally started on the diet!

The lowered metabolism, which is causing the more rapid weight gain, may persist for as long as 1 year after stopping the very low calorie diet. This phenomenon explains to me why many of my obese patients complain after frequent dieting that they gain weight more easily than they ever have before. Apparently, they aren't imagining things: They really can gain weight on minimal calories. So to avoid this problem, stay clear of the crash diets and stick to a dietary-exercise program. Also, arrange your diet program so as to consume your calories in the 25-50-25 percentages discussed in Principle Two. This approach will enable you to lose 2 to 3 pounds per week, no more, no less, and the weight you lose this way will be much more likely to stay off!

It's neither wise nor necessary to get on the weight-gain-and-loss roller coaster. At least, it's not necessary if you establish your own Positive Eating Plan of the type that has been developed by nutritionists and registered dietitians like Georgia Kostas, director of our nutrition programs at the Aerobics Center.

A P.E.P. plan consists of an individualized, sensible, well-balanced eating pattern that can be followed for life. It emphasizes eating habits that are conducive to lifelong weight control. Here are some of the basics of the P.E.P. approach:

1. Eat a well-balanced diet, with a variety of foods at each meal. "Balanced" here means eating foods containing carbohydrates (fruits, vegetables, grains, starches); protein (meat or dairy products, beans, or peas); fats (oil or margarine); and fluids at each meal. This combination will allow more long-lasting energy throughout a day. Carbohydrates are burned first (thus giving you a burst of energy for 3–4 hours). Protein then boosts your energy for the next 1–2 hours; and fats pick up the remaining fifth or sixth hour, right up to your next meal!

Also, be sure to keep in mind the 50-20-30 percent concept, described in Principle One, when you're distributing your calories in these first three food categories over the course of the day.

2.   *Establish consistent eating patterns, including three meals a day.* The old tradition of the importance of three square meals a day has a great deal of truth in it. This kind of regular eating promotes sound nutrition through more variety in your food and nutrients. It prevents broad fluctuations in blood sugar (which regulates appetite and influences your personal energy levels and your ability to handle stress well). And it prevents a "starve-stuff" eating pattern which often results in overeating. So don't skip meals—especially breakfast. And once again, remember Principle Two, which calls for following the 25-50-25 percent rule for those involved in serious weight reduction programs. This approach will spread out your calories in the healthiest way during the three meals you eat each day.

3.   *Decrease calorie intake and increase calorie expenditure.* One pound of stored fat equals 3,500 calories. To lose 2 pounds (7,000 calories) weekly, you should omit 1,000 calories of your food intake daily. To achieve even faster weight loss and lose primarily fat rather than muscle mass, you should increase your physical activity, including aerobic exercises like walking and jogging. But don't overdo the weight reduction program. A loss of 1–2 pounds each week is the best rate at which you should lose weight if you intend to keep it off.

4.   *Eat fewer foods high in fat.* The ones you should limit include: fried foods, butter, margarine, mayonnaise, oils, sauces, salad dressings, nuts, avocado, olives, granola, party crackers and dips, fast foods, convenience foods, commercial pastries, fatty meat products (bacon, sausage, cold cuts, hot dogs), marbled beef, lamb, pork, high-fat dairy products (whole milk, sour or sweet cream, most cheeses, ice cream).

Also, use low-calorie salad dressings; limit intake of regular salad dressing; use low-fat yogurt in place of sour cream; drink skim milk; and eat skim milk or low-fat cheeses. Finally, choose dishes like chicken, turkey, and tuna sandwiches instead of hamburgers, cold cuts, fast foods, and pizza. Keep in mind that each gram of fat you eat contains double the calories of each gram of protein or carbohydrate! (1 gram of fat = 9 calories; 1 gram of protein or carbohydrate = 4 calories.)

5.   *Eat less sugar.* You'll find refined sugar in foods like table sugar, honey, jam, jelly, soft drinks, desserts, candy, cookies, cakes, pastries, processed foods and beverages, sweetened juices and canned fruit, and sugar-coated cereals. Important: Get in the habit of reading food labels to identify sugar content. In this regard, "sugar" is also labeled as "glucose," "corn sugar (sweeteners)," "dextrose," "fructose," and "lactose." Finally, limit yourself to one or two desserts a week. Sugar is a non-

nutritive, calorie-dense food, which means it adds a lot of calories in a very small volume, yet provides not a single vitamin or mineral.

6.   *Eat more low-calorie, high-volume, high-fiber foods.* Some examples are raw fruits and vegetables (eat the peels and seeds as well), baked potatoes, whole-grain cereals and breads, bran, popcorn, and broth-based soups.

7.   *Eat smaller meat portions.* I would suggest that you eat no more than 5 to 8 ounces (about two medium-sized servings) of lean meat, or poultry and fish, daily.

8.   *Eat more lean meats, poultry and fish.* If you're trying to lose or even maintain a good weight, it's especially important to arrange your diet heavily in favor of poultry, fish, and veal. Limit beef, lamb, pork, and cheese. When you do occasionally eat beef, concentrate on lean beef cuts, such as flank steak, tenderloin (filet, sirloin, T-bone), chuck, round, sirloin tip, and rump.

9.   *Prepare foods in a way that minimizes the use of fat.* Broil or bake meats on a rack. Drain off fat. For gravies, use meat drippings with fat skimmed off. Sauté foods in water (not fat). Steam vegetables or eat them raw—without sauces and dips. Use fat-free butter substitutes, such as butter-flavored granules and seasonings, calorie-free non-stick cooking sprays, and butter-flavored extract.

10.   *Limit alcohol.* One beer, a 2-ounce cocktail, or 6 ounces of wine contain 150 nonnutritive calories.

11.   *Eat low-calorie snacks.* These snacks encompass such foods as raw fruit and vegetables, popcorn (unbuttered), diet beverages, water, broth, tomato juice, and salads.

12.   *Drink six to eight glasses of fluids daily.* Water is still one of the best. Other fluids include low-fat milk, natural beverages such as unsweetened fruit juices, low-salt soups, and some dietary drinks (particularly those low in caffeine).

13.   *Eat slowly in a relaxed, pleasant environment.* Resolve to enjoy your food, and structure the atmosphere at each meal so that you do. Chew each bite thoroughly and allow at least 20 minutes to finish each meal. Remember: It takes 20 minutes to feel "full" after eating, so the more slowly you eat, the less likely you'll be to overeat.

14.   *Choose "crunchy" foods over "soft" foods.* Crunchy foods, like apples, take longer to chew than soft foods, like bananas, and therefore they can be more satisfying. Another bonus: Psychologically, we *need* to chew! It relieves stress and tension. Our dentist tells us he often observes marks on patients' teeth when they grind them together during sleep and at other times when they are under stress.

15.   *Preplan meals.* To avoid "impulse eating," have appropriate

low-calorie foods on hand. Planned meals and carefully practiced eating strategies prevent emotional moods, unexpected circumstances, parties, weekends, holidays, and vacations from interfering with your weight-loss goals.

16.   Limit sodium. Sources of sodium, which may be associated with hypertension, are salt, pickles, olives, luncheon meats, hot dogs, ham, bacon, sausage, cheeses, processed foods, fast foods, snack foods (chips, crackers, dips, pretzels), canned soups and vegetables, sauces (chili, barbecue, soy, steak), pizza, many "instant" products, TV dinners, and commercial bakery products. Suprisingly, some diet drinks are also high in salt. A 12-ounce diet drink contains 40–60 milligrams of sodium. This is not much compared to a pickle (1,900) or a cup of commercially prepared soup (1,100), but several drinks do add up. So limit yourself to two or three a day if you are limiting your sodium intake closely.

Remember: The body needs only 2 grams of sodium daily to meet its needs, and the average American consumption is between 12 and 20 grams per day!

17.   Eliminate external food "cues." Many outside influences may cause you to eat too much. For example, it's best to store extra food out of sight so you won't be tempted. Also, serve food from the stove in the portions you actually expect to eat, rather than putting excessive amounts on the table in food containers. Don't combine meals with TV, reading, or other activities that may distract you from being aware of how much you're actually eating. Finally, try to concentrate more on the meal you're eating, and don't let your mind wander to the dessert or other snack you plan to eat at some point in the future.

18.   Incorporate more activity into your daily schedule, and establish a regular exercise program. Regular exercise burns calories, depresses the appetite, and promotes cardiovascular and pulmonary health. In one study of overweight women who continued to put on extra pounds, it was discovered that they were consuming exactly the same number of calories per day as a lean group of women, whose weight was stable. But the heavier women walked an average of only 2 miles a day in their routine activities, whereas the lighter women were covering 5 miles. These activities included taking stairs instead of elevators, parking in the most remote spaces in the parking lot, walking to the neighborhood store for errands and taking an "after dinner" walk as a daily routine.

This difference of 3 miles of walking was equal to about 200 calories of energy expenditure daily. And remember, vigorous exercise immediately preceding a meal can effectively depress the appetite and assist in not only controlling weight, but *losing* weight (see Principle Three).

19. *Find ways to deal with stress effectively, without food or alcohol.* Problems with overeating and drinking too much can often be traced back to frustrations arising from your daily routine or a need to "relax" after the pressures from a hard day's work. But there are other ways, such as exercise and spiritual pursuits, that can help you deal with stress more effectively—and also help you avoid indulging in those extra calories.

20. *Establish lifelong eating and exercise habits for permanent weight control.* This is the essence of the P.E.P. approach to proper diet. Your ultimate goal should be to take off those pounds and then embark on a life-style that will enable you to *keep* them off. One simple but highly effective way of monitoring your progress is to weigh yourself regularly. Then, never allow yourself a weight gain of more than 2 to 3 pounds over your ideal weight, as you've determined it by using the formula described under Principle Six.

These, then, are some of the most important basic principles of nutritional balance for anyone who hopes to develop a healthy lifetime eating plan. We've seen that if you eat *too much*, even of the right sort of foods, you're going to start adding pounds and be confronted with all the problems, present and future, that accompany obesity. On the other hand, if you eat *too little*, you may also run into serious health problems. And finally, if your diet *isn't well-balanced*—even if the number of calories is about right—you may very well experience a marked lack of energy and even certain emotional problems from deficiencies of certain important nutrients.

But on a happier note, if you do eat properly, your energy levels will soar and you'll lay a firm foundation to get involved in enjoyable aerobic activities. What's more, you'll be well on your way to achieving that ultimate state we all desire, total well-being.

But before we leave this subject of good nutrition, it's necessary to spend some time examining a couple of the most controversial topics involving the body's proper balance that are being bruited about these days. The first of these is the all-important question of cholesterol and its relationship to heart disease and other ailments. The second is the issue of food supplements and special foods like fiber.

4

Is Your Blood in Balance? The Great Cholesterol Controversy

Are you one of those lucky people who enjoys:

- A glowing skin and healthy-colored complexion?
- Sharp vision?
- Warm toes and fingers, even on chilly days or nights?
- An incisive, agile intellect that enables you to grapple enthusiastically with tough problems?
- Supple leg and arm muscles?
- A clear-headed alertness during most of your daily tasks?
- Normal blood pressure?
- Sharp mental functioning and good memory, even though you may be approaching "senior citizenship" or actually be well into your late sixties, seventies, or eighties?

If these descriptions fit you, then you may well have a couple of the most valuable elements of physical well-being that a human being can possess—good blood quality and good circulation.

On the other hand, have you ever noticed any of these problems:

- Excessive fatigue, especially in the arms and legs?
- Mental confusion?
- Dizziness?
- Blurred vision?
- Cramps in your muscles after light exercise?
- High blood pressure?
- Signs of early senility?

If any of these problems has bothered you, especially on a consistent basis, you may be a victim of poor blood quality or inadequate circulation, and that could mean big trouble for your present and future well-being.

Long thought of as a difficulty faced only by the elderly, circulation problems are now affecting an astonishing number of relatively young people as well. But unfortunately, by the time it becomes clear that the problem is in the circulatory system, the individual may already have suffered a severe or even fatal stroke or heart attack.

Circulation problems can often be traced to atherosclerosis or arteriosclerosis—an ailment often called "hardening of the arteries" which involves a build-up in the blood vessels of fatty cholesterol deposits. And when this clogging gets too serious, all sorts of unpleasant symptoms may crop up.

For example, when key arteries in the neck get partially obstructed, that causes a decreased blood flow to the brain—with the result that a person's mental faculties don't work quite as well as they should. An inability to think as clearly as you could in the past, a poor memory, or a tendency toward dizziness or light-headedness may be the result.

Also, if atherosclerosis causes a decrease in blood flow in the small vessels supplying blood to the eyes, there may be a decrease in visual acuity. This is one reason the physician looks into your eyes during a physical examination. In other cases, an artery in the neck becomes clogged and impaired vision may result. But then with a "reaming out" operation to clear the cholesterol and other deposits—or a more complicated vessel grafting or bypass operation—the vision may improve substantially. Let me hasten to say, however, that the overwhelming majority of impaired vision that occurs with aging is not the result of poor circulation, but is the result of a change in the lens in the eye that occurs as part of the aging process.

Sometimes, there are much more dangerous consequences of the poor circulation that stems from hardening of the arteries. Without warning, this clogging process may precipitate a massive heart attack or stroke, and death may be the first and only symptom that appears.

In the past, it was generally believed that hardening of the arteries was just something that happened to people with advancing age and there was nothing that could be done to prevent it. Some people were younger than others when the circulatory problems struck, but that was just regarded as the "luck of the draw," so to speak.

But there is evidence now that you can maintain or recapture a feeling of well-being and greatly reduce your chances of future circulatory disease by slowing down, stopping, or even possibly *reversing,* the process of atherosclerosis that at this very moment is occurring in your body!

In a report by David Blankenhorn, a physician at the University of Southern California in Los Angeles, it was shown that the yearly progress of atherosclerosis in heart attack patients who stop smoking is about 6 percent less than in those who continue to smoke. He studied 10 men, all younger than 50 years of age, who had experienced a heart attack. Five continued to smoke a pack a day during the 13-month period following their heart attacks, while the other five stopped smoking. By performing angiograms at 3-month intervals, Dr. Blankenhorn was able to show that the coronary artery obstruction in the smokers increased by an average rate of 4.8 percent per year, while among the nonsmokers, it decreased by a rate of 1.8 percent per year. The net effect between the smoking and nonsmoking groups was 6.6 percent per year!

And remember, cholesterol is the major component of the plaques that cause atherosclerosis. As with everything else that involves physical and emotional health, it's all a matter of balance—in this case, the proper amount and type of cholesterol in your blood.

As we said earlier, cholesterol is a waxy, fatty substance in body tissues and the blood which is absolutely essential to many physical functions, including the efficient operation of the brain. But too much of a good thing can often create major problems—and that's what sometimes happens with cholesterol. An imbalance of the cholesterol in your body can contribute directly to heart disease.

The HDLs (high-density lipoproteins) in the blood are believed to serve two important functions: (1) They coat the inside of the artery walls and thus provide a kind of protective layer of grease to prevent fatty deposits from building up; and (2) they serve as scavengers by actually helping dissolve fatty deposits when they do occur.

LDLs (low-density lipoproteins) are quite responsive to dietary habits and form dangerous deposits on the walls of blood vessels and are the primary culprits in clogged arteries and atherosclerosis.

The basic rule of balance for your blood is that it's necessary to have a relatively high amount of HDLs in your body, in relation to your total amount of cholesterol.

So, if your HDLs are relatively high, your risk of heart disease will be correspondingly lower. And if your HDLs are relatively low, your risk of heart disease will increase. In adult men, the HDLs should be above 45, and in women above 55. This normally higher HDL that women have genetically may be the most important factor in protecting them from heart disease. Now, here are some more details to help you understand this key principle of balance in your blood:

The *ratio* of a man's *total* cholesterol (HDLs plus LDLs) to his HDL should always be less than 5.0, and preferably less than 4.5.(If his total cholesterol is 200, then his HDLs should be at least 40, and preferably 45 or above.) For women, the ratio should be lower: always be under 4.0 and preferably under 3.5.

Another way of putting this is that for a man, the HDLs should always represent at least 20 percent of the total cholesterol count, and preferably should be 25 percent or greater. For a woman, the HDL cholesterol should make up at least 25 percent of the total cholesterol in her blood, and preferably should be 30 percent or higher.

If you have more than the *preferred* percentage of HDLs in your blood, then very likely, the chances are minimal that any hardening of the arteries is occurring, and perhaps there is even some dissolving of cholesterol obstructions. On the other hand, if you have less than the *minimum* percentage of HDLs, then the chances are that you are steadily developing atherosclerosis, or hardening of the arteries, and you are probably well on your way to serious problems associated with arteriosclerosis and coronary artery disease.

But more needs to be said about this principle of balance in your blood before you can understand how it can be applied in a practical way in your own life.

First of all, there has been considerable controversy about the role that fatty substances play in the development of coronary disease and in other life-threatening ailments. For example, for a while, some experts felt that in addition to cholesterol, another type of fat, triglycerides, might play a role in heart disease. But after extensive studies during the past few years, the role of triglycerides in cardiovascular disease is still uncertain.

In contrast, cholesterol has emerged as a major villain. But even the precise role of cholesterol has been surrounded by considerable controversy.

As medical researchers have offered evidence that high levels of cholesterol in the blood—or "serum cholesterol"—are associated with an increased risk of coronary disease, sentiment has built up in favor of cutting down on cholesterol-laden foods. But this movement has produced a highly vocal opposition of procholesterol forces.

Some food manufacturers, for example, have pointed to studies that purport to show that the amount of cholesterol consumed in your diet has little relationship to the concentration of cholesterol in the blood. In other words, cholesterol may be bad in some cases, but there's no way you can control it adequately through your diet.

In this same vein, no less a group than the Food and Nutrition Board of the respected National Academy of Sciences has recommended that otherwise healthy Americans need not restrict the intake of cholesterol in their food—though the Board did suggest that there should be a reduction in a person's consumption of saturated fats.

But these recommendations have been attacked vehemently by anticholesterol forces. Specifically, the anticholesterol people argue that both the food manufacturers, and also Food and Nutrition Board members who had strong connections with the food industry, can't be objective because they have an interest in seeing cholesterol-laden foods sold to consumers.

Another area of controversy has developed around a recent study suggesting that very low cholesterol levels may increase the risk of cancer in men—especially cancer of the colon, or large intestine. But so far, there have been no studies which say specifically that low cholesterol *causes* cancer. It's just that the rate of cancer appears to be higher in men with an unusually low serum cholesterol level.

As far as this cancer issue is concerned, some researchers have suggested that a genetic linkage between cancer and low cholesterol is to blame. In other words, inherited genes predispose some people both to low cholesterol levels and also to an accompanying tendency toward cancer.

Others believe that the bodily mechanisms responsible for excreting cholesterol may be overactive in some people and that this tendency causes cancer. Still other investigators have pointed out that people who have a lower risk of heart disease because of their low cholesterol levels simply live long enough to suffer from cancer: If they died earlier from a heart attack, they wouldn't have to worry about the cancer problem!

The final word isn't yet in on this issue of the relationship between cancer and low cholesterol levels. But in the meantime, I would suggest you follow the guidelines offered by the *Harvard Health Letter* of October 1981.

This report recommends that *if the total cholesterol count in your blood is less than 180,* "it *may* be wise to avoid further reductions until the matter of unusually low cholesterol levels and cancer is further clarified. And to put this whole matter in ultimate perspective, it is important to stress that the association between high blood cholesterol and heart disease appears to be far greater than the possible relationship of low cholesterol levels to cancer."

So to summarize, at this point we believe that:

- Cholesterol does play an important, deadly role in the development of the hardening of the arteries (arteriosclerosis or atherosclerosis).
- It's more important to be concerned about high cholesterol as a cause of heart disease than low cholesterol as a cause of cancer.

But now, let's return to that all-important matter of the ratio of the total cholesterol to HDLs, which we considered briefly a few pages back. This balance is perhaps the single most important factor in predicting your susceptibility to heart attacks, and in determining your total well-being, both now and in the future.

If you hope to live a long, alert, and productive life, it's absolutely essential, first of all, that you get regular analyses of your blood from a reliable laboratory, with a breakdown of the count for your total cholesterol and your HDL cholesterol. Then, armed with the knowledge of the balance of the cholesterol in your own blood, you'll be in a better position to assess the latest findings on what that balance really means for you personally.

Here are some of the most recent findings at the Aerobics Center and elsewhere about the cholesterol balance issue, and particularly about the importance of HDL cholesterol:

A very low total cholesterol count offers no guaranteed protection against heart disease. One 61-year-old man who had been under observation at our clinic for 5 years had a total cholesterol count from 185 to 147, which was far below our suggested safe range of less than 200. But one day he suffered a massive heart attack and required a five-vessel bypass operation to save his life. The physicians found that his coronary disease was far advanced, with evidence of atherosclerosis everywhere.

How could such a thing happen?

The answer lay in his very low HDL levels, which we had measured at 22. In other words, the ratio of his total cholesterol (147) to HDL cholesterol (22) was nearly 7.0—far above the minimally safe ratio of 5.0, or the preferred ratio of 4.5.

A high HDL level alone is no guarantee against heart disease. In another case we handled at our clinic, a 51-year-old runner came in for an evaluation. He had been running for about 15 years, was seemingly in excellent physical condition, and had an HDL count of 60—rather high for a man by any standards. Yet, in conjunction with his physical examination, a disturbing change in his stress electrocardiogram appeared, and further study showed that he had severe hardening of the arteries which eventually required bypass surgery.

What was the problem here?

Even though his HDLs were high, his total cholesterol was out of control, approaching 400. As you can see, his ratio of total cholesterol (400) to HDL cholesterol (60) was also pushing 7.0, and even though he was running regularly, he was steadily developing atherosclerosis.

A low concentration of HDLs has been linked in some studies to gallbladder disorders. In one California study of women with a history of gallbladder disease, one of the key factors that many of them lacked was a high level of HDLs. So if you have a tendency toward gallstones or other gallbladder problems, a low HDL level may be the key.

High HDL levels are associated with longevity. A study of families who tend to live longer than 80 years of age has found that the average HDLs for both men and women were 75.

But for most people, advancing age means an increasingly unhealthy balance of the cholesterol readings. In a group we observed at the Aerobics Center, the levels of total cholesterol, including both LDLs and HDLs, were monitored in relation to the person's age. We found that the HDL level didn't change significantly among the younger and older people tested. But the total cholesterol levels (and the LDLs) were higher in the older persons.

In the following chart, this phenomenon is clearly shown:

Age versus Cholesterol
(2,928 men, average age 44.6 years)

Age	under 30	30–39	40–49	50–59	60–plus
Total cholesterol	186	200	210	216	216
HDL	44	43	44	44	45
LDL	142	157	166	172	171

In women, the relationship with age is comparable to that observed in men, except that HDL cholesterol seems to increase with age:

Age versus Cholesterol
(589 women, average age 39.4 years)

Age	under 30	30–39	40–49	50–59	60–plus
Total cholesterol	179	186	194	219	221
HDL	53	57	58	60	62
LDL	126	129	136	159	159

In trying to understand this difference, we discovered that as the people we studied aged, their percentage of body fat increased—even though their weight might remain the same. And as their body fat went up, so did their LDLs. In other words, the LDLs went up in direct proportion to the increasing amount of body fat as the individual got older.

Again, this can be documented in both men and women in the study we just cited:

Age versus Body Weight and % Body Fat

Age	under 30	30–39	40–49	50–59	60–plus
2,928 men:					
Body weight	176	180	181	179	174
% body fat	17%	20%	21%	22%	22%
589 women:					
Body weight	129	129	135	137	134
% body fat	26%	26%	27%	30%	29%

People who keep fit by exercising regularly generally have high levels of HDL cholesterol. In one study, a group of tennis players was observed in relation to a separate "control" group of people. The men in the tennis group had been playing for an average of 10 years, and in the previous 6 months had played an average of 4.5 days a week. The women in the tennis group had been playing for an average of 7 years, and in the previous 6 months had played 4.9 days a week.

When the tennis players were compared with the non-tennis-playing control group, the HDL levels in the tennis group were found to be significantly higher, particularly among the male players.

Animal studies confirm what our research is demonstrating among humans. In dogs and rabbits—animals which normally don't develop hardening of the arteries—75 percent of the total cholesterol is in HDL form. And in some sea mammals, such as dolphins, the total cholesterol level is high, with HDL counts of 800 which represent 90 percent of their total body cholesterol. There is virtually no atherosclerosis among dolphins, by the way.

The more physically fit you are, the better your cholesterol balance. In a study of more than 700 men at our clinic, we noted their ages and fitness levels on their first visit. They averaged almost 45 years of age, and their fitness levels ran the spectrum from poor to excellent. In the course of our research, we determined the ratio of total cholesterol to HDL cholesterol for each person, and we found consistently that the fitter they were, the lower the ratio (i.e., the better their cholesterol balance).

Fitness versus Cholesterol/HDL Ratio
(732 men, average age 44.6 years)

Fitness Category*	Cholesterol/HDL
Very poor	6.1
Poor	5.7
Fair	5.1
Good	4.9
Excellent	4.3

* as determined by age-adjusted treadmill times

This important relationship between fitness and the cholesterol/ HDL also is shown in women:

Fitness versus Cholesterol/HDL Ratio
(346 women, average age 39.4 years)

Fitness Category*	Cholesterol/HDL
Very poor	4.0
Poor	3.9
Fair	3.9
Good	3.3
Excellent	3.2

* as determined by age-adjusted treadmill times

The ratio of your total cholesterol to HDL cholesterol is probably the best predictor of future coronary disease. The U.S. Air Force School of Aerospace Medicine conducted a study which screened nearly 600 aircrew members for risk of coronary artery disease, even though none of the subjects showed any symptoms. Some level of coronary artery disease was predicted for about 14 percent of the total group in light of their age, family histories, weight, and other factors.

But among those who had a cholesterol-to-HDL ratio of more than 6.0, the risk of coronary disease—when all the risk factors were taken into account—was 78 percent, no matter what their age was.

Active people with low levels of body fat tend to show the best cholesterol balance in their blood. The American Airlines Medical Department evaluated more than 2,000 candidates for employment as pilots during a 3-year period which ended in January 1980. They were evaluated according to their cholesterol and HDL levels and other coronary risk factors, and 900 were eventually accepted into the program.

Then, these final 900 were separated into three groups according to their weight, that is, whether they were (1) at or below their "ideal weight" based on a widely used table of ideal weights issued by the Metropolitan Life Insurance Company; (2) within 10 pounds of their ideal weight; or (3) within 20 pounds of the ideal.

Next, the select group of 900 pilots were categorized in three more groups in terms of their exercise habits: (1) those who ran a total of 10 or more miles per week; (2) those who maintained a regular aerobics exercise program at least 20 to 30 minutes, three times a week; and (3) those who exercised only occasionally.

Finally, the total cholesterol-to-HDL ratios were correlated to the findings in both the body weight and exercise categories, and the results were quite instructive. In the group as a whole, the pilots who were at or below their ideal weight also showed the lowest average cholesterol-to-HDL ratios (i.e., they had the best cholesterol balance in their blood). Those pilots who were within 10 pounds of their ideal weight showed slightly higher ratios; and those within 20 pounds showed still higher ratios.

When the cholesterol ratios were compared to the three levels of exercise habits, a similar set of correlations emerged. The serious runners showed the lowest (healthiest) average cholesterol ratios; the regular exercisers showed slightly higher ratios; and those who exercised only occasionally showed the highest ratios of total cholesterol to HDL cholesterol.

Because of the naturally higher levels of HDL cholesterol in women, coronary disease is less of a problem with them until they go through menopause. We expect that a normal, healthy HDL level in men will be about 45 or higher, while the level in women will be 55. The higher levels in women automatically lower their ratios of total cholesterol to HDL cholesterol, and consequently lower their risk of heart disease (see previous charts in this chapter).

In a recent study of Japanese men and women, there was no significant difference in the HDL cholesterol between the sexes; both averaged above 50. Of interest in this regard is that the incidence of fatal heart attacks among Japanese men or women is considerably less than in the United States.

These, then, are some of the latest findings about the proper cholesterol balance in our blood. And the basic message comes across loud and clear: The lower you can keep the ratio of your total cholesterol to your HDLs, the healthier your cardiovascular system will be.

In fact, I would go so far as to say that the total amount of cholesterol probably doesn't make much difference at all. I would recommend that you keep yours below 200, but even if it goes as high as 300 or 400, you're most likely still on safe ground—*so long as your HDL cholesterol count is high enough to keep the ratio below 5.0 for men and 4.0 for women.*

If your total cholesterol count is rather low, you are still in trouble if the ratio is out of balance. According to an evaluation of data from long-term heart studies such as the Framingham Project in Massachusetts, you don't have an increased risk of coronary heart disease if your total cholesterol, divided by your HDL level, is 5.0 or less. But if your ratio is 10.0, your risk of heart disease doubles. And if the ratio rises to 15.0, the coronary risk triples; and serious heart trouble is a definite possibility.

In the Appendix, you will find sex- and age-adjusted coronary risk factor charts. In these charts, you can readily see how your cholesterol/ HDL compares with that of other people in your age group. Remember:

You should be above the fiftieth percentile level, and the ratio does vary according to sex and age.

But now that you have the latest facts on cholesterol at your fingertips, what, in practical terms, can you do to adjust your blood balance so that your circulatory system is in a healthy state of equipoise?

In light of the most recent research, here is a three-step action plan to help you find that proper blood balance and enhance your personal well-being.

STEP ONE: LOWER THE LDLs IN YOUR BLOOD

If you can lower the low-density lipoproteins (LDLs) in your blood, you'll lower your total cholesterol readings without also lowering the high-density lipoproteins (HDLs). As a result, your ratio of total cholesterol to HDLs will go down, and your blood will be in better balance.

To illustrate, suppose your total cholesterol is 250, but your HDL cholesterol is 40, which would give you an unacceptable ratio of 6.25. In this example, the LDLs would be about 210 (250 minus 40 equals 210). (I'm including in the LDL cholesterol another type of cholesterol, called "very low-density lipoprotein" or VLDL.) If you can lower the LDLs in your total cholesterol count without also lowering your HDLs, so that your total is 180 instead of 250, then your ratio of total cholesterol to HDLs also will drop to 4.5—or the preferred ratio in preventing hardening of the arteries.

But how do you go about lowering the LDLs in your system?

There are four main ways: a restricted diet; losing weight; exercise; and the use of certain drugs. Let's examine each of these methods in turn.

First of all, by going on a *low-cholesterol diet*, you can reduce your LDL count, and as a result, lower your total cholesterol level. Most important of all, these adjustments in your blood balance will also lower your total cholesterol-to-HDL ratio.

Dietary cholesterol is supplied through foods that come from animal and animal fat sources. Egg yolks, organ meats, lard, meat, and dairy products (butter, cream, cheese, and whole milk) are high in cholesterol. Shrimp is moderately high. In contrast, foods of plant origin (grains, vegetables, beans, and peas) contain no cholesterol.

Saturated fats, which usually are of animal origin, contribute to elevated blood cholesterol and therefore should be restricted. Major sources of saturated fat include visible and "hidden" fat in meat (such as beef, lamb, pork, sausage, bacon, and hot dogs) and fat in dairy products made from whole milk or cream (such as butter and cheese).

Also, a few vegetable fats are saturated: These include coconut and palm (kernel) oils (used in nondairy creamers and some frozen desserts, cake mixes, crackers, and breakfast cereals), and cocoa butter (the fat in chocolate).

"Hydrogenated" or "hardened" vegetable oils contain more saturated fat than the liquid oils from which they are made—so avoid these. Also, select soft, tub margarines, which usually are less saturated than stick margarines.

Polyunsaturated fats, which are fats of plant origin, are thought to help lower blood cholesterol. Safflower, corn, sunflower, soybean, and cottonseed oils are polyunsaturated.

While there has been some controversy about whether or not reducing dietary cholesterol will lower the concentration of LDLs in the blood, the most solid studies seem to support the importance of diet in striking the right blood balance. For example, in one recent study, some vegetarians were fed meat during the 4-week experiment, and there was a dramatic rise in the amount of cholesterol in their blood just as a result of the diet. When the meat was eliminated from the diet, the cholesterol levels returned to their previous levels.

So it's a good idea to avoid foods with excessive saturated fats and cholesterols. And when you do start restricting your diet in this way, you can expect the cholesterol balance in your blood to begin shifting in a healthier direction within a month. The Fat-Cholesterol Chart in the Appendix has specific information about foods.

As we've already seen, loss of weight is also associated with a decrease in the total cholesterol in your blood. This can be achieved through a weight-reduction diet, and also through weight loss that results from an increase in exercise.

Both cross-sectional and longitudinal studies conducted at the Institute for Aerobics Research have shown a correlation between measured levels of physical fitness and total cholesterol levels, as well as a reduction in the total cholesterol levels in response to physical activity. This response can be shown even though body weight and age are held constant.

Finally, if all else fails, there are a number of prescription drugs on the market which have been shown to be effective in lowering total cholesterol levels. For example, in one set of tests conducted with rhesus monkeys, a combination of certain drugs, including Cholestramine and Probucol, reduced total blood cholesterol by about 20 percent. This method also actually reduced fatty deposits in the vessels within a year, even though the animals continued to eat the same high cholesterol diet that had caused their hardening of the arteries in the first place.

In humans, promising results in reversing atherosclerosis have been achieved with Probucol used with Colestipol, and also Colestipol used with niacin. The Japanese have recently reported success with the drug Compactin. An even newer drug is Lopid. But this drug-oriented approach must be used with extreme care and under the direction of a qualified physician because of the possible side effects of these medications.

There is the tendency to believe that it takes great changes in diets or habits to obtain results in reducing deaths from coronary disease. But apparently, that is not true. A group of over 1,200 men, 40–49 years of age, participated in the 5-year Oslo study. To enter into the program, the men must have been smoking at least a pack of cigarettes daily and have cholesterol levels between 290 and 380.

Fifty percent of the men constituted a control group, who did nothing to change these habits. The other 50 percent tried to break the cigarette-smoking habit and also reduce the cholesterol intake in their diets.

Moderate success was achieved in limiting the smoking and changing the eating habits of the experimental group: About 45 percent of the men in the experimental group reduced the number of cigarettes smoked daily, and 25 percent of them quit altogether. Dietary changes resulted in a 13 percent reduction in the serum cholesterol.

At the end of the 5-year study, it could be shown that the control group who did nothing of a preventive nature had a 47 percent higher incidence of fatal and nonfatal heart attacks than did the experimental group. Apparently, great changes are not necessary to see highly beneficial results!

STEP TWO: INCREASE THE LEVELS OF HDLs IN YOUR BODY

This second way of improving your blood balance is somewhat more limited than that described in Step One, but it can still be a great help in improving the state of your cardiovascular system.

There is considerable evidence, for example, that aerobic exercise can raise the amount of HDLs in your body. In one study, investigators found that running 11 miles per week was associated with a 35 percent increase in the HDLs. Our own studies have shown a good correlation between fitness and HDLs. Here's a chart that shows the findings from one of our studies:

Fitness versus HDL Cholesterol

Fitness Category*	HDL Cholesterol	
	347 women	731 men
Very poor	50.0	37.0
Poor	55.0	40.0
Fair	54.0	41.5
Good	61.0	44.5
Excellent	62.0	49.3

* as determined by age-adjusted treadmill times

As part of another study, people who ran more than 11 miles per day were also monitored to see if their HDL levels would increase even more—and they did, indeed, increase. For example, marathoners who ran in excess of 50 to 60 miles per week showed the highest average levels of HDLs, or a count of 65. In contrast, joggers who covered 12 to 15 miles per week had an HDL average of 58; and an inactive control group maintained their average HDL levels of 43.

It also has been suggested that running increases HDLs only to a certain point. Then, according to some examinations we have done of individual long-distance runners, the HDLs may level off and possibly even decrease. Generally speaking, though, most studies of both men and women runners support the idea that those who run up to 15 miles a week will have significantly higher levels of HDL than people who are similar in every other aspect, but who are inactive.

But even though most of our studies and examples involve runners and joggers, it would be a mistake to assume that these benefits can be achieved only by running and jogging. In fact, it appears that *any* aerobic exercise can improve HDL levels.

For example, one group of men who had suffered heart attacks was observed during a 13-week walking program. Their average age was 53, and the program required that they walk only 1.7 miles, three times per week, for a total of 5.1 miles a week. By the end of the 13 weeks, their walking rate had increased slightly, but there was no visible change in their physical condition. As a matter of fact, their total cholesterol levels had even increased somewhat.

But more significantly, the HDL levels in these walkers rose significantly. Similarly, in a study of tennis players that we considered earlier in this chapter, HDL levels rose with the regular sports actitivity—and it's generally recognized that tennis is less strenuous than distance running. So there is evidence that even modest exercise can help raise your HDL level, and consequently decrease your ratio of total cholesterol to HDL cholesterol.

Finally, there have been some research findings that moderate amounts of alcohol—about 6 to 8 ounces of alcohol per week, or about the equivalent of one cocktail a day—will increase HDL levels in the blood. Also, studies have shown that runners who consume alcohol have higher HDL levels than runners who don't.

The problem with emphasizing the "alcohol solution" to the blood balance problem is that the cure may well be worse than the disease. In other words, there are too many problems associated with drinking in our society for anyone to emphasize this approach over aerobic exercise and a low-cholesterol diet. Cirrhosis of the liver, for example, is the fastest-rising cause of death in the United States. And it's estimated that by 1983, deaths from cirrhosis of the liver in the working population, ages 25–64 years, will rank as the third leading cause of death in this country.

Also, alcoholic drinks add nonnutritive calories to your diet and thus promote unnecessary weight gains—which can cause the level of LDLs in your blood to rise. In addition, some studies have linked the consumption of three or more alcoholic drinks each day to the development of high blood pressure. Finally, there is the well-known problem of alcoholism which can creep up on drinkers before they realize what is happening to them.

So I suppose I'll have to put myself in the camp of those doctors who warn, in one way or another throughout the medical literature, "Physicians, don't give your patients the license to drink!"

STEP THREE: AVOID PRACTICES WHICH ARE KNOWN TO LOWER HDL CHOLESTEROL

This third major way of redressing the balance of cholesterol in your blood can have many other beneficial side effects, including reducing other coronary risk factors and reducing the possibility of contracting certain types of cancer. The three most important negative forces which tend to lower the HDL levels, and thus raise the crucial ratio of total cholesterol to HDL cholesterol, are certain medications, cigarette smoking, and the use of the birth control pill.

Medications such as Inderal and other types of beta-blockers used in the management of high blood pressure and heart disease lower the HDL cholesterol, whereas beta-agonists such as Brethine, used by asthmatics, may actually increase the HDL cholesterol. More recently, it has been shown that epileptics using Dilantin to control seizures have high HDL cholesterols—most likely a result of the anticonvulsant medication. Certainly, I would not recommend the routine use of these medicines as a means of increasing the HDL cholesterol. But research developments in this field will be well worth watching in the future.

Here's a dramatic example of how a combination of two factors can operate against your health. If a woman smokes a pack of cigarettes a day, this lowers her HDL level by at least five points. If she uses the birth control pill, another five points should be subtracted. So, taking the average female HDL count of 55, a woman who both smokes and uses the pill will find her HDL levels dropping to 45, or the average level for men. As a result, the natural protection she enjoys against heart disease is significantly reduced.

But the consequences of both smoking and taking the pill are even more ominous than this example might suggest. In one study of women 30 to 39 years of age, the researchers found that smokers had two to three times the risk of dying from cardiovascular disease than nonsmokers. If the women were using the birth control pill only, there was also some risk of getting heart disease.

But if the women *combined* smoking cigarettes with use of the birth control pill, there was an astonishing elevenfold increase in risk of death! And for women 40 to 44 years old who combined the pill with cigarettes, there was an incredible fifty-five-fold increase in the risk of getting cardiovascular disease!

There is now a growing body of opinion that these dramatic effects of smoking and using the pill may be directly related to the fact that both habits lower HDL cholesterol and thus dangerously elevate the crucial cholesterol ratio.

So now you have a practical action plan to get your blood in a better state of balance, which will put you another important step closer to achieving your ultimate goal of total well-being. But before we move on to the important question of exercise, let's take some time to examine one more nutrition-related topic—the question of the extent to which you should consider using stimulants, supplements, and drugs which are not on everyone's daily meal menu.

5

Supplements, "Super Foods"...and Super Advertising

A well-balanced diet, which is based on the principles in the previous chapters, will provide enough energy and nutrition for most people to cover all their basic "human fuel" needs—regardless of advertising claims to the contrary. But everybody wants a little extra bit of health, pep, and vitality now and then, and that desire has given rise to the term "super foods"—substances that theoretically can give us that little additional something that an ordinary diet can't provide.

For example, when some people begin to start dragging at the end of a hard day or week, they may turn to more caffeine, nicotine, alcohol, or laxatives to provide an extra punch in their system. Or, more ominously, they may start relying on various kinds of "pep-up" pills or "uppers" to pick them up and give them the energy to clear that final hurdle that's facing them. If they tend to be anxious, rather than exhausted, they may turn to tranquilizers or sedatives.

Also, along these same lines, there is a tremendous desire among many segments of the population in our society to relax and forget the troubles of a hard day by "getting high." The means may be quite varied—alcohol, marijuana, drugs, special spiritual techniques, or even certain forms of exercise. But the ultimate goal is often the same: to move from the humdrum, stressful, everyday world of problems and pressures into a more pleasant or even exciting inner dimension of consciousness.

I can sympathize with this desire to escape into another reality. Sometimes, the stresses and strains of my own schedule make me look for ways to reduce the stress that weakens my system and makes me more susceptible to disease. Or I may want to energize my body and mind when excessive work and social commitments threaten to drain the extra zip out of my life.

But the problem with many of the supplements that people ingest is that they do little if any good, and may actually cause harm. And if people rely primarily on alcohol and other drugs, pep-up pills, caffeine, or laxatives, it may throw their bodies out of balance and make it difficult, if not impossible, to achieve total well-being.

But having offered these cautionary words, I now want to look at possible benefits of supplements that may help to "tip the balance" toward total well-being, especially when our diets are not what they should be. The three groups that I want to focus upon here are (1) vitamins,

(2) fiber, and (3) minerals, which are present in our ordinary foods, but perhaps not in the quantities we may need at any given point in time.

I realize, by the way, that many other foods and food supplements might be classified in this category. For example, the complex carbohydrates, such as fruits and certain vegetables which we discussed in previous chapters are among the most important kinds of "fuel" we can take into our bodies to increase our energy levels. But that subject has already been treated adequately. Now, I'd like to move on to these other three substances which may have an even greater impact on long-term health.

GROUP # 1: VITAMINS

Vitamins have been at the center of a controversy for the past few years. Some physicians and nutritionists have argued that if a person's diet is balanced, supplements shouldn't be necessary. Others, though, have contended that some regular vitamin supplementation may be helpful in encouraging good health. Because I tend to maintain a neutral position, let me explain both sides of the discussion.

Certain trace elements of vitamins and minerals, known as "micronutrients," are present in tiny amounts in many of our foods. According to Dr. David P. Rose, professor of human oncology at the Wisconsin Clinical Cancer Center, these micronutrients appear to play a role in reducing the risk of lung, colon and breast cancer.

In addition, he puts vitamins A and C at the top of his cancer-fighting list. As further indication of this interest, the National Cancer Institute (NCI) launched a cancer "chemoprevention" program in mid-1982, which included broad-scale support of basic research and chemical trials with vitamins.

Previously, the American Cancer Society (ACS) established a study that, among other things, seeks to identify chemicals in foods that inhibit development of cancers. Among the prime anticancer food candidates are carrots, brussels sprouts, cabbage, fruit, green coffee beans, and black tea.

NCI's Dr. Peter Greenwald sums up these findings as follows: "There is considerable information from laboratory studies to suggest that certain vitamins or synthetic analogues have an inhibitory effect on cancer. In addition, there are some human data consistent with this, although we need a great deal more."

Furthermore, there is mounting evidence that vitamins A, C, and E somehow enhance various immune functions which may provide protection from infectious disease. For many years, I have taken 1,000 milligrams of vitamin C daily, and during that time, I've experienced almost complete protection from colds and other upper respiratory infections. Coincidental? I don't know, but I've seen many patients respond the same way.

Until more research is available, my recommendation is that you consume a good multiple vitamin capsule daily, which includes adequate amounts of vitamins A and E, and also a 500- or 1,000-milligram tablet of vitamin C each day. (Women require a minimum daily amount of 4,000 International Units [IU] of vitamin A; men require 5,000 IU. Women require 11 IU of vitamin E; men, 15 IU.) The most likely deficiencies, especially for those eating 1,800 calories a day, include the following minerals: iron (women); magnesium; zinc; and the vitamin folic acid. By taking a multiple vitamin that contains 100% of the R.D.A.'s, you won't suffer any harm, and you may well derive great benefits, particularly if you are eating less than 1,800 calories a day.

But now, before we move on, let's focus on the controversial subject of taking vitamin C supplements. This issue continues to remain in the news, and it's important that you understand exactly what the latest scientific studies have to say about this supplement.

Let me admit right away that I realize there is a great deal of dispute about the validity of taking *large* doses of vitamin C. Dr. Linus Pauling and others have recommended huge daily amounts to combat the common cold, and these recommendations have brought forth a barrage of criticism from the medical community on the grounds that scientific research doesn't substantiate the claims for the vitamin.

But despite the negative reactions, there are some studies and personal experiences that suggest additional dosages of vitamin C each day may contribute to a more energetic, efficient life. In one research project conducted by Drs. H. Howald and B. Segesser in Switzerland, the researchers tried to answer the question: Does vitamin C help athletes to improve their performances? From their research, they concluded: "Our present knowledge allows us only to recommend that they have a normal or a slightly increased intake of ascorbic acid, since doses of 1 gram daily have been shown to bring beneficial effects in both cardiovascular and metabolic parameters during exercise."

Dr. Howald explained further, "When helping athletes to train and prepare for competition, we usually give them small amounts of additional vitamin C because we see that a lot of athletes are in bad nutritional states. I know athletes who eat just a sausage and a roll for lunch, so with their increased caloric needs there might be the risk that they do not get enough vitamin C. We usually give up to 1 gram a day."

Other studies indicate that when there is a deficiency of vitamin C, performances of athletes in endurance activities may be adversely affected. But when the diet is adequate, these studies say, vitamin supplements don't improve a person's performance.

As I've already said, my own personal practice is to take a 1-gram dose of vitamin C each day. There are a couple of reasons for my decision: First of all, I run 3 miles a day, 4 or 5 days a week, and I'm quite active in other aspects of my life. So I believe I fall into the category of the athletic person who may need extra amounts of vitamin C to keep my work performance levels at a peak.

But also, my opinion on this subject has another strong personal dimension. Before I began to take this dosage, I regularly had two or three major colds each year. After I started taking some extra vitamin C each day, however, the number of colds declined dramatically. In my opinion, there is probably a causal connection between the vitamin C supplement and my good health, although it is impossible to draw a valid conclusion based on a study of one patient!

Of course, I realize there are studies relating to vitamin C and colds which don't support this position. In fact, I conducted one in the Air Force in the 1960s in which we gave 450 men 1 gram (1,000 milligrams) of vitamin C daily to see whether it would reduce colds or help in the healing of athletic injuries, or both.

We told all the men that they were getting vitamin C, but in reality half of them were placed on placebos—i.e., salt or sugar tablets. This was a "double blind" study, in the sense that neither the participants nor the investigators knew who was on the placebo.

After 12 weeks, we looked at the results and concluded we were unable to find any difference whatsoever between the two groups. But one of the criticisms of this particular study was that these were young men—28 years old, on the average—who probably weren't deficient in vitamin C in the first place. In contrast, in another, older group, we might have found a number who were somewhat deficient in vitamin C, and the dosage might have helped them tremendously. Certainly, this would have been a possibility in those people who skip or minimize breakfast where vitamin C intake should be substantial.

Finally, it's known that vitamin C aids in the absorption of iron, which is an especially important mineral that is often recommended in extra quantities for both men and women distance runners and for many women in general. In my opinion, it's also likely that there are still other benefits of taking vitamin C supplements that will be discovered through future research. So even though there may be no hard scientific evidence right now to support my personal position about vitamin C being helpful in combating colds, I remain an advocate of reasonable amounts of supplemental vitamin C.

Before leaving the vitamins, however, let me say a word about vitamin E. Currently, it is being used in the treatment of a neurological disease which has been diagnosed in young children and teenagers. (M.A. Guggenheim, M.D., at the University of Colorado School of Medicine is one of the main figures in this research.) Symptoms include a staggering gait, eye-muscle imbalance, and abnormal reflexes. In one study, injections of vitamin E were used and improvement took place over periods of 12 to 20 months.

Vitamin E is being investigated as a means of treating fibrocystic disease of the breast, which is characterized by a painful lumpiness. Dr. Robert London at Baltimore's Sinai Hospital has been studying this relationship for several years, and he has found a number of women who experienced improvement after receiving 600 IU of synthetic vitamin E for a period of 2 months.

You should be aware, by the way, that fibrocystic breast disease affects almost one-fifth of all women at some point in their lives and carries with it at least twice the normal risk of breast cancer. Current experiments involve lower doses of vitamin E, although no side effects were noted at the 600 IU level.

Another, less documented use of vitamin E is as a protection against the damaging effects of environmental pollution and aging. Even less proven is its effect on reducing or preventing cardiovascular problems, such as heart attacks and strokes—and despite the lack of solid evidence, such claims have been made for years.

GROUP # 2: FIBER

A lot of good things have been written about high-fiber diets, and as far as I'm concerned, many of them are true. In fact, when I'm traveling around the world on speaking engagements, I like to take a supply of bran to give me the additional roughage I feel I need, over and above that derived from the typical hotel or restaurant fare. This bran is particularly useful when you elect to avoid fresh vegetables and salads to guard against intestinal infections.

Why is fiber so important?

Various studies have shown that an increase in fiber in your diet can help prevent constipation and other colon problems, including the irritable bowel syndrome and spastic colitis. Also, a high level of dietary fiber in diets in certain countries has been associated with a lower incidence of cancer of the colon.

Certain types of fiber such as pectins in fruit and the fiber in oatmeal have been associated with a cholesterol-lowering effect. Another interesting finding is that the addition of fiber in the diet may aid in blood sugar control in mild diabetes.

Fiber can be found in many foods—particularly fruits, vegetables, and beans—but is in greatest abundance in certain breakfast cereals that contain large amounts of bran. These include Kellogg's All-Bran, Bran Buds, and Nabisco 100% Bran. The only food with higher fiber content than these cereals is baked beans. But it is important to eat a variety of food to get different types of fiber.

GROUP # 3: MINERAL SUPPLEMENTS

The most important of the mineral supplements that I would recommend is iron. As our nutritionist at the Aerobics Center, Georgia Kostas, says, "Women do generally need an extra iron supplement because it's very hard for women to get enough iron in the diet. A woman would have to eat about 3,000 calories a day to meet her requirement of 18 milligrams of iron a day. But most women don't eat 3,000 calories a day. They usually maintain their weight at 1,500-1,700 calories a day. So most women do often need an iron supplement."

The type of iron supplement is important since many women cannot easily digest iron in the ferrous sulfate form, even though it is the most available type. Splitting up the doses or using other iron compounds such as ferrous gluconate can help. The supplement can be taken after a meal, but absorption is best accomplished with a meal. Customarily, we absorb only 10 percent of a supplement of iron, and it must be in ferrous form to be absorbed best.

To determine whether your body is absorbing iron, the easiest way is to document if there is a change in your blood—that is, an increase in the hemoglobin or hematocrit. Unless there is an indication of an iron deficiency in the body (or anemia), I would not use an iron supplement.

One exception, though, would be in hard-training athletes, who may need iron supplementation as well as extra vitamin C. Also, I recommend that people who are running and sweating excessively during the summer months should supplement their diet with a multiple vitamin containing iron.

Magnesium is another mineral that is lost in excessive amounts with this sort of athletic activity. Common sources of magnesium are seeds, nuts, and green vegetables. A magnesium deficiency may be related to muscle cramping and cardiac irritability (arrhythmia). But I wouldn't advise you to take special magnesium supplements (other than what you can get through ordinary foods) or any other supplements without medical supervision. If you take too much of one mineral, you may offset the effect of another and develop relative deficiencies that can harm your health.

For example, copper and zinc should be taken into the diet in a certain ratio. But if you take a zinc supplementation and fail to ingest the right amount of copper along with it, you may offset the ratio of zinc to copper. The result may be a *relative* deficiency of copper, with the attendant medical problems of such a deficiency, even though your regular diet, minus these supplements, is entirely adequate.

So these are a few of the substances that may have medical benefit. They include actual foods as well as vitamin and mineral supplements, which can have the potential of improving the quality and quantity of your life. But foods, special supplements, and bodily secretions can only go so far in advancing you toward your ultimate goal of total well-being.

In addition to needing a special balance of foods and the fine-tuned inner chemical support systems that respond to them, the human body was intended to be active. And to achieve the overall physical balance that well-being requires, it's necessary to move beyond nutrition to that special realm of activity that I have already alluded to on several occasions.

I'm speaking, of course, about the realm of aerobic exercise.

PART THREE

THE FITNESS FACTOR IN TOTAL WELL-BEING

6

Aerobic Exercise: The Key to Achieving Balance in Body and Mind

For me, the quest for total well-being began with the discovery of the amazing wonders of aerobic exercise—that is, endurance exercise which takes place over a relatively long time period and depends on establishing a balance between the intake and expenditure of oxygen. And the more deeply involved I get with conducting research into the benefits of aerobic activity, the more amazed I become.

When you become so totally committed to a concept or belief as I am to aerobics, it's easy to become so enthusiastic that people think you're getting lost in your own hyperbole. At the risk of appearing to have become carried away, let me share with you a few of the latest wonders—all documented by scientific research—of this aerobics phenomenon.

For example, how would you like to know you could have:

- Higher levels of energy for longer periods during the day?
- Improved digestion and control of constipation?
- A realistic way to lose and control weight?
- Bones that will continue to be strong and healthy as you grow old?
- Improved intellectual capacity and increased productivity?
- Better and more effective sleep?
- A very effective way to control depression and other emotional disturbances?
- Relief from stress at the end of a pressure-packed day, without resorting to the use of alcohol or drugs?
- Significant added protection from heart disease?
- Maximum benefits of exercise for a minimum output of your time—say about 1 hour and 20 minutes a week?

The list could go on and on, but these are just a few of the solid benefits that have been uncovered at the Aerobics Center and other research facilities, and more are being discovered regularly.

In this chapter, I want to give you an overview of what aerobic exercise is all about, and exactly how it compares with other kinds of common athletic activity. Then, we'll discuss some of the benefits in more detail. Finally, in the next two chapters, we'll get into the nuts and bolts of exactly how you can set up a personal exercise program that can totally transform your life—a program which, along with good nutrition, can give you a tasty serving of total well-being on a silver platter.

Now, step back for a few moments and ponder not what you'd like to be, but what you *are*—at least in physical terms.

Have you been noticing increased susceptibility to lower back pain? A little more difficulty taking a couple of flights of stairs two at a time? A sagging of your chest muscles; some extra flab on the back of your arms; or fat shimmering more than you'd like on your thighs?

If you see these or similar signs, you can be sure there's a clear-cut explanation. You see, the human body is constructed in such a way that prolonged inactivity—such as sitting for hours or moving about a few steps every now and then in a limited space—will cause it to deteriorate more rapidly.

You may be one of those lucky people who can make it to age 40 or 50 before you start noticing any definite symptoms of the fact that your physique is falling apart. But believe me, if you're basically a sedentary person—in the sense that your job and/or household responsibilities require that you stay in one location most of the day—a gradual decaying and eroding of your physical as well as your intellectual and emotional powers is occurring day by day.

Of course, we are *all* deteriorating in the sense that as we get older, our physical and mental powers lessen, until finally we die. But different people fall apart at different rates of speed. And the message I want to get across is that you can retard or even temporarily *reverse* that aging process—and recapture some of the verve and energy of your youth— if you'll just give a pleasant, exhilarating, and relatively undemanding aerobics program a try.

The late cardiologist Paul Dudley White summarized this subject when he said: "It is fascinating to know that one can grow healthier as one grows older and not necessarily the reverse!" And aerobic exercise is a major factor in growing healthier as you grow older.

Now, let me explain in more detail what aerobic exercise is all about. There are five basic types of exercise programs in which most people become involved, and it's important for you to know something about each if you hope to understand why aerobic exercise is so different and so important.

ISOMETRIC EXERCISE

These activities are characterized by physical exercise that contracts muscles, yet doesn't move joints or extremities. For example, if you stand in front of a mirror, contract your biceps or upper arm muscle for 10 to 20 seconds, and then relax the muscle, you have completed a typical isometric exercise. Also, pushing against an immovable object, such as a doorjamb, or pulling up on the chair in which you are sitting are all classic examples of isometrics.

Years ago, body-builder Charles Atlas sold an exercise program through the mail—often by advertising in comic books—which concentrated on building up muscle mass through what he called "dynamic tension." And that approach was nothing more than a form of isometric exercise.

Studies have shown that it's possible to increase your muscle size and strength with isometric exercise. But such exercises have little if any beneficial effect on the cardiovascular system. To the contrary, an isometric contraction of the hand, as by gripping something tightly for several seconds, may cause a brief increase in blood pressure that would potentially be dangerous for a person with hypertensive problems.

Over the years, we have advised our cardiac patients not to engage in any exercise that is associated with isometrics because this sort of activity could trigger cardiac irregularity, or even a heart attack. For example, lifting a heavy object, putting a spare tire on a car, or pushing or pulling against any immovable or nearly immovable object would fall into the category of dangerous isometric-type exercise for the person with moderate to severe heart disease.

ISOTONIC OR ISOPHASIC EXERCISE

These are exercises that require contraction of a muscle and then movement of a joint, an extremity, or both in the process of the contraction. Classic examples would be weight lifting and calisthenics.

These exercises help to build greater muscle mass and strength, but as with isometrics, they have little if any effect on the cardiovascular system. In other words, they don't build long-distance endurance, increase blood volume, increase lung capacity, or contribute to lower blood pressure and pulse rates.

Also, we've discovered that it's possible to build up exceptional muscle mass and strength, and yet be in very poor physical condition from the standpoint of cardiovascular or endurance fitness. Let me give you a rather startling illustration.

A few years ago, "Mr. Texas" came to our clinic for an evaluation. At 28 years of age, he had just won the state championship and was on his way to national competition. When he walked into our offices, you can imagine what he looked like. The circumference of one of his biceps was larger than my thigh, and his chest was absolutely unbelievable in size. In fact, it was so large that the female technicians in our lab were drawing straws to see who was going to put the EKG electrodes on his chest.

Noticing their response, I cautioned them, "Don't expect too much. He may not be in shape!" (At least, I was hoping he wasn't in shape!)

As it happened, the test proved me to be right. After walking only 16 minutes on the treadmill, he was totally exhausted, his heart rate reached 192 beats per minute, and he was nauseated because he had pushed himself so hard! For his age this performance classified him in the "poor" fitness category, or the bottom 15 percentile.

This man, and many others who to one degree or another rely exclusively on weight lifting, suffer from what I call the "specificity of training." In other words, they concentrate heavily on muscular development to the exclusion of exercises that strengthen the heart and circulatory systems. And the body responds accordingly. There is little if any cross-over training effect in this type of exercise. (In other words, the benefits you gain from one exercise don't transfer to another.)

ISOKINETIC EXERCISE

This is a relatively new category of exercise which involves weight lifting through an entire range of motion. For example, in ordinary isotonic exercise, you lift a barbell, and then the gravity pulls it back down. But with isokinetic exercise, you have to work not only to lift the weight but also to pull it back down to the starting point.

Some of the very complex exercise machinery, such as the Nautilus and even some of the stations on the Universal Gym, could be classified as promoting isokinetic activity. Studies at our Institute for Aerobics Research in Dallas have indicated that this sort of exercise, if used properly, can strengthen muscles, as does weight lifting. But also, it can produce a beneficial endurance training effect similar to that which accompanies an aerobic exercise like distance running or swimming.

A combination of various types of isotonic and isokinetic exercise for short periods is gaining popularity and scientific support. It is called "circuit weight training" and is accomplished as follows:

Ten stations are set up around a room or gymnasium, and at each station, 30 seconds of activity is performed. Approximately twelve to fifteen repetitions at a resistance equal to 40 percent of a one-repetition maximum is the goal during the 30 seconds, followed by 30 seconds of rest before beginning the next exercise. Two sets of ten exercises are completed in 20 minutes, and exercise sessions are scheduled a minimum of four times per week.

A further modification of this approach has been called "the supercircuit." The only difference is that with the supercircuit, the 30-second rest period is eliminated and the exerciser is required to run in place for 30 seconds, or to run 80 to 160 yards around a gymnasium floor between stations. Such a program is comparable to a ten-station parcourse, set up over a distance of 800 to 1,600 yards. (A parcourse is an exercise course involving short runs punctuated by different types of calisthenics and muscle-building routines.)

Both circuit weight training and supercircuit programs are associated with significant increases in both strength and aerobic capacity or endurance fitness.

The ten weight-training stations used during the studies at the Aerobics Center were: squats, shoulder presses, leg curls, pull-downs, leg presses, chest presses, sit-ups, low pulley curls, hyperextension, and the vertical fly. The absolute results measured as improvement in strength and endurance capacity will be given later in this chapter (see chart on page 115).

ANAEROBIC EXERCISE

Anaerobic means "without oxygen," and so exercise of this type requires that the activity be performed without utilizing the oxygen that you are breathing. In other words, any exercise like sprinting which is limited by exhaustion in the first 2 to 3 minutes would be strictly anaerobic.

The threshold between anaerobic and aerobic exercise depends on the person's level of conditioning in relation to the distance or time period during which he or she runs or otherwise exercises. For example, a 100-yard dash is nearly entirely anaerobic, while a marathon would be 99 percent aerobic. To put it another way, the sprinter may run an entire race holding his or her breath, while the long-distance runner must strike a balance over at least a couple of hours between the consumption and expenditure of oxygen. The distance runner may only get involved in anaerobic exercise in the last hundred yards or so as he or she sprints all out toward the finish line.

As far as the intermediate distances are concerned, if a runner runs a mile in, say, 6 to 8 minutes, that exercise is roughly 50 percent anaerobic and 50 percent aerobic. In other words, he or she is running hard enough to expend slightly more oxygen than is taken in, and eventually the runner will "run out of steam" and have to slow down or stop to catch his or her breath. But if he or she runs nonstop for 12 minutes, you can assume that the workout is 80 percent aerobic and 20 percent anaerobic. For this reason, the 12-minute test is used as a test of aerobic, not anaerobic, capacity.

One good example of how a person can be in top shape anaerobically, but bad shape aerobically, involved some tests done on Hasely Crawford, the Trinidadian who won the gold medal in the 100-meter dash at the Montreal Olympic games. His time was 10.06 seconds. The year after his victory, I heard that he would be coming through Dallas on his way to the Texas Relays in Austin, and so I encouraged him to come by our clinic for an evaluation.

He agreed, and we found that in many ways he was an outstanding physical specimen. At 6 feet 2 inches, he weighed 190 pounds and his percentage of body fat was quite low—only 9 percent. He was a very powerful, muscular man, but at that time, his athletic training had been limited almost exclusively to sprinting.

When we put him on the treadmill to test his cardiovascular endurance, he reached a maximum heart rate of 187 beats per minute and total exhaustion after only 16½ minutes of walking. In other words, like our previous Mr. Texas example, he received only a "poor" rating for cardiovascular fitness.

Is it possible, then, to be a world champion sprinter and not be in shape?

The answer is yes. *Aerobically* speaking, he wasn't in shape. And to round out the irony, only a few days later, he won the exhibition 100-meter run at the Texas Relays.

But you may ask, "How can this be?" The answer, as with our weight-lifting examples, goes back to that concept of specificity of training. Crawford and many other world-class sprinters concentrate only on building those muscles and skills that relate to short bursts of speed, and not to aerobic fitness.

To understand this point a little better, let's now turn to the fifth form of exercise, aerobics.

AEROBIC EXERCISE

I've defined aerobic exercise several times in this book as referring to those exercises which demand large quantities of oxygen for prolonged periods and ultimately force the body to improve those systems responsible for the transportation of oxygen. In other words, the exercise is being performed with the body in a "steady state."

To illustrate this in a slightly different way, you should be aware that as you sit there reading this book, you're in an aerobic steady state. Why? Because you're breathing regularly and you will continue inhaling and exhaling air as long as there is life.

The main difference between what you're doing and what a marathoner is doing is that your steady state of energy expenditure is at a level much lower than that of the marathoner. The marathoner will fatigue ultimately, due to the fact that his or her energy expenditure is 12–15 times above your basal, or resting, rate. And your resting heart and respiratory rates are not operating at a level high enough to place demands on the body, whereas in the runner, this *is* occurring. Such a high-demand response can occur from many types of aerobic exercise and together they are called the "training effect," or the positive physical changes that accompany aerobic exercise.

Some of these beneficial physical effects that accompany aerobic exercise include the following:

- The total blood volume increases so that the body is better equipped to transport oxygen—and thus the individual has more endurance when engaging in strenuous physical activities;
- The capacity of the lungs increases, and some studies have associated this increase in "vital capacity" with a greater longevity;
- The heart muscle grows stronger, is better supplied with blood, and with each stroke, the heart can pump more blood (increased stroke volume);
- High-density lipoprotein (HDL) increases, the total cholesterol : HDL ratio decreases, and thus there is a reduction in the person's risk of developing atherosclerosis, or hardening of the arteries.

Aerobic exercise characteristically involves covering long slow distances (L.S.D.) rather than short bursts of speed. But once an "aerobic base" is built up through distance training, athletes who are engaged in anaerobic sports often find that their overall performance improves.

The training of football players is a good example of this principle. Until the aerobics era burst upon us in the late 1960s, football players were customarily told by their coaches to concentrate only on sprinting and muscle building. As a result, the players were strong, muscular, and prepared for short bursts of energy. But their energy dwindled during the third and fourth quarters of the game. Perhaps for this reason, the incidence of injuries in football is often higher in the third and fourth quarters than in the first half.

Similarly, it's been well known for years that the greatest number of injuries for skiers occur at the end of a hard day of activity, just before the closing of the ski lifts. Again, this fact points up the relationship between fatigue and injuries—and it also indicates the need for all athletes, regardless of their sport, to develop an aerobic base during their training.

My experience in advising various professional athletes and their coaches has convinced me that a more serious year-round aerobic exercise program for most team sports would result in at least four major benefits:

1. A reduction in injuries. As I said, the fatigued athlete is more susceptible to injuries, and if you can delay the onset of fatigue with a good aerobic conditioning program, the injuries should decrease. The Dallas Cowboys under the training supervision of Dr. Bob Ward have employed an aerobic training principle for some time. And they had one of the lowest injury rates for any team in the National Football League from 1977–1982.

2. Better performance in the third and fourth quarter of games. Historically, the Dallas Cowboys have been a better "second half" team.

3. Better performance in the latter games of the season. As many NFL coaches have observed, what determines the winner at the end of the season is a slight edge over the other teams. Practically any coach you can corner would tell you, "Any professional team can defeat any other team on any given Sunday." So the goal of good off-season conditioning for an athletic team should be to have that edge at the beginning of the season. Then, as performance decreases during the season as a result of injuries and less adherence to a regular aerobic program, the team that has the edge at the beginning of the season will be most likely to keep that edge at the end, too.

4. Finally, an aerobic program can prolong a professional athlete's career. Certainly this was true of Roger Staubach's experience as the quarterback of the Dallas Cowboys. His decision to retire at age 38 was not a mandatory decision because of his condition. In fact, at age 40, he was in much better aerobic condition than he had been even while he was playing football. (Recently, he ran 4 miles in less than 27 minutes and walked 30:00 minutes on the Balke treadmill stress test.)

So now you have an overview of the five major categories of exercise, but it's important to remember that they are not mutually exclusive. As I've mentioned already, there are anaerobic components to almost any aerobic exercise. As a result, it's usually essential for those who are engaged in aerobic sports like running, swimming, or racketball to supplement their basic endurance training with strength and muscle building.

Why is this? There are at least two reasons: First of all, improving the strength and flexibility of key muscle groups can improve your performance in any sport. And secondly, paying attention to muscular development and flexibility can reduce your susceptibility to injury in your chosen sport.

You simply can't run or play many sports safely and efficiently without engaging in some isometric and isotonic activity as well. For example, you almost always have to engage in calisthenics, weight lifting, or muscle building if you hope to be in the best condition to turn on the speed abruptly, to turn sharply as you chase a racketball, or to continue running without incapacitating musculoskeletal injuries as you grow older.

But special muscle-building and flexibility exercises must be done in addition to or in combination with—and *not* in place of—one of the primary aerobic programs.

As I mentioned earlier in this chapter, circuit weight training may be used as a means of improving both strength and aerobic capacity. Studies done at the Aerobics Center are summarized in the following chart:

	Aerobic Capacity	Strength
Weight training only	No change, may even decrease	Over 30% increase
Aerobic training only	15–25% increase	0–12% increase
Circuit weight training	5% increase	18% increase
Supercircuit training	12% increase	23% increase

As you can see, the aerobic capacity will increase if you utilize more than one type of exercise, but aerobic training alone is overall the most effective.

In general, aerobic exercise programs have the greatest impact on your cardiovascular fitness, and hence your total well-being. In more specific terms, however, it's possible to identify at least seven key benefits of aerobic exercise that can enhance your total well-being. They were referred to briefly at the beginning of this chapter, but let me go into several of them in a little more detail at this point.

BENEFIT #1: AEROBIC EXERCISE PROMOTES STRONG AND HEALTHY BONES

As you grow older, there's a tendency for your bones to demineralize, or lose calcium, and to become so weak and brittle that fractures and breaks become a real threat, such as when you sustain a moderate fall or even as you step off a curb into the street. But various studies have shown that to some extent bone strength is related to physical activity. Bone, like muscle, tends to get stronger and thicker the more it's used and exercised.

For example, one study has shown that serious tennis players tend to have larger and stronger bones in their "playing arm" than in their other arm. Also, weight lifters tend to have thicker arm bones than runners; and runners' leg bones are thicker than those of swimmers, who sustain less gravity pressure during their aquatic workouts.

So everyone who wants a more solid bone structure—and that means especially both men and women in their forties and fifties and older—should seriously consider a regular weight-bearing exercise program. The more exercise the bones get, the stronger they will be. And the stronger and thicker the bones, the less prone to fractures the individual will become as he or she gets older.

Women who have passed through menopause are especially susceptible to osteoporosis, or deterioration of the bones, because of a loss of estrogen from their systems. So they should pay particular attention to exercise programs, such as calisthenics, weight training, walking, or running.

BENEFIT #2: AEROBIC EXERCISE WILL HELP YOU CONTROL THE PHYSICAL AND EMOTIONAL STRESS IN YOUR LIFE

This is a very important benefit which will be discussed in some detail in Chapter 9, which deals with emotional balance.

BENEFIT #3: AEROBIC EXERCISE ACTS AS AN ANTIDOTE FOR EMOTIONAL DISTURBANCES

This also is a significant benefit of aerobic exercise, and like Benefit #2, it will be treated in Chapter 9.

BENEFIT #4: AEROBIC EXERCISE CAN IMPROVE YOUR INTELLECTUAL CAPACITY AND INCREASE YOUR PRODUCTIVITY

Now, I realize this is a rather dramatic, sweeping statement. But the evidence we have so far has convinced me that it is justified.

My experience in testing fitness and intellectual capacity began rather early in my career, while I was still an officer in the Air Force. While at Maxwell Air Force Base, Alabama, I conducted physical fitness field studies three times a year on a group of young second and first lieutenants who also were involved in academic work. We were able to show some rather interesting correlations—such as the fact that their performance on a 12-minute aerobic endurance test varied in direct proportion to the grades in their academic course. In other words, the correlation was almost perfect in showing that those who made the best grades academically also performed best on the 12-minute test—that is, they had the greatest endurance capacity.

Other reports, including one by Florida psychiatrist Dr. Ray Killinger, have indicated that in conjunction with exercise, greater originality of thought is shown, the duration of concentration increases, and the mental response time is quicker. Also, a person who is aerobically fit has the ability to change subject material quickly and more effectively than an unconditioned person. A fit individual can carry more ideas simultaneously and has greater mental tenacity when trying to resolve tough and prolonged problems.

BENEFIT #5: AEROBIC EXERCISE IS A REALISTIC WAY TO LOSE WEIGHT AND KEEP IT OFF

I want to emphasize that, generally speaking, exercise should be only an *aid* to weight reduction, not the exclusive technique. If you really need to lose 5 pounds or more, it's important to make your diet the crown jewel of your weight reduction program, and use exercise as an adjunct method.

The reason for this approach is that exercise alone is not an effective way to lose weight rapidly. For example, if you walk a mile in 20 minutes, you'll burn about 70 calories. And if you run 1 mile in 6 minutes, you'll still burn only about 100 calories. The problem is that to lose 1 pound through exercise, you have to burn up 3,500 calories—and that represents a lot of walking or running!

But many times, a serious aerobic exercise program pursued along with a sensible diet can tip the balance in favor of your maintaining or losing poundage. For that reason if for no other, I think it's important always to combine the two approaches when you're attacking that extra flab.

One method I advise people to take is to think in terms of losing 1 pound every 2 weeks exclusively through their exercise program. To do this, you must burn 200–250 calories daily with physical activity. Here are some examples of how a 150-pound person can achieve this goal. If you weigh more than 150, you'll have to burn more calories in the same time periods indicated; if you weigh less, you'll have to burn fewer calories.

Calories Burned from Physical Activity

Activity	Calories/hour	Time to Burn 250 Cal.
Skating (moderate)	354	45 min.
Walking (4.5 mph)	400	37 min.
Tennis (moderate)	425	35 min.
Swimming (crawl, 45 yd/min)	530	30 min.
Downhill skiing	585	27 min.
Handball, squash	600	25 min.
Tennis (vigorous)	600	25 min.
Jogging (5.5 mph)	650	22 min.
Biking (13 mph)	850	18 min.

BENEFIT #6: AEROBIC EXERCISE PROVIDES SIGNIFICANT PROTECTION FROM HEART DISEASE

We've already discussed several aspects of this issue in other chapters, but let me summarize a few of these points again.

Aerobic exercise tends to increase the level of HDLs in the blood, and as a result also helps to put your crucial ratio of total cholesterol to HDL cholesterol in a healthier balance, which is increasingly being associated with a lower risk of developing atherosclerosis.

In addition, high levels of aerobic fitness are associated with an increased vital capacity, or lung capacity. And a high vital capacity is associated with greater longevity.

A good level of aerobic fitness also promotes less clotting in the blood, and this is especially valuable when we're treating patients with coronary artery disease after they have a heart attack. In other words, the less likelihood a person in this position has of developing a blood clot, the safer he or she is while recovering from the cardiac problems.

In general at the Aerobics Center, when we're drawing up a person's coronary risk profile to predict the likelihood of heart trouble in the future, we give great weight to performance on our treadmill stress test. And it's impossible to do well on this test without being in above-average aerobic condition.

BENEFIT #7: YOU CAN GET THE MAXIMUM BENEFITS IN A MINIMUM AMOUNT OF TIME IN A VARIETY OF AEROBICS PROGRAMS

Contrary to what many people think, you don't have to commit your life to marathon competition to get the maximum benefits from an aerobics conditioning program. On the contrary, I strongly recommend that the average person who chooses running as his or her aerobic activity, should stay away from working out over extremely long distances.

You can get all the physical benefits listed above, and many more, just by devoting about 80 to 90 minutes a week to an aerobics program. If you're a jogger, that means devoting 20 minutes, four times a week, or 30 minutes three times a week to a jogging program. If you run any farther, the additional benefits you'll gain—other than increased weight loss—probably won't outweigh the danger that you'll suffer injuries to your bones, joints, and muscles.

Remember: If you run more than 3 miles five times per week (or a combination totaling 15 miles per week), you are running for something other than fitness, such as competition or ego-building.

Of course, if you want to go into competition and run in races such as the marathon, then you'll need to spend more time with your aerobics activity. But for the average person who only wants the important fringe benefits of aerobics, without the excitement and accolades of competition, 90 minutes or about 10 to 15 miles a week is entirely adequate.

It's also important to remember that there are many aerobic exercises besides running that qualify for an effective aerobics program. I've mentioned a few of them in the list in this chapter on losing weight through exercise. You can add aerobic dancing, roller skating, and almost any other activity that will get your heart rate up to a level where, over a sustained period of time, beneficial changes can take place in your cardiovascular system.

Now we will leave this general discussion of what exercise is and what benefits it can give you. Instead, let's move on now to the nuts and bolts of setting up your own highly enjoyable exercise program which will enable you to embark on a lifetime plan of keeping your body in an ultimate state of balance.

7

The Secret of Enjoying Exercise

The secret of enjoying exercise is rather simple. First of all, it's important for you to understand what kind of exercise will do the most to promote total well-being in your life. And you already know the answer to that—aerobic exercise wins hands down.

Secondly, you should pick an aerobic activity that really interests you—one that you can stick with indefinitely—perhaps for the rest of your life. I'll offer some specific suggestions later in this chapter, and you may well come up with some entirely new ideas of your own.

Finally, after you've decided on your basic aerobic exercise, you should schedule a definite program for pursuing that activity and commit yourself to following it *for at least 6 weeks*. Now, I'll admit that I fully expect you to stick with this program for much longer than a month and a half. But I find that most people tend to drop out of a program after a few days or perhaps the first week. On the other hand, most who stay with it for a month or more begin to taste some of the tantalizing benefits that are available—and they get excited about bringing more and more of these great feelings into their lives.

So, as I say, the secret of enjoying exercise is fairly straightforward and simple to understand. But there are a few important guidelines you should know about in setting up your own program. Now, let's spend some time discussing the practicalities.

The most fundamental concept in the aerobics program that I have formulated and that millions around the world have been using since the 1960s is the *aerobic points system*. You'll find many of the details about how specific sports activities relate to this concept in Chapter 8 and in the Appendix after you select the kind of exercise program you want to follow. But at this point, let me give you an overview of what the aerobic points idea is all about.

The main problem in setting up an exercise program that can apply to many different types of activities is finding a basis for comparing the aerobic value of those activities with each other. I decided long ago that the best way to compare the many activities that are available would be to find a way to establish the "energy cost" of each.

In other words, how much energy do you expend to run at a certain speed? And how much energy is required to walk a certain distance at a certain rate? If you can establish these values and come up with an underlying numerical system to express their relationship to one another in basically the same terms, then you have a standard for comparison.

One of the simplest analogies I can think of is the popular practice of rating a person's physical looks on a scale of one to ten, with one being the most unattractive and ten being the most handsome or beautiful. If you decide that one individual is worth an "eight" and another is worth a "five," then you're saying that in comparison with an absolute scale of beauty, one person is significantly more attractive than the other.

The same principle applies with the aerobic points system. One exercise, when performed at a certain intensity during a certain duration of time, may be worth a twelve, while another may only be worth a six. In making this comparison, we are saying that the aerobic benefit of the first is worth twice as much as the second.

The way we determined the energy cost of and points to be assigned to each exercise was to collect all the expired air during experiments with subjects who were performing exercises at a certain intensity over a certain period of time. For example, we first studied the energy costs for walking and running. We discovered that walking on a treadmill for a distance of 1 mile in 20 minutes required an average oxygen consumption of about 3.4 calories per minute over and above a resting state. Therefore, walking 1 mile burned up about 68 calories.

On the other hand, running a mile in 6 minutes and 15 seconds on a treadmill—the fastest time we considered in our research—revealed an energy cost of 16.6 calories per minute, or a total of almost 100 calories for running a mile at that pace.

Frequently, I am asked to explain the statement that if you run or walk a mile, there is not that much difference in the energy cost. In reality, that statement is true, but the total expenditure per unit of time is considerably different. For example, if you walk 1 mile in 20 minutes, you burn up about 70 calories (over and above resting), whereas running a mile in 6:15 minutes burns about 100 calories. Yet in 20 minutes, our walker has burned a total of 70 calories, and our runner would have covered 3.2 miles and burned 320 calories. So running is a much more efficient way to burn up calories.

But there is one exception to this generalization: In between the 20-minute-mile walk and the 6:15-mile run, there is a progressive increase in calorie cost for walking and a decrease for running. And at the energy-cost "threshold" between walking and running—or the point where the energy expended in running slowly and walking at a fast pace tended to converge—we discovered that the oxygen cost for walking a mile in 12 minutes was actually *higher* than it was for running a mile at that speed.

We derived the point system for comparing the relative energy costs of walking, running, and other aerobic activities from the mathematical relationships between the oxygen expenditures assigned to each exercise at a given intensity and duration. So we found that if you ran a mile in slightly less than 8 minutes, your oxygen consumption during that activity would give you an aerobic exercise value of 5 points.

But then the issue arose, how should your points be awarded if you run several consecutive miles?

At first, we assigned points in a strictly linear fashion, with a set number of points for a set number of miles. So, if you ran 3 miles in less than 24 minutes, that could be slightly less than 8 minutes a mile, or 3 times 5 points, for a total of 15 points.

But our later studies revealed that you use more energy if you run 3 miles continuously than if you run a mile, rest a few minutes, run another mile, rest, and so on for the 3-mile total. So for continuous exercise, we began to award "endurance points." In the 3-mile-run example we've been using, then, instead of giving 15 points for 3 miles in less than 24 minutes, we gave 17 points, or the basic 15 points plus 2 endurance points.

I'm going into this detail explaining the aerobic point concept because if you look through the charts and programs in Chapter 8 and in the Appendix and try to figure out why points are assigned in the way they are, you may be puzzled unless you understand the scientific basis on which we have done our calculations. In any case, you can be assured that the points for each of the exercises we've included have been derived after painstaking research into the precise energy cost of each activity.

Now that you have some of the background about how the aerobic point system came about and what it means, let's get started in setting up your personal exercise program. There are four major steps involved in tailoring a program for your particular needs, and now I want to explain each of these in some detail.

STEP ONE: HAVE A THOROUGH MEDICAL EXAMINATION, WITH A PROPERLY ADMINISTERED STRESS TEST, BEFORE YOU BEGIN YOUR EXERCISE PROGRAM

It's especially important to have a complete medical exam if you're 30 or older, and it's essential if you're over 40. But the exam will be less meaningful unless it involves a stress test, with an electrocardiogram, to see how your heart performs under exercise conditions. Some guidelines for what's involved in a thorough physical are included in a later chapter in this book, and I would suggest you go over that material just prior to your medical appointment to be certain you're being evaluated properly.

I realize the impracticality of all people being evaluated and having a stress electrocardiogram prior to entering a vigorous exercise program. To compensate partially, in all the progressive exercise programs listed in this book, the 6-week starter concept is used. (See the explanation of the various programs in Chapter 8.)

As you'll see, the programs are so slowly progressive during that time that dangerous cardiac events are unlikely even in people with diagnosed or undiagnosed heart problems. Remember: Many heart patients have successfully completed 26-mile marathons, but their key to safe running was starting very slowly into their program. So, if you can't have medical screening prior to beginning your program, start and progress very slowly into it! If at any time unusual symptoms occur, then you must seek medical consultation before continuing.

One reason we have outstanding safety statistics here at the Aerobics Center, is because all of our participants over 30 years of age must have a stress electrocardiogram before beginning their programs, and they must be reevaluated at regular intervals. Don't make the mistake of thinking, "I couldn't run the way I run without symptoms and still have significant heart disease!" That, surprisingly, is not a safe assumption.

STEP TWO: DETERMINE YOUR "TARGET HEART RATE"

To get the maximum benefits from aerobic activity, it's necessary that you maintain a sufficiently high heart rate during your exercise to get a "training effect," or certain beneficial cardiovascular changes in the body. This is where the concept of the "target heart rate" comes in. This is the minimum rate at which your heart should be beating to get the optimum aerobic conditioning effect.

Our aerobic point system is structured in such a way that if you earn a minimum number of points per week, you'll get an adequate training effect without having to worry about what your heart rate is during exercise. But there are a number of new aerobic activities, like aerobic dancing and roller skating, which are sometimes hard to quantify in terms of aerobic points.

So, because you may be interested in working these activities into your personal exercise program, I think it's important for you to understand how the target heart rate concept works. Then, even if we haven't been able to set up an aerobic point chart for a given form of exercise you may have chosen, you'll still be in a position to evaluate whether or not this activity is valuable as a means to aerobic conditioning.

Here's an easy procedure to determine your personal target heart rate:

First, take your resting heart rate. To get this figure, monitor your pulse at the wrist, at the neck, or by placing your hand over your heart. Count every beat for 15 seconds, and then multiply that figure by 4 to get the number of heartbeats per minute.

If you measure the number of beats for a shorter period than 15 seconds—say 6 or 10 seconds—the possibility of committing a major error is greatly magnified. For example, if you're off one beat over a 15-second period, you'll only be off four beats over the 1-minute period. But if you make one error during a 6-second count, your error over the minute period could be plus or minus 10 heartbeats.

Finally, I would recommend that you take your heart rate at the heart itself or the wrist, rather than at the carotid artery at the neck. The reason for this is that some studies have shown that if you press too hard on the neck you may actually slow down your rate by as much as 3 to 4 beats per minute.

For the purposes of illustrating the way to calculate your target heart rate, let's assume for the rest of this discussion that you are a 50-year-old man or woman.

Next, use the formula that we use for men: Predicted Maximum Heart Rate (PMHR) = 205 minus 1/2 your age. (For women use PMHR = 220 minus age.) For example, at 50 years of age, a man's predicted maximum heart rate would be 205 minus 25 = 180. For women, it would be 220 minus 50 = 170.

The third step is a rather simple calculation: Take 80 percent of 180, and you get 144 beats per minute. If your heart rate exceeds that figure for a minimum of 20 minutes, four times per week, then you will get an aerobic training effect. In fact, combinations of a heart rate of 130 for 30 minutes, or 150 for 10 minutes, four times a week, will in general give you the same results.

Finally, there is the problem of how to accurately *monitor* your heart rate during exercise to be sure you're reaching your target heart rate and getting the full aerobic benefits. The problem here is that it usually takes at least 20 seconds to take your pulse after you stop exercising. That includes 5 to 10 seconds just to find the pulse, waiting a few seconds for the second hand to be just right, and then another 10 seconds to count the beats.

In addition, if you are in good condition, your heart rate may drop at a rate of a beat per minute for the first 15 to 20 seconds after exercise. So it's necessary to correct your reading upward to find your true heart rate during exercise. The technique I would suggest for the highly conditioned person is to go ahead and take your pulse rate within 20 seconds after you stop your aerobic exercise. Then, add 10 percent to this pulse rate to get your heart rate during exercise. For example, if you counted a heart rate of 160, in reality it was probably 10 percent higher at maximum, or 176.

And now, armed with this knowledge of your target heart rate, let's move on to the next step in setting up your personal aerobics program—the choice of an appropriate aerobic exercise.

STEP THREE: CHOOSE A BASIC AEROBIC EXERCISE

The aerobic activity you choose should have two primary characteristics: (1) It should provide enough exercise to allow you to get your body functioning up around your target heart rate for a period of at least 20 to 30 minutes at a time; and (2) it should be an activity that interests you enough to motivate you to continue with it over an indefinite number of years, and preferably over your entire lifetime.

As far as this second characteristic is concerned, I don't mean to imply that you have to love the activity you've chosen more than any of your other recreational or sports interests—just that you have to be sufficiently interested, perhaps because you see the fitness value of the exercise, to keep at it. In other words, if you absolutely hate swimming or running, or you get totally embarrassed every time you step on a racketball court because you're so uncoordinated, I certainly wouldn't recommend one of those sports as your basic aerobic activity.

Among the common athletic activities that our research has shown provide the best aerobic conditioning potential, here are the top five, listed in descending order of exercise value.

1. Cross-country skiing.

Why is this the top aerobics activity? The answer is relatively simple: With cross-country skiing, you have more muscles involved than just the legs, and any time you get more muscles involved, you get more aerobic benefit.

But there are other advantages that cross-country skiing has over most other aerobic sports. The fact that this activity is usually done at relatively high altitudes and in cold weather adds additional strain on the body, and that means a more rigorous workout. Finally, it's necessary to wear heavier clothing in cross-country skiing than in most other aerobic activities, and so you have an overload principle at work—an added weight on the body which further enhances the aerobic effect.

2. Swimming.

As the second most effective aerobic exercise, swimming involves all of the major muscles in the body, and as a result, it gives you more of a total conditioning effect than many other sports. Also, swimmers tend to have fewer problems with injuries than runners because the buoyancy of the water helps reduce excessive pressure on the joints and bones.

For this reason, swimmers can swim up to 10 miles per day and get in excess of 1,300 aerobic points per week without any great danger of pulling a muscle or harming a joint. This level of exercise would be practically impossible for a runner, who would have to run almost 300 miles per week to get 1,300 points. If a runner could achieve such distances on a regular basis, he or she could be expected to seriously damage the bone and joint system in the process. On the other hand, swimmers must be on their guard to avoid ear or eye infections, sinus problems, and other physical maladies that may accompany serious water-sport workouts.

3. Jogging or running.

The activity that we put in third place for aerobic value is jogging or running. The difference between the two, by the way, is usually defined in terms of how fast you go. Those who run faster than 9 minutes per mile I consider to be running; and those who run slower than 9 minutes per mile are jogging. Of course, other people have other definitions which may be either faster or slower than the ones I've suggested.

Most people who get into aerobic conditioning choose jogging because it's the most convenient—there's always an available street or sidewalk just outside your door. Also, you get some of the greatest benefits from this sport in the shortest period of time. Finally, jogging is popular because the level of skill required is quite low in comparison to swimming, cross-country skiing, and most of the other top-level aerobic activities.

The problem with jogging, as we've seen already, lies in the injuries that may occur if you do not warm up properly, or if you begin to run excessive distances—say, 25 miles or more per week. Certainly, there are exceptions; some runners have routinely run 50 or more miles each week for many years, with no apparent harm. In these cases, I am not advocating that the number of miles be reduced. The important thing is just to listen to your body: If it rebels, respond accordingly.

Also, the potential danger of subjecting your feet and legs to pounding on the ground is the other side of the coin of a major strength of jogging: Because the bones and joints get more pressure exerted on them in this sport, they tend to get thicker and stronger and thus become better protected from the onset of osteoporosis, or deterioration of the bones that occurs with aging.

4. Outdoor cycling.

This exercise causes less wear and tear on the joints and muscles than does jogging, and so people with joint problems—particularly older people—can benefit from this approach to exercise. Generally speaking, speeds of less than 10 miles per hour are worth very little from an aerobic standpoint, whereas speeds in excess of 20 miles per hour are racing speeds. For the average person, we've found that a cycling speed slightly greater than 15 miles per hour is the optimum rate for a good training effect.

Finally, let me say a word or two about indoor cycling: If you use a stationary bicycle, you'll put out considerably more effort to get the same benefit as you will with outdoor cycling. Perhaps the reason for this is that in outdoor cycling you are not only overcoming the resistance of the bicycle, but you are propelling your body weight. In contrast, with indoor cycling you are merely cycling against the resistance in the bicycle. Consequently, the legs play out faster; so almost invariably, exercise heart rates are higher with outdoor than with indoor cycling.

With some of the new exercise bicycles (e.g., Schwinn Air-Dyne Ergometer), a pumping action of the arms is required along with the leg movement. Such self-propelled exercise bikes are of great aerobic benefit and are comparable to the type of physical activity achieved with cross-country skiing. Yet you should be aware that the points awarded for stationary cycling in the Appendix are for standard cycling, in which the arms remain motionless. A separate table in the Appendix gives point information about the Schwinn Air-Dyne Ergometer.

So although I'm not saying that it's impossible to get an adequate aerobic benefit from stationary cycling, I do feel that it requires more effort and greater resistance than the average person's legs can handle. In any case, it's important to use the heart rate monitoring technique we discussed in Step Two to be sure that you're exercising at your target heart rate.

5. Walking.

The last of the five major exercises is walking, and the great advantage of walking is that it can be done anywhere by anyone, regardless of age or sex. The disadvantage is that it takes about three times as long to get the same aerobic benefit from walking as from running. To see what the benefits are of walking at various speeds, for various distances, check the aerobic point charts in the Appendix of this book.

In addition to these five main aerobic exercises, there are many others which you can use to get the desired conditioning effect. For example, you may prefer a racket sport like squash, tennis, or handball, roller skating, or aerobic dancing. The important thing is to pick an activity which you can truly *enjoy*—one which you can remain enthusiastic about for many years into the future.

Also, it's not at all necessary to do only one aerobic activity. You may want to shift back and forth among several (particularly for seasonal activities such as skiing) and that's perfectly acceptable. The only consideration is that you should do the activity at an intensity and for a duration which will give you an adequate aerobic conditioning effect. And that means being sure that you keep your heart rate up well above normal—at least at 130 beats per minute and preferably up close to your target heart rate—for the duration of the exercise.

Now, let's examine the important characteristics of some of the less traditional, but quite popular, aerobic activities on the current scene.

Roller skating.

Recent research has shown that roller skating at a speed of 10 miles per hour is the aerobic equivalent of jogging at 5 miles per hour. Using this finding as a basic guideline, we would award 1.5 aerobic points for every 6 minutes of roller skating, or a total of 15 points for 1 hour of this activity.

But remember: To qualify for this number of points, it's necessary to keep skating continuously, so that your legs and arms are constantly in motion and your heart rate stays up close to the target rate. If you begin to coast along—as is often the temptation with cycling or any other activity that involves vehicles on wheels—the aerobic benefit will be less.

Aerobic dancing.

We have examined this activity in some detail and have found that it's quite difficult to quantify the energy cost of aerobic dancing accurately because of the different intensities with which it can be practiced.

For example, there is only one way you can run a mile in 8 minutes. But two women standing side-by-side in the same aerobic dance class can be expending considerably different amounts of energy. One woman may really be putting her heart and soul into it, while the other may barely be going through the motions.

But even with these difficulties, we've tried to estimate the average energy cost involved, and we've awarded aerobic dancing 6 points for every 30 minutes, or 9 points for a standard 45-minute class. But even with this point system as a guideline, I would advise you to monitor your heart rate a few times if you begin to participate in aerobic dancing to see just how it is responding to the amount of energy you're expending. If your rate is not up to at least 130 beats a minute, then you probably need to put more effort into your workout.

There are many good aerobic dance programs on the market, in the form of classes, tapes, and books. And the only way to evaluate how good they are is to try some of them out and see if you enjoy one well enough to stick with it. Then, monitor your exercise heart rate to be sure you're expending enough energy—but without pushing yourself too hard. (For detailed guidelines regarding a slowly progressive exercise program conducted to music, see Chapter 8.)

Handball, racketball, squash, and basketball.

I lump these together because they provide about the same amount of exercise as a group. We award 9 points for an hour of these activities—mainly because there is a lot of stopping and starting, and so the heart rate goes up and down and prevents you from getting the continuous aerobic effect that's available in a sport like jogging. A detailed summary of how to award yourself points with these sports is on the charts in the Appendix.

Tennis.

We have decided to award only 4.5 points for an hour of tennis singles play. But as with many of the other activities, this can vary considerably as a result of the intensity at which the game can be played. Some people are earning more than 4.5 points per hour; others earn less. Yet overall, a good average is 4.5 points per hour. Dr. R. Donald Hagan of our Institute for Aerobics Research conducted a survey that showed that the aerobic capabilities of top-ranked female singles players, ages 11 to 16, were higher than those of players ranked lower. Hagan believes that the study supports the idea that a talented player who ignores aerobic training is often the one who wins big in the first set but invariably loses in three.

As far as the implications for your own tennis playing are concerned, I would suggest that you resolve to play your singles at as high a pitch as you can maintain, with minimal resting between points. Also, if you are playing doubles, reduce the aerobic points by one half. It is difficult to use tennis exclusively in an aerobics program because the sport requires too many hours per week, unless you are a competitive player. And many professional tennis players jog regularly to improve their stamina and their game.

The minitrampoline.

This device, which is a small trampoline just large enough to enable a person to run in place on its surface, is one of the latest of the highly touted exercise devices. Advertisements indicate, first of all, that exercise on the minitrampoline is much better than jogging since the trampoline reduces the hard impact on the floor and therefore reduces the incidence of muscle injuries and joint problems. I would agree that, to some extent, this may be a valid claim, and for a person who is suffering from serious muscular or bone problems, the trampoline may be preferable to regular jogging.

But some of the advertisements also claim that the minitrampoline provides unusually good conditioning benefits in a very short period of time. For example, it's been stated that 10 minutes on the small trampoline is roughly the equivalent of running 2 miles. But that's completely untrue. As a matter of fact, studies performed in several laboratories have shown that the energy cost for running on the trampoline is even less than the energy cost for running in place.

The problem with the minitrampoline is that it reduces the pull of gravity, and this decreases the workload. In other words, instead of the requirement of pulling the legs up, the trampoliner's legs are "sprung up" in such a way that the overall physical effort is reduced.

As far as aerobic points are concerned, we have determined that continuous running in place on the minitrampoline is worth 1.6 points per 10 minutes, or 5 points for 30 minutes. This is the equivalent of running a mile in between 12 and 13 minutes.

Horseback riding.

I just threw this one in for fun: A few years ago, a woman wrote and asked, "I enjoy horseback riding and I'd like to know how many points I get for riding a horse?"

I said, "None. But give the horse a bunch!"

The horseback-riding question is symbolic of an issue you should constantly keep in mind if you're planning to use an untraditional exercise for your aerobic activity. Just make sure—by monitoring your heart rate immediately after exercise—that you really are exercising *aerobically*, and not involved in an exercise which is more isotonic or isometric or anaerobic than it is aerobic.

You can see from this brief list that there are a wide variety of possibilities, as you look around for an aerobic activity, that will enable you to get your heart and circulatory system in good shape. But after you've picked your activity, the time has arrived to put it into effect. And so now, we move on to the crucial final step in getting your personal aerobics program off the ground.

STEP FOUR: EMBARK ON A REGULAR AEROBICS PROGRAM

There are four important parts to any effective aerobics conditioning program: (1) warm-up; (2) aerobic phase; (3) cool-down; and (4) musculoskeletal conditioning through calisthenics and/or weight training. Now, let's look at each of these four components and see how, in practical terms, you can incorporate them as an exciting, enjoyable part of your own approach.

1. Warm-up.

The warm-up phase is extremely important, but unfortunately, it's often an activity that is ignored—and painful, frustrating muscle pulls or strains may be the result.

There are two goals for the warm-up: The first is to stretch and warm up the muscles of the back and the extremities. And the second is to encourage a slight acceleration of the heart rate so that the body can move more gradually into the high heart rate of the aerobic phase. It's been shown that even patients with severe heart disease, characterized by angina or chest pains, can always do more aerobic work without chest pains if they warm up slowly.

In general, warm-ups should consist of 2 to 3 minutes of exercises that are not very demanding. Stretching, such as touching your toes, is quite important. But difficult exercises like pull-ups, push-ups, or weight lifting should be avoided because they may create an "oxygen debt." This sort of debt leads to a state of fatigue before you start into the aerobic phase of the workout. Such exercise is not advisable and at times may not be safe, particularly in the patient with heart problems.

One particularly good stretching routine which I always use during my warm-up also happens to be one of the best sets of exercises to help prevent low-back pain. Called the Williams exercises, these involve lying flat on your back and then raising one of your knees up toward your chest, holding it tight into the chest for a count of five. Then, you straighten the leg and repeat the exercise with the other leg. The third step is to pull both knees to the chest, hold tight for a count of five, and then straighten both legs and relax. The final exercise is called the "pelvic tilt" and consists of pushing the lower back into the floor, thereby eliminating the normal curvature. Again, hold for a count of at least five. These exercises should be repeated for at least 3–4 minutes, and throughout the exercises the head should be flat on the floor.

If I happen to be short of time in running my customary 3 miles, I may do my warm-up in a slightly different way. Instead of taking time to do calisthenics, I may run the first quarter mile at a very slow pace—that is, about 10 minutes per mile or slower. During that time, I'll swing my arms, bend my body up and down, and incorporate a modified stretching warm-up into that quarter-mile. But I don't recommend this as a routine type of warm-up.

2. Aerobic phase.

This second part of your exercise program is the meat-and-potatoes of your conditioning efforts. For this particular part of your workout, you should take the aerobic activity or activities you've chosen in Step Three and make them a regular part of your weekly schedule—as regular as brushing your teeth or going to work in the morning.

I'm frequently asked, "How much aerobic exercise is really necessary?"

There are several ways of answering this question, and, as I've already indicated elsewhere, the answer depends on the kind of exercise you've chosen and how intensely you go at it. For the top four aerobic exercises I listed earlier—cross-country skiing, swimming, jogging, and outdoor cycling—you could get adequate aerobic conditioning from a minimum of 20 minutes a day, 4 days a week.

In recommending this amount of activity, though, I'm assuming that you would exercise at a minimum level of intensity in each sport. For example, a 20-minute workout would be fine if you run 2 miles in under 20 minutes; if you swim 800 yards in 20 minutes; or if you cycle 5 miles in less than 20 minutes. On the other hand, if you're playing competitive sports, it's going to take a full 1-hour session of such activities as handball, racketball, squash, basketball, or football to get enough exercise with four workouts a week.

But even as I talk about working out for 20 minutes in these most effective aerobic activities, I should mention that that's only a minimum. The optimum workout would be more like 30 minutes, three to four times a week.

Another way of describing how much exercise is necessary for you is to focus on the aerobic points concept. Our most recent research at the Aerobics Center has convinced us that a man should work up to a minimum of 35 aerobics points per week, and a woman should get at least 27 points. There are many ways in which you can achieve those points, as you can see from the charts at the back of the book. But it's important to understand that it's necessary to exercise at least three times per week. Trying to cram 30 points into two workouts per week may actually be more dangerous than it is beneficial. And certainly vigorous activity once a week for the man or woman past 40 years of age is, to use the strongest negative medical term, contraindicated. In other words, you're crazy if you try it!

Of course, it is possible to get 30 or 35 points in a day, but our studies have shown that if you reduce the frequency to only twice weekly, not only is it potentially dangerous, but you can expect to lose aerobic capacity.

At three times a week, on the other hand, you can maintain an adequate aerobic capacity. And for four sessions a week, you can get even more significant improvements in your conditioning.

But there are limits to every good thing. It's not at all necessary to work out five or more times per week, and in fact, I discourage vigorous physical activity seven times per week. Even on a 5-day schedule, I recommend alternating hard days and easy days. It's simply not wise to go out and push yourself to your maximum performance every day because if you do, you'll almost certainly begin to suffer from cumulative fatigue and also be prone to more muscle, joint, and bone injuries.

3. Cool-down.

This third phase of a complete conditioning program should take a minimum of 5 minutes, and during that time, you don't just remain motionless. Rather, you should keep moving, but at a slow enough pace to let your heart rate decline gradually. If you're running, as soon as you cross the finish line, walk one additional quarter-mile—or if you don't have the distance measured, go by the 5-minute cool-down guideline.

If you're walking, just amble around slowly for 5 minutes more. Or if you're swimming, walk back and forth across the shallow end of the pool. Finally, if you're cycling, cycle slowly on a flat surface or get off and walk for 5 minutes. But the important thing at the end of any aerobic exercise is just to keep moving around so that the blood can be pumped from your lower extremities back into the central circulatory system. Otherwise, you could get dizzy or lightheaded, or possibly even lose consciousness. Remember, too, that the majority of severe cardiac irregularities that can be dangerous, occur following the exercise, not during it.

4. Calisthenics or weight training.

This phase of your workout, which should last a minimum of 10 minutes, should involve activities that will build up your muscles and increase your flexibility. I would concentrate on the main muscle groups, like different parts of the legs, the stomach, the back, and the chest. Weight training of various types, or calisthenics like push-ups, sit-ups, pull-ups, or any other kind of weight training will suffice.

One of the main reasons you want to pursue this muscle-building phase of your workout is that the added strength and toughness you'll gain will make you less prone to injuries during the aerobic aspect of your program.

If you follow each of these four phases of your conditioning program faithfully, I think you'll find you can avoid most exercise-related injuries. Because we stress this approach, we've enjoyed great success in achieving safety at the Aerobics Center. Our runners have covered in excess of 4.5 million miles on their various programs—without a single fatality and only minimal musculoskeletal problems.

And here's another important point, especially if you're one of those people who worries that he doesn't have enough time to exercise: When you think about it, it doesn't take much time at all, does it? If you add up the recommended times for each of the four phases of your conditioning program, you'll find that you can get by on less than 40 minutes for a *complete* workout, including weight training or calisthenics, with a minimum of three and preferably four sessions a week.

Moreover, if you've chosen your aerobic activity carefully—and it's an activity that you really are interested in and want to become proficient in doing—that 40 minutes can become something you'll look forward to as much as anything else you do during the average day. Most of the people who exercise regularly at our Dallas facility can't wait to arrive here and get out on our running trails, or into our pool, or onto our courts.

Now we're ready to examine the exercise programs and aerobics equations in detail.

8

The Plan: The Chart Pack and the Aerobics Equations

After you have chosen your aerobic exercise by following the guidelines suggested in Chapter 7, you're ready to embark upon a step-by-step, lifetime program of vigorous activity. And that's the ultimate goal this newly organized chart pack and the never-before-published formulas accompanying it have been designed to help you achieve.

The charts in this section have been scientifically formulated in accordance with the aerobics points system that we've already discussed in some detail. As in my past books, the charts are all age-adjusted, so that you can fit right into the exercise program that is best suited for your age level. But as I've indicated, there is also a great deal of new, and I think exciting, information in these charts that hasn't been included in earlier books that I've written.

First of all, some of the point values have been adjusted in light of new information we've discovered in our research at the Aerobics Center during the last few years.

Secondly, you'll note that aerobic dancing, circuit weight training and minitrampoline exercise programs have been included for the first time here.

In the third place, if you happen to want to run, cycle, or otherwise exercise over a distance or time period that is not specifically included in these chart packs, you can become an aerobics points expert yourself! By using some new "do-it-yourself" equations in this chapter, you can formulate your own point system. The equations follow the progressive exercise and maintenance programs.

For example, I've received many letters over the years saying things like, "I like to cycle 24.5 miles [or 17.5 miles, or some other odd figure], but those distances aren't included in the chart pack. How can I figure the number of points I'll earn if I go that distance?"

Up to this point, I've had to respond personally to each of these inquiries. But now, with these new equations, you can figure out for yourself how many points you're entitled to for whatever level of exercise you've chosen. Also, if you use a personal computer to keep track of the points you earn at various distances, as we do at the Aerobics Center in Dallas, you can just plug the equation into your computer program. In this way, you can figure your points each day rather easily by inserting the appropriate values into the formula.

The procedure you should use to apply these equations is self-explanatory, with examples to demonstrate exactly how they work.

The way we arrived at these equations, by the way, was to look at the concrete results of our research, and then work our way backwards until we had the formula that was consistent with that research. These equations, in other words, are not some pie-in-the-sky mathematical theory: To the contrary, they are solidly based in empirical research and evidence.

We first decided, from observing people's responses on treadmill tests and in other situations, the number of points a given activity was worth. The person's physical responses, in light of the intensity and duration of each activity, were a key factor in determining how many points were awarded. Then, we found that it was necessary to add "endurance points" as individuals exercised over longer periods of time.

In other words, if you run 1 mile in a certain time—assume 10 minutes—you'll earn a certain number of points, say 4 points. But if you run 3 miles in 30 minutes, you'll earn more than 3 times 4, or 12 points because of the "endurance point" factor. So, running 3 miles in 30 minutes would give you 14 points instead of 12 points (or two extra "endurance points").

Finally, because some people wanted to be more precise than our charts in determining their points over odd distances or times, we took what we had learned from our research in developing the chart packs and derived some simple equations. These are the formulas that we have included in this chapter to enable you to build your own precise aerobics points program, if you so desire.

So this is the background for our new, do-it-yourself, highly personalized approach to aerobic exercise. Before we plunge into the chart packs and formulas that deal with the type of exercise you've chosen for your lifetime aerobics plan, let's review the 12-minute test.

THE 12-MINUTE TEST

Field testing of physical fitness is no longer a required part of the aerobics program and is in fact contraindicated initially in the deconditioned person over 35 years of age. Yet it is an easy way to measure the success of your program and continues to be a popular feature of the aerobics system. It gives you a reliable estimate of your aerobic capacity, or oxygen consumption, yet does not require expensive laboratory equipment. It can be used by people of all ages, and large groups can be tested at one time. It has also been used as a measuring tool to compare levels of fitness among people of different countries. Included here are 12-minute tests for running, walking, swimming, and cycling.

But do not go out and take any 12-minute test or other field test of fitness requiring maximal effort unless you are under 35 years of age, are already conditioned, or have progressed through at least the first 6 weeks of one of the programs.

If you qualify to take the test, you will find that it is quite simple. You cover the greatest distance that you can in 12 minutes, walking and running on a level surface, or just walking, or swimming, or cycling. Warm up before and cool down properly, as described in the preceding chapter. If any unusual symptoms occur during the test, *do not continue.*

Based on the distance you cover in 12 minutes, you can measure your fitness level from the following tables.

12-Minute Walking/Running Test
Distance (Miles) Covered in 12 Minutes

Fitness Category		13-19	20-29	30-39	40-49	50-59	60+
				Age (years)			
I. Very Poor	(men)	<1.30*	<1.22	<1.18	<1.14	<1.03	<.87
	(women)	<1.0	<.96	<.94	<.88	<.84	<.78
II. Poor	(men)	1.30-1.37	1.22-1.31	1.18-1.30	1.14-1.24	1.03-1.16	.87-1.02
	(women)	1.00-1.18	.96-1.11	.95-1.05	.88-.98	.84-.93	.78-.86
III. Fair	(men)	1.38-1.56	1.32-1.49	1.31-1.45	1.25-1.39	1.17-1.30	1.03-1.20
	(women)	1.19-1.29	1.12-1.22	1.06-1.18	.99-1.11	.94-1.05	.87-.98
IV. Good	(men)	1.57-1.72	1.50-1.64	1.46-1.56	1.40-1.53	1.31-1.44	1.21-1.32
	(women)	1.30-1.43	1.23-1.34	1.19-1.29	1.12-1.24	1.06-1.18	.99-1.09
V. Excellent	(men)	1.73-1.86	1.65-1.76	1.57-1.69	1.54-1.65	1.45-1.58	1.33-1.55
	(women)	1.44-1.51	1.35-1.45	1.30-1.39	1.25-1.34	1.19-1.30	1.10-1.18
VI. Superior	(men)	>1.87	>1.77	>1.70	>1.66	>1.59	>1.56
	(women)	>1.52	>1.46	>1.40	>1.35	>1.31	>1.19

* < Means "less than"; > means "more than."

1.5-Mile Run Test
Time (Minutes)

Fitness Category		13-19	20-29	30-39	40-49	50-59	60+
				Age (years)			
I. Very poor	(men)	>15:31*	>16:01	>16:31	>17:31	>19:01	>20:01
	(women)	>18:31	>19:01	>19:31	>20:01	>20:31	>21:01
II. Poor	(men)	12:11-15:30	14:01-16:00	14:44-16:30	15:36-17:30	17:01-19:00	19:01-20:00
	(women)	16:55-18:30	18:31-19:00	19:01-19:30	19:31-20:00	20:01-20:30	21:00-21:31
III. Fair	(men)	10:49-12:10	12:01-14:00	12:31-14:45	13:01-15:35	14:31-17:00	16:16-19:00
	(women)	14:31-16:54	15:55-18:30	16:31-19:00	17:31-19:30	19:01-20:00	19:31-20:30
IV. Good	(men)	9:41-10:48	10:46-12:00	11:01-12:30	11:31-13:00	12:31-14:30	14:00-16:15
	(women)	12:30-14:30	13:31-15:54	14:31-16:30	15:56-17:30	16:31-19:00	17:31-19:30
V. Excellent	(men)	8:37-9:40	9:45-10:45	10:00-11:00	10:30-11:30	11:00-12:30	11:15-13:59
	(women)	11:50-12:29	12:30-13:30	13:00-14:30	13:45-15:55	14:30-16:30	16:30-17:30
VI. Superior	(men)	<8:37	<9:45	<10:00	<10:30	<11:00	<11:15
	(women)	<11:50	<12:30	<13:00	<13:45	<14:30	<16:30

* < Means "less than"; > means "more than."

3-Mile Walking Test (No Running)
Time (Minutes)

Fitness Category		13–19	20–29	30–39	40–49	50–59	60+
I. Very poor	(men)	>45:00*	>46:00	>49:00	>52:00	>55:00	>60:00
	(women)	>47:00	>48:00	>51:00	>54:00	>57:00	>63:00
II. Poor	(men)	41:01–45:00	42:01–46:00	44:31–49:00	47:01–52:00	50:01–55:00	54:01–60:00
	(women)	43:01–47:00	44:01–48:00	46:31–51:00	49:01–54:00	52:01–57:00	57:01–63:00
III. Fair	(men)	37:31–41:00	38:31–42:00	40:01–44:30	42:01–47:00	45:01–50:00	48:01–54:00
	(women)	39:31–43:00	40:31–44:00	42:01–46:30	44:01–49:00	47:01–52:00	51:01–57:00
IV. Good	(men)	33:00–37:30	34:00–38:30	35:00–40:00	36:30–42:00	39:00–45:00	41:00–48:00
	(women)	35:00–39:30	36:00–40:30	37:30–42:00	39:00–44:00	42:00–47:00	45:00–51:00
V. Excellent	(men)	<33:00	<34:00	<35:00	<36:30	<39:00	<41:00
	(women)	<35:00	<36:00	<37:30	<39:00	<42:00	<45:00

Age (years)

* < Means "less than"; > means "more than."
The Walking test, covering 3 miles in the fastest time possible *without running*, can be done on a track over any accurately measured distance. As with running, take the test after you have been training for at least 6 weeks, when you feel rested, and dress to be comfortable.

12-Minute Swimming Test
Distance (Yards) Swum in 12 Minutes

Fitness Category		13–19	20–29	30–39	40–49	50–59	60+
I. Very poor	(men)	<500*	<400	<350	<300	<250	<250
	(women)	<400	<300	<250	<200	<150	<150
II. Poor	(men)	500–599	400–499	350–449	300–399	250–349	250–299
	(women)	400–499	300–399	250–349	200–299	150–249	150–199
III. Fair	(men)	600–699	500–599	450–549	400–499	350–449	300–399
	(women)	500–599	400–499	350–449	300–399	250–349	200–299
IV. Good	(men)	700–799	600–699	550–649	500–599	450–549	400–499
	(women)	600–699	500–599	450–549	400–499	350–449	300–399
V. Excellent	(men)	>800	>700	>650	>600	>550	>500
	(women)	>700	>600	>550	>500	>450	>400

Age (years)

* < Means "less than"; > means "more than."
The Swimming test requires you to swim as far as you can in 12 minutes, using whatever stroke you prefer and resting as necessary, but trying for a maximum effort. The easiest way to take the test is in a pool with known dimensions, and it helps to have another person record the laps and time. Be sure to use a watch with a sweep second hand.

12-Minute Cycling Test
(3-Speed or less)
Distance (Miles) Cycled in 12 Minutes

Fitness Category		13–19	20–29	Age (years) 30–39	40–49	50–59	60+
I. Very poor	(men)	<2.75*	<2.5	<2.25	<2.0	<1.75	<1.75
	(women)	<1.75	<1.5	<1.25	<1.0	<0.75	<0.75
II. Poor	(men)	2.75–3.74	2.5–3.49	2.25–3.24	2.0–2.99	1.75–2.49	1.75–2.24
	(women)	1.75–2.74	1.5–2.49	1.25–2.24	1.0–1.99	0.75–1.49	0.75–1.24
III. Fair	(men)	3.75–4.74	3.5–4.49	3.25–4.24	3.0–3.99	2.50–3.49	2.25–2.99
	(women)	2.75–3.74	2.5–3.49	2.25–3.24	2.0–2.99	1.50–2.49	1.25–1.99
IV. Good	(men)	4.75–5.74	4.5–5.49	4.25–5.24	4.0–4.99	3.50–4.49	3.0–3.99
	(women)	3.75–4.74	3.5–4.49	3.25–4.24	3.0–3.99	2.50–3.49	2.0–2.99
V. Excellent	(men)	>5.75	>5.5	>5.25	>5.0	>4.5	>4.0
	(women)	>4.75	>4.5	>4.25	>4.0	>3.5	>3.0

* < Means "less than"; > means "more than."

The Cycling test can be used as a test of fitness if you are utilizing the cycling program. Cycle as far as you can in 12 minutes in an area where traffic is not a problem. Try to cycle on a hard, flat surface, with the wind (less than 10 mph), and use a bike with no more than 3 gears. If the wind is blowing harder than 10 mph take the test another day. Measure the distance you cycle in 12 minutes by either the speedometer/odometer on the bike (which may not be too accurate) or by another means, such as a car odometer or an engineering wheel.

THE AEROBICS CHART PACK

1. Read all the chapters preceding this chart pack before starting one of the following progressive exercise programs.

2. Then select one of the eleven programs compatible with your age, health, and personal desires. The programs are grouped basically by age, so that the programs for people under thirty, for example, are found together. A few programs do cover several decades, however.

3. Remember, the time goals are to be reached at the end, not at the beginning, of the week. If you have a problem with the requirements of the week, repeat it until that week's goals can be met.

4. When you have completed one of the age-adjusted programs, continue averaging a minimum of 27 to 32 points a week, utilizing one or a variety of different exercises. Either continue with the final program in a chosen exercise, or select one of the maintenance programs that follow the progressive programs, or develop a program of your own from the aerobics equations at the end of this chapter or from the point value charts in the Appendix.

5. Remember the objective of aerobics is to get the required number of points per week, not to exercise in any particular way or at any particular speed or intensity. Accept the fact that your condition is good even without testing if you are averaging 27 points per week (women) or 32 points per week (men). The number of weekly points you earn correlates well with your level of physical fitness.

Aerobic Fitness Categories

Fitness Classifications	Average Points Per Week Men	Women
Very Poor	less than 10	less than 8
Poor	10–20	8–15
Fair	21–31	16–26
Good	32–50	27–40
Excellent	51–74	41–64
Superior	75+	65+

Definitions For Walking, Jogging, Running

Activity	Speed/Mile
Walk	14:01 min. or longer
Walk–Jog	12:01–14:00 min.
Jog	9:00–12:00 min.
Run	under 9:00 min.

PROGRESSIVE EXERCISE PROGRAMS BY AGE

Walking Exercise Program
(Under 30 Years of Age)

Week	Distance (miles)	Time Goal (minutes)	Freq/Wk	Points/Wk
1	2.0	34:00	3	12.2
2	2.0	32:00	4	18.0
3	2.0	30:00	5	25.0
4	2.5	38:00	5	31.8
5	2.5	37:00	5	33.2
6	2.5	36:00	5	34.6
7	3.0	45:00	5	40.0
8	3.0	44:00	5	41.3
9	3.0	43:00	5	42.9
10	3.0	42:00	4	35.4

By the tenth week, an adequate level of aerobic condition has been reached and can be maintained with a four-time-per-week schedule. This level of exercise equals 35 aerobic points per week, consistent with the good category of aerobic fitness.

Note: Points determined from the equations for walking, jogging, and running. If the point charts in the Appendix are used, the total point values may vary slightly.

Running/Jogging Exercise Program
(Under 30 Years of Age)

Week	Activity	Distance (miles)	Time Goal (min)	Freq/Wk	Points/Wk
1	walk	2.0	32:00	3	13.5
2	walk	3.0	48:00	3	21.7
3	walk/jog	2.0	26:00	4	24.9
4	walk/jog	2.0	24:00	4	28.0
5	jog	2.0	22:00	4	31.6
*6	jog	2.0	20:00	4	36.0
7	jog	2.5	25:00	4	46.0
8	jog	2.5	23:00	4	49.5
9	jog	3.0	30:00	4	56.0
10	jog	3.0	27:00	4	61.3

* By the sixth week, a minimum aerobic fitness level has been reached (36 aerobic points per week), but it is suggested that a higher level of fitness be achieved. By the tenth week of the above program, a total of 61 points per week is being earned, consistent with the excellent category of aerobic fitness.

Note: Points determined from the equations for walking, jogging and running. If the point charts in the Appendix are used, the point values may vary slightly.

Cycling Exercise Program
(Under 30 Years of Age)

Week	Distance (miles)	Time Goal (min)	Freq/Wk	Points/Wk
1	5.0	30:00	3	10.5
2	5.0	25:00	3	13.5
3	5.0	20:00	4	24.0
4	6.0	26:00	4	27.2
5	6.0	24:00	4	30.0
6	7.0	30:00	4	33.2
*7	7.0	27:45	4	36.4
8	8.0	35:00	4	37.9
9	8.0	34:00	4	39.2
10	8.0	32:00	4	42.0

* By the seventh week, an adequate level of aerobic fitness has been reached and can be maintained with a four-day-a-week exercise program. This level of exercise equals 36 aerobic points per week. It is suggested that a higher level be achieved and following the above program, by the tenth week, 42 aerobic points per week will be earned.

Note: Points determined from the equation for cycling. If the point charts in the Appendix are used, the point values may vary slightly.

Swimming Exercise Program
(Under 30 Years of Age)

Week	Distance (yards)	Time Goal (min)	Freq/Wk	Points/Wk
1	400	15:00	4	8.9
2	400	13:00	4	10.2
3	500	15:00	4	13.9
4	500	13:00	4	16.0
5	600	18:00	4	16.7
6	600	16:00	4	18.8
7	700	19:00	4	23.5
8	800	21:00	4	29.4
9	900	23:30	4	34.7
10	1000	25:00	4	41.3

Use whatever stroke enables you to swim the required distance in the time given. Resting is permissible during the initial weeks. By the tenth week, an adequate level of aerobic fitness has been reached (41 points) but it is suggested that higher levels of fitness be achieved by swimming faster or swimming further. Also, swimming 5 days per week may be desirable to increase fitness.

Note: Points determined from the equations for swimming. If the point charts in the Appendix are used, the point values may vary slightly.

Progressive Treadmill Exercise Program
(Under 30 Years of Age)

Week	Activity	Treadmill Speed (mph)	Incline (%)	Time (min)	Freq/Wk	Points/Wk
1	walk	4	flat	20:00	4	12.0
2	walk	4	flat	30:00	4	20.0
3	walk	4.5	flat	30:00	4	27.5
4	walk	4.5	5%	25:00	4	24.4
*5	walk/jog	5.0	flat	30:00	4	36.0
6	walk/jog	5.0	5%	25:00	4	32.2
7	jog	5.5	flat	30:00	4	45.5
8	jog	5.5	5%	25:00	4	41.0
9	jog	6.0	flat	30:00	4	56.0
10	jog	6.0	5%	30:00	4	61.6

* By the fifth week, adequate aerobic fitness has been reached (36 aerobic points per week) and it is permissible to continue at the exercise level.

By the tenth week, the excellent category has been achieved (61.6 aerobic points per week). Other combinations of speed, incline, duration, and frequency per week can be used to maintain the good or excellent categories of fitness.

Note: Points determined from the equation for treadmill exercising. If the point charts in the Appendix are used, the point values may vary slightly.

Aerobic Dancing and Other Exercise Programs Conducted to Music
(Under 30 Years of Age)

Week	Time (min)	Heart Rate Max* (beats/min)	Freq/Wk	Points/Wk
1	15:00	120–130	3	9.0
2	21:00	120–130	3	12.6
3	21:00	130–140	3	12.6
4	27:00	130–140	3	16.2
5	27:00	140–150	3	16.2
6	36:00	140–150	3	21.6
7	36:00	150–160	3	21.6
8	45:00	150–160	3	27.0

By the eighth week, an adequate level of aerobic conditioning has been reached (27 aerobic points) and this is consistent with the good category of fitness for women. Exercising five times per week would earn 45 points, consistent with the excellent category of fitness.

* Heart rates determined at 3 or more equal intervals during the exercise based on a 10 second × 6 count.

Note: Points determined from the equation for aerobic dancing.

Handball/Racketball/Squash/Basketball/Soccer/Hockey/ Lacrosse Exercise Program
(Under 30 Years of Age)

Week	Time Goal (min)	Freq/Wk	Points/Wk
1	30:00	3	0
2	30:00	3	0
3	30:00	3	0
4	45:00	3	0
5	45:00	3	0
6	45:00	3	0
7	20:00	4	12
8	25:00	4	15
9	30:00	4	18
10	40:00	4	24
11	45:00	4	27
12	60:00	4	36

During the first six weeks, the objective is to exercise the required time, *but not continuously*. Rest frequently. The time goals represent the combined exercise and rest periods. Beginning with the seventh week, the time goals represent continuous exercise. Do not count breaks, time-outs, etc.

Stationary Running Exercise Program
(Under 30 Years of Age)

Week	Time Goal (min)	Steps/Min*	Freq/Wk	Points/Wk
1	10:00	70–80	3	0
2	10:00	70–80	3	0
3	10:00	70–80	3	0
4	15:00	70–80	3	0
5	15:00	70–80	3	0
6	15:00	70–80	3	0
7	10:00	70–80	4	14.0
8	10:00	70–80	5	17.5
9	12:30	80–90	4	24.5
10	12:30	80–90	5	30.6
11	15:00	80–90	4	31.0
12	15:00	90–100	4	37.0

During the first six weeks, the requirement is to exercise the required number of minutes, *but not continuously*. Rest frequently and as long as necessary, *but continue to walk slowly while resting*. The time goals represent the combined stationary running and rest periods. Beginning with the seventh week, the time goals represent continuous exercise. Warm up for 3:00 minutes by walking briskly. Cool down for 3:00 minutes after exercise by walking slowly. Exercise on a cushioned surface (e.g., a thick carpet) in athletic shoes that have either a ripple or deep-cushioned sole.

* Count only when left foot hits the floor. Feet must be lifted at least eight inches off the floor.

Stationary Cycling Exercise Program
(Under 30 Years of Age)

Week	Speed (mph/rpm)	Time Goal (min)	PR After Exercise*	Freq/Wk	Points/Wk
1	15/55	8:00	<140*	3	3.0
2	15/55	10:00	<140	3	3.75
3	15/55	12:00	<140	3	4.13
4	17.5/65	12:00	<150	4	6.5
5	17.5/65	14:00	<150	4	8.0
6	17.5/65	16:00	<150	4	9.0
7	17.5/65	16:00	>150	5	11.25
8	17.5/65	16:00	>150	5	11.25
9	20/75	18:00	>160	5	18.13
10	20/75	18:00	>160	5	18.13
11	25/90	20:00	>160	5	28.33
12	25/90	25:00	>160	4	30.0

During the first six weeks, warm up by cycling for 3:00 minutes, 17.5 to 20 mph, with no resistance, before beginning the actual workout. At the conclusion of the exercise, cool down by cycling for 3:00 minutes with no resistance.

* Add enough resistance so that the pulse rate (PR) counted for 10 seconds immediately after exercise and multiplied by 6 equals the rate specified. If it is higher, lower the resistance before cycling again; if it is lower, increase the resistance.

Stair-Climbing Exercise Program
(Under 30 Years of Age)

Week	Round Trips (average number per min)	Time Goal (min)	Freq/Wk	Points/Wk
1	5	10:00	3	0
2	5	10:00	3	0
3	5	10:00	3	0
4	5	12:00	3	0
5	5	12:00	3	0
6	5	12:00	3	0
7	6	8:30	4	7.84
8	6	9:30	4	8.77
9	7	10:00	5	16.67
10	7	10:30	5	17.5
11	8	11:30	5	26.13
12	8	13:00	5	29.54

During the first six weeks, the requirement is to exercise the required number of minutes, *but not continuously.* Rest frequently, and as long as necessary, but walk slowly while resting. The time goal is the combined time for both stair climbing and resting. Beginning with the seventh week, the time goals refer to continuous exercise. Warm up for 3:00 minutes by walking briskly. Cool down for 3:00 minutes after exercise by walking slowly.

This program applies to 10 steps, 6″ to 7″ in height, 25° to 30° incline. Use of banister is encouraged.

Rope-Skipping Exercise Program
(Under 30 Years of Age)

Week	Time Goal (min)	Steps/Min	Freq/Wk	Points/Wk
1	10:00	70–90	3	0
2	10:00	70–90	3	0
3	10:00	70–90	3	0
4	15:00	70–90	3	0
5	15:00	70–90	3	0
6	15:00	70–90	3	0
7	7:30	90–110	4	12
8	7:30	90–110	5	15
9	10:00	90–110	4	16
10	10:00	90–110	5	20
11	12:30	90–110	5	27.5
12	15:00	90–110	5	35.0

During the first six weeks, the requirement is to exercise the required number of minutes, *but not continuously.* Rest frequently, and as long as necessary, but continue either to skip very slowly or to walk while resting; the time goals represent the combined time for rope skipping and resting. Beginning with the seventh week, the time goals refer to continuous exercise. Warm up for 3:00 minutes by slow skipping or walking briskly. Cool down for 3:00 minutes after exercise by slow walking.

Exercise on a cushioned surface (e.g., a thick carpet) in athletic shoes. Skip with both feet together, or step over the rope, alternating feet.

Walking Exercise Program
(30–49 Years of Age)

Week	Distance (miles)	Time Goal (min)	Freq/Wk	Points/Wk
1	2.0	36:00	3	11.0
2	2.0	34:00	3	12.2
3	2.0	32:00	4	18.0
4	2.0	30:00	4	20.0
5	2.5	39:00	4	24.5
6	2.5	38:00	5	31.8
7	2.5	37:00	5	33.2
8	3.0	46:00	5	38.7
9	3.0	45:00	5	40.0
10	3.0	44:00	4	33.1

By the tenth week, an adequate level of aerobic conditioning has been reached and can be maintained with a four-time-per-week schedule. This level of exercise equals 33 aerobic points per week, consistent with the good category of aerobic fitness.

Note: Points determined from the equations for walking, jogging and running. If the point charts in the Appendix are used, the point values may vary slightly.

Running/Jogging Exercise Program
(30–49 Years of Age)

Week	Activity	Distance (miles)	Time Goal (min)	Freq/Wk	Points/Wk
1	walk	2.0	34:00	3	12.2
2	walk	2.5	42:00	3	16.3
3	walk	3.0	50:00	3	20.4
4	walk/jog	2.0	25:00	4	26.4
5	walk/jog	2.0	24:00	4	28.0
6	jog	2.0	22:00	4	31.6
*7	jog	2.0	20:00	4	36.0
8	jog	2.5	26:00	4	43.7
9	jog	2.5	25:00	4	46.0
10	jog	3.0	31:00	4	53.7
11	jog	3.0	29:00	4	57.6
12	jog	3.0	27:00	4	61.3

* By the seventh week, a minimum aerobic fitness level has been reached (36 aerobic points per week) but it is suggested that a higher level of fitness be achieved. By the twelfth week of the above program, a total of 61 points per week is being earned, consistent with the excellent category of aerobic fitness.

Note: Points determined from the equations for walking, jogging, running. If the point charts in the Appendix are used, the point values may vary slightly.

Cycling Exercise Program
(30–49 Years of Age)

Week	Distance (miles)	Time Goal (min)	Freq/Wk	Points/Wk
1	4.0	20:00	3	10.0
2	4.0	18:00	3	11.5
3	5.0	24:00	4	19.0
4	5.0	22:00	4	21.3
5	5.0	20:00	4	24.0
6	6.0	26:00	4	27.2
7	6.0	24:00	4	30.0
8	7.0	30:00	4	33.2
9	7.0	28:00	4	36.0
10	7.0	27:55	4	36.1

By the tenth week, an adequate level of aerobic fitness has been reached and can be maintained with a four-day-a-week exercise program. This level of exercise equals 36 aerobic points per week. If desired, cycling faster, further or more frequently each week will increase both the aerobic points and fitness level.

Note: Points determined from the equation for cycling. If the point charts in the Appendix are used, the point values may vary slightly.

Swimming Exercise Program
(30–49 Years of Age)

Week	Distance (yards)	Time Goal (min)	Freq/Wk	Points/Wk
1	300	12:00	4	6.2
2	300	10:00	4	7.5
3	400	13:00	4	10.2
4	400	12:00	4	11.1
5	500	14:00	4	14.9
6	500	13:00	4	16.0
7	600	16:00	4	18.8
8	700	19:00	4	23.5
9	800	22:00	4	28.2
10	900	22:30	4	36.0

Use whatever stroke enables you to swim the required distance in the prescribed time. Resting is encouraged during the first few weeks. By the tenth week, adequate aerobic fitness is achieved (36 points) but it is suggested that higher levels of fitness be reached by swimming longer or faster or more frequently.

Note: Points determined from the equations for swimming. If the point charts in the Appendix are used, the point values may vary slightly.

Progressive Treadmill Exercise Program
(30–49 Years of Age)

Week	Activity	Treadmill Speed (mph)	Incline (%)	Time (min.)	Freq/Wk	Points/Wk
1	walk	3.5	flat	20:00	4	7.6
2	walk	4.0	flat	25:00	4	15.9
3	walk	4.0	flat	30:00	4	20.0
4	walk	4.5	flat	25:00	4	22.2
5	walk	4.5	5%	30:00	4	30.2
6	walk/jog	5.0	flat	25:00	4	29.3
*7	walk/jog	5.0	flat	30:00	4	36.0
8	jog	5.5	flat	25:00	4	37.2
9	jog	5.5	5%	25:00	4	41.0
10	jog	6.0	flat	30:00	4	56.0

* By the seventh week, adequate aerobic fitness has been reached (36 aerobic points per week) and it is permissible to continue at this exercise level. By the tenth week, the excellent category has been achieved (56 aerobic points per week). Other combinations of speed, incline, duration and frequency per week can be used to maintain the good or excellent categories of fitness.

Note: Points determined from the equation for treadmill exercising. If the point charts in the Appendix are used, the point values may vary slightly.

Aerobic Dancing and Other Exercise Programs Conducted to Music
(30–49 Years of Age)

Week	Time (min)	Heart Rate Max* (beats/min)	Freq/Wk	Points/Wk
1	15:00	110–120	3	9.0
2	21:00	110–120	3	12.6
3	21:00	120–130	3	12.6
4	27:00	120–130	3	16.2
5	27:00	130–140	3	16.2
6	36:00	130–140	3	21.6
7	36:00	140–150	3	21.6
8	45:00	140–150	3	27.0

By the eighth week, an adequate level of aerobic conditioning has been reached (27 aerobic points) and this is consistent with the good category of fitness for women. Exercising five times per week would earn 45 points, consistent with the excellent category of fitness.

* Heart rates determined at 3 or more equal intervals during the exercise based on a 10 second × 6 count.

Note: Points determined from the equation for aerobic dancing.

Handball/Racketball/Squash/Basketball/Soccer/Hockey/ Lacrosse Exercise Program
(30–49 Years of Age)

Week	Time Goal (min)	Freq/Wk	Points/Wk
1	20:00	3	0
2	25:00	3	0
3	30:00	3	0
4	30:00	3	0
5	40:00	3	0
6	40:00	3	0
7	20:00	4	12
8	25:00	4	15
9	25:00	4	15
10	30:00	4	18
11	35:00	4	21
12	40:00	4	24
13	45:00	4	27
14	60:00	4	36

During the first six weeks, the objective is to exercise the required time, *but not continuously*. Rest frequently. The time goal represents the combined exercise and rest periods. Beginning with the seventh week, the time goal represents continuous exercise. Do not count breaks, time-outs, etc.

Stationary Running Exercise Program
(30–49 Years of Age)

Week	Time Goal (min)	Steps/Min*	Freq/Wk	Points/Wk
1	7:30	70–80	3	0
2	10:00	70–80	3	0
3	10:00	70–80	3	0
4	12:30	70–80	3	0
5	12:30	70–80	3	0
6	15:00	70–80	3	0
7	7:30	70–80	4	10.5
8	7:30	70–80	5	13.13
9	10:00	70–80	4	14.0
10	10:00	80–90	4	18.0
11	12:30	70–80	5	24.38
12	12:30	80–90	4	24.5
13	15:00	80–90	4	31.0
14	15:00	90–100	4	37.0

During the first six weeks, the requirement is to exercise the required number of minutes, *but not continuously.* Rest frequently and as long as necessary, *but continue to walk slowly while resting.* The time goals represent the combined stationary running and rest periods. Beginning with the seventh week, the time goals represent continuous exercise. Warm up for 3:00 minutes by walking briskly. Cool down for 3:00 minutes after exercise by walking slowly. Exercise on a cushioned surface (e.g., a thick carpet) in athletic shoes that have either a ripple or deep-cushioned sole.

* Count only when left foot hits the floor. Feet must be raised at least eight inches off the floor.

Stationary Cycling Program
(30–49 Years of Age)

Week	Speed (mph/rpm)	Time Goal (min)	PR After Exercise*	Freq/Wk	Points/Wk
1	15/55	6:00	<140	3	2.25
2	15/55	8:00	<140	3	3.0
3	15/55	10:00	<140	3	3.75
4	15/55	12:00	<150	4	5.5
5	15/55	14:00	<150	4	7.0
6	15/55	16:00	<150	4	8.0
7	15/55	18:00	<150	5	11.25
8	15/55	20:00	<150	5	12.5
9	17.5/65	18:00	>150	5	13.0
10	17.5/65	20:00	>150	5	14.5
11	20/75	18:00	>150	5	18.13
12	20/75	20:00	>150	5	19.38
13	20/75	22:30	>150	5	22.5
14	25/90	25:00	>150	5	30.0

During the first six weeks, warm up by cycling for 3:00 minutes, 17.5 to 20 mph, with no resistance, before beginning the actual workout. At the conclusion of the exercise, cool down by cycling for 3:00 minutes with no resistance.

* Add enough resistance so that the pulse rate (PR) counted for 10 seconds immediately after exercise and multiplied by 6 equals the rate specified. If it is higher, lower the resistance before cycling again; if it is lower, increase the resistance.

Stair-Climbing Exercise Program
(30–49 Years of Age)

Week	Round Trips (average number per min)	Time Goal (min)	Freq/Wk	Points/Wk
1	5	7:30	3	0
2	5	7:30	3	0
3	5	10:00	3	0
4	5	10:00	3	0
5	5	12:00	3	0
6	5	12:00	3	0
7	6	6:30	4	6.0
8	6	7:30	4	6.92
9	6	8:30	5	9.81
10	7	9:00	4	12.0
11	7	10:30	4	14.0
12	7	10:30	5	17.5
13	8	11:00	5	25.0
14	8	13:00	5	29.54

During the first six weeks, the requirement is to exercise the required number of minutes, *but not continuously.* Rest frequently, and as long as necessary, but walk slowly while resting. The time goal is the combined time for both stair climbing and resting. Beginning with the seventh week, the time goals refer to continuous exercise. Warm up for 3:00 minutes by walking briskly. Cool down for 3:00 minutes after exercise by walking slowly.

This program applies to 10 steps, 6″ to 7″ in height, 25° to 30° incline. Use of banister is encouraged.

Rope-Skipping Exercise Program
(30–49 Years of Age)

Week	Time Goal (min)	Steps/Min	Freq/Wk	Points/Wk
1	7:30	70–90	3	0
2	10:00	70–90	3	0
3	10:00	70–90	3	0
4	12:30	70–90	3	0
5	12:30	70–90	3	0
6	15:00	70–90	3	0
7	5:00	90–110	4	8
8	7:30	90–110	4	12
9	7:30	90–110	4	12
10	10:00	90–110	4	16
11	10:00	90–110	5	20
12	12:30	90–110	5	27.5
13	12:30	90–110	5	27.5
14	15:00	90–110	5	30

During the first six weeks, the requirement is to exercise the required number of minutes, *but not continuously.* Rest frequently, and as long as necessary, but continue either to skip very slowly or to walk while resting; the time goals represent the combined time for rope skipping and resting. Beginning with the seventh week, the time goals refer to continuous exercise. Warm up for 3:00 minutes by slow skipping or walking briskly. Cool down for 3:00 minutes after exercise by slow walking.

Exercise on a cushioned surface (e.g., a thick carpet) in athletic shoes. Skip with both feet together, or step over the rope, alternating feet.

Walking Exercise Program
(50 Years of Age and Older)

Week	Distance (miles)	Time Goal (min)	Freq/Wk	Points/Wk
1	1.0	20:00	4	4.0
2	1.5	30:00	4	8.0
3	2.0	40:00	4	12.0
4	2.0	38:00	4	13.3
5	2.0	36:00	4	14.7
6	2.0	34:00	4	16.2
7	2.5	42:00	4	21.7
8	2.5	40:00	4	23.5
9	2.5	38:00	4	25.5
10	3.0	47:00	4	30.0
11	3.0	46:00	4	31.0
12	3.0	45:00	4	32.0

By the twelfth week, an adequate level of aerobic conditioning has been reached and can be maintained with four exercise periods each week. This level of exercise equals 32 aerobic points per week, consistent with the good category of aerobic fitness.

Note: Points determined from the equations for walking, jogging and running. If the point charts in the Appendix are used, the point values may vary slightly.

Jogging Exercise Program
(50–59 Years of Age)

Week	Activity	Distance (miles)	Time Goal (min)	Freq/Wk	Points/Wk
1	walk	1.0	18:00	5	5.3
2	walk	2.0	36:00	4	14.7
3	walk	3.0	54:00	3	18.0
4	walk	3.0	52:00	4	25.6
5	walk/jog	2.0	26:00	4	24.9
6	walk/jog	2.0	24:00	4	28.0
7	jog	2.0	22:00	4	31.6
*8	jog	2.0	20:00	4	36.0
9	jog	2.5	27:00	4	41.6
10	jog	2.5	25:00	4	46.0
11	jog	3.0	32:00	4	51.5
12	jog	3.0	30:00	4	56.0

*By the eighth week, a minimum aerobic fitness level has been reached (36 aerobic points per week) but it is suggested that a higher level of fitness be achieved. By the twelfth week of the above program, a total of 56 points per week is being earned, consistent with the excellent category of aerobic fitness.

Note: Points determined from the equations for walking, jogging and running. If the point charts in the Appendix are used, the point values may vary slightly.

Cycling Exercise Program
(50–59 Years of Age)

Week	Distance (miles)	Time Goal (min)	Freq/Wk	Points/Wk
1	3.0	20:00	3	3.6
2	3.0	18:00	3	4.5
3	4.0	25:00	4	9.4
4	4.0	24:00	4	10.0
5	5.0	32:00	4	12.8
6	5.0	28:00	4	15.4
7	5.0	24:00	4	19.0
8	6.0	30:00	4	22.8
9	6.0	26:00	4	27.2
10	7.0	32:00	4	30.8
11	7.0	30:00	4	33.2
12	7.0	28:00	4	36.0

By the twelfth week, adequate aerobic fitness has been achieved and can be maintained with a four-day-a-week exercise program. This level of exercise equals 36 aerobic points per week. If a higher level of fitness is desired, cycling further, faster, or more frequently each week will increase the fitness level.

Note: Points determined from the equation for cycling. If the point charts in the Appendix are used, the point values may vary slightly.

Swimming Exercise Program
(50 Years of Age and Older)

Week	Distance (yards)	Time Goal (min)	Freq/Wk	Points/Wk
1	300	15:00	4	5.0
2	300	12:00	4	6.2
3	400	15:00	4	8.9
4	400	13:00	4	10.2
5	500	16:00	4	13.0
6	500	14:00	4	14.9
7	600	17:00	4	17.6
8	600	15:00	4	20.0
9	700	20:00	4	22.4
10	700	18:00	4	24.7
11	800	22:00	4	28.2
12	800	20:00	4	30.7

Use the stroke that enables you to swim the required distance in the required time. Resting is encouraged during the initial weeks. By the twelfth week, adequate fitness has been achieved (31 aerobic points per week) but higher levels of aerobic fitness are encouraged by swimming longer or faster or more frequently.

Note: Points determined from the equations for swimming. If the point charts in the Appendix are used, the point values may vary slightly.

Progressive Treadmill Exercise Program
(50 Years of Age and Older)

Week	Activity	Treadmill Speed (mph)	Incline (%)	Time (min)	Freq/Wk	Points/Wk
1	walk	3.0	flat	20:00	4	4.0
2	walk	3.0	flat	25:00	4	6.0
3	walk	3.0	flat	30:00	4	8.0
4	walk	3.5	flat	25:00	4	10.5
5	walk	3.5	flat	30:00	4	13.5
6	walk	3.75	flat	25:00	4	13.2
7	walk	3.75	flat	30:00	5	20.7
8	walk	4.0	flat	30:00	5	25.0
9	walk	4.0	flat	45:00	5	40.0
10	walk	4.0	5%	45:00	4	35.2

Either 4.0 mph at no incline for 45:00 minutes, 5 times per week, or 45:00 minutes with a 5% incline, 4 times per week can be used to achieve adequate fitness. Both training programs will produce the good category of aerobic fitness. For individuals over 60 years of age, fast walking or slow jogging on a treadmill is discouraged unless the subject has been exercising regularly prior to age 60. In such cases, continued treadmill exercise is permissible past 60 years of age.

Note: Points determined from the equation for treadmill exercising. If the point charts in the Appendix are used, the point values may vary slightly.

Aerobic Dancing and Other Exercise Programs Conducted to Music
(50–59 Years of Age)

Week	Time (min)	Heart Rate Max* (beats/min)	Freq/Wk	Points/Wk
1	12:00	100–110	3	7.2
2	15:00	100–110	3	9.0
3	18:00	110–120	3	10.8
4	21:00	110–120	3	12.6
5	24:00	120–130	3	14.4
6	27:00	120–130	3	16.2
7	30:00	130–140	3	18.0
8	33:00	130–140	3	19.8
9	36:00	130–140	3	21.6
10	39:00	140–145	3	23.4
11	42:00	140–145	3	25.2
12	45:00	140–145	3	27.0

By the twelfth week, an adequate level of aerobic fitness has been reached (27 aerobic points) and is consistent with the good category of fitness for women. Exercising five times per week would earn 45 points, consistent with the excellent category of fitness.

*Heart rates determined at 3 or more intervals during the exercise based on a 10 second × 6 count.

Note: Points determined from the equation for aerobic dancing.

Handball/Racketball/Squash/Basketball/Soccer/Hockey/ Lacrosse Exercise Program
(50–59 Years of Age)

Week	Time Goal (min)	Freq/Wk	Points/Wk
1	10:00	3	0
2	15:00	3	0
3	20:00	3	0
4	25:00	3	0
5	30:00	3	0
6	30:00	3	0
7	15:00	4	9
8	20:00	4	12
9	25:00	4	15
10	30:00	4	18
11	35:00	4	21
12	40:00	4	24
13	45:00	4	27
14	45:00	4	27
15	45:00	4	27
16	60:00	4	36

During the first six weeks, the objective is to exercise the required time, *but not continuously.* Rest frequently. The time goal represents the combined exercise and rest periods. Beginning with the seventh week, the time goal represents continuous exercise. Do not count breaks, time-outs, etc.

Stationary Running Exercise Program
(50–59 Years of Age)

Week	Time Goal (min)	Steps/Min*	Freq/Wk	Points/Wk
1	5:00	70–80	3	0
2	7:30	70–80	3	0
3	10:00	70–80	3	0
4	10:00	70–80	3	0
5	12:30	70–80	3	0
6	12:30	70–80	3	0
7	5:00	70–80	4	7.0
8	7:30	70–80	4	10.5
9	10:00	70–80	4	14.0
10	10:00	70–80	5	17.5
11	10:00	70–80	5	17.5
12	12:30	70–80	5	24.38
13	12:30	70–80	5	24.38
14	15:00	70–80	5	31.25
15	15:00	70–80	5	31.25
16	17:30	80–90	4	37.5

During the first six weeks, the requirement is to exercise the required number of minutes, *but not continuously.* Rest frequently and as long as necessary, *but continue to walk slowly while resting.* The time goals represent the combined stationary running and rest periods. Beginning with the seventh week, the time goals represent continuous exercise. Warm up for 3:00 minutes by walking briskly. Cool down for 3:00 minutes after exercise by walking slowly. Exercise on a cushioned surface (e.g., a thick carpet) in athletic shoes that have either a ripple or deep-cushioned sole.

* Count only when left foot hits the floor. Feet must be raised at least eight inches off the floor.

Stationary Cycling Exercise Program
(50–59 Years of Age)

Week	Speed (mph/rpm)	Time Goal (min)	PR After Exercise*	Freq/Wk	Points/Wk
1	15/55	4:00	<135	3	1.5
2	15/55	6:00	<135	3	2.25
3	15/55	8:00	<135	3	3.0
4	15/55	10:00	<140	4	5.0
5	15/55	10:00	<140	4	5.0
6	15/55	12:00	<140	4	5.5
7	15/55	14:00	<140	5	8.75
8	15/55	16:00	<140	5	10.0
9	15/55	18:00	<140	5	11.25
10	15/55	20:00	<140	5	12.6
11	17.5/65	18:00	<150	5	13.13
12	17.5/65	20:00	<150	5	14.38
13	20/75	20:00	<150	5	19.38
14	20/75	20:00	>150	5	19.38
15	20/75	25:00	>150	5	25.0
16	20/75	30:00	>150	4	26.0

During the first six weeks, warm up by cycling for 3:00 minutes, 17.5 to 20 mph, with no resistance, before beginning the actual workout. At the conclusion of the exercise, cool down by cycling for 3:00 minutes with no resistance.

From the tenth week on, the exercise periods can be divided into two equal periods, performed twice daily.

* Add enough resistance so that the pulse rate (PR) counted for 10 seconds immediately after exercise and multiplied by 6 equals the rate specified. If it is higher, lower the resistance before cycling again; if it is lower, increase the resistance.

Stair-Climbing Exercise Program
(50–59 Years of Age)

Week	Round Trips (average number per min)	Time Goal (min)	Freq/Wk	Points/Wk
1	4	5:00	3	0
2	4	5:00	3	0
3	4	7:30	3	0
4	4	7:30	3	0
5	4	10:00	3	0
6	4	10:00	3	0
7	5	5:00	4	2.86
8	5	7:00	5	5.0
9	5	9:00	5	6.43
10	5	11:00	5	7.86
11	6	9:30	5	10.96
12	6	11:00	5	12.69
13	7	10:30	5	17.5
14	7	12:00	5	20.0
15	8	11:00	5	25.0
16	8	13:00	5	29.54

During the first six weeks, the requirement is to exercise the required number of minutes, *but not continuously*. Rest frequently, and as long as necessary, but walk slowly while resting. The time goal is the combined time for both stair climbing and resting. Beginning with the seventh week, the time goals refer to continuous exercise. Warm up for 3:00 minutes by walking briskly. Cool down for 3:00 minutes after exercise by walking slowly.

This program applies to 10 steps, 6″ to 7″ in height, 25° to 30° incline. Use of banister is encouraged.

Rope-Skipping Exercise Program
(50–59 Years of Age)

Week	Time Goal (min)	Steps/Min	Freq/Wk	Points/Wk
1	5:00	70–90	3	0
2	7:30	70–90	3	0
3	10:00	70–90	3	0
4	10:00	70–90	3	0
5	12:30	70–90	3	0
6	12:30	70–90	3	0
7	5:00	70–90	4	6.0
8	5:00	70–90	5	7.5
9	7:30	70–90	4	9.0
10	7:30	70–90	5	11.25
11	10:00	70–90	4	12.0
12	10:00	70–90	5	15.0
13	12:30	70–90	5	21.25
14	12:30	70–90	5	21.25
15	15:00	70–90	5	27.5
16	15:00	90–110	5	35.0

During the first six weeks, the requirement is to exercise the required number of minutes, *but not continuously.* Rest frequently, and as long as necessary, but continue either to skip very slowly or to walk while resting; the time goals represent the combined time for rope skipping and resting. Beginning with the seventh week, the time goals refer to continuous exercise. Warm up for 3:00 minutes by slow skipping or walking briskly. Cool down for 3:00 minutes after exercise by slow walking.

Exercise on a cushioned surface (e.g., a thick carpet) in athletic shoes. Skip with both feet together, or step over the rope, alternating feet.

Jogging Exercise Program
(60 Years of Age and Older)

This type of physical activity is *not recommended* for the totally inactive individual. But jogging is not contraindicated in the individual who has been jogging/running prior to age 60 and wishes to continue. Even progressive jogging programs are permitted past 60 years of age, provided the exercise can be conducted in a medically supervised environment preceded by adequate testing.

Cycling Exercise Program
(60 Years of Age and Older)

For subjects past 60 years of age, it is *not recommended* that a progressive cycling program be used such as those recommended for younger ages. But when a regular cyclist reaches 60, it is recommended that the cycling be continued with no restrictions. To avoid problems including falls and fractures, 3-wheeled cycling is encouraged at slower speeds and longer distances.

Walking, Swimming, and Progressive Treadmill Exercise Programs

(60 Years of Age and Older—Use Programs for 50 Years of Age and Older)

Aerobic Dancing and Other Exercise Programs Conducted to Music

(60 Years of Age and Older)

This type of physical activity is *not recommended* in the totally inactive individual. But it is encouraged in the individual who has been involved in aerobic dancing prior to age 60 and wishes to continue. Even the progressive programs are permitted past 60 years of age, provided the exercise can be conducted in a medically supervised environment preceded by an adequate examination.

Stationary Running Exercise Program

(Age 60 and Over)

NOT RECOMMENDED

Stationary Cycling Exercise Program

(Age 60 and Over)

Week	Speed (mph/rpm)	Time Goal (min)	PR After Exercise*	Freq/Wk	Points/Wk
1	15/55	4:00	<100	3	1.5
2	15/55	4:00	<100	3	1.5
3	15/55	6:00	<100	3	2.25
4	15/55	6:00	<110	4	3.0
5	15/55	8:00	<110	4	4.0
6	15/55	10:00	<110	4	5.0
7	15/55	12:00	<110	4	5.5
8	15/55	14:00	<110	4	7.0
9	15/55	16:00	<110	4	8.0
10	15/55	16:00	<120	5	10.0
11	15/55	18:00	<120	5	11.25
12	15/55	20:00	<120	5	12.5
13	17.5/65	18:00	<120	5	13.13
14	17.5/65	20:00	<120	5	14.38
15	20/75	20:00	<130	5	19.38
16	20/75	22:30	<130	5	22.5
17	20/75	25:00	<130	5	25.0
18	20/75	30:00	<130	4	26.0

During the first six weeks, warm up by cycling for 3:00 minutes, 17.5 to 20 mph, with no resistance, before beginning the actual workout. At the conclusion of the exercise, cool down by cycling for 3:00 minutes with no resistance.

From the tenth week on, the exercise periods can be divided into two equal periods, performed twice daily.

* Add enough resistance so that the pulse rate (PR) counted for 10 seconds immediately after exercise and multiplied by 6 equals the rate specified. If it is higher, lower the resistance before cycling again; if it is lower, increase the resistance.

Stair-Climbing Exercise Program
(Age 60 and Over)

NOT RECOMMENDED

Rope-Skipping Exercise Program
(Age 60 and Over)

NOT RECOMMENDED

Handball/Racketball/Squash/Basketball/Soccer/Hockey/Lacrosse Exercise Program
(Age 60 and Over)

NOT RECOMMENDED

Progressive Walking Program for the Excessively Overweight Individual*
(To Be Used in Conjunction with Dieting)

Week	Distance (miles)	Time Goal (min)	Freq/Wk	Points/Wk
1	2.0	40:30	3	3
2	2.0	39:00	3	9
3	2.0	38:00	4	12
4	2.0	37:00	4	12
5	2.0	36:00	5	15
6	2.0	35:00	5	15
7	2.5	45:00	5	20
8	2.5	43:00	5	20
9	3.0	52:00	5	25
10	3.0	51:00	5	25
11	3.0	50:00	5	25
12	3.0	49:00	5	25
13	3.0	48:00	5	25
14	3.0	47:00	5	25
15	3.0	46:00	5	25
16	3.0	<45:00	4	32

After completing the progressive program, either continue with the final program listed above, or select one of the maintenance programs that follow the progressive programs; or develop a program of your own from the point value charts in the Appendix or the aerobics equations at the end of this chapter.

* At least 50 pounds above ideal weight (as calculated using the formula given in Principle 6 in Chapter 3).

Progressive Walking Program Following Uncomplicated Coronary Artery Bypass Surgery*

Week	Distance (miles)	Time Goal (min)	Freq/Wk	Points/Wk
1	0.5	12:00	3	0
2	0.5	10:00	3	0
3	1.0	22:00	3	0
4	1.0	20:00	3	3
5	1.0	19:00	4	4
6	1.0	18:00	4	4
7	1.5	29:30	4	8
8	1.5	28:00	4	8
9	1.5	26:00	5	10
10	1.5	24:00	5	10
11	2.0	32:00	5	15
12	2.0	31:00	5	15
13	2.5	38:00	5	20
14	2.5	37:00	5	20
15	3.0	48:00	5	25
16	3.0	47:00	5	25
17	3.0	46:00	5	25
18	3.0 or 4.0	<45:00 <60:00	4 3	32 33

*This program should not be started until at least three weeks following surgery. After this 18-week program, some patients can progress to a standard running program, *but only with their physician's approval!* If approval is given, start the progressive program at the 2.0-miles-in-25:00-minutes level in your age-adjusted category (e.g., week 4 of the 30–49 age group).

Progressive Walking Program Following an Uncomplicated Heart Attack and for Cardiac Patients with Minimal Disease*

Week	Distance (miles)	Time Goal (min)	Freq/Wk	Points/Wk
1	1.0	22:00	3	0
2	1.0	21:00	3	0
3	1.0	20:00	3	3
4	1.0	18:00	4	4
5	1.0	17:00	4	4
6	1.0	16:00	4	4
7	1.5	24:00	4	8
8	1.5	23:00	4	8
9	2.0	32:00	4	12
10	2.0	31:30	5	15
11	2.0	31:00	5	15
12	2.5	39:00	5	20
13	2.5	38:00	5	20
14	2.5	37:45	5	20
15	3.0	48:00	5	25
16	3.0	47:00	5	25
17	3.0	46:00	5	25
18	3.0	<45:00	4	32
	or			
	4.0	<60:00	3	33

*This program is to be started two months following the heart attack, *only with physician's approval*, and only if the patient is asymptomatic and not requiring medication for relief of pain or prevention of heart irregularities. If these prerequisites cannot be met, the program for patients with moderate to severe heart disease should be used. After this 18-week program, some patients can progress to a standard running program, *but only with their physician's approval!* If approval is given, start the progressive running program at the 2.0-miles-in-25:00-minutes level in your age-adjusted category (e.g., week 4 of the 30–49 age group).

*Progressive Exercise Program for Cardiac Patients, Moderate to Severe Disease (Symptomatic)**

Week	*Distance (miles)*	*Max HR†*	*Freq/Wk*
1	1/8	100	
	rest 1:00		
	1/8	100	
	rest 1:00		3
	1/8	100	
	rest 1:00		
	1/8	100	
2	1/8	105	
	rest 1:00		
	2/8	105	
	rest 1:00		3
	2/8	105	
	rest 1:00		
	1/8	105	
3	1/8	110	
	rest 1:00		
	2/8	110	
	rest 1:00		3
	2/8	110	
	rest 1:00		
	1/8	110	
4	1/8	110	
	rest 1:00		
	3/8	115	
	rest 1:00		3
	3/8	115	
	rest 1:00		
	1/8	110	
5	1/8	110	
	rest 1:00		
	4/8	120	
	rest 1:00		3–4
	4/8	120	
	rest 1:00		
	1/8	100	

* This program is designed for those patients with symptoms requiring medication for relief, and should be used only in a medically supervised class.

† Maximum heart rate is determined during the rest periods by counting the pulse for 10 seconds and multiplying by 6.

Moderate to Severe Disease Program (continued)

Week	*Distance (miles)*	*Max HR*	*Freq/Wk*
6	1/8	110	
	rest 1:00		
	5/8	120	
	rest 1:00		3–4
	5/8	120	
	rest 1:00		
	1/8	100	
7	1/8	110	
	rest 1:00		
	6/8	125	
	rest 1:00		3–4
	6/8	125	
	rest 1:00		
	1/8	100	
8	1/8	110	
	rest 1:00		
	7/8	125	
	rest 0:30		3–4
	1/8	100	
9	1/8	110	
	rest 1:00		
	7/8	130	
	rest 0:30		3–5
	1/8	100	
10	1/8	110	
	rest 1:00		
	1	130	
	rest 0:30		3–5
	1/8	110	
11	2/8	110	
	rest 1:00		
	1	130	
	rest 0:30		3–5
	1/8	120	
12	2/8	110	
	rest 1:00		
	1	135	
	rest 0:30		3–5
	1/8	120	

At the conclusion of this program, progress to the program of cardiac patients with minimal disease (if no problems or complications have occurred).

Maintenance Programs for the Person Already Conditioned
(all ages)

Walking

Distance (miles)	Time Requirement (min)	Freq/Wk	Points/Wk
2.0	24:01–30:00	6	30
or			
3.0	36:01–45:00	4	32
or			
4.0	48:01–60:00	3	33
or			
4.0	60:01–80:00	5	35

Running

Distance (miles)	Time Requirement (min)	Freq/Wk	Points/Wk
1.0	6:41–8:00	6	30
or			
1.5	10:01–12:00	4	32
or			
1.5	12:01–15:00	5	32.5
or			
2.0	16:01–20:00	4	36
or			
2.0	13:21–16:00	3	33

Cycling

Distance (miles)	Time Requirement (min)	Freq/Wk	Points/Wk
5.0	15:01–20:00	5	30
or			
6.0	18:01–24:00	4	30
or			
7.0	21:01–28:00	4	36
or			
8.0	24:01–32:00	3	31.5

Maintenance Programs (continued)
Swimming

Distance (yards)	Time Requirement (min)	Freq/Wk	Points/Wk
600	10:01–15:00	6	30
or			
800	13:21–20:00	4	30.5
or			
900	15:01–22:30	4	36
or			
1000	16:41–25:00	3	31

Progressive Treadmill Exercise

Treadmill Speed (mph)	Incline (%)	Time (min)	Freq/Wk	Points/Wk
6.0	flat	30:00	3	42
5.0	flat	30:00	4	36
4.5	5%	30:00	4	30
4.0	flat	45:00	5	40
4.0	5%	45:00	4	35

Aerobic Dancing and Other Exercise Programs Conducted to Music

Time (min)	Heart Rate Max* (beats/min)	Freq/Wk	Points/Wk
45:00	above 140	3	27
40:00	above 140	4	32
30:00	above 140	5	30

* Heart rate determined at 3 or more equal intervals during the exercise based on a 10 second × 6 count.

Maintenance Programs (continued)
Handball/Racketball/Squash/Basketball/Soccer/Hockey/ Lacrosse

Time Requirement (min)	Freq/Wk	Points/Wk
30:00	6	27.0
35:00	5	26.25
45:00	4	27.0
60:00	4	36.0

Stationary Running

Time Requirement (min)	Steps/Min*	Freq/Wk	Points/Wk
12:30 or	80–90	6	33
15:00 or	80–90	5	35
15:00 or	90–100	4	34
20:00 or	70–80	4	32
20:00	80–90	3	30

* Count only when left foot hits the floor. Feet must be lifted at least eight inches off the floor.

Stationary Cycling

Speed (mph/rpm)	Time Requirement (min)	Freq/Wk	Points/Wk
17.5/65 or	30:00	6	30
17.5/65 or	35:00	5	30
20/75 or	30:00	5	32.5
25/90 or	20:00	5	28.5
25/90 or	25:00	4	30
30/105	25:00	3	30

Add enough resistance so that the pulse rate counted for 10 seconds immediately after exercise and multiplied by 6 equals or exceeds 140 beats per minute.

Stair Climbing

Round Trips (min)*	Time Requirement (min)	Freq/Wk	Points/Wk
7	12:00	8	32
or			
7	15:00	6	30
or			
8	11:00	6	30
or			
8	13:00	5	30
or			
9	14:30	4	35

* Count round trips on 10 steps, 6″ to 7″ in height, 25° to 30° incline.

Rope Skipping

Time Requirement (min)	Steps/Min	Freq/Wk	Points/Wk
12:30	90–110	6	30.0
or			
15:00	90–110	5	31.25
or			
17:30	70–90	5	30.0
or			
17:30	90–100	4	30.5
or			
20:00	90–110	3	27.0

THE AEROBICS EQUATIONS

Walking/Jogging/Running

1. For distances less than or equal to 1 mile at speeds slower than or equal to 6 mph (10:00/mile)

    POINTS = (velocity* − 2) × distance in miles

    EXAMPLE: Walking 0.75 miles in 15:00 minutes

    $$\text{POINTS} = \left(\frac{0.75 \times 60}{15} \right) - 2 \times 0.75$$

    $$= 3 - 2 \times 0.75$$

    $$= 1 \times 0.75$$

    $$= .75$$

2. For distances less than or equal to 1 mile at speeds faster than 6 mph (10:00/mile)

$$\text{POINTS} = \left(\frac{2 \times \text{velocity}^*}{3}\right) \times \text{distance in miles}$$

EXAMPLE: Running 0.5 miles in 4:00 minutes

$$\text{POINTS} = \frac{2 \times \left(\dfrac{0.5 \times 60}{4}\right)}{3} \times 0.5$$

$$= \frac{2 \times 7.5}{3} \times 0.5$$

$$= \frac{15}{3} \times 0.5$$

$$= 2.5$$

3. For distances greater than 1 mile at speeds slower than or equal to 6 mph (10:00/mile)

$$\text{POINTS} = [(\text{velocity}^* - 1) \times \text{distance in miles}] - 1$$

EXAMPLE: Walking 2 miles in 36:00 minutes

$$\text{POINTS} = \left[\left(\frac{2 \times 60}{36} - 1\right) \times 2\right] - 1$$

$$= [(3.33 - 1) \times 2] - 1$$

$$= [2.33 \times 2] - 1$$

$$= 3.66$$

4. For distances greater than 1 mile at speeds faster than 6 mph (10:00/mile)

$$\text{POINTS} = \left\{\left[\left(\frac{2 \times \text{velocity}^*}{3}\right) + 1\right] \times \text{distance in miles}\right\} - 1$$

EXAMPLE: Running 3 miles in 19:00 minutes

$$\text{POINTS} = \left\{\left(\frac{\left[2 \times \left(\dfrac{3 \times 60}{19}\right)\right]}{3} + 1\right) \times 3\right\} - 1$$

$$= \left\{\left[\left(\frac{2 \times 9.47}{3}\right) + 1\right] \times 3\right\} - 1$$

$$= [(6.31 + 1) \times 3] - 1$$

$$= (7.31 \times 3) - 1$$

$$= 20.93$$

---

* velocity $= \dfrac{(\text{Distance in miles} \times 60)}{\text{Duration in minutes}}$

For detailed breakdown for points awarded for various distance and multiple walking and running speeds, refer to the point system in the Appendix.

Cycling (Outdoors)

$$POINTS = \left(\frac{6 \times \text{distance}^2}{\text{duration}} \right) - 1.5$$

EXAMPLE: Cycled 6 miles in 36:00 minutes

$$POINTS = \left(\frac{6 \times 6^2}{36} \right) - 1.5$$

$$= \left(\frac{216}{36} \right) - 1.5$$

$$= 6 - 1.5$$

$$= 4.5$$

Swimming

1. For less than 600 yards of swimming, variable speed

$$POINTS = \left(\frac{\text{velocity}^*}{4800} \right) \times \text{yards}$$

EXAMPLE: Swam 500 yards in 15:00 minutes

$$POINTS = \left(\frac{\frac{500}{15}}{4800} \right) \times 500$$

$$= \left(\frac{33.33}{4800} \right) \times 500$$

$$= .0069 \times 500$$

$$= 3.45$$

2. For more than or equal to 600 yards of swimming, variable speeds

$$POINTS = \left\{ \left[\left(\frac{\text{velocity}^*}{4800} \right) + .005 \right] \times \text{yards} \right\} - 3$$

EXAMPLE: Swam 1500 yards in 30:00 minutes

$$POINTS = \left\{ \left[\left(\frac{\frac{1500}{30}}{4800} \right) + .005 \right] \times 1500 \right\} - 3$$

$$= \left\{ \left[\left(\frac{50}{4800} \right) + .005 \right] \times 1500 \right\} - 3$$

$$= ([.0104 + .005] \times 1500) - 3$$

$$= (.0154 \times 1500) - 3$$

$$= 23.1 - 3$$

$$= 20.1$$

* velocity $= \dfrac{\text{yards}}{\text{duration in minutes}}$

For detailed breakdown for points awarded for various distances and multiple swimming speeds, refer to the point charts in the Appendix.

Hockey/Soccer/Lacrosse

POINTS = Duration in minutes × 0.15
EXAMPLE: 1 hour and 30 minutes of soccer
POINTS = 90 min × 0.15
$\qquad$ = 13.5

Handball/Basketball/Squash/Racketball

POINTS = Duration in minutes × 0.15
EXAMPLE: 2 hours of basketball
POINTS = 120 min × 0.15
$\qquad$ = 18.0

Stationary Running

1. For stationary running less than 10:00 minutes

$$POINTS = \left[\frac{(steps/min - 40)}{100}\right] \times duration\ in\ minutes$$

EXAMPLE: Running in place for 5 minutes at 60 steps per minute

$$POINTS = \left(\frac{60 - 40}{100}\right) \times 5$$

$$= \left(\frac{20}{100}\right) \times 5$$

$$= 0.2 \times 5$$

$$= 1.0$$

2. For stationary running longer than or equal to 10:00 minutes

$$POINTS = \left[\left(\frac{steps/min - 20}{100}\right)\right] \times duration - 2$$

EXAMPLE: Running in place for 15 minutes at 70 steps per minute

$$POINTS = \left[\left(\frac{70 - 20}{100}\right) \times 15\right] - 2$$

$$POINTS = \left[\left(\frac{50}{100}\right) \times 15\right] - 2$$

$$= [0.5 \times 15] - 2$$

$$= 7.5 - 2$$

$$= 5.5$$

Stationary Cycling
To compute points, use the two charts in the Appendix.

Stair Climbing

$$POINTS = \left(\frac{Round\ Trips/min - 3}{19 - Round\ Trips/min}\right) \times duration$$

EXAMPLE: Climbed 8 round trips* per minute for 9:00 minutes

$$POINTS = \left(\frac{8 - 3}{19 - 8}\right) \times 9$$

$$= \frac{5}{11} \times 9$$

$$= .4545 \times 9$$

$$= 4.09$$

* Assuming a single flight of stairs with 10 steps.

Rope Skipping

1. For rope skipping less than 10:00 minutes

    POINTS = [(.005 × steps/min) − 0.1] × duration in min.

    EXAMPLE: Rope skipping at 100 steps per minute for 5:00 minutes

    POINTS = [(.005 × 100) − 0.1] × 5

    = [0.5 − 0.1 × 5]

    = 0.4 × 5

    = 2.0

2. For rope skipping longer than or equal to 10:00 minutes

    POINTS = {[(0.005 × steps/min) + 0.1] × duration} − 2

    EXAMPLE: Rope skipping for 15:00 minutes at 100 steps/min.

    POINTS = {[(.005 × 100) + 0.1] × 15} − 2

    = [(0.5 + 0.1) × 15] − 2

    = (0.6 × 15) −2

    = 9 − 2

    = 7.0

Golf
(walking only, carrying a golf bag, or towing a golf bag cart)

$$POINTS = \frac{\text{Number of holes played}}{6}$$

EXAMPLE: Played 18 holes of golf

$$POINTS = \frac{18}{6}$$

$$= 3$$

At least 4 holes and no more than 60 must be played to calculate points.

Rowing
(2 oars, 20 strokes/min)

POINTS = Duration in minutes × 0.233
EXAMPLE: 20 minutes of rowing
POINTS = 20 × 0.233
$$= 4.66$$

Tennis/Aerial Tennis/Badminton
(Singles only)

$$POINTS = \frac{\text{Duration in minutes}}{15}$$

EXAMPLE: 1 hour and 20 minutes of singles tennis

$$POINTS = \frac{80 \text{ min}}{15}$$

$$= 5.33$$

Tennis/Aerial Tennis/Badminton
(Doubles only)

POINTS = Duration in minutes × 0.025
EXAMPLE: 45 minutes of doubles tennis
POINTS = 45 × 0.025
$$= 1.125$$

Snow Skiing
(Downhill)

POINTS = Duration in minutes × 0.1

EXAMPLE: 2 hours of downhill skiing

POINTS = 120 min × 0.1

= 12

Consider only the time spent actually skiing. The usual requirement is 3:1, that is, three hours on the slopes to actually ski one hour.

Snow Skiing
(Cross Country)

POINTS = Duration in minutes × 0.3

EXAMPLE: 3 hours of cross-country skiing

POINTS = 180 min × 0.3

= 54

Depending upon terrain, altitude and weather conditions, points may actually be more or less than those given above.

Skating
(Either ice or roller skating)

POINTS = Duration in minutes × 0.075

EXAMPLE: 30 minutes of leisure skating

POINTS = 30 × 0.075

= 2.25

Volleyball

$$\text{POINTS} = \frac{\text{Duration in minutes}}{15}$$

EXAMPLE: 1 hour of volleyball

$$\text{POINTS} = \frac{60 \text{ min}}{15}$$

$$= 4.0$$

Fencing

POINTS = Duration in minutes × 0.1
EXAMPLE: 1 hour of fencing
POINTS = 60 min × 0.1
      = 6

Football

POINTS = Duration in minutes × 0.1
EXAMPLE: 2 hours of football
POINTS = 120 min × 0.1
      = 12

Wrestling

POINTS = Duration in minutes × 0.4
EXAMPLE: 30 minutes of wrestling
POINTS = 30 min × 0.4
      = 12

Calisthenics

POINTS = Duration in minutes × 0.025
EXAMPLE: 60 minutes of calisthenics
POINTS = 60 × 0.025
      = 1.50

Treadmill Exercise at Variable Speeds and Inclines

1. For distances less than or equal to 1 mile and at speeds slower than or equal to 6 mph

    POINTS = [(Velocity* − 2) × Elevation Factor**] × distance in miles

2. For distances less than or equal to 1 mile and at speeds greater than 6 mph

    $$\text{POINTS} = \left[\left(\frac{2 \times \text{Velocity}}{3} \right) \times \text{Elevation Factor} \right] \times \text{distance in miles}$$

3. For distances greater than 1 mile and at speeds slower than or equal to 6 mph

POINTS = $\{ [(\text{Velocity} - 1) \times \text{distance in miles}] - 1 \} \times \text{Elevation Factor}$

4. For distances greater than 1 mile and at speeds greater than 6 mph

POINTS = $\left\{ \left[\left(\dfrac{2 \times \text{Velocity}}{3} \right) + 1 \right] \times \text{distance} \right\} - 1 \times \text{Elevation Factor}$

---

* VELOCITY = $\left(\dfrac{\text{Distance in miles} \times 60}{\text{Duration in minutes}} \right)$

** ELEVATION FACTOR = $\dfrac{\% \text{ Elevation}^3 + 15 \times \% \text{ Elevation}^2 + 50 \times \% \text{ Elevation} + 1}{7500}$

Since the above formulas are very complicated, a point chart that considers speed in mph, time in minutes and elevation in percentages can be found in the Appendix.

Circuit Weight Training

POINTS = Duration in minutes × 0.1679

EXAMPLE: 20 minutes of circuit weight training

* POINTS = 20 min × 0.1679

   = 3.358

---

* This point value assumes 30 seconds of activity followed by 30 seconds of rest for 20 minutes.

Super Circuit Weight Training

POINTS = Duration in minutes × 0.2605

EXAMPLE: 20 minutes of super circuit weight training

* POINTS = 20 min × 0.2605

   = 5.21

---

* This point value assumes 30 seconds of activity followed by 30 seconds of brisk walking or running between stations, that is, no rest during the 20 minutes.

Minitrampoline Exercise

POINTS = Duration in minutes × 0.25

EXAMPLE: 30 minutes of continuous exercise

* POINTS = 30 min × 0.25

   = 7.50

---

* Exercising at a rate of at least 60 steps/min, counting only when the left foot strikes the surface.

Aerobic Dancing & Other Dancing Exercise Programs Conducted to Music

POINTS = Duration in minutes × 0.2

EXAMPLE: Danced 45 minutes with breaks only to check heart rate

* POINTS = 45 min × 0.2

= 9

---

* Depending upon the effort expended, the point value may be more or less than that given above.

Note: If you need a detailed breakdown of points earned or are interested in sports for which equations are not available, consult the point charts in the Appendix.

PART FOUR

THE EMOTIONAL FACTOR IN TOTAL WELL-BEING

9

The Aerobics Way to Emotional Balance

The middle-aged insurance agent was burned out.

He had been one of the top salesmen in his area when he was in his late twenties and early thirties, and it seemed in those days that the sky was the limit. There was nothing he couldn't achieve in his field, no height of salesmanship he couldn't reach.

But then, things started to go wrong. He began to lose interest in his work, and his sales gradually began to fall off—or maybe it was the other way around. He couldn't remember, and, quite frankly, he really didn't care. He tired more easily, his energy levels were down, and he was depressed more often than not. In fact, most days, he would just as soon have stayed in bed if he hadn't had to go out and earn money for his family's needs.

In the past, he had thought he had nothing at all in common with that unfortunate, suicidal salesman Willy Loman in Arthur Miller's play, *Death of a Salesman*. But now he wasn't so sure. His dreams, like Willy's, seemed dead. In fact, his spirits were so low sometimes that he wondered if *he* wouldn't be better off dead than alive.

This insurance man's wife became deeply concerned about him. She thought he looked unhealthy, and she knew he was at a low ebb emotionally. So she kept urging him to see a doctor. Finally, he reluctantly agreed.

At his medical exam, the physician immediately sized this salesman up as an out-of-shape fellow who was about 20 pounds overweight and was also a prime candidate for heart trouble. So he prescribed a reasonable, weight-loss diet and a graduated exercise program—and the results were nothing less than miraculous.

The man began by alternating walking and jogging for a 20- to 30-minute period, 3 to 4 days a week. Before long, he found he could run the entire time. And within 6 months, he had dropped 20 pounds, firmed up his muscles, and looked 10 years younger.

But perhaps even more important—and to his complete surprise—he experienced a startling change for the better in his emotional outlook. The result was that his self-confidence and interest in his work soared, and so did his list of sales prospects. Before long, he was back at the highest level of productivity he had achieved as a younger man.

This sort of story is being recounted over and over these days by those who have discovered aerobic exercise. Self-confidence increases;

self-esteem reaches new highs; and emotional problems, including anxiety and depression, drop to new lows.

It's often hard to quantify the connection between exercise and emotional well-being. In many cases, personal testimonies about "what exercise has done for me" are the only evidence we have of the phenomenon. But still, there is every reason to believe that the psychological advantages of vigorous exercise are quite real. And in the last few years, studies by physicians and exercise physiologists have begun to contribute a much needed scientific dimension to the understanding of this important aerobic benefit of greater emotional balance.

Here are some interesting findings by various experts who have done research into this fascinating topic:

In a study conducted at Purdue University, 58 men were put into a physical fitness program, which included three 90-minute work-out sessions, three times a week. At each session, the participants jogged for 10 minutes to warm up, did calisthenics for 25 minutes, jogged for 25 minutes, and engaged in a recreational physical activity for 25 minutes.

In addition to certain changes in body chemistry as a result of becoming more physically fit, the participants in this study showed some definite personality changes. As they improved in their capacity to jog faster for longer distances, they showed increases in self-confidence and self-assurance. Also, as the individual improved in jogging ability, "not only does he visibly improve in self-confidence, but he also becomes more outgoing, more involved with the group and appears to be more stable emotionally from the psychological point of view," according to Professor A. H. Ismail, author of the study.

In studies both of prison and jail inmates in California and Texas and also of male police officers from Dallas, Dr. Michael Pollock, formerly the Director of the Institute for Aerobics Research, reported that participants in aerobic exercise programs showed a number of beneficial personality changes. In general, their ability to sleep improved markedly, their sense of well-being increased, and they experienced less tension and depression. Also, those individuals with low self-esteem showed definite improvement.

Another study involving 48 university students who experienced "test anxiety," or stress and tension before and during written exams, showed that meditative relaxation techniques and aerobic exercise had similar benefits in reducing anxiety. Dr. Wesley E. Sime, an exercise physiologist with the University of Nebraska, concluded, "It is possible that jogging may be a very appropriate prescriptive treatment for the individual with high . . . anxiety. . . ."

Finally, our Institute for Aerobics Research in Dallas did some extensive research with teachers and administrators of the Dallas Independent School District into the relationship between physical fitness and stress management. This study, which was sponsored by a private foundation and completed in July, 1982, involved a six-month period of testing the effect of exercise and good nutrition on 100 participants and 60 "controls" (teachers and administrators who didn't do anything to change their exercise or dietary habits).

The results showed, among other things, that those who engaged in a regular aerobics conditioning program and who altered their diets to the Institute's specifications experienced certain beneficial changes in their outlook on life. These changes included the following: (1) participants demonstrated significant gains in self-concept, feelings of well-being, satisfaction, and reduced depression when compared with the control sample; (2) participants rated their changed ability to handle job stress significantly more positive than the control sample; and (3) principals rated participants (teachers) as having improved more significantly in the ability to handle job stress, as compared with the control sample.

These and other studies show that aerobic exercise can, indeed, have a beneficial effect on a person's emotional and psychological balance. To understand this phenomenon more fully—and also to learn what practical steps you can take to alleviate your own inner tensions and problems—let's take a closer look at three major elements I've identified in aerobic emotional balance: (1) the stress-reduction factor; (2) the endorphin effect; and (3) the more nebulous "personality change principle."

THE STRESS-REDUCTION FACTOR

There are at least two levels on which this principle operates: (1) your ability to deal with specific stress situations that occur during the course of each ordinary day, and (2) your ability to relieve yourself of stress at the end of an especially pressure-filled day, so that you're more relaxed and energized and ready to work or play, even into the evening hours.

First of all, let's talk about ways to deal with specific stress situations through aerobic exercise.

Various studies have demonstrated that aerobic activity helps individuals control anxiety reactions in the course of their normal daily work and leisure pursuits. Many of these studies focus on the change in heart rates of individuals who shift from a resting, unpressured state to a high-anxiety situation. So before we get into specific illustrations, let me give you some background on the heart rate concept as it relates to exercise.

The average American male who is not in condition has a resting heart rate of about 70 beats per minute, and the average American woman's rate is about 75 to 80 beats per minute. In response to minimal aerobic conditioning there is a significant decrease in the average resting heart rate.

For example, in one study involving middle-aged men, 45 to 55 years old, there was a decrease from 72 beats per minute to 55 beats after only 3 months of aerobic conditioning. And women have shown a comparable decrease in response to an aerobic program. Highly conditioned world-class distance runners whom we evaluated in a 1975 study, had average resting heart rates in the mid-40s. Some marathon runners, women as well as men, are in the high to mid-30s; and the slowest resting heart rate I've ever seen documented was in a marathoner by the name of Hal Higdon—whose resting heart rate was 28 beats per minute!

In addition to a lower resting heart rate, the rate tends to stay lower and rise more slowly in a fit person when anxiety strikes or when the individual begins to increase the level of his or her physical activity.

What accounts for these low levels in the heart rate?

There are at least two answers. First of all, after aerobic conditioning, there is a slight increase in the size of the heart and a significant increase in the internal volume of the heart. As a result, the heart pumps out more blood with each stroke. In medical terminology this is called an "increase in stroke volume," and what it means is that there is a conservation of energy. In other words, the heart doesn't have to work as hard to pump the same volume of blood throughout the body.

The second reason that the resting heart rate goes down and stays down is that better cardiovascular fitness tends to put a "governor" on the effect that the adrenal gland's secretions can have on the heart. In response to intense emotion, anxiety or fear, the resting heart rate increases to some extent. This is the result of the outpouring of adrenaline into the body.

The adrenal gland stimulates the heart to beat faster and thus prepares us for "fight or flight." And in our primitive ancestors, this response was probably an internal danger signal that put them on edge when danger threatened and often saved their lives because it enabled them to react quickly.

But in our more sedentary society, this same adrenal response may well push a poorly conditioned person's heart beyond its capacity. Here are some examples:

In a study of student teachers in a fourth-grade classroom, the average heart rate for the teachers while they were sitting behind their desks was 75 beats per minute. Then, when they stood up and began to speak to the class, the rate jumped up to 110 beats per minute. Next, the regular teacher, who was more familiar with the classroom situation, was monitored. Her resting heart rate was 75 beats per minute, and her "teaching rate" was 95.

Finally, in a related study, a very fit male college instructor was evaluated. His resting heart rate was 65 beats per minute, and the rate rose to only 67 beats per minute during the teaching phase. At one point, he became involved in an argument with a student, and in that stressful situation, his heart rate went up to only 70 beats per minute. Here, then, is an excellent example of how aerobic fitness can put a governor on the adrenal response of the body.

But perhaps the classic example of an anxiety response in this study was shown in a fourth-grade boy known to have a reading problem. Using a technique known as "telemetry monitoring," the researchers found his heart rate averaged 85 beats per minute while sitting in the classroom. When the teacher unexpectedly called upon the young boy to come to the front of the class and read to his fellow students, he became excited—"stage fright" gripped him. During the 10 minutes he was reading to his fellow students, his heart rate averaged 171 beats per minute! I had no idea that the anxiety response could be that great. But if he had been aerobically fit, most likely his heart rate response would have been less.

What is the significance of the lower heart rate response in the well-conditioned subjects? For one thing, a lower heart rate during stress means you tend to stay calmer and more in control of your emotions. But there are even more important consequences: To put it bluntly, a well-conditioned heart may save the person's life—as we'll see in this next set of examples.

There are numerous cases demonstrating how a quick jump in heart rate as a result of intense physical or emotional stress can lead directly to a lethal heart attack. For example, a couple of years ago, while flying out to the West Coast, I began talking to one of the flight attendants who happened to be a runner and was familiar with my "Aerobics" books.

"Boy, did we have an example of what you talk about in your books!" she said. I asked her to tell me about it.

"Just a few days ago," she said, "our plane had pulled away from the terminal and was being disconnected from the tow truck when an agent radioed to say that he had to get a late passenger on board.

"I went to the back of the airplane, lowered the rear stairs, and assisted this 40-year-old man onto the plane. I noticed that he was breathing heavily, sweating profusely, and was as pale as a sheet! He had a large briefcase in one hand and a heavy hang-up bag in the other.

"I helped him into a seat in the rear of the plane—smoking section, of course—and then resumed my position. But no sooner did I sit down when suddenly, all the call lights started coming on. I told the captain, 'Just a minute—we may have a problem,' and then I rushed to the back of the plane, where I found the passenger unconscious in his seat.

"I tried mouth-to-mouth resuscitation and closed chest massage as the pilot taxied the aircraft back to the terminal. But there was nothing that could be done." So another busy executive, rushing to catch an airplane, died of a heart attack. The chances are, if he had been in good aerobic condition, he could have tolerated that stress and would still be alive today.

In a related incident, a 39-year-old newspaper reporter was assigned to do a story on a new roller coaster called the "Python" in a Tampa, Florida, amusement park. The ride was advertised as a "real thriller" because it went up exceptionally high and then made several spiral loops before it arrived back at the starting point.

The reporter rode the Python, as he had been requested to do, stepped off at the end of the ride, collapsed, and could not be resuscitated. He had literally been "scared to death."

In reality, this is nothing new, since in the Bible it says, "Men's hearts can fail them from fear!" But now, we know the medical explanation for this phenomenon: With our reporter, the adrenaline response had driven his heart rate up to a point that he could not tolerate because of his poor physical condition. This sort of thing is reported periodically when older people are frightened by burglars or when someone is informed of the death of a loved one.

Another example of this phenomenon centers on our nation's firemen, whose physical condition often deteriorates. Their big problem is that periodically they have to overextend themselves when an alarm comes and they find they must respond with vigorous physical activity.

In one 15-month study, the purpose was to determine how many firemen died while on the job and what were the causes of death. There were 101 deaths during this 15-month period, and you might naturally assume that nearly all of the deaths would be fire-related—such as by being burned to death or fatally injured by a collapsing building.

But out of the 101 deaths, 45—or nearly half—died from heart attacks, and their average age was 51 years.

Finally, there have been studies done on the effect of watching an exciting sporting event on television. In one case, an EKG monitoring system was placed on a man with known heart disease while he was watching the Boston Celtics, his favorite team in the playoffs.

From the late morning until midafternoon, just before the game started, his heart rate ranged from 60 to 80 beats per minute. But then when the game started at 4 P.M., his heart rate began to vary from 80 to 120, and he was showing increasing "irritability" or irregularities in his heart rate.

During the next hour, as the game got more exciting, his heart rate increased to 150 beats per minute, and in conjunction with the high heart rate, there were multiple episodes of heart irregularities. If they had been persistent, these irregularities could easily have been fatal. It wasn't until 2 hours after the game that his heart rate returned to normal and the irregularities disappeared.

These are just a few examples to show you how an unconditioned person may compare with a person with a well-conditioned heart and vascular system under stressful conditions. But there's another important point that needs to be made about aerobic exercise as a means to control stress.

We've already considered how a generally high level of fitness can help you handle stress on the job or in leisure activities, and how a lack of conditioning can hurt you in these situations. But also, we are finding that the *timing* of aerobic exercise can provide an additional benefit in controlling stress. If you exercise at the *end of a high pressure day*— prior to the evening meal—aerobic activity can help to dissipate the stress you feel, relax you more, and even energize you so that you can continue to work or play much later into the evening than might be possible otherwise. Also, this sort of late afternoon exercise helps to depress the appetite if you are constantly fighting a weight problem.

I've noticed this particular benefit of exercise consistently in my interviews with patients and in my own personal observations at the Aerobics Center. One of the busiest times of the day we have at our Dallas facility is between the hours of 4:30 P.M. and 7:00 P.M. One reason for this is that I've taught many of my keyed-up executives, both men and women, to exercise at the end of the day as a means of "burning up" the stress physiologically, the way nature meant for it to be handled.

Why should exercise at the end of the day be such a great benefit in reducing stress and anxiety levels?

For one thing, it's likely that increasing the metabolism helps you dissipate the effect of the accumulated adrenal secretions that are still readying you for a fight or flight response. If you're keyed up from a high level of these hormones, your body is chemically out of balance, and you can't hope to achieve a relaxed feeling of well-being until that situation is corrected. Exercise apparently acts as nature's waste-removal process and helps your body return to a more relaxed state of equilibrium.

THE ENDORPHIN EFFECT

Many of the feelings of well-being and even euphoria often associated with running and other aerobic exercise have been traced in recent years to a powerful secretion of hormones called endorphins, which the body produces during endurance activities. Endorphins are morphinelike substances that are released from the pituitary gland in a variety of situations, including vigorous exercise.

I say endorphins are like morphine, and that's true, in that they can act to control pain. But at comparable dosages, they are about 200 times more powerful than morphine, and the effects they can have on the body are nothing short of phenomenal in terms of producing a *natural* feeling of well-being.

As a result of some research conducted by Scottish and British investigators back in the mid-1970s, the endorphin molecule was identified and associated with the feeling of euphoria and well-being that occurs after vigorous exercise. This feeling may last with a fair degree of intensity for 30 minutes to an hour or longer.

Studies on endorphins have revealed some of these findings:

In an experiment on dogs, researchers found that immediately after vigorous exercise, the endorphin levels were high and they remained high for as long as 1–1½ hours.

In a number of cases, endorphins have been shown to be powerful pain-killers. It's been speculated that the presence of endorphins in the body may explain why a football player can break his ankle in the first half of a game, play the whole second half and not realize until later that evening that he actually has a fractured bone.

In the 1982 Boston Marathon, Guy Gerisch, a runner from Salt Lake City, apparently sustained a stress fracture of the thigh bone (femur) at the seventh mile. Even though the bone was completely fractured, he completed the 26.2 mile race before collapsing. Then, several hours of surgery were required to stabilize the bone with a steel rod running from his hip to his knee. The surgeons theorized that the thigh muscles in this 38-year-old man were so powerful that they acted as a splint for the bone during the run; and obviously the endorphins were a factor enabling him to tolerate the pain and continue running at a 6:30-minute-per-mile pace.

The effectiveness of the medicinal powers of acupuncture has also been related to the release of endorphins in the body. For many years, the Chinese have used acupuncture as an anesthetic during surgery, including open heart surgery. And several studies exploring "electro-acupuncture" (EAP) have shown that pain relief is associated with elevated endorphin levels in the body.

After all-out exercise, there is a marked increase in the body's endorphin levels—as much as a fivefold increase as documented in a 1980 Italian study. In this study, eight world-class male athletes averaging 21 years of age, were tested while exercising to exhaustion on a treadmill. Before beginning the exercise, their endorphin levels were measured at an average level of 320. Immediately after their all-out, 12-minute effort, the endorphin levels rose to 1,620. Fifteen minutes later, they were still 1,080. And 30 minutes later, they were still at 420, which was above the resting level.

Endorphin levels tend to be higher during pregnancy and much higher during delivery. This fact probably explains how a woman can tolerate the multitude of aches and pains that occur normally during pregnancy; and it also explains the ability to tolerate what could be severe pain associated with natural childbirth. If a woman is highly conditioned aerobically, her potential endorphin level is higher, and this fact could make the childbirth experience easier for her than for the unconditioned woman. Certainly, this would suggest that a conditioning program could be of value prior to pregnancy, but a woman should never enter into a vigorous exercise program, which includes jogging, *after* the diagnosis of pregnancy has been made.

Endorphins may have a direct relationship to the relief of some mental problems. Psychiatrists throughout the world have been using exercise as a standard treatment for depression for years. In some cases of depression, the endorphin levels are abnormally low, and in such situations, physical activity should be of value with its exercise-induced endorphin "high."

Many physicians believe that exercise is nature's best physiological tranquilizer. And in addition to using exercise as a means of controlling depression, psychiatrists are using it as a way of relieving some types of stress and emotional anxiety.

One of the most dramatic, life-or-death cases I've had in my own practice involved a man whom I've counseled for several years and whom I still see regularly. He has used exercise effectively in controlling a multitude of very stressful situations in his career and personal life.

"Exercise is what has kept me alive," he told me recently.

When I asked him to explain his feelings in detail, here's what he said:

"It all started several years ago when, as a relatively young man, I had a major heart attack. Prior to that time, I was totally caught up in achieving success in my business, spending long hours, lots of entertaining—you know, the typical ambitious executive cycle. But after the heart attack, I began to exercise as a part of my rehabilitation program and I found it was valuable in other areas.

"For example, after many years of successful and harmonious marriage, separation and divorce occurred, and it was a long and painful process. At times, I became severely depressed, and ultimately found that I was becoming dependent upon running and association with my running friends as the means of getting through this period. It worked, but unfortunately, the story is not over yet.

"One of my sons had a nervous breakdown, and I had to confine him to a mental hospital. And then my brother, who was my partner in business, died suddenly. We were experiencing some financial reversals prior to his death, but these were all exaggerated and almost led to bankruptcy.

"During this turmoil in my life, I became even more regular with my running and that regularity, or obsession, has continued. In fact, recently I was having dinner with a business associate, and between 6 and 7 P.M., the guilt feeling was so bad, it was almost unbearable. I knew this was the time for my physiological tranquilizer, running." An exaggerated response? Perhaps. But it's a lot better than resorting to alcohol, drugs, or perhaps even ending it all.

Here's a man, then, who over the past 5 to 7 years of his life has wrestled with overwhelming stress and depression, and exercise has literally been the thing that has kept him alive.

As a result of cases I've encountered like this, I firmly believe that the person who is exercising regularly is psychologically healthier than the person who is not involved in a regular physical activity program. And there is some scientific support for this position.

For example, some research by Dr. G. H. Hartung at the Baylor College of Medicine in 1977 involved a comparison of forty-eight healthy male runners and joggers, 48 to 59 years of age, with a comparable number of nonrunners drawn from the general population. When compared with the nonrunners, it was obvious that the joggers were significantly more intelligent, imaginative, reserved, self-sufficient, sober, and shy than the general population. The conclusion was that middle-aged runners and joggers possess or develop high levels of self-sufficiency and imagination, and tend toward introversion in their personality makeup.

Our own psychological studies of patients at the Aerobics Center agree in general with the work of Hartung, except I doubt his conclusion that the joggers are more introverts than extroverts. Our more highly conditioned people have the reverse tendency: They are inclined to be extroverts, rather than introverts.

During the past 20 years that I have been involved in research in aerobics, I've seen some remarkable psychological changes among friends and patients, once they have become involved in a jogging program. And some of the most dramatic responses are evident in women.

One case that comes to mind involved a woman who was a classic introvert. For example, she always stayed in the background in conversations and social gatherings and was so self-conscious that she would never have been seen on a track running in shorts.

But then she became involved in our programs at the Aerobics Center, and immediately her attitude changed. She began to run regularly, performed exceedingly well on the treadmill stress test, and completely reversed her personality traits to the extent that she became a classic extrovert.

The change in this woman's personality—as well as in the personalities of countless other patients I've worked with—was primarily the result of an improved self-image. In fact, one of the things that can be most easily documented about people's responses to our exercise programs is an improvement in the self-image.

And along with an improved self-image, I have come to expect a transformation of the person into an outgoing, self-confident personality. This conclusion of mine is based on the cumulative results of a rather sophisticated personality profile that we give our patients to test any trends in their emotional makeup.

Relatively high endorphin levels are probably also present in the body after exercise sessions of relatively mild intensity. According to individual accounts we have received from people who work out at our Aerobics Center, it seems that most runners who run for about 3 miles at a rate of 7½ to 9 minutes per mile, get at least a transient feeling of euphoria during and after the experience. And these feelings are most likely related to a release of endorphins—though we can't always document such a phenomenon with scientific studies at these less intense exercise levels. And we don't know yet whether the "second wind" is in any way endorphin-related.

But one recent set of findings from Loma Linda University, as presented by Lee S. Berk, D.H.Sc., and his associates, offers some scientific support for this position. Studies were conducted with men 45 years old, some of them in good physical condition and some not. The two groups were exercised to exhaustion on a treadmill with the "Bruce multilevel test," which involved increasing the angle and speed of the treadmill after each 3 minutes of exercise.

In the highly conditioned men, the endorphin levels went up right away but reached a peak after a 12- to 15-minute run. Even when these men kept on exercising for 2 to 3 minutes longer, the endorphin levels didn't go up any further, and as soon as they stopped their activity, the endorphins dropped off rapidly within 15 to 30 minutes.

In the unconditioned people, the endorphins reached a peak lower than that of the conditioned men, at a point 3 to 6 minutes before the end of the run. Then, their endorphin levels dropped off for the remainder of the exercise period. But when these unconditioned people stopped exercising, their endorphin shot up to a second, higher peak and took longer in coming down than the men who were in better shape.

So it seems that exercise helps you get more endorphins into your system sooner and hold them longer during the exercise session if you're in condition. But if you're not in condition, the body apparently has some sort of system to compensate for the pain that you would experience normally after exercise, such as pain from sore or strained muscles and ligaments.

A related hypothesis on *physical* stress focuses on the idea that the soreness or stiffness in muscles or joints that may precede aerobic exercise often disappears after the exercise is under way.

Why should this be? Endorphins may be the answer. In other words, these morphinelike substances may spread through the body and suppress pain you would normally be feeling. The problem here is that if a person is suffering from a real injury and not just transient soreness, the endorphins may mask the pain. The result may be even greater injury and more intense pain once the endorphin effect wears off.

So, "running through the pain," as athletes have often been advised to do, may not be that wise.

A good rule of thumb may be that if you're feeling only minor pain or soreness, you might go ahead and work out. Then, if with exercise the pain disappears but comes back later at a greater level of intensity, you should rest for a few days, and consult with your physician if the pain doesn't subside.

THE "PERSONALITY-CHANGE PRINCIPLE"

In some ways, this last element of emotional balance is a catch-all term which includes many nebulous but still quite beneficial effects of aerobic exercise. Some people describe the effect as a general increase in self-confidence or self-esteem. Others say that the strengths they have developed from their aerobic activities have carried over into other aspects of their lives—qualities such as perseverance and a sense that seemingly impossible tasks are really quite possible.

For example, one executive I know said, "Even though I had first thought it was impossible for me, I finally achieved a 2-mile run. It was a struggle getting there, as I worked out over a period of several months and gradually built up my distance. But when I finally made the 2-mile mark, that achievement became a metaphor for other areas of my life.

Suddenly, overwhelming amounts of work I faced didn't seem so overwhelming any more. I seemed to have more tolerance for emotional stress."

This person went on to describe some of his running experience in almost mystical terms: "Now, many days when I run several miles, I have a much greater awareness of my body than I ever had before. Sometimes, at the end of a good run, my body seems to be working like a well-oiled machine. I may start the run in a fragmented emotional state, with many concerns and worries about various things. But by the end of such a run, I feel whole. My mind and my body become one."

Now, it's possible that the release of endorphins has something to do with these feelings. But the momentum that this individual feels when he moves from his running into his regular work seems to involve something that goes well beyond the endorphin effect. There does, indeed, seem to be some sort of broader positive personality-changing principle that begins to operate in the minds and emotions of experienced runners—a principle which helps hold their inner beings in a state of balance.

10

The Aerobic Family: A Study in Balance

As we've seen, total well-being depends on total balance—balance in what we eat and in the way we exercise. But there's another kind of balance that goes beyond the individual and concerns the way we relate to one another. This kind of community-oriented balance can be just as important a factor in promoting total well-being as anything else that we've discussed, in part because it provides a fertile environment in which our individual commitment to fitness can grow more rapidly.

For example, if your entire family is as devoted to good nutrition and aerobic conditioning as you are, it becomes much easier to stay on a healthy diet or stick to a regular exercise schedule. In addition, one fascinating thing I've discovered in recent years is that a balanced diet and aerobic exercise program can do wonders in helping to establish interpersonal harmony, especially within the family.

Unfortunately I think most people would agree that one of the weakest links in trying to achieve any sort of overall well-being in our society is our shaky family structure. Just as our general culture has changed over the years, so has the character of the family. We've all heard theories regarding the need for a return to a "extended family," or the importance of strengthening the "nuclear family." But one thing that seems to come across loud and clear in all the theorizing is that for lack of enough cohesive, binding forces, the extended family has become *over*extended. And the nuclear family is in the process of blowing itself to bits, with parents and children often becoming strangers to each other.

Despite all this chaos—this radical imbalance in our family structure—I have a dream about what family relationships could be like. There is a new label that I would like to see attached to the families of the future: the *aerobic family*.

In my personal dream, the members of these aerobic families would be linked in more intimate relationships by a concern for their mutual health and well-being. They would exercise together, share their daily progress in moving toward individual health goals, and feel free to share their problems and release their tensions and stresses in a constructive, healing way in one another's presence.

The possible family benefits from regular exercise are enormous. Here are just a few that I'm aware of:

EXERCISE PROMOTES FAMILY TOGETHERNESS

The family that exercises together—or at least that shares and supports one another in individual exercise programs—frequently possesses a much greater level of well-being and unity.

Of course, there are always dangers of excess exercise in the family, especially if the commitment to exercise among different individuals isn't in balance. If mom is out training for a marathon while dad, a non-exerciser, stews about her absence, there are going to be frictions. A number of divorces have occurred because of the "runner's widower or widow syndrome." But if dad runs a bit himself, he'll probably be able to understand his wife better, and the relationships in the family will be the better for it.

Of course, if your entire family runs, that doesn't mean they must all run together. Not only would that be rather cumbersome to organize, but it probably wouldn't be a workable arrangement. Everyone has his or her own pace or favorite running route. And there will always be those who don't like running or swimming or whatever sport the rest of the family engages in. Yet, the very fact that all or most of the family members are involved in serious aerobic activity gives them a common tie that they wouldn't otherwise have, and as a result, they are drawn closer together.

This is certainly the way it is in my own family—we usually exercise separately, but then come together to share our individual experiences. Occasionally, I do enjoy running with my wife, but it's not our normal practice. Her speed is considerably less than mine, and she complains that I push her too hard. For my part, I complain that it makes my legs sore to run that slow. So running side-by-side isn't always practical, and it can even be divisive.

On the other hand, I have trouble keeping up with my young daughter. When she was just 6 or 7, she used to love to go out running moderate distances with mom or dad. But now that she is a state champion in the 2-mile and cross-country, she's gone a bit beyond the scope of her 50-year-old father.

It's much the same with my son. He is interested in a variety of athletic activities, such as soccer, snow and water-skiing, and sometimes we'll work out together. But more often, we don't. Yet these diverse athletic interests and habits don't draw us apart; on the contrary, they draw us together under the common umbrella of a mutual interest in good health.

PHYSICAL FITNESS MAY ENHANCE A COUPLE'S SEX LIFE

This is a subject for which quantifiable data are lacking, yet there does seem to be a positive relationship between aerobic conditioning and a satisfying sex life. Many times over the past 20 years, I have had patients volunteer the information that their sex lives have improved in response to regular physical exercise, and when both partners are involved, this relationship seems to be enhanced even more.

The only exception might be where chronic fatigue sets in as a result of running. In that case, exercise may actually have a detrimental effect. Also, when only one partner exercises regularly and reaches a high level of fitness, there may be a noticeable decrease in the level of sexual compatibility.

STRESS LEVELS IN AEROBIC FAMILIES

We've already seen ample evidence of how such factors as endorphins and exercise at the end of a pressure-packed day can greatly reduce stress levels in individuals. This being the case, it logically follows that with fewer stress-laden people around, family relationships will suffer less from stress.

For example, how often have you witnessed, or personally experienced, a father or mother with problems at work or in the home taking out those problems on the kids? Exercise can help reduce those frustrations and pressures. It can also function as a mood elevator which will have a kind of domino effect. When you feel good about yourself, it's apparent to those around you, and your sense of well-being will tend to rub off on others.

A TOTAL FAMILY EXERCISE HABIT ENHANCES COMMUNICATION BETWEEN PARENTS AND CHILDREN—AND ESPECIALLY PARENTS AND TEENAGERS

In my practice at the Aerobics Center, I've had countless families come into my offices with many stories about how their mutual commitment to regular exercise, good diet, and other aspects of good health has broken down barriers between them.

All too often, parents lose contact with their children because they lack experiences to share and talk about with them. But family members who exercise individually or together have much more to share, and better communication and relationships are the inevitable result. In many cases, I've seen parents establish and maintain relationships with their kids even during the difficult teenage years—simply because both parent and child have a deep interest in good health and physical conditioning.

During the spring of 1982, our 16-year-old daughter Berkley developed into a top-quality, competitive runner. Our entire family attended every track meet: I rushed back from some trips to get to the track just in time to see her finish the mile. But during most of her meets, I was down on the track with a stopwatch.

At times, I think my heart was beating faster than hers! What fun for the entire family this experience was. It brought my daughter a feeling of accomplishment and self-esteem that was truly remarkable. I wish every family could experience the thrill in the accomplishments of one of their members, that the Cooper family experienced during the spring of 1982.

But let me offer one word of warning here: Children can't be forced into exercise, just as they can't be forced into anything else. Instead of enjoying themselves, kids who are pushed too hard will learn to hate exercise, and they'll look for any opportunity to escape from it. As soon as they leave their parents, they'll leave their exercise program.

Some parents with good intentions may push their children too far in trying to promote fitness. A friend of mine who tried to motivate his children to work out regularly had a track in his backyard. It was a nice little set-up—about fifteen laps to the mile—and under any other circumstances it would probably have attracted his kids like flies. But he decided to pay the children a nickel or so for every lap they completed. It seemed to work at first: They ran a lot and earned a bit of money. But as soon as he stopped paying them, they stopped running. Apparently, they had just not learned to like it. They had been running, but for all the wrong reasons.

The *right* way to motivate kids, from what I've seen among the families that have a balanced exercise relationship, is for the parents to serve as models for the kids, without trying to promote the exercise idea too strongly. Kids are likely to mimic adult activities anyway—whether cigarette smoking, drinking, or exercising.

In my own family, I've encouraged my children to exercise, but I've never tried to push them. Our son has never been too enthusiastic about running, but he enjoys soccer, football, and other competitive sports. The main goal the parents should have for the child should be the same as the parent has for him- or herself: Find and encourage those aerobic activities that the youngster takes to naturally and seems to enjoy. Then, exercise for the entire family will come naturally and happily.

PROPER EXERCISE AND DIET ARE VITAL FOR YOUR CHILD'S HEALTH AND HAPPINESS

As you know, Americans are prone to an unusually high rate of atherosclerosis, or hardening of the arteries. And whether it's from the high dependence on junk food or a widespread lack of aerobic activity, this same malady begins to afflict our children at an astonishingly early age.

In studies of American servicemen killed in the Korean conflict in 1953, fully 77 percent already showed signs of coronary artery disease and some had obstructive disease—at an average age of only 22. This study was repeated in 1975 with casualties from the Vietnam War, and the average age once again was 22. Incredibly, 55 percent already had some signs of obstructive coronary disease that must have set in much earlier in life.

Just how early atherosclerosis may start in children can't be easily determined. But autopsies of children as young as 10 who have died in accidents or from other causes show that even at that age there are at times streaks of cholesterol on the walls of some of their major arteries.

Simply stated, fat children tend to become fat adults. And by continuing the bad diets and inadequate exercise habits of their formative years, they lessen their chances of a healthy future. So a regular program of physical activity for kids is vital from a very young age.

These, then, are some of the considerations that make it so vital that you bring a balanced diet and exercise program into your home in a big way to enhance your family's total well-being. Because your biggest problem may be in shaping your children's exercise and dietary habits, I'd like to devote the rest of this discussion to some practical observations about how you might get your kids started off on the right track toward total well-being.

First of all, how young should they start exercising?

My answer is, start them exercising as soon as they are born! Encourage them to move about, use their little legs and arms, catch balls, and do whatever else they are capable of doing at each age level.

As far as aerobic exercise is concerned, however, I would hold off until they are at least 10 years old before encouraging them to embark on a disciplined, long-distance program. In my opinion, their bone and muscular development is just not far enough along before that to warrant subjecting them to the stresses of a full-blown aerobic exercise activity.

A few years ago, there was a craze for young kids running 26-mile marathons. On one of the national news programs, it was announced that a 5-year-old boy had just established the "world's record for 5-year-olds for running a marathon." Immediately after that, young children (encouraged by their parents) began entering marathons all over the country.

Our White Rock Marathon in Dallas was no exception. Against my better judgment, the marathon committee consented to allow a 6-year-old to enter in light of his training history, which was provided by his father. The child, astonishingly, was able to complete 17 miles before being forced to quit. But then, he began to suffer severe cramps because of fluid loss and electrolyte depletion. His temperature shot up, and he lapsed into a state of mental confusion.

Fortunately, after a few days of rehydration with intravenous fluids in the hospital, he recovered without problems. But we all learned our lesson, and I can better understand now why the Boston Marathon has an age minimum of 18 years.

Even though marathon training is unwise for young children, by the time a child reaches the fourth grade, he or she is ready for a more disciplined program of conditioning and should undergo regular tests for fitness.

And by the time kids get into junior high school, participation in an aerobically oriented progressive exercise program should be part of their life-style. After all, atherosclerosis begins in these early years and it may take 20 years or more before any outward symptoms show—and the first symptom may be sudden death. So you may, indeed, be saving your child from an early grave if you encourage him or her to start a balanced diet and aerobics program right now.

But there's a major problem in your guidance of your child's conditioning program. When your child reaches the junior high and high school years, much of the responsibility and initiative for his or her physical conditioning program goes out of your control into the hands of school officials. And it's at this point that the aerobic family must begin to look beyond itself and take action, if necessary, to promote better community and school fitness programs.

What I'm saying here is that it may be necessary for you to get political—to begin to apply pressure and to formally lobby your local school board to get essential changes in your school's gym programs.

While some schools have active physical education programs, too many others regard "gym" as just an institutionalized form of recess. Ironically, just as the benefits of preventive conditioning are being demonstrated and exercise as an integral part of our society's life-style is coming into its own, many school systems are being pressured to eliminate gym programs entirely.

In other words, at a time when many foreign countries are mandating that their youth participate in conditioning programs, we are cutting them out. There's no question in my mind that this deemphasis on good conditioning is a trend that must be reversed immediately. In my view, the strength of our country tomorrow depends to a large degree on the physical strength and energy of our youth today.

And the kids themselves know they are getting short-changed. In a survey of New England high school students a few years ago, 87 percent acknowledged they were not getting enough exercise in their daily lives. One student said, "Personally, I am concerned because when my parents were my age, they exercised a great deal more than I am exercising. Look at them now. If they look that bad, what am *I* going to look like when I'm their age?"

But is there any evidence that conditioning programs in secondary schools really work when they are established?

Emphatically, yes! When we tested 18- and 19-year-old recruits in the United States Air Force, we found that the individual's fitness often depended on what state he or she was from.

For example, recruits coming from California were clearly fitter than those from other states. Also, it was evident that environmental factors such as the weather weren't responsible for the difference: When we compared the California recruits with those from the southern states with similar weather conditions, the southerners were far less fit than the westerners.

What California had that the southern states didn't have was a *mandatory physical education program*. And the payoff in increased levels of fitness was remarkable. Unfortunately, though, California discontinued its mandatory program, and in a short period of time, the fitness of California recruits dropped markedly.

In cooperation with the President's Council on Physical Fitness and Sports and the Institute for Aerobics Research, a national study of the fitness of American youth will start soon. The project is being funded by the Campbell Soup Company and will last 3 years. Students in the fourth to twelfth grades will be tested in three areas—strength, flexibility, and endurance. Percentile rankings will be established so that studies comparing students of exactly the same age can be conducted.

For example, a boy or girl 10 years and 9 months of age in California can be compared with boys and girls exactly the same age in all other states. If there are differences, efforts will be made to determine why, and appropriate suggestions will be offered.

Nine thousand students will be involved the first year; the second year, 200,000 students; and the third year, 12,900,000 students. It is hoped that this study will produce an awareness of youth fitness that will result in major changes in school programs and eventually in the improvement of the health and fitness of all Americans.

But what about the school system where you live? Is the physical education program there up to par?

Most likely, the gym program is regarded as no more than a fun-and-games hour—not a serious conditioning program in which progress can be charted and evaluated. If that's the case, and you want to try to change things, here are some steps you might take:

- Discuss the problem with the school's parent–teacher association.
- Bring in an exercise expert to explain to the PTA the implications of the problem, and the serious threat to the health and well-being of the children involved.
- Bring the matter before the school board, with a concrete proposal about what they can do to correct the situation.
- Get the support of the school staff (the PE teachers are sure to support your efforts if they are truly interested in physical education).
- Make arrangement for some type of physical fitness testing program to begin.

On this last point, some individual states, such as Texas, already have an ongoing study of students' strength, flexibility, and endurance capacities. The response of students to that particular program has been quite impressive and enthusiastic. They are compared with a general standard of fitness and placed in various percentiles, depending on how well they perform. Those who make the 75th percentile or higher receive a special "Governor's Commission Award," established by the Texas Governor's Commission on Fitness. And there is a special gold award for those reaching the 90th percentile or higher. For more details on the Texas program, contact: Mr. Sonny Rooker, Executive Director, Governor's Commission on Fitness, 4200 North Lamar Blvd., Austin, Texas 78756.

Giving awards for fitness as part of programs such as the one in Texas can serve as a tremendous motivational tool to get kids to work toward higher levels of personal fitness. And the better habits they establish as youngsters, the more likely they will be to achieve high levels of well-being throughout their lives.

So, as you can see, starting a conditioning program in your family may well have broader implications for your community as well. In the last analysis, becoming an "aerobic family" may not solve all your problems. But establishing this sort of approach to health in your home will certainly serve as a form of "family insurance" in the sense that the marital and parental bonds that now exist will almost certainly get stronger and remain stronger.

Before I leave the subject of family and marital harmony, let me offer a few final comments:

Remember, as I tell my busy executives, a good marriage requires a lot of attention, just as being successful in your job requires a lot of work. According to the Holmes Life Change Score, the ten most stressful things you may experience in your life include five that are related to your marriage. Number one is death of a spouse; number two is divorce; and number three is marital separation. Number seven is marriage; and number nine is marital reconciliation. The statement that they were married and "lived happily ever after" doesn't occur often unless there is a bilateral willingness to want to work and make it successful.

And "as for me and my family, we serve the Lord." A home without a spiritual base has no foundation regardless of the emphasis on fitness and well-being. If the family works together toward both physical and spiritual fitness, a state of joy, happiness, and contentment is waiting that exceeds the imagination. My wife and I refer to this common spiritual orientation as the "joy of living," which without question is the basis of our success, family harmony, and total well-being.

Finally, as we'll see in the next chapter, the habits that develop in the family may also spill over into your job and make the workplace, as well, a home for total well-being.

11

The Joys of Fitness on the Job

Acquiring the kind of physical and emotional balance that is necessary to achieve total well-being is an infectious thing. When you develop a personal equilibrium, that automatically leads to greater family equilibrium. And this family balance flows naturally into a more balanced state in the world at large, including the workplace.

If you find you're not quite happy or satisfied with your job, that is probably because something, somewhere in your work life is in a state of imbalance. It may just be that you're a square peg in a round hole. But the reason for your dissatisfaction may also be that something is wrong with some other aspects of your life. Something may be out of kilter in your body or in your family. And so your feelings on the job may just be a symptom of a much deeper personal difficulty.

Probably a person's absenteeism from work is the best barometer to illustrate the presence or absence of a proper balance among bosses and employees at work. A Canadian research team discovered that the four major reasons that people don't show up for work are (1) indifference and boredom; (2) domestic problems; (3) drug and alcohol abuse; and (4) infectious diseases—in that order.

In other words, as you might expect, absences are directly related to emotional or physical problems, or both. But in addition, this study revealed that different "illnesses"—if they can really be called that—typically occurred on particular days. For instance:

- Monday absences are usually caused by problems with drugs or alcohol;
- Friday absences occur most often because of boredom or indifference toward work;
- Midweek absences are frequently the result of domestic problems or infectious disease.

Boredom on the job, alcohol, troubles at home—if this sounds all too familiar to you, it may be a signal that your life is out of balance. And the problem may not be with your job, but with your body, your spirit, and your emotions, because the condition you're in can be the key to happiness.

Take a cue from your fellow workers. Look at those who are in good physical condition: They're the ones who most often are not overweight; they watch their diets; they exercise often; and they don't smoke.

They are probably also the most active, reliable, and productive people at work.

Generally speaking, studies of workers show that those who are physically fit face each day with more enthusiasm and a better sense of well-being than those who are out of condition. The fit people can eliminate much of the boredom from their lives because their high degree of stamina helps them to maintain a much higher level of energy, and hence interest in what they're doing throughout the day. They tend to be more alert and more outgoing—and they call in sick less often than their flabby friends.

In addition, workers who are in shape are less likely to be careless on the job, and that means fewer industrial accidents. Finally, exercise promotes productivity. Employees who are in an aerobic program tend to take fewer breaks during the workday, they do their jobs faster, and they operate more efficiently.

A couple of recent studies illustrate what I'm talking about here:

A three-times-a-week exercise program conducted for NASA employees improved attitudes and job performance in more than half of the workers. Almost 90 percent said their stamina had gone up, and 60 percent lost excess weight.

Workers in the Soviet Union who started an exercise program showed greater productivity, fewer doctor visits, and fewer industrial accidents than before they began exercising.

And there are many "fall-out" effects to exercise and a balanced diet that can improve your productivity and help reduce absenteeism. For example, even though exercise can't act directly to eliminate the effects of alcohol or drug abuse, the desire to exercise and improve your health may provide a strong incentive to cut down on their use. Many of my patients have been able to quit or cut down on smoking as a result of a regular exercise regimen. And it's likely that the increased feeling of well-being that comes with regular exercise is a strong factor in lessening the dependence on drugs as well.

Absenteeism due to infectious disease may also be affected by an ongoing exercise program. Although you may catch the flu whether you exercise or not, some studies have shown that your body's resistance to some colds and sore throats may increase as a result of exercise and fitness. According to a report by University of Michigan researchers J. G. Cannon and M. J. Kluger, joggers and other enthusiasts may get sick less often because of an increase in body heat caused by exercise. The increase in body temperature which lingers after the exercise may make it harder for invading bacteria to grow in the body. So your aerobics program may help you ward off some illnesses or decrease their severity.

In a similar vein, one important study of New York state employees who participated in a 5-year exercise program showed the participating individuals had a significant reduction in their risk of cardiac disease. Also, other health problems decreased, and the rate of absenteeism dropped.

Finally, absenteeism as a result of marital problems can certainly be reduced by a commitment to fitness. We've already seen that spouses who are in good physical shape are more likely to be sexually compatible. And because exercise helps to relieve individual stresses and tensions, this means that there are less pressures and frustrations floating around the home which could lead to marital disruptions.

But there are some other very attractive "fringe benefits" that go along with this idea of fitness on the job, in addition to improving your performance and cutting down on your absenteeism. One of the most important of these may be the fact that your higher level of physical fitness, with the accompanying good looks and improved self-image, can put you in a better position to get a promotion.

To enhance employee appearance, some corporations have provided bonuses to those employees who lose weight and keep it off. I worked with one excessively overweight man who was being given $5.00 per pound for every pound he lost, with the understanding that for each pound he gained back, $10.00 would be withdrawn from his weekly paycheck. Needless to say, this was an effective motivator, and it worked!

I know of other corporations who place a premium on good physical fitness and proper weight. If two candidates for a job or a promotion within the company are equally qualified, except that one is overweight and inactive, they will always select the one in the best physical condition. And when you think about it, it makes sense to select the one who is most likely to be with you the longest.

In other cases, I have been asked about an employee's health and fitness when additional schooling was being considered or when promotions requiring more hours and greater responsibility were at stake. Obviously, a lot of talented people have been "passed over" because they didn't take better care of themselves physically.

As you're looking around your workplace, try analyzing the lifestyles of your fellow employees and see if you can identify who is getting ahead most quickly, and why. People are often evaluated for promotions both by what they have done and what their present level of work indicates about their potential. And the future prospects of any individual—including his or her probable physical condition several years from now—are a very important consideration. After all, what good is a "great mind" if you aren't going to be around long enough to use it? So an out-of-condition person who goes about his or her work sluggishly for months at a time, who has a poor attitude, and who calls in sick often, is likely to be passed over if a higher position opens in his or her department.

Instead, the job will go to the more energetic person, who may also appear to be more of a self-starter and a leader. And getting into good shape can be a key factor in energizing you and building up the good self-image and self-confidence that often characterize the leader in business.

But so far, we've been concentrating on fitness at work mainly from the perspective of the employee. Now, what about the boss? If you're a boss, you should be aware that you can save your company a lot of money and greatly increase the productivity of those under you just by promoting fitness among your workers. Here are some of the startling statistics that tell part of the story:

- Industry pays out nearly $10 billion each year for sick pay.
- Total annual cost of health care in the U.S. now exceeds $225 billion, which equals about 9 percent of the Gross National Product—and that figure escalates every year.
- One hundred thousand worker deaths each year are caused by cardiovascular disease.
- Seven hundred million dollars are spent annually by business to replace workers who are out sick.

The burden to business and consumers alike of the astronomical costs of employee health care is illustrated rather dramatically by still another example: Except for wages, the highest single monetary component of the cost of a new General Motors automobile is the health insurance premium! For the past 3 years, General Motors has paid more for its employees' health insurance premiums than it has paid for purchasing steel to go into the automobiles! Realizing that bad health on the job is getting out of hand, many American executives are taking a cue from abroad to ways to solve their problems.

For example, the Japanese have long recognized the joys of fitness and of well-balanced health on the job. Their employees regularly participate in "exercise breaks" rather than in the traditional American-style coffee break. Upon coming to work first thing in the morning, Japanese workers gather together for stretching and light calisthenics, and then they go up to their desks or work places to start their day fresh and alert. Another exercise session in the middle of the afternoon steams them up enough to get through the afternoon doldrums that so often lull American workers into lethargy and make them look forward to 5 o'clock more than to the tasks at hand.

In November 1981, I visited Japan as a guest of several corporations, including Yamaha Motor Company. It was most impressive to observe the employer/employee relationship and to visit one of their rest and conditioning centers in Sendai, Japan. Employees and families are encouraged to use these facilities, and certainly, they are first-class! With such personal attention to their needs, it is easy to see why an employee feels so strongly about his or her company and why Japanese productivity is the highest in the world.

And the Japanese are not the only foreign nation to see the benefits of fitness. Workers in the Soviet Union have *mandatory* exercise sessions at their work places. So you can see the value of an alert, healthy worker hasn't been lost on the Soviet government.

As I say, then, some American companies have seen that part of the answer to their productivity and absenteeism problems may lie in the experience of the Japanese and Russians in promoting exercise. And the result has been an increase in the number of American businesses that have started aerobic fitness programs, which are often called *"wellness" programs.*

Wellness programs, which are being implemented in both the hospital environment and in industry, consist of much more than just initiating an exercise program. They must concentrate on at least five things:

1. Proper weight, diet, and nutrition.
2. Properly implemented and supervised exercise programs.
3. Reduction and/or elimination of cigarette smoking.
4. Prevention and rehabilitation of alcoholism.
5. Stress management.

Corporations have found success in implementing one or more of these programs, and the employee response to them has been quite positive.

Generally speaking, an American wellness program is designed both to perk up employees during work hours and also to increase their overall health so that company health costs and absenteeism go down.

More specifically, wellness programs have been shown to improve employee attitudes and morale at work, reduce turnover, and decrease sick pay and the cost of company health insurance premiums. The more sophisticated of these programs screen employees for potential risk of diseases; they provide a thorough physical examination; and they make recommendations for improving a person's coronary risk profile, with diet and exercise suggestions.

Here are some encouraging signs, which may make you want to try to start a similar program in your own company:

Between 1979 and 1982 businesses invested nearly $2 billion to establish and maintain wellness programs. But they don't have to be supersophisticated to work. All that's really required is good employer leadership to motivate the employees to use the facilities regularly. Also, it's important to make arrangements for monitoring and developing a person's fitness through aerobic conditioning techniques.

Doctors who scoff at the value of preventive medicine in reducing employee absences—and there are still far too many of these medical skeptics—haven't talked to the Canadian Life Assurance Company, whose results have been particularly impressive. After a fitness program was started at the company, employee absentee rates were cut by 42.9 percent, and the savings to the company were $175,000 in 1 year. Also, employee turnover dropped by 13.5 percent, with savings estimated at $510,000.

Another large insurance company, Prudential, also needs no convincing about the benefits of wellness programs. After starting their program, they reported sharp declines in absenteeism (down 59 percent), with estimated savings to the company in 1 year of $284,744.

Kennecott Copper showed a 55 percent decrease in medical costs, a savings they attributed to their program.

New York Telephone carefully analyzed the results of its health promotion program to see exactly how much money they were saving in employee absences and in cost of medical treatment. Smoking cessation programs were credited with savings of $645,000, with additional savings from the program in lower costs of lung disease treatment of $1.4 million. Also, reduction in cholesterol levels saved them $250,000 in medical costs, and hypertension control programs meant another $663,000 in savings.

Some companies also manage to save money through refunds on health insurance premiums. For example, Bonne Bell Cosmetics, which has for years been promoting exercise and fitness among its employees, reported that for two consecutive years, their health insurance carrier gave the company a $43,000 refund on their premiums. The reason for this is that as the claims against the insurer decreased within their company, the cost of carrying the insurance became less—and so the savings were passed on to the company.

Another refund success story involved Forney Engineering in Dallas. This company instituted a wide-ranging wellness program which encourages exercise, proper diet, and control of cigarette smoking. Because of their dramatically improved record of health claims, their insurance carrier recently gave them a $92,000 refund on their hospitalization insurance.

In an interesting twist on motivating employees to participate in these wellness programs, Bob Schwartz of the Schwartz Meat Company in Norman, Oklahoma, started an aerobics program among his 75 employees several years ago. He offered bonuses to workers who earned a minimum number of points from using the program every week for 6 months. At the end of the 6 months, the employee received an additional week's pay if he or she had participated fully in the fitness program.

To sweeten the deal further, Schwartz offered another week's pay if the employee's spouse participated in the program. And for every child under 18 who participated, one-half week's pay was added. If an employee, his or her spouse, and two children faithfully participated in the program for 1 year, at the end of that time there would be a 1½-month salary bonus. Is such a program realistic?

This answer is a resounding "yes!" The results of this incentive program were dramatic, with productivity shooting up and absenteeism dropping sharply. And perhaps the best indication of employee morale came from the employees themselves. While many other companies are having labor battles, Bob Schwartz's employees saved up enough money out of their own pockets to send him and his wife to Europe for 4 weeks—all expenses paid!

So there is a great deal to be said for wellness programs in corporations from everyone's point of view, boss and employee alike. If your company doesn't have such a program, you may be able to help organize one. Here are some points based on suggestions by Blue Cross/Blue Shield to help you along:

- Talk to people in companies that have programs. Find out how much their approach to fitness costs and whether or not they would change anything they've set up.
- Organize a committee, draft a wellness program proposal, and set a deadline within which you want to accomplish your goals.
- Take advantage of in-house expertise of company doctors and employees trained in fitness-related fields and nutrition.
- Publicize your idea to gain support among the employees in the company.
- Include employees' families in the program: Remember that they, too, are on your company health plan.
- Get top executives committed to the program since they will be the ones who will have the greatest influence in getting the idea approved.
- Evaluate and change your wellness program periodically to suit your evolving needs.
- Use community resources whenever possible. Local schools and gyms may be able to help provide facilities and instruction, thus reducing your costs.

Many corporations are hiring their own staffs and building their own facilities, but that may be an unnecessary luxury. IBM started a national program for its employees two years ago that has been highly successful without involving an expensive building program. Instead of erecting facilities or paying for memberships in various clubs, contractual arrangements are made with local groups to provide educational and training programs for employees and families.

For example, if ten or more employees and family members want a 5-day, quit-smoking program, IBM will make all the arrangements and pay the bill. Likewise, if there is interest in an aerobic dance class (which has been one of the most frequently requested courses), IBM will contract with an instructor, make arrangements for a place, and pay the total bill. Direct contractual arrangements with YMCAs, driver education courses, and weight-loss programs have all been highly successful. It is a new approach to employee wellness programs that is enjoying great popularity among IBM personnel.

But even though the business community is beginning to come around to the idea that a physically fit body reaps many corporate rewards, the biggest changes yet to be made will focus on the life and health insurers. Some life insurance companies already offer discounts on premiums to people who do well on a physical exam, exercise regularly, and don't smoke. Why the premium breaks? It's simply that those who take care of their health have a lower risk of early death.

But health insurers so far don't offer the same incentives. Even if you watch your weight and diet, don't smoke, and exercise regularly, you still pay the same premium as the person who isn't as conscientious. Most insurers won't even pick up the tab for an annual physical unless it's in response to a medical problem—and this is the case even though the evidence shows that people who have annual physicals live longer and suffer less from catastrophic illnesses.

An old Chinese custom was for the people to pay their physician only when they were well. If they got sick, the doctor had to care for the patient without any pay. That was quite an incentive for doctors to work hard at keeping people well! If we could only come up with similar incentives to get *our* doctors and insurers to motivate people to keep well and not just care for them when they're sick, the payoffs in good health and productivity would be unbelievable.

So you can see that establishing a personal balance that will lead to total well-being on the job is not limited to one individual's commitment to fitness. No, if we hope to create an environment where good health and productivity become the order of the day, we must all work together—to achieve a community equilibrium, based on good nutrition and aerobic conditioning, that will accrue to the benefit of all.

PART FIVE

HOW TO MONITOR YOUR BODY'S OVERALL BALANCE

12

Taking the Mystery out of Your Medical Exam

There's a notion being propagated these days that going in for a regular medical examination, when there's nothing hurting you, is a waste of time and money. And it's certainly true that the haphazard, superficial way many exams are conducted makes them virtually useless.

But the evidence of the results of *comprehensive* medical exams demonstrates clearly that they are an absolutely essential part of any program of total well-being—especially as the individual gets older.

Once again, the concept of balance is the key.

One of your major goals in life should be to achieve the balance of body and emotions that will result in total well-being. But without a regular physical exam to *determine* that state of balance, there's no way to know exactly where you stand. You may feel all right, as you sit there reading this book. But we've already seen a number of examples of people who felt good—and then suffered major health problems because, unknown to them, something was dreadfully wrong! Perhaps it was a very high blood pressure, markedly elevated cholesterol, or insufficiency of the blood supply to the heart or brain. Many of these maladies could have been detected at an early stage during a thorough medical check-up.

Already, I've given you a number of examples of how heart problems can be detected before they cause symptoms through blood tests or electrocardiograms taken during treadmill stress testing. But there are many other potentially devastating maladies that an exam may reveal which are relatively simple to correct. Here are a few examples:

A Dallas schoolteacher no longer suffers daily from severe headaches because she learned from a routine dental exam that the majority of tension headaches, including her own, could be traced back to a "bad bite"—and could be successfully treated by a procedure known as dental equilibration.

A man avoided total blindness in one eye because a routine eye exam showed a problem developing *before* he noticed any symptoms.

A 36-year-old man is alive and well today because a malignant tumor in his thyroid gland was detected during a routine physical exam—even though he had never felt anything unusual. The tumor was encapsulated and easily removed before it had a chance to spread.

Our bodies are in a state of constant motion and change, and as a result, they frequently go out of balance in one way or another, especially as we get older. But usually, that imbalance begins in a small way—and therein lies the strength and importance of the medical exam.

Simply stated, a small problem can be treated most successfully before it becomes a big problem. And a regular physical exam will make it unnecessary for your preventive medicine specialist to tell you, "I wish you'd come to me sooner."

So how often should you get a physical?

The answer to this question depends entirely on your past medical history, your age, and what shape you're in. If you're generally healthy and under 30, you probably don't need a physical more frequently than once every 2 to 3 years. From ages 30 to 35, examinations should be done every 2 years. When you are this young, some tests aren't too important, but at least one resting electrocardiogram should be taken to use as a reference in future years.

If you're between 35 and 40, you should get a physical every 18 months. The exam should include a resting electrocardiogram each time, and this is also the best time to start maximum performance stress testing on a treadmill.

For anyone over 40, a thorough physical, including a stress test, is preferable every year to 18 months. Women should have a baseline mammogram done at this age for future reference because the risk for breast cancer increases as they get older. While a mammography in younger women is not usually in order, it's recommended for women over 40 and is so sensitive that a mass in the breast often can be picked up 2 years before it can be felt. At that stage, most breast cancer usually can be completely corrected by surgery.

Remember, too, that the majority of breast malignancies are found by the women themselves. At least one time each month (not at the premenstrual period when the breasts may be swollen and sore), a woman should palpate her breast for nodules, masses, or areas of tenderness. The ideal way is to lather up the breast when bathing, place the arm above the head, and then with the opposite hand, reach over and palpate the breast in a clockwise fashion. Begin at the nipple and work outward in a spiral fashion. If there are questionable abnormalities, check with your physician.

As a part of the annual exam, the breast examination by the physician is still one of the most important parts of the exam. In American women 35–54 years of age, breast malignancies rank close to the top among the various causes of death, the majority of which are preventable if diagnosed early.

After age 50, men and women can benefit from an annual exam that includes both a resting and a stress electrocardiogram, as well as mammography for women. Also at this age, men and women should have an exam with a proctosigmoidoscope (an intestinal exam conducted by inserting a long, thin, metallic device up through the rectum) or a colonoscopy (involving a much longer, but flexible, tube) every 1 to 2 years. This rectal exam should be conducted every 2 years for people over 40.

Generally speaking, except for the mammogram and Pap test, there shouldn't be any difference in the examination schedule for men or women after the age of 40. But for women under 40, it's not as important to have regular stress testing since the incidence of coronary disease is much less in this age category for women than it is for men.

Many people aren't used to the idea of going to the doctor as often as I'm suggesting when they are well. In fact, some put off going for as long as they can even when they are very sick. But the sense of tranquillity that can come from knowing that you're in good health and doing all you can to stay that way far outweighs the expense, minor inconvenience, and discomfort of a few hours in the doctor's office.

To help you evaluate whether or not the exams you're now getting are thorough enough, you might want to use the following twenty-two points, which represent the twenty-two phases of a complete physical exam at the Aerobics Center, as a checklist. Although each of these phases is important, it's not necessary that they be conducted in any particular order.

Phase 1: Before the actual exam begins, the patient should be required to fill out a comprehensive health history. This includes a description of how the patient is feeling now, his or her personal health history of diseases or operations, and any family history of disease. For instance, he or she should note if a parent suffered a heart attack, and at what age, to alert the examining doctor to any family tendency toward coronary disease.

Also, it's helpful to fill out a questionnaire about eating habits, including types of foods typically eaten, quantities, vitamins, drinking habits, and other relevant information. Then, a qualified nutritionist may evaluate this diet and make suggestions in light of the final results of the exam.

Phase 2: The actual physical inspection of the patient starts with routine measurements and observations. These include height, weight, percentage of body fat, blood pressure, pulse rate, chest and waist measurements, and bone size.

These measurements, taken as a whole, help us determine a person's level of fitness. Life insurance companies often require such a physical before giving a person a policy. Did you ever wonder why they want waist and chest measurements? One reason is that they have learned from experience that in a man, for every inch his stomach measurement exceeds his chest size, 2 years can be subtracted from his expected life span.

Body fat percentage, as we saw in an earlier chapter, is determined in a variety of ways—skinfolds, using a caliperlike instrument to pinch the outside fat; underwater measurements to determine specific gravity; total body volumetric determinations; and ultrasonic measurement of fat thickness. You'll recall that a normal body fat for males is less than 19 percent, and normal athletic weight is less than 15 percent. For women, the normal body fat should be less than 22 percent, or 18 percent for athletic women.

Phase 3: The doctor should examine your head and neck to see that they are of normal size and show no signs of swelling in the lymph nodes—a condition which could indicate a variety of health problems. Pulse beat in the carotid arteries of the neck is also checked to make sure it's strong, regular, and without unusual sounds. Next, I always examine the thyroid gland simply by feeling it to see that it's of normal size and that no nodules, or lumps, can be felt.

Some people may get a little uneasy about being prodded, poked, or felt, but this aspect of the exam can be an extremely effective and safe method of finding masses of tissue that shouldn't be there. Over the past 10 years, I've discovered a number of nodules, or tissue masses, in the thyroid. While they are more common in women than in men, the ones in women are usually benign and represent no danger. But the ones found in men are often malignant, and early discovery is essential for effective treatment.

For example, as I mentioned before, when we first started physical screening at our clinic about 10 years ago, a 36-year-old man was found to have a nodule on his thyroid gland, which was completely unknown to him. We did a radioactive scan of the gland to see if the nodule was "hot" or "cold." A cold nodule is possibly malignant and needs to be removed surgically.

As it turned out, the scan showed the nodule was cold, and it was removed. It proved to be malignant, but because it was taken out at the earliest stage of development, it did not have a chance to spread all over the body. Because that man had undergone a comprehensive preventive examination, he is alive today!

Phase 4: The next thing to check is the eyes. They are truly the body's windows and allow the examining doctor to see much about your state of health. For example, it's possible, by looking into the eyes, to see indications of high blood pressure. Or we may see evidence of eye diseases that may seriously impair the vision. There may even be signs of brain tumors or diabetes.

As a part of the examination, the accommodation of the eyes to changes in light and distance should be checked, and the lens evaluated for cataracts. Early changes that can occur in the back of the eyes sometimes warn of more serious problems.

In a routine exam of a 30-year-old man, I discovered that he had a complete loss of vision in one half of his eye—and he didn't even know it! By testing his peripheral or field of vision, I detected the problem almost immediately. Both of us were surprised to find that he couldn't see my finger until it got all the way over to the center of his face.

Upon further examination, I discovered that part of his retina had separated, and he was referred to a retinal specialist for laser treatment. The separation or tear in the retina was very close to the macula—the most sensitive part of the eye for vision. Had the tear gone just a little farther, this man probably would have been totally blind in that eye. Fortunately, though, we were able to catch this condition early enough, the problem was treated, and his vision was saved.

Another important eye test is to check the internal eye pressure—which is called the "intraocular tension"—to see that it's within normal limits. By using a little device that painlessly aims puffs of air at the eye, a doctor or technician can determine whether you may be developing glaucoma without even knowing what is happening. In fact, most people who do have glaucoma in its early stages often aren't aware of it because the symptoms are so minor—such as seeing vague halos around lights or suffering a partial, almost imperceptible change in vision called "tunnel vision."

But most people wait too long to get their eyes checked, and so they don't realize they are developing glaucoma until it's too late. As a result, they may suffer irreversible damage, which can deteriorate into complete blindness. The tragedy of this is that by early detection, glaucoma is easily treated. All you have to do is put drops in your eyes. During the past 10 years, we've screened more than 22,000 people in this way, and we've sent hundreds to ophthalmologists for further diagnostic studies.

Phase 5: Lymph nodes throughout the body are carefully palpated during this phase of the exam. The key areas of the body to focus on are the neck, underarms, and groin. Whenever we find a lymph node that is unusually firm or that hadn't previously been in the spot where we've found it, we take it out and examine it. These little kernels under the skin often give us a good clue to what's happening elsewhere in your body, and they can be an excellent indicator of early malignancy.

One time when I was undergoing an annual exam, the physician noticed a firm lump that had developed in the back of my neck. It could have been a cyst, which is common and not dangerous, or it could have been a lymph node.

If the lump was a lymph node, that might have meant that a malignancy had developed somewhere in my body and would have required immediate treatment. So you can imagine my delight when the surgeon removed it in a simple operation and found it was only a benign cyst. Even if it had been a malignant node, my chances would have been better because the disease would have been diagnosed at an early stage.

Phase 6: Your physician can often pick up signs of emphysema, asthma, or even such infectious diseases as tuberculosis simply by listening to your chest with a stethoscope. This exam causes no discomfort at all, and it can help ward off serious disease.

In addition to listening to the lungs, he or she will also listen to the heart to make sure the beat sounds regular and normal. We often find sounds that aren't necessarily considered normal, but when we check them against your overall fitness and other factors in your exam, we can often rule out any serious problem. Most abnormal sounds really are of little clinical significance. But because some require corrective treatment, this is a very important phase of your physical.

For questionable heart sounds, your physician may request an echocardiogram or ultrasonic examination. This is a painless, noninvasive examination of the heart that can determine the extent of the abnormality of heart valves; measure the thickness of the heart muscles; and even determine the internal volume of the heart. It is a very valuable diagnostic tool which eventually may become a part of a routine cardiovascular examination.

Phase 7: Next, the doctor will feel your abdominal area, including the liver. Often, an enlargement of the liver indicates cirrhosis, though there are some other infections which can cause a swelling to develop. Cancers which have developed in other parts of the body sometimes show up in the liver as well, and their presence can often be detected simply by feeling for lumps on the liver's surface.

On the other side of the body, we feel the spleen to see if it's normal or enlarged. If it is enlarged, that would indicate another range of possibilities that would have to be checked.

About 7 years ago, a man in his early forties came to the clinic, and even though he didn't suspect any problems, as part of his complete exam I found a suspicious mass in his lower abdomen. It could have been a full bladder, so I asked him to void and come back to the examining room. But when he was reexamined, the mass was still present.

An X ray was ordered which confirmed the presence of a mass of some kind, so he was referred to his personal physician for follow-up studies. As a result, the man found himself in a hospital operating room within 36 hours. The mass turned out to be a severe malignancy the size of a grapefruit. Luckily, it was caught early, and had not spread to other parts of his body. The mass was removed, and the man recovered remarkably well.

But that's not the end of the story. We followed this man's case closely for the next several years because this type of cancer is notorious for flaring up again in other parts of the body. There was no problem until 6 years later, when an ultrasound examination of the abdomen revealed a lemon-sized cyst in his liver.

We assumed that this cyst was related to the previous disease because it has a history of spreading to the liver. Sure enough, it was malignant, but even this lesion was removed successfully by surgery. The man is now back at work and doing remarkably well. There are no signs that the disease has spread to any other parts of the body, and we attribute this to early diagnosis. In fact, I'm sure there is no way this man would be alive today if that first cancerous mass hadn't been picked up at the time that it was.

The abdominal sonogram mentioned above is becoming popular with diagnosticians. This is an entirely painless exam with no potentially dangerous radiation such as that which occurs with extensive X-ray studies of the abdomen. It consists of placing an ultrasonic probe on the abdomen. Then, by careful direction of ultrasonic rays, the various organs can be identified and screened for abnormalities.

The test includes the liver, gall bladder, spleen, kidneys, and pancreas. Masses within the abdomen can be seen, and even the exact dimensions of the abdominal aorta, or artery, can be determined. In this way, an aneurysm or other problem with this artery can be identified early and corrected before it might rupture. In the near future, we'll probably add abdominal sonography to our routine exams for people over 40, most likely at 2-year intervals.

Phase 8: The next procedure is the rectal examination, which also includes a prostate examination for men. While many people tend to avoid this, the only simple way to detect a malignancy in the prostate is by means of digital (finger) examination. When there is a malignancy, the doctor feels a small nodule, and then refers the patient to a urologist for a needle biopsy for confirmation.

It's quite possible to take corrective action that can be life-saving in some of these early malignancies. So men over 60 should be checked regularly for this problem, because it's at this age that prostate malignancies increase in frequency. In fact, cancers of the prostate account for 17 percent of all cancers, and in men that makes them second only to lung cancer in their incidence of occurrence. But with early detection, they can be treated successfully.

During the past 3 years, there have been articles in newspapers and magazines calling our attention to a blood test described as the "male PAP test." The letters "PAP" in this instance stand for "prostatic acid phosphatase," and this test has been used for years as a means of determining the spread of prostatic cancer.

As a mass screening method, however, it has not been effective. I can recall a 70-year-old gentleman who, judging from a rectal prostate examination, had a classic malignancy. The diagnosis was confirmed by needle biopsy and the prostate later was removed surgically. Yet at no time was the male PAP test abnormal, even though we tested him several times. So the annual rectal exam is still the most reliable method for early detection of cancer of the prostate.

Next, it's important to be quite thorough with the additional examinations of the bowels and colon because many serious cancers begin there—and they can be nipped in the bud if they are caught early enough. A popular and inexpensive screen for cancer of the colon is called hemocult testing. Over 3 days, the patient is asked to take a specimen of stool and apply it to a paper. Then, he or she sends all three specimens to the laboratory for evaluation. In a few seconds, the stool can be tested for blood—a common early sign of a cancer somewhere in the lower intestines.

It is estimated that 55 percent of all bowel cancers can be diagnosed in this way, at a stage when most are correctable. And remember: Of the nearly 60,000 deaths from cancer of the colon and rectum that occur each year, it is estimated that up to 90 percent could be prevented if the diagnosis could be made early.

Then, there is the exam that many people seem to fear most—the all-important sigmoidoscopic procedure. Sometimes called "the silver bullet," the device used in this exam is an inflexible, metal tube that is inserted 25 centimeters (about 9¾ inches) into the intestine to allow the physician to view the walls of the upper and lower colon.

This test is given to everyone at our clinic who is over 40 years of age at 2-year intervals to help detect any polyps or early malignancies. It's believed that between 50 and 80 percent of all cancers in the colon can be detected by this procedure, usually at a stage in which complete cure is possible. As a matter of fact, the American Cancer Society says that if every person over 40 without symptoms of cancer had this exam performed every 1 to 2 years, 27,000 lives could be saved annually! Indeed, cancers in this area account for 14 percent of all cancers in men and 15 percent in women, and represent the most common cancer known to mankind.

Admittedly, the sigmoidoscopic exam is a mildly uncomfortable procedure. But I want to emphasize the "mildly" because it's certainly not painful, and the anticipation is usually much worse than the exam itself.

Phase 9: In the 1930s, cancer of the cervix was the number one cause of malignant death in American women. In 1981, it had dropped to number five. What accounted for this change? Better personal hygiene, and most important, the annual pelvic examination and Pap test.

Without question, I feel that the annual test in women, beginning in their childbearing years, is very valuable. Yes, this is a debatable statement in that some physicians feel that "the annual Pap smear does not reveal enough cancers to be worth the price." Yet the Pap smear is only the tip of the medical iceberg.

The annual visit to the gynecologist can be valuable in many ways. For example, that is the time when the nurse or physician can ask essential questions concerning major diseases. Also, the patient learns the importance of vaginal, rectal, or urinary bleeding; the coughing up of blood; hoarseness; or a mass in the breast or elsewhere in the body. In addition, the woman can learn about diet, fiber, sugar, salt content of foods, supplemental vitamins and minerals.

So there is considerable benefit in addition to the exam itself. Preventive medicine and early detection of disease are the ultimate goals, and the annual pelvic exam and Pap smear are convenient mechanisms for achieving this.

Phase 10: Next, it's important to check the health of the person's bone structure and musculature. In this phase of your exam, your doctor will examine the range of motion in your limbs to see whether there is any weakness, restriction of movement, or other abnormality. If there is, he or she will try to determine why. For instance, in examining skeletal structure, we often find people are flat-footed or slightly bow-legged. While these are not life-threatening conditions, people with these characteristics are more likely to develop foot and ankle problems when they jog.

Phase 11: Skin examinations frequently turn up skin lesions and minor malignancies that are often the result of too much sun. An alert physician usually is able to pick these up at a very early stage because they are easily identifiable. In many cases, they are treated rapidly and effectively in a doctor's office.

Phase 12: It's also important to check the central nervous system to screen the person for neurological problems and brain tumors. Reflex tests often are the key.

For instance, one of the most interesting reflexes we check is the ankle. Often, if there is a difference in the reflex response of one ankle as compared with the other, this may indicate a disc problem in the back. The absent ankle reflex plus an area of numbness on the lower leg or foot is a classic sign of disc disease, regardless of whether or not a person has other symptoms.

People are sometimes bewildered when their doctor asks them to assume various positions, such as standing with their feet together and their eyes closed. But the way people respond to tests while in these positions provides clues as to how the various parts of the brain function.

Their response can signal the presence of any disorders such as tumors.

Phase 13: Laboratory analyses of the blood and urine are extremely helpful indicators of your body's state of balance.

Many clinics use a test called the SMAC-20, which refers to the type of machine used in the blood analysis. There are twenty different blood studies done, in addition to separate tests for triglycerides and various types of cholesterol, including HDLs.

At this point, you should recall how important the ratio of total cholesterol to HDL cholesterol is in predicting your likelihood of developing hardening of the arteries. Remember: the ratio must be less than 5.0 and preferably less than 4.5 in men; and less than 4.0 and preferably less than 3.5 in women (see Chapter 4).

A thorough check-up will include examination of a urine specimen to make sure there are no suspicious levels of protein or glucose that could signal diabetes or kidney disorders. Also, the blood should be checked for syphilis. It's astonishing how often people have syphilis without ever suspecting it. If we find a patient does have this venereal disease, we tend to look more closely for heart and blood vessel problems that often accompany it.

During these laboratory procedures, there should be a test to see if there are elevated levels of uric acid, which is associated with gout. Potassium levels, if they are too low, can cause muscle cramping and may even result in an abnormal EKG during stress testing. In addition, salt content, magnesium, and calcium are checked to see if they could be tied in with potential heart problems.

So there are a variety of problems that can be detected through the blood, and a thorough screening can alert the doctor to the possibility of anemia, leukemia, diabetes, cirrhosis of the liver, and a host of other ailments. Blood studies aren't considered conclusive, however, and so they must be followed up with other tests if anything abnormal comes back in the laboratory analysis. But early detection is the key to maintaining a healthy balance, and the blood and urine tests can contribute a great deal to keeping you in good condition by alerting your doctor to early signals of imbalance.

Phase 14: In addition to a physical inspection of the eyes, your vision and hearing should be checked to see if they need to be corrected through glasses or hearing aids.

A 26-year-old accountant who tired easily when reading thought that he might need glasses. But when he went for an eye exam, the doctor found that he had a "converging" problem: His eyes had difficulty centering on an object. His eye problem might have become progressively worse if it hadn't been detected early. But he was helped by therapy which strengthened his eye muscles, and he may avoid or at least delay the need for glasses.

Phase 15: A spirometry test is next on our list. This is a test for pulmonary, or lung, functions, in which you take a deep breath and blow it all out into a special canister. We check both the total amount of air expelled (vital capacity) and also the rapidity with which you do it (timed vital capacity). Tests of this type are useful for detecting emphysema, and also obstructions in the lungs or throat.

You should be able to blow out at least 75 percent of the air in your lungs in the first second, though this capacity differs according to age. This test for "vital capacity" is very important since, according to some studies, it is the best predictor of longevity. If timed vital capacity is less than predicted, it may indicate asthma, bronchitis or perhaps emphysema. If any of these problems are indicated, the test may be used as a good motivator to encourage someone to stop smoking.

Phase 16: Also, we strongly recommend that our patients over 40 have a barium enema, which involves injecting a barium solution into the bowels through the rectum so that X rays can be taken to check the entire intestinal system more thoroughly. It's necessary to clear your bowels through a series of small enemas during the 24 hours preceding this test, but this relatively mild discomfort is well worth the benefits of the test in detecting early cancer.

In addition to the barium enema, we give an "upper GI series" in which the patient drinks a nearly tasteless, milkshake-type liquid barium concoction. This enables us to do X rays on the stomach and esophagus, and can help in detection of abnormalities like ulcers. These examinations are repeated only at 4-year intervals.

Phase 17: Chest X rays should be performed to check the heart, lungs, and other organs. This procedure helps the doctor ascertain whether these parts of the body are within normal size limits and are otherwise in good shape.

Phase 18: The next part of the exam, which is perhaps the most important in evaluating your heart and cardiovascular fitness, is the treadmill stress test.

This test has come into increasing use in recent years, but it's being misused too often by doctors who seem to be solely concerned with the electrocardiographic results of the test. Consequently, these physicians are likely to make recommendations for bypass surgery which may be unnecessary.

Instead of focusing exclusively on the abnormalities of the electro-cardiogram, which are, of course, important, I believe in putting a big emphasis as well on other factors, such as the *time* the person can stay on the treadmill. This measure of fitness is one of the most sensitive tools we now have to predict whether or not disease is going to occur.

In our 10 years of testing more than 43,000 people on treadmills at the Aerobics Center, we found 126 patients who subsequently had a major coronary attack or had serious problems which led to surgery. But the illnesses and deaths of those 126 were of great concern to us. So we've studied their cases and discovered the following:

- Some had high blood sugar;
- One out of four had an abnormal resting EKG;
- One third smoked at the time of their visit;
- Many showed a relatively high level of triglycerides and cholesterol;
- Almost three-quarters showed abnormal stress electrocardiograms;
- A majority of the people who died were overweight (i.e., the men had more than 19 percent body fat, the women had more than 22 percent).

But in addition to these factors, there was one other that was the most reliable predictor of all of their upcoming heart attacks—and that was *the time they walked on the treadmill.*

The treadmill test I prefer is called the Balke protocol. This approach involves increasing elevation of the treadmill every minute, with the speed remaining constant so that the workload on the patient goes up gradually. We've established a minimum standard for the average middle-aged patient of walking 15 minutes or longer on the treadmill, which is roughly equivalent to running 2 miles in 20 minutes. This is the first threshold of fitness beyond which there appears to be some protection from coronary heart disease. For more detailed levels of fitness adjusted to age and sex, see the Definition of Fitness Categories for Males and Females charts in the Appendix.

Unless you have reached this minimum fitness level, it doesn't appear that you have any protection from coronary disease. One hundred and one of the 126 patients who had the major heart problems mentioned earlier were unable to walk 15 minutes on the Balke treadmill test.

In another study performed at Duke University Medical Center, patients complaining of chest pain were given coronary arteriograms (pictures taken of their blood vessels by injecting a dye into the blood system), and in addition were given treadmill stress tests. Of the 1,200 patients involved, 744 were proven by coronary arteriography to have obstructive coronary disease, or hardening of the arteries, in one or more vessels. Of those 744 patients, the ones who were able to walk 15 minutes or more on the Balke treadmill test or its equivalent on the Bruce test, showed a remarkable survival rate of 98 percent over the next 3 years.

On the other hand, those who could walk only 7 minutes or less (level one on the Bruce test) were far less fortunate: In the next 2 years,

41 percent died. Both groups had proven coronary artery disease; the only difference between them was their level of fitness. The most logical conclusion I draw from all this is that those who could walk the longest on the treadmill were in the best shape and this fact afforded them some protection from coronary heart disease.

But because there are so many ways to give treadmill stress tests, and because these tests are sometimes misused, how can you know if the test you take is valid and safe?

Here are a number of factors to keep in mind:

Patients should be selected carefully for the tests. Not all people can be stress-tested. Those with severe chest pain should never be tested, especially if the pain is getting worse. So if your chest hurts, stay off the treadmill, or at least ask for a second medical opinion before you agree to a test. There are several absolute contraindications to stress testing.

Proper treadmill techniques should be used. The technique most commonly used in this country is known as the Bruce protocol, which consists of increasing both the speed and the incline of the treadmill every 3 minutes. The other popular technique, mentioned earlier, is the Balke protocol, which takes about twice as long to perform. On the other hand, the Balke approach allows more of a warm-up and for that reason it may be a safer test. Yet this point hasn't been proven by any studies: It's just a personal assumption I'm making. In any case either test can be used effectively.

The test should begin gradually to warm the patient's body up, and it should wind down gradually, with a 3- to 5-minute cool-down period. At the beginning and end of the test, patients are asked to grab onto the bar for safety, but they are discouraged from holding on during the test. It is impossible to quantify levels of fitness if the subject is holding onto the bar throughout the test because this significantly decreases the energy expended.

At least seven electrodes should be attached to the chest for adequate monitoring. One young doctor told me that he stopped stress testing because one of his patients almost died. It seems that, in addition to other things he was doing wrong, this physician was using only three electrodes for monitoring.

We use twelve electrodes or wires attached to the body to monitor fifteen leads, in order to obtain a complete picture of what's happening to the heart during the test. If you use only a three-lead system, as the young doctor did, you'll miss about 22 percent of the abnormal responses that would be diagnosed with more leads. The absolute minimum number of electrodes for adequate monitoring is seven.

In those cases in which there is a strong suspicion of coronary artery obstruction, additional testing may be necessary, particularly if coronary artery bypass surgery is contemplated. In such cases, the first step might be a thalium scan which consists of injecting a radioactive material into the blood and then scanning it as it goes through the heart. This is another rather simple screening test, and if it's abnormal, it may be followed by a coronary arteriogram. A coronary arteriogram is always necessary before bypass surgery to determine the extent and location of the coronary artery obstructions and whether or not bypass surgery is a viable option.

The patient should be exercised to the point he or she approaches his or her predicted maximum heart rate. Another misconception by many who administer the stress test is that the patient should be taken to a heart rate that is no more than 85 percent of his or her predicted maximum rate. In contrast, our studies have shown that at least a third of the abnormalities would have been missed if we had stopped at this point. Also, if the test is terminated too soon, this may give the patient a false sense of security.

Some doctors feel that taking the patient close to his or her maximum heart rate increases the likelihood of a heart attack, but we've found that this isn't true. As I've mentioned elsewhere, we've conducted more than 43,000 maximum performance stress tests in more than a decade, and we've never had a death during stress testing. If done properly by competent personnel, treadmill stress testing can be quite safe.

Finally, physicians and technicians administering the stress test must be adequately trained. Too often, I've seen physicians, business executives, or attorneys buy a treadmill, put it into their offices and then suddenly assume they're experts on stress testing. I recommend that physicians go through additional training to be qualified to perform a safe, sensitive treadmill stress test.

To increase sensitivity, several baseline electrocardiograms must be taken prior to beginning the treadmill phase of the test. Complete electrocardiograms should be taken at rest in the supine position, after a few seconds of standing, and certainly after 30 seconds of hyperventilation (breathing rapidly). At the conclusion of the active phase of the test, the subject should cool down for 3 to 5 minutes, and then additional monitoring in the supine position should occur for another 5 to 10 minutes. In this way, accuracy of testing can be increased.

Phase 19: Special strength and flexibility tests can often pinpoint muscular or other physical problems. For example, one man who scored in the superior category on the treadmill stress test was found to have a weakness in the muscles at the back of his thighs. We determined that this weakness was contributing to periodic lower back pains he was experiencing, and a set of corrective exercises helped him overcome that problem.

Phase 20: A dental exam is a "must" if you hope to monitor adequately your movement toward total well-being. In our case, a visit to our staff dentist often proves to be one of the most important for many patients. There are several reasons that this check-up is so important:

Self-image. All you have to do is take any magazine, find an attractive, smiling model in any ad, and blacken in one of the teeth with a pencil. This will totally change the way you perceive that person, and it would obviously change that person's image about himself or herself. It's certainly not necessary that your teeth fall out or become unattractive as you get older, and that's part of what a regular dental exam is all about.

Headaches. It's been estimated that a high percentage of all tension headaches are probably caused by a bad bite. About 60 percent to 85 percent of all people have a bad bite—or a condition where their teeth come together improperly or unevenly when the mouth is closed. But some are worse than others, and it's in the worst cases that headaches may occur.

For example, one woman who came to see our staff dentist had been having headaches all her life, and she thought they were migraines. When she woke up with one of these headaches, she'd literally get sick and be unable to go to work.

After spending several thousand dollars to have brain scans done in an effort to find out if there was some neurological problem, she finally began to wonder if the problem could be her teeth. Sure enough, when our dentist examined her, he found her bite to be off. When this problem was corrected through a series of simple procedures, including the temporary insertion of an artificial bite, her chewing muscles relaxed and she was able to sleep through the entire night without awakening with a headache. Finally, through a simple dental procedure which involved grinding down the high spots on her teeth on one side of her mouth, her problem was corrected.

Another important part of the dental exam is the laryngoscopic exam, in which an instrument is placed in the back of the throat to enable the doctor to see the vocal cords. This painless procedure is very important in detecting cancer of the larynx. Just as cigarette smokers have a tenfold increase in risk of cancer of the lungs over the nonsmoker, they also have a tenfold increase in risk of cancer of the larynx. With the laryngoscope, the dentist or physician can see if there are any nodules developing on the vocal cords, and if there are, they need to be removed surgically.

Phase 21: I believe a psychological examination is an important part of a comprehensive examination and should be conducted at least once. From this test, a person can get some idea of his or her psychological makeup, anxieties, and frustrations, and how much stress is present in his or her life and how well it is being handled. As you know, stress is beginning to be regarded as an important risk factor in heart disease, cancer, and other maladies. So the better you manage that stress—through spiritual and psychological techniques, exercise, and proper rest—the less your chances will be of suffering serious physical problems.

Phase 22: This last phase of your examination procedure focuses on a meeting between the patient and the doctor to go over the results and evaluation of the entire medical exam. This is the very important educational and motivational part of the exam. As a part of this "debriefing," we present the patient with his or her coronary risk profile chart, examples of which are included in the Appendix at the back of this book. By taking such things as performance on the stress test, level of cholesterol and HDLs in the blood, family history of heart disease, and percentage of body fat, it is possible to predict accurately the patient's likelihood of developing heart problems. And at this stage, the patient and his or her physician can take corrective action which may be very important, even life-saving.

So these are the twenty-two different components in a complete medical exam. I'm convinced that each of them is quite important in helping you to monitor the total balance in your body—the balance on which your goal of total well-being so heavily depends. The entire examination should only take a day to a day and a half, and the benefits you'll derive from knowing what may be wrong with you and how to correct it are virtually limitless.

Indeed, a regular physical can contribute significantly to your long life, as well. But there are other factors which will contribute even more, and that's the final topic I'd like to explore with you.

13

Total Well-Being and Your Future

have told audiences all over the world, "Biblically, our bodies are designed to last us 120 years. The reason they don't is not because of a design deficiency, but because of the way we treat our bodies."

Furthermore, I am convinced that what we have been taught about physiological aging is probably not completely correct. So many changes that we see in our bodies which may be attributed to aging are in reality not physiological responses but rather "adaptive responses." What I mean by this is that the reason our bodies deteriorate rapidly as we grow older is not so much that we are growing older, as it is that we are doing less as we grow older.

Almost daily, I am surprised and delighted to see the performances of older people. Even 10 years ago, some of the performances I've observed more recently would not have been considered a possibility. Let me give you an example:

In the 1981 Tyler Cup (a corporate track meet held each year at the Aerobics Center in Dallas), one of our participants was very disappointed because for the first time in 5 years, he was unable to run the 2.0 miles in less than 16:00 minutes. His time was 16:10.

What was so unusual about that? Nothing, except for the fact that this active chairman of the board of a large corporation was 81 years of age.

So remember: Our bodies don't have to age as rapidly as they do. Who determines how fast they age? You do! And here are the three main things, mostly likely in this order, that accelerate the aging process:

- Cigarette smoking
- Inactivity
- Obesity

If you wish to slow down the aging process in your own life, I am convinced that you must eliminate all three of these factors.

Throughout this book I've talked at great length about the harmful effects of obesity and inactivity, and I've given guidelines about how to change these enemies of good health. But I've said little, if anything, about what is probably the worst health hazard in America today—cigarette smoking! So now, I want to discuss at some length why I feel so strongly that the control of cigarette smoking is mandatory for total well-being.

A recent report on smoking and health released by the Surgeon

General of the U.S. Public Health Service stated that in 1982, we could expect approximately 400,000 deaths in some way related to the use of tobacco—through lung cancer, bronchitis, emphysema, and heart disease. In 90 percent of the estimated 90,000 deaths from lung cancer, there is a history of tobacco usage. Not only are cigarette smokers ten times more likely to die of lung cancer than nonsmokers, but they are ten times as likely to die of cancer of the larynx, five times as likely to die of cancer of the esophagus, twice as likely to die of cancer of the pancreas, and twice as likely to die of cancer of the bladder.

If you smoke a pipe or cigar, you are less likely to have a problem unless you inhale, but if you do inhale, there is even a greater chance of your developing problems.

So how can you go about cutting out the cigarette habit? I think the best way to tackle this question is first to consider some of the excuses we all hear with great regularity.

Excuse #1: "I've been smoking so long that stopping now wouldn't do any good." There is evidence that by cutting out smoking entirely, right now, a person can cut his or her risk for having a heart attack down to the level of the nonsmoker in as short a period of time as 10 to 12 weeks. The damage to your lungs may still be present, but at least your coronary risk profile will show a dramatic improvement. And there are six times as many people who die of heart attacks each year as die of lung cancer.

Excuse #2: "Women don't have to worry as much as men about the danger of tobacco." New evidence dispels any myths about protection against lung cancer in women who smoke. As the rate of smoking has increased among women in recent years, so has the incidence of the disease. In fact, it's likely that by 1983 or 1984, lung cancer and not breast cancer will be the leading cause of malignant death among American women. There is an epidemic of lung cancer deaths among women because they have now been smoking long enough to have the same problem as men. Remember: It takes about 20 years for a lung cancer to develop, and only recently have enough women been smoking long enough to have a problem.

The effects of smoking are especially insidious for pregnant women. Smoking has been linked to a higher rate of spontaneous abortions and to a greater possibility of infants of low birth weight. Some studies have implied that there is a possible relationship between mental retardation in the child and heavy cigarette smoking by the mother during pregnancy.

As for heart trouble, fully 75 percent of the heart attacks suffered by otherwise healthy women under the age of 50 have been shown in one study to be related to cigarette smoking.

Excuse #3: "I only smoke a half a pack a day. That can't harm me." The evidence tells a different story. In a study of women smokers, just 25 cigarettes a day increased the risk of heart attacks by 21 times over nonsmokers. Smoking 14 to 25 cigarettes a day increased the risk by 14 times; and one to 14 cigarettes results in a fourfold increase in risk over nonsmokers.

Excuse #4: "I don't smoke. I just chew tobacco." Don't think for a minute that it's just the smoke that's harmful. There has been a phenomenal increase in the use of "smokeless" tobacco, especially among teenagers who believe they can avoid the dangers of inhaled tar and nicotine. But snuff and chewing tobacco still contain nicotine, which can be absorbed into the body through nasal membranes and the lining of the mouth.

And there are some common problems associated with smokeless tobacco that aren't found in ordinary cigarettes. One is the leatherlike appearance within the cheek, which is called leukoplakia and can lead to oral cancer. About 24,000 new cases are discovered each year. Another problem is excessive wear on the teeth, and the gums tend to recede from the teeth in those areas where the tobacco is held in the mouth. The exposed roots then become more susceptible to decay, and also more sensitive to heat, cold, foods, and chemicals.

Even snuff dipping can give the heart rate and blood pressure a kick. Twenty male athlete volunteers abstained from tobacco use for 72 hours to allow baseline EKG and blood pressure measures to be made. Then, a 2.5-gram pinch of oral tobacco was placed in each man's mouth. Within 20 minutes, the heart rates increased from 69 to 88 beats per minute. Mean blood pressure values rose from 118/72 to 126/78. Both functions returned to their original levels after the tobacco was removed.

Other studies have shown that side effects of oral tobacco use may include mouth lesions, nausea, dizziness, hiccoughs, and mouth and throat irritation.

Unfortunately, since 1971 there has been an enormous increase in the dollars spent to advertise smokeless tobacco. This development has been accompanied by two big problems: (1) a 33 percent increase in the production of smokeless tobacco; and (2) a corresponding increase in the mouth and throat cancer rates.

None of this sounds much like total well-being, does it? The solution is just to keep away from this smokeless tobacco.

Excuse #5: "I don't smoke." Ironically, even though this is the best excuse, it still doesn't always completely protect you.

There is a growing body of evidence that suggests that by merely inhaling the smoke from another person's cigarette you may be subjecting yourself to an increased risk of various diseases. One study of this "sidestream" smoke revealed that cancer-causing tars were still present, along with nicotine which has been associated with heart disease.

In one recent study in the *New England Journal of Medicine*, non-smokers who worked daily in a smoke-filled office, had a measurable decrease in lung functions, even though many had never smoked in their lives. Although the evidence still isn't completely in on this subject, what we do know is that some people are markedly affected by sidestream smoke and should avoid it whenever possible. They include:

- People who are allergic to tobacco smoke;
- People with chronic heart or lung disease;
- Some contact lens wearers who have an allergy to tobacco smoke which results in watery and itching eyes;
- Children and infants.

On this last point, it's been well documented that if a mother smokes, her children are more likely to be admitted to the hospital with bronchitis or pneumonia. And the kids are twice as likely to be admitted if both parents smoke.

Now, here are a few tips which we have found helpful from our experiences at the Aerobics Center:

- Stop all at once. Don't just taper off.
- Quit when you aren't under a lot of stress or tension. In other words, don't try to break the habit when you've just lost your job or when you are going through a divorce.
- Involve someone else in your effort to stop—misery loves company!
- Drink six to eight glasses of water a day, and especially drink water or fruit juice when your craving for a cigarette reaches a level where you think you can't resist.
- Get at least 7 to 8 hours of sleep each night during the time you're breaking the habit.
- Avoid alcoholic beverages during this time as well. Also, drink only noncaffeinated beverages—no coffee, tea, or cola drinks. It's easy to move from one habit to another when you're in this transition phase.
- Exercise. After meals, get outside and walk briskly and breathe deeply for 15 to 30 minutes.
- Cut out spices and rich desserts. Eat all you want at regular meal hours in the way of fruit, grains, vegetables, and nuts. But snack only on carrots or celery sticks. When you break the cigarette habit, there is a tendency to replace cigarette smoking with food. (Yet, if you are at a normal body weight when you

quit smoking. to have a comparable risk as you have while smoking one pack of cigarettes per day, you would have to gain almost 100 pounds!)

- Find something else to occupy your hands and your mind.
- Join an organized quit-smoking program. Most of the recommendations in this chapter come from the 5-day quit-smoking plans as developed by the Seventh-Day Adventist Church. Without question, the Adventist program is one of the best available, and it's also very economical. The American Cancer Society has comparable organized plans, and so does the American Heart Association. Commercial programs available include Smokenders and Schick Laboratories.

For more information, you can get in touch with these and other such organizations at the following addresses:

1. American Cancer Society, 777 Third Avenue, New York, N.Y. 10017
2. American Heart Association, 7320 Greenville Avenue, Dallas, Texas 75231
3. American Lung Association, 1740 Broadway, New York, N.Y. 10019
4. General Headquarters, 5-Day Plan To Stop Smoking, Seventh-Day Adventist Church, Narcotics Education Division, 6840 Eastern Avenue, N.W., Washington, D.C. 20012
5. Office on Smoking and Health, U.S. Department of Health, Education and Welfare, Room 1-58, 5600 Fishers Land, Rockville, Maryland 20857
6. National Interagency Council on Smoking and Health, Room 1005, 291 Broadway, New York, N.Y. 10017
7. Schick Laboratories, 1901 Avenue of the Stars, Suite 1530, Los Angeles, Calif. 90067
8. Smokenders, 50 Washington St., Norwalk, Conn. 06854
9. Office of Cancer Communications, National Cancer Institute, National Institutes of Health, Bethesda, Md. 20205

With this discussion of smoking, you now have enough information to know how best to increase your chances of living a longer life. As I said at the beginning of this chapter, the three keys to greater longevity are (1) avoiding tobacco; (2) regular aerobic activity; and (3) keeping normal body weight. So now that you have the requisite knowledge to add years to your life, it's time to act upon it!

And you can indeed slow down the aging process. Although there is no such thing as a fountain of youth, which will completely halt or reverse aging, the rapid rate at which people age in this country simply isn't necessary. And if present preventive medicine trends continue, there's every reason to believe that by the year 2000, U.S. citizens should attain an average life span of 80 years. This may seem hard to believe right now, but it's a definite possibility.

As for you personally, if you follow all the guidelines of preventive medicine that we've been discussing—including not only the three keys to longevity but also all the elements of good diet, exercise, and physical exams—your possibilities could be even more dramatic. You may even be able to approach that proverbial 120-year maximum age for humans that I mentioned earlier. I myself believe that, if we balance our lives completely through physical and spiritual fitness, the ultimate age limit may well be that high.

CONCLUSION

By now, you can see that the quest for total well-being is a comprehensive, all-consuming, lifelong saga which can touch every habit and activity that is part of your existence. The great thing about this quest is that you don't have to wait for years or until you get too old to enjoy the process.

Total well-being is not like a retirement program, where you put your treasures away and then take them out to sustain you in your twilight years. A personal program of total well-being will certainly have a beneficial impact on your later years, but at the same time, you can enjoy it and revel in it right now, in the present moment.

One of the things that amazes me most about this notion of total well-being is that it's an ever-expanding concept in every immediate moment of our existence. Every time I think that maybe we've reached the limits of what proper diet and exercise can do, I'm setting myself up to be surprised—and pleasantly so, I might add.

For example, one of the things that has been impressing me most in recent years about the principles of balance that underlie total well-being is that they don't apply just to the young and the beautiful. Granted, if you're young and in reasonably good health, the ideas that have been discussed in this book will put you in top form and bestow on you a beauty and vigor that you wouldn't otherwise attain. But those who are older—or who are seriously handicapped—can also take full advantage of the principles of total well-being.

For example, in an article by Dr. Keith Johnsgard entitled "You're Never Too Old" in *Runner's World* magazine, runners in a Fifty-Plus Runners Association were asked what caused them to run. The responses offered a classic study in total well-being for the women, who averaged 55 years of age, and the men, who averaged 57:

- Many wanted to assume greater responsibility for their own health.
- Of the males, 13 percent said hypertension was the main thing that started them running.
- Half the women and a third of the men began running to reduce or control weight.
- One fourth of the women and one fifth of the men ran to find relief from depression or anxiety.
- Many also began an aerobic running program to find or affirm their own sense of personal identity.

Many of these responses sound familiar, don't they? The motivations for older people, as well as those who are much younger, center on maintaining a healthy, energetic body, an alert mind, and stable, tranquil emotions. And the motivations aren't much different for those who are handicapped.

In this regard, I'm reminded of a fellow named Harry Cordellos, whom I met many years ago while I was speaking in San Francisco. He was a classic product of a balanced aerobics program: He carefully watched his diet, controlled his weight, didn't smoke, and had recently run 10 miles in 63 minutes.

The unusual thing about Harry was that he was completely blind. When he ran, he had to keep on the right path by rubbing elbows with another runner.

A few weeks after I had met him, he wrote to me and said, "Dr. Cooper, I just wanted you to know that I entered and successfully completed my first marathon—The Golden Gate Marathon! I ran the 26 miles, 385 yards and only fell down twice!"

Harry went on to become the holder of the national record for the blind with a sub-3-hour marathon, and believe me, with his vibrant, energetic personality, he was one of the best advertisements for total well-being you could find. But like a lot of other handicapped people, he had some special problems arranging an adequate aerobic schedule. The main difficulty was that he continued to have trouble lining up running partners to accompany him in his races and his work-outs. But he so impressed some of the runners at our Aerobics Center that they chipped in to commission the design of a special treadmill for blind runners. Bob Parker, President of Pacer Industries, responded by building the treadmill. And thus, another step was taken to put total well-being through aerobic exercise within the reach of a handicapped group that faced difficulties participating in regular running because of a lack of partners.

Mike Levine is another person who has had to overcome a major handicap in order to run. I believe it was 1976 at the White Rock Marathon in Dallas when Mike and I first met. I was impressed with his running style since every step was a limp. Mike had cerebral palsy, and his right side had not fully developed. The right leg was at least 4 inches shorter than the left.

As I saw him warm up, I thought to myself, "There is no way he can complete a marathon, limping all the way."

Yet, he started with the group, and with unbelievable tenacity and determination he finished the 26.2 miles in a little more than 4 hours. At the conclusion of the race, I rushed over to congratulate him, admittedly impressed to the point of tears.

I asked, "Is this the first time you have completed a marathon?"

As long as I live, I will never forget his answer. He pulled that handicapped and fatigued body up to a position of attention, and with a sense of pride such as I have never heard before, he said, "No sir! This is my twenty-fourth marathon!"

What would you do if you had the problems of a Harry Cordellos or a Mike Levine? Would you give up, or continue in the same way to "glorify God in your body and in your spirit, which are His?"

To list all the amazing people I have met over the years or to acknowledge all the various groups and programs involved in active rehabilitation of the handicapped would be impossible. But it is possible to generalize about what the future most likely has in store for those diverse individuals who have embarked on the quest for total well-being: In every sense of the word, no matter who you are and what your age or special personal qualities, the balance you establish in your body now will lead inexorably to well-being in the future as well.

But of course, as we've seen already, the many benefits are not limited to the future. As far as your health is concerned, the future is only another dimension, a long-term result of what you're doing for yourself in a concrete way in the present. And a present state of physical and emotional equilibrium will mean greater tranquility, energy, intellectual capacity, and overall happiness for you in the exciting here-and-now.

I love to talk about the "now"—the present benefits—of preventive medicine because that is where the greatest interest lies. Of course, I can lecture to audiences for hours about their need to do something that will affect their *future* well-being; but that message just doesn't seem to get through. People instinctively feel that they have some divine protection and that they can continue to ignore the laws of well-being and not reap the consequences.

You see, fear is simply not a good, long-term motivator, because most of us can rationalize that "it will never happen to me." One of the reasons we can fool ourselves is that our rationalizations are often partially true: For some heavy-smoking, overweight, inactive people reading this book, "it" never will happen. In other words, they won't die young or suffer some debilitating, premature illness no matter how much they mistreat their bodies. But even though some will escape the physical consequences of poor diet and exercise habits, most of us won't. So for the average person who wants to increase his or her odds of living long and productively, it's important to begin a program of total well-being such as the one outlined in these pages, and then stick with it.

Yet, if the only reason you practice preventive medicine is to delay or reduce the possibility of having a heart attack or even to prolong life, you have missed the whole point of this book. The main reason to exercise and follow the concepts we've been discussing is that this approach will enhance your *present* sense of well-being, make you feel good, and give you a greater zest for life.

Whether you live one day longer is really not the ultimate goal. What *is* important is the quality of your life—a life that is happy, healthy, and productive. If you practice the *now* of total well-being, you can feel the best you have ever felt in your life in the near, not just the distant, future!

So let me encourage you to plan for a long and enjoyable life by living wisely and intensely each day through a balanced program of total well-being. For if you plan wisely for each day, the morrow will plan for itself.

APPENDIX

THE POINT SYSTEM

Walking/Running

Time (hr:min:sec)	Point Value	Time (hr:min:sec)	Point Value	Time (hr:min:sec)	Point Value
1.0 Mile		**1.1 Miles**		**1.2 Miles**	
over 20:01	0	over 33:01	0	over 36:01	0
20:00–15:01	1.0	33:00–22:01	0.1	36:00–24:01	0.2
15:00–12:01	2.0	22:00–16:31	1.2	24:00–18:01	1.4
12:00–10:01	3.0	16:30–13:13	2.3	18:00–14:25	2.6
10:00– 8:01	4.0	13:12–11:01	3.4	14:24–12:01	3.8
8:00– 6:41	5.0	11:00– 8:49	4.5	12:00– 9:37	5.0
6:40– 5:44	6.0	8:48– 7:21	5.6	9:36– 8:01	6.2
under 5:43	7.0	7:20– 6:19	6.7	8:00– 6:53	7.4
		under 6:18	7.8	under 6:52	8.6
1.3 Miles		**1.4 Miles**		**1.5 Miles**	
over 39:01	0	over 42:01	0	over 45:01	0
39:00–26:01	0.3	42:00–28:01	0.4	45:00–30:01	0.5
26:00–19:31	1.6	28:00–21:01	1.8	30:00–22:31	2.0
19:30–15:37	2.9	21:00–16:49	3.2	22:30–18:01	3.5
15:36–13:01	4.2	16:48–14:01	4.6	18:00–15:01	5.0
13:00–10:25	5.5	14:00–11:13	6.0	15:00–12:01	6.5
10:24– 8:41	6.8	11:12– 9:21	7.4	12:00–10:01	8.0
8:40– 7:27	8.1	9:20– 8:01	8.8	10:00– 8:35	9.5
under 7:26	9.4	under 8:00	10.2	under 8:34	11.0
1.6 Miles		**1.7 Miles**		**1.8 Miles**	
over 48:01	0	over 51:01	0	over 54:01	0
48:00–32:01	0.6	51:00–34:01	0.7	54:00–36:01	0.8
32:00–24:01	2.2	34:00–25:31	2.4	36:00–27:01	2.6
24:00–19:13	3.8	25:30–20:25	4.1	27:00–21:37	4.4
19:12–16:01	5.4	20:24–17:01	5.8	21:36–18:01	6.2
16:00–12:49	7.0	17:00–13:37	7.5	18:00–14:25	8.0
12:48–10:41	8.6	13:36–11:21	9.2	14:24–12:01	9.8
10:40– 9:10	10.2	11:20– 9:44	10.9	12:00–10:19	11.6
under 9:09	11.8	under 9:43	12.6	under 10:18	13.4

Walking/Running (continued)

Time (hr:min:sec)	Point Value	Time (hr:min:sec)	Point Value	Time (hr:min:sec)	Point Value
1.9 Miles		*2.0 Miles*		*2.1 Miles*	
over 57:01	0	over 40:01	1.0	over 42:01	1.1
57:00–38:01	0.9	40:00–30:01	3.0	42:00–31:31	3.2
38:00–28:31	2.8	30:00–24:01	5.0	31:30–25:13	5.3
28:30–22:49	4.7	24:00–20:01	7.0	25:12–21:01	7.4
22:48–19:01	6.6	20:00–16:01	9.0	21:00–16:49	9.5
19:00–15:13	8.5	16:00–13:21	11.0	16:48–14:01	11.6
15:12–12:41	10.4	13:20–11:27	13.0	14:00–12:01	13.7
12:40–10:53	12.3	under 11:26	15.0	under 12:00	15.8
under 10:52	14.2				
2.2 Miles		*2.3 Miles*		*2.4 Miles*	
over 44:01	1.2	over 46:01	1.3	over 48:01	1.4
44:00–33:01	3.4	46:00–34:31	3.6	48:00–36:01	3.8
33:00–26:25	5.6	34:30–27:37	5.9	36:00–28:49	6.2
26:24–22:01	7.8	27:36–23:01	8.2	28:48–24:01	8.6
22:00–17:37	10.0	23:00–18:25	10.5	24:00–19:13	11.0
17:36–14:41	12.2	18:24–15:21	12.8	19:12–16:01	13.4
14:40–12:35	14.4	15:20–13:10	15.1	16:00–13:44	15.8
under 12:34	16.6	under 13:09	17.4	under 13:43	18.2
2.5 Miles		*2.6 Miles*		*2.7 Miles*	
over 50:01	1.5	over 52:01	1.6	over 54:01	1.7
50:00–37:31	4.0	52:00–39:01	4.2	54:00–40:31	4.4
37:30–30:01	6.5	39:00–31:13	6.8	40:30–32:25	7.1
30:00–25:01	9.0	31:12–26:01	9.4	32:24–27:01	9.8
25:00–20:01	11.5	26:00–20:49	12.0	27:00–21:37	12.5
20:00–16:41	14.0	20:48–17:21	14.6	21:36–18:01	15.2
16:40–14:19	16.5	17:20–14:53	17.2	18:00–15:27	17.9
under 14:18	19.0	under 14:52	19.8	under 15:26	20.6
2.8 Miles		*2.9 Miles*		*3.0 Miles*	
over 56:01	1.8	over 58:01	1.9	over 1:00:01	2.0
56:00–42:01	4.6	58:00–43:31	4.8	1:00:00– 45:01	5.0
42:00–33:37	7.4	43:30–34:49	7.7	45:00– 36:01	8.0
33:36–28:01	10.2	34:48–29:01	10.6	36:00– 30:01	11.0
28:00–22:25	13.0	29:00–23:13	13.5	30:00– 24:01	14.0
22:24–18:41	15.8	23:12–19:21	16.4	24:00– 20:01	17.0
18:40–16:01	18.6	19:20–16:35	19.3	20:00– 17:10	20.0
under 16:00	21.4	under 16:34	22.2	under 17:09	23.0

Walking/Running (continued)

Time (hr:min:sec)	Point Value	Time (hr:min:sec)	Point Value	Time (hr:min:sec)	Point Value
3.1 Miles		**3.2 Miles**		**3.3 Miles**	
over 1:02:01	2.1	over 1:04:01	2.2	over 1:06:01	2.3
1:02:00– 46:31	5.2	1:04:00– 48:01	5.4	1:06:00– 49:31	5.6
46:30– 37:13	8.3	48:00– 38:25	8.6	49:30– 39:37	8.9
37:12– 31:01	11.4	38:24– 32:01	11.8	39:36– 33:01	12.2
31:00– 24:49	14.5	32:00– 25:37	15.0	33:00– 26:25	15.5
24:48– 20:41	17.6	25:36– 21:21	18.2	26:24– 22:01	18.8
20:40– 17:44	20.7	21:20– 18:19	21.4	22:00– 18:53	22.1
under 17:43	23.8	under 18:18	24.6	under 18:52	25.4
3.4 Miles		**3.5 Miles**		**3.6 Miles**	
over 1:08:01	2.4	over 1:10:01	2.5	over 1:12:01	2.6
1:08:00– 51:01	5.8	1:10:00– 52:31	6.0	1:12:00– 54:01	6.2
51:00– 40:49	9.2	52:30– 42:01	9.5	54:00– 43:13	9.8
40:48– 34:01	12.6	42:00– 35:01	13.0	43:12– 36:01	13.4
34:00– 27:13	16.0	35:00– 28:01	16.5	36:00– 28:49	17.0
27:12– 22:41	19.4	28:00– 23:21	20.0	28:48– 24:01	20.6
22:40– 19:27	22.8	23:20– 20:01	23.5	24:00– 20:35	24.2
under 19:26	26.2	under 20:00	27.0	under 20:34	27.8
3.7 Miles		**3.8 Miles**		**3.9 Miles**	
over 1:14:01	2.7	over 1:16:01	2.8	over 1:18:01	2.9
1:14:00– 55:31	6.4	1:16:00– 57:01	6.6	1:18:00– 58:31	6.8
55:30– 44:25	10.1	57:00– 45:37	10.4	58:30– 46:49	10.7
44:24– 37:01	13.8	45:36– 38:01	14.2	46:48– 39:01	14.6
37:00– 29:37	17.5	38:00– 30:25	18.0	39:00– 31:13	18.5
29:36– 24:41	21.2	30:24– 25:21	21.8	31:12– 26:01	22.4
24:40– 21:10	24.9	25:20– 21:44	25.6	26:00– 22:19	26.3
under 21:09	28.6	under 21:43	29.4	under 22:18	30.2
4.0 Miles		**4.1 Miles**		**4.2 Miles**	
over 1:20:01	3.0	over 1:22:01	3.1	over 1:24:01	3.2
1:20:00–1:00:01	7.0	1:22:00–1:01:31	7.2	1:24:00–1:03:01	7.4
1:00:00– 48:01	11.0	1:01:30– 49:13	11.3	1:03:00– 50:25	11.6
48:00– 40:01	15.0	49:12– 41:01	15.4	50:24– 42:01	15.8
40:00– 32:01	19.0	41:00– 32:49	19.5	42:00– 33:37	20.0
32:00– 26:41	23.0	32:48– 27:21	23.6	33:36– 28:01	24.2
26:40– 22:53	27.0	27:20– 23:27	27.7	28:00– 24:01	28.4
under 22:52	31.0	under 23:26	31.8	under 24:00	32.6

Walking/Running (continued)

Time (hr:min:sec)	Point Value	Time (hr:min:sec)	Point Value	Time (hr:min:sec)	Point Value
4.3 Miles		*4.4 Miles*		*4.5 Miles*	
over 1:26:01	3.3	over 1:28:01	3.4	over 1:30:01	3.5
1:26:00–1:04:31	7.6	1:28:00–1:06:01	7.8	1:30:00–1:07:31	8.0
1:04:30– 51:37	11.9	1:06:00– 52:49	12.2	1:07:30– 54:01	12.5
51:36– 43:01	16.2	52:48– 44:01	16.6	54:00– 45:01	17.0
43:00– 34:25	20.5	44:00– 35:13	21.0	45:00– 36:01	21.5
34:24– 28:41	24.8	35:12– 29:21	25.4	36:00– 30:01	26.0
28:40– 24:35	29.1	29:20– 25:10	29.8	30:00– 25:44	30.5
under 24:34	33.4	under 25:09	34.2	under 25:43	35.0
4.6 Miles		*4.7 Miles*		*4.8 Miles*	
over 1:32:01	3.6	over 1:34:01	3.7	over 1:36:01	3.8
1:32:00–1:09:01	8.2	1:34:00–1:10:31	8.4	1:36:00–1:12:01	8.6
1:09:00– 55:13	12.8	1:10:30– 56:25	13.1	1:12:00– 57:37	13.4
55:12– 46:01	17.4	56:24– 47:01	17.8	57:36– 48:01	18.2
46:00– 36:49	22.0	47:00– 37:37	22.5	48:00– 38:25	23.0
36:48– 30:41	26.6	37:36– 31:21	27.2	38:24– 32:01	27.8
30:40– 26:19	31.2	31:20– 26:53	31.9	32:00– 27:27	32.6
under 26:18	35.8	under 26:52	36.6	under 27:26	37.4
4.9 Miles		*5.0 Miles*		*5.5 Miles*	
over 1:38:01	3.9	over 1:40:01	4.0	over 1:50:01	4.5
1:38:00–1:13:31	8.8	1:40:00–1:15:01	9.0	1:50:00–1:22:31	10.0
1:13:30– 58:49	13.7	1:15:00–1:00:01	14.0	1:22:30–1:06:01	15.5
58:48– 49:01	18.6	1:00:00– 50:01	19.0	1:06:00– 55:01	21.0
49:00– 39:13	23.5	50:00– 40:01	24.0	55:00– 44:01	26.5
39:12– 32:41	28.4	40:00– 33:21	29.0	44:00– 36:41	32.0
32:40– 28:01	33.3	33:20– 28:35	34.0	36:40– 31:27	37.5
under 28:00	38.2	under 28:34	39.0	under 31:26	43.0
6.0 Miles		*6.5 Miles*		*7.0 Miles*	
over 2:00:01	5.0	over 2:10:01	5.5	over 2:20:01	6.0
2:00:00–1:30:01	11.0	2:10:00–1:37:31	12.0	2:20:00–1:45:01	13.0
1:30:00–1:12:01	17.0	1:37:30–1:18:01	18.5	1:45:00–1:24:01	20.0
1:12:00–1:00:01	23.0	1:18:00–1:05:01	25.0	1:24:00–1:10:01	27.0
1:00:00– 48:01	29.0	1:05:00– 52:01	31.5	1:10:00– 56:01	34.0
48:00– 40:01	35.0	52:00– 43:21	38.0	56:00– 46:41	41.0
40:00– 34:19	41.0	43:20– 37:10	44.5	46:40– 40:01	48.0
under 34:18	47.0	under 37:09	51.0	under 40:00	55.0

Walking/Running (continued)

Time (hr:min:sec)	Point Value	Time (hr:min:sec)	Point Value	Time (hr:min:sec)	Point Value
7.5 Miles		**8.0 Miles**		**8.5 Miles**	
over 2:30:01	6.5	over 2:40:01	7.0	over 2:50:01	7.5
2:30:00–1:52:31	14.0	2:40:00–2:00:01	15.0	2:50:00–2:07:31	16.0
1:52:30–1:30:01	21.5	2:00:00–1:36:01	23.0	2:07:30–1:42:01	24.5
1:30:00–1:15:01	29.0	1:36:00–1:20:01	31.0	1:42:00–1:25:01	33.0
1:15:00–1:00:01	36.5	1:20:00–1:04:01	39.0	1:25:00–1:08:01	41.5
1:00:00– 50:01	44.0	1:04:00– 53:21	47.0	1:08:00– 56:41	50.0
50:00– 42:53	51.5	53:20– 45:44	55.0	56:40– 48:35	58.5
under 42:52	59.0	under 45:43	63.0	under 48.34	67.0
9.0 Miles		**9.5 Miles**		**10.0 Miles**	
over 3:00:01	8.0	over 3:10:01	8.5	over 3:20:01	9.0
3:00:00–2:15:01	17.0	3:10:00–2:22:31	18.0	3:20:00–2:30:01	19.0
2:15:00–1:48:01	26.0	2:22:30–1:54:01	27.5	2:30:00–2:00:01	29.0
1:48:00–1:30:01	35.0	1:54:00–1:35:01	37.0	2:00:00–1:40:01	39.0
1:30:00–1:12:01	44.0	1:35:00–1:16:01	46.5	1:40:00–1:20:01	49.0
1:12:00–1:00:01	53.0	1:16:00–1:03:21	56.0	1:20:00–1:06:41	59.0
1:00:00– 51:27	62.0	1:03:20– 54:19	65.5	1:06:40– 57:10	69.0
under 51:26	71.0	under 54:18	75.0	under 57:09	79.0
11.0 Miles		**12.0 Miles**		**13.0 Miles**	
over 3:40:01	10.0	over 4:00:01	11.0	over 4:20:01	12.0
3:40:00–2:45:01	21.0	4:00:00–3:00:01	23.0	4:20:00–3:15:01	25.0
2:45:00–2:12:01	32.0	3:00:00–2:24:01	35.0	3:15:00–2:36:01	38.0
2:12:00–1:50:01	43.0	2:24:00–2:00:01	47.0	2:36:00–2:10:01	51.0
1:50:00–1:28:01	54.0	2:00:00–1:36:01	59.0	2:10:00–1:44:01	64.0
1:28:00–1:13:21	65.0	1:36:00–1:20:01	71.0	1:44:00–1:26:41	77.0
1:13:20–1:02:53	76.0	1:20:00–1:08:35	83.0	1:26:40–1:14:19	90.0
under 1:02:52	87.0	under 1:08:34	95.0	under 1:14:18	103.0
14.0 Miles		**15.0 Miles**		**16.0 Miles**	
over 4:40:01	13.0	over 5:00:01	14.0	over 5:20:01	15.0
4:40:00–3:30:01	27.0	5:00:00–3:45:01	29.0	5:20:00–4:00:01	31.0
3:30:00–2:48:01	41.0	3:45:00–3:00:01	44.0	4:00:00–3:12:01	47.0
2:48:00–2:20:01	55.0	3:00:00–2:30:01	59.0	3:12:00–2:40:01	63.0
2:20:00–1:52:01	69.0	2:30:00–2:00:01	74.0	2:40:00–2:08:01	79.0
1:52:00–1:33:21	83.0	2:00:00–1:40:01	89.0	2:08:00–1:46:41	95.0
1:33:20–1:20:01	97.0	1:40:00–1:25:44	104.0	1:46:40–1:31:27	111.0
under 1:20:00	111.0	under 1:25:43	119.0	under 1:31:26	127.0

Walking / Running (continued)

Time (hr:min:sec)	Point Value	Time (hr:min:sec)	Point Value	Time (hr:min:sec)	Point Value
17.0 Miles		**18.0 Miles**		**19.0 Miles**	
over 5:40:01	16.0	over 6:00:01	17.0	over 6:20:01	18.0
5:40:00–4:15:01	33.0	6:00:00–4:30:01	35.0	6:20:00–4:45:01	37.0
4:15:00–3:24:01	50.0	4:30:00–3:36:01	53.0	4:45:00–3:48:01	56.0
3:24:00–2:50:01	67.0	3:36:00–3:00:01	71.0	3:48:00–3:10:01	75.0
2:50:00–2:16:01	84.0	3:00:00–2:24:01	89.0	3:10:00–2:32:01	94.0
2:16:00–1:53:21	101.0	2:24:00–2:00:01	107.0	2:32:00–2:06:41	113.0
1:53:20–1:37:10	118.0	2:00:00–1:42:53	125.0	2:06:40–1:48:35	132.0
under 1:37:09	135.0	under 1:42:52	143.0	under 1:48:34	151.0
20.0 Miles		**21.0 Miles**		**22.0 Miles**	
over 6:40:01	19.0	over 7:00:01	20.0	over 7:20:01	21.0
6:40:00–5:00:01	39.0	7:00:00–5:15:01	41.0	7:20:00–5:30:01	43.0
5:00:00–4:00:01	59.0	5:15:00–4:12:01	62.0	5:30:00–4:24:01	65.0
4:00:00–3:20:01	79.0	4:12:00–3:30:01	83.0	4:24:00–3:40:01	87.0
3:20:00–2:40:01	99.0	3:30:00–2:48:01	104.0	3:40:00–2:56:01	109.0
2:40:00–2:13:21	119.0	2:48:00–2:20:01	125.0	2:56:00–2:26:41	131.0
2:13:20–1:54:19	139.0	2:20:00–2:00:01	146.0	2:26:40–2:05:44	153.0
under 1:54:18	159.0	under 2:00:00	167.0	under 2:05:43	175.0
23.0 Miles		**24.0 Miles**		**25.0 Miles**	
over 7:40:01	22.0	over 8:00:01	23.0	over 8:20:01	24.0
7:40:00–5:45:01	45.0	8:00:00–6:00:01	47.0	8:20:00–6:15:01	49.0
5:45:00–4:36:01	68.0	6:00:00–4:48:01	71.0	6:15:00–5:00:01	74.0
4:36:00–3:50:01	91.0	4:48:00–4:00:01	95.0	5:00:00–4:10:01	99.0
3:50:00–3:04:01	114.0	4:00:00–3:12:01	119.0	4:10:00–3:20:01	124.0
3:04:00–2:33:21	137.0	3:12:00–2:40:01	143.0	3:20:00–2:46:41	149.0
2:33:20–2:11:27	160.0	2:40:00–2:17:10	167.0	2:46:40–2:22:53	174.0
under 2:11:26	183.0	under 2:17:09	191.0	under 2:22:52	199.0
26.22 Miles					
over 8:44:25	25.22				
8:44:24–6:33:19	51.44				
6:33:18–5:14:40	77.66				
5:14:39–4:22:13	103.88				
4:22:12–3:29:47	130.10				
3:29:46–2:54:49	156.32				
2:54:48–2:29:51	182.54				
under 2:29:50	208.76				

Cycling

Time (hr:min:sec)	Point Value	Time (hr:min:sec)	Point Value	Time (hr:min:sec)	Point Value
2.0 Miles		**3.0 Miles**		**4.0 Miles**	
over 12:01	0	over 18:01	0	over 24:01	0
12:00– 8:01	0.5	18:00–12:01	1.5	24:00–16:01	2.5
8:00– 6:01	1.5	12:00– 9:01	3.0	16:00–12:01	4.5
under 6:00	2.5	under 9:00	4.5	under 12:00	6.5
5.0 Miles		**6.0 Miles**		**7.0 Miles**	
over 30:01	2.0	over 36:01	2.7	over 42:01	3.4
30:00–20:01	3.5	36:00–24:01	4.5	42:00–28:01	5.5
20:00–15:01	6.0	24:00–18:01	7.5	28:00–21:01	9.0
under 15:00	8.5	under 18:00	10.5	under 21:00	12.5
8.0 Miles		**9.0 Miles**		**10.0 Miles**	
over 48:01	4.1	over 54:01	4.8	over 1:00:01	5.5
48:00–32:01	6.5	54:00–36:01	7.5	1:00:00– 40:01	8.5
32:00–24:01	10.5	36:00–27:01	12.0	40:00– 30:01	13.5
under 24:00	14.5	under 27:00	16.5	under 30:00	18.5
11.0 Miles		**12.0 Miles**		**13.0 Miles**	
over 1:06:01	6.2	over 1:12:01	6.9	over 1:18:01	7.6
1:06:00– 44:01	9.5	1:12:00– 48:01	10.5	1:18:00– 52:01	11.5
44:00– 33:01	15.0	48:00– 36:01	16.5	52:00– 39:01	18.0
under 33:00	20.5	under 36:00	22.5	under 39:00	24.5
14.0 Miles		**15.0 Miles**		**16.0 Miles**	
over 1:24:01	8.3	over 1:30:01	9.0	over 1:36:01	9.7
1:24:00– 56:01	12.5	1:30:00–1:00:01	13.5	1:36:00–1:04:01	14.5
56:00– 42:01	19.5	1:00:00– 45:01	21.0	1:04:00– 48:01	22.5
under 42:00	26.5	under 45:00	28.5	under 48:00	30.5
17.0 Miles		**18.0 Miles**		**19.0 Miles**	
over 1:42:01	10.4	over 1:48:01	11.1	over 1:54:01	11.8
1:42:00–1:08:01	15.5	1:48:00–1:12:01	16.5	1:54:00–1:16:01	17.5
1:08:00– 51:01	24.0	1:12:00– 54:01	25.5	1:16:00– 57:01	27.0
under 51:00	32.5	under 54:00	34.5	under 57:00	36.5

Cycling (continued)

Time (hr:min:sec)	Point Value	Time (hr:min:sec)	Point Value	Time (hr:min:sec)	Point Value
20.0 Miles		**21.0 Miles**		**22.0 Miles**	
over 2:00:01	12.5	over 2:06:01	13.2	over 2:12:01	13.9
2:00:00–1:20:01	18.5	2:06:00–1:24:01	19.5	2:12:00–1:28:01	20.5
1:20:00–1:00:01	28.5	1:24:00–1:03:01	30.0	1:28:00–1:06:01	31.5
under 1:00:00	38.5	under 1:03:00	40.5	under 1:06:00	42.5
23.0 Miles		**24.0 Miles**		**25.0 Miles**	
over 2:18:01	14.6	over 2:24:01	15.3	over 2:30:01	16.0
2:18:00–1:32:01	21.5	2:24:00–1:36:01	22.5	2:30:00–1:40:01	23.5
1:32:00–1:09:01	33.0	1:36:00–1:12:01	34.5	1:40:00–1:15:01	36.0
under 1:09:00	44.5	under 1:12:00	46.5	under 1:15:00	48.5
26.0 Miles		**27.0 Miles**		**28.0 Miles**	
over 2:36:01	16.7	over 2:42:01	17.4	over 2:48:01	18.1
2:36:00–1:44:01	24.5	2:42:00–1:48:01	25.5	2:48:00–1:52:01	26.5
1:44:00–1:18:01	37.5	1:48:00–1:21:01	39.0	1:52:00–1:24:01	40.5
under 1:18:00	50.5	under 1:21:00	52.5	under 1:24:00	54.5
29.0 Miles		**30.0 Miles**		**35.0 Miles**	
over 2:54:01	18.8	over 3:00:01	19.5	over 3:30:01	23.0
2:54:00–1:56:01	27.5	3:00:00–2:00:01	28.5	3:30:00–2:20:01	33.5
1:56:00–1:27:01	42.0	2:00:00–1:30:01	43.5	2:20:00–1:45:01	51.0
under 1:27:00	56.5	under 1:30:00	58.5	under 1:45:00	68.5
40.0 Miles		**45.0 Miles**		**50.0 Miles**	
over 4:00:01	26.5	over 4:30:01	30.0	over 5:00:01	33.5
4:00:00–2:40:01	38.5	4:30:00–3:00:01	43.5	5:00:00–3:20:01	48.5
2:40:00–2:00:01	58.5	3:00:00–2:15:01	66.0	3:20:00–2:30:01	73.5
under 2:00:00	78.5	under 2:15:00	88.5	under 2:30:00	98.5
55.0 Miles		**60.0 Miles**		**65.0 Miles**	
over 5:30:01	37.0	over 6:00:01	40.5	over 6:30:01	44.0
5:30:00–3:40:01	53.5	6:00:00–4:00:01	58.5	6:30:00–4:20:01	63.5
3:40:00–2:45:01	81.0	4:00:00–3:00:01	88.5	4:20:00–3:15:01	96.0
under 2:45:00	108.5	under 3:00:00	118.5	under 3:15:00	128.5

Cycling (continued)

Time (hr:min:sec)	Point Value	Time (hr:min:sec)	Point Value	Time (hr:min:sec)	Point Value
70.0 Miles		*75.0 Miles*		*80.0 Miles*	
over 7:00:01	47.5	over 7:30:01	51.0	over 8:00:01	54.5
7:00:00–4:40:01	68.5	7:30:00–5:00:01	73.5	8:00:00–5:20:01	78.5
4:40:00–3:30:01	103.5	5:00:00–3:45:01	111.0	5:20:00–4:00:01	118.5
under 3:30:00	138.5	under 3:45:00	148.5	under 4:00:00	158.5
85.0 Miles		*90.0 Miles*		*95.0 Miles*	
over 8:30:01	58.0	over 9:00:01	61.5	over 9:30:01	65.0
8:30:00–5:40:01	83.5	9:00:00–6:00:01	88.5	9:30:00–6:20:01	93.5
5:40:00–4:15:01	126.0	6:00:00–4:30:01	133.5	6:20:00–4:45:01	141.0
under 4:15:00	168.5	under 4:30:00	178.5	under 4:45:00	188.5
100.0 Miles					
over 10:00:01	68.5				
10:00:00–6:40:01	98.5				
6:40:00–5:00:01	148.5				
under 5:00:00	198.5				

Note: Points are determined considering an equal uphill and downhill course, and considering an equal time with and against the wind. For cycling a one-way course against a wind exceeding 5 mph, add ½ point per mile to the total point value.

Swimming

Time (hr:min:sec)	Point Value	Time (hr:min:sec)	Point Value	Time (hr:min:sec)	Point Value
200 Yards		*250 Yards*		*300 Yards*	
over 6:41	0	over 8:21	0	over 10:01	0
6:40–5:01	1.25	8:20–6:16	1.56	10:00–7:31	1.88
5:00–3:21	1.67	6:15–4:11	2.08	7:30–5:01	2.50
under 3:20	2.50	under 4:10	3.12	under 5:00	3.75
350 Yards		*400 Yards*		*450 Yards*	
over 11:41	0	over 13:21	0	over 15:01	0
11:40–8:46	2.19	13:20–10:01	2.50	15:00–11:16	2.81
8:45–5:51	2.92	10:00–6:41	3.33	11:15–7:31	3.75
under 5:50	4.38	under 6:40	5.00	under 7:30	5.63

Swimming (continued)

Time (hr:min:sec)	Point Value	Time (hr:min:sec)	Point Value	Time (hr:min:sec)	Point Value
500 Yards		**550 Yards**		**600 Yards**	
over 16:41	0	over 18:21	0	over 20:01	0
16:40–12:31	3.12	18:20–13:46	3.44	20:00–15:01	3.75
12:30– 8:21	4.17	13:45– 9:11	4.58	15:00–10:01	5.00
under 8:20	6.25	under 9:10	6.87	under 10:00	7.50
650 Yards		**700 Yards**		**750 Yards**	
over 21:41	0	over 23:21	0	over 25:01	0
21:40–16:16	4.31	23:20–17:31	4.88	25:00–18:46	5.44
16:15–10:51	5.67	17:30–11:41	6.33	18:45–12:31	7.00
under 10:50	8.38	under 11:40	9.25	under 12:30	10.13
800 Yards		**850 Yards**		**900 Yards**	
over 26:41	0	over 28:21	0	over 30:01	0
26:40–20:01	6.00	28:20–21:16	6.56	30:00–22:31	7.13
20:00–13:21	7.67	21:15–14:11	8.33	22:30–15:01	9.00
under 13:20	11.00	under 14:10	11.87	under 15:00	12.75
950 Yards		**1000 Yards**		**1050 Yards**	
over 31:41	0	over 33:21	0	over 35:01	0
31:40–23:46	7.69	33:20–25:01	8.25	35:00–26:16	8.81
23:45–15:51	9.67	25:00–16:41	10.33	26:15–17:31	11.00
under 15:50	13.63	under 16:40	14.50	under 17:30	15.38
1100 Yards		**1150 Yards**		**1200 Yards**	
over 36:41	0	over 38:21	0	over 40:01	0
36:40–27:31	9.37	38:20–28:46	9.94	40:00–30:01	10.50
27:30–18:21	11.67	28:45–19:11	12.33	30:00–20:01	13.00
under 18:20	16.25	under 19:10	17.12	under 20:00	18.00
1250 Yards		**1300 Yards**		**1350 Yards**	
over 41:41	0	over 43:21	0	over 45:01	0
41:40–31:16	11.06	43:20–32:31	11.63	45:00–33:46	12.19
31:15–20:51	13.67	32:30–21:41	14.33	33:45–22:31	15.00
under 20:50	18.88	under 21:40	19.75	under 22:30	20.63

Swimming (continued)

Time (hr:min:sec)	Point Value	Time (hr:min:sec)	Point Value	Time (hr:min:sec)	Point Value
1400 Yards		**1450 Yards**		**1500 Yards**	
over 46:41	0	over 48:21	0	over 50:01	0
46:40–35:01	12.75	48:20–36:16	13.31	50:00–37:31	13.88
35:00–23:21	15.67	36:15–24:11	16.33	37:30–25:01	17.00
under 23:20	21.50	under 24:10	22.37	under 25:00	23.25
1550 Yards		**1600 Yards**		**1650 Yards**	
over 51:41	0	over 53:21	0	over 55:01	0
51:40–38:46	14.44	53:20–40:01	15.00	55:00–41:16	15.56
38:45–25:51	17.67	40:00–26:41	18.33	41:15 27:31	19.00
under 25:50	24.13	under 26:40	25.00	under 27:30	25.88
1700 Yards		**1750 Yards**		**1800 Yards**	
over 56:41	0	over 58:21	0	over 1:00:01	0
56:40–42:31	16.12	58:20–43:46	16.69	1:00:00– 45:01	17.25
42:30 28:21	19.67	43:45–29:11	20.33	45:00– 30:01	21.00
under 28:20	26.75	under 29:10	27.62	under 30:00	28.50
1850 Yards		**1900 Yards**		**2000 Yards**	
over 1:01:41	0	over 1:03:21	0	over 1:06:41	0
1:01:40– 46:16	17.81	1:03:20– 47:31	18.38	1:06:40– 50:01	19.50
46:15– 30:51	21.67	47:30– 31:41	22.33	50:00– 33:21	23.67
under 30:50	29.38	under 31:40	30.25	under 33:20	32.00
2100 Yards		**2200 Yards**		**2300 Yards**	
over 1:10:01	0	over 1:13:21	0	over 1:16:41	0
1:10:00– 52:31	20.63	1:13:20– 55:01	21.75	1:16:40– 57:31	22.87
53:30– 35:01	25.00	55:00– 36:41	26.33	57:30– 38:21	27.67
under 35:00	33.75	under 36:40	35.50	under 38:20	37.25
2400 Yards		**2500 Yards**		**2600 Yards**	
over 1:20:01	0	over 1:23:21	0	over 1:26:41	0
1:20:00–1:00:01	24.00	1:23:20–1:02:31	25.13	1:26:40–1:05:01	26.25
1:00:00– 40:01	29.00	1:02:30– 41:41	30.33	1:05:00– 43:21	31.67
under 40:00	39.00	under 41:40	40.75	under 43:20	42.50

Swimming (continued)

Time (hr:min:sec)	Point Value	Time (hr:min:sec)	Point Value	Time (hr:min:sec)	Point Value
2700 Yards		*2800 Yards*		*2900 Yards*	
over 1:30:01	0	over 1:33:21	0	over 1:36:41	0
1:30:00–1:07:31	27.38	1:33:20–1:10:01	28.50	1:36:40–1:12:31	29.62
1:07:30– 45:01	33.00	1:10:00– 46:41	34.33	1:12:30– 48:21	35.67
under 45:00	44.25	under 46:40	46.00	under 48:20	47.75

Time (hr:min:sec)	Point Value
3000 Yards	
over 1:40:01	0
1:40:00–1:15:01	30.75
1:15:00– 50:01	37.00
under 50:00	49.50

Note: Points are calculated on overhand crawl, considering average skill in swimming, i.e., 9.0 kcal (kilo calories) per minute. Breaststroke is less demanding: 7.0 kcal per minute. Backstroke, a little more than breaststroke: 8.0 kcal per minute. Butterfly is the most demanding, i.e., 12.0 kcal per minute.

Handball/Racketball/Squash/Basketball/Soccer/Hockey/Lacrosse*

Time (hr:min:sec)	Point Value	Time (hr:min:sec)	Point Value
under 4:59	0	1:05:00	9.75
5:00	0.75	1:10:00	10.50
10:00	1.50	1:15:00	11.25
15:00	2.25	1:20:00	12.00
20:00	3.00	1:25:00	12.75
25:00	3.75	1:30:00	13.50
30:00	4.50	1:35:00	14.25
35:00	5.25	1:40:00	15.00
40:00	6.00	1:45:00	15.75
45:00	6.75	1:50:00	16.50
50:00	7.50	1:55:00	17.25
55:00	8.25	over 2:00:00	18.00
1:00:00	9.00		

* Continuous exercise. Do not count breaks, time-outs, etc.

Stationary Running

Time (min:sec)	60–70* Steps/Min	Point Value	70–80* Steps/Min	Point Value	80–90* Steps/Min	Point Value	90–100* Steps/Min	Point Value	100–110* Steps/Min	Point Value
2:30			175–200	.88	200–225	1.13	225–250	1.38	250–275	1.63
5:00	300–350	1.25	350–400	1.75	400–450	2.25	450–500	2.75	500–550	3.25
7:30		1.88	525–600	2.63	600–675	3.38	675–750	4.13	750–825	4.88
10:00	600–700	2.50	700–800	3.50	800–900	4.50	900–1000	5.50	1000–1100	6.50
12:30		3.63	875–1000	4.88	1000–1125	6.13	1125–1250	7.38	1250–1375	8.63
15:00	900–1050	4.75	1050–1200	6.25	1200–1350	7.75	1350–1500	9.25	1500–1650	10.75
17:30		5.88	1225–1400	7.63	1400–1575	9.38	1575–1750	11.13	1750–1925	12.88
20:00	1200–1400	7.00	1400–1600	9.00	1600–1800	11.00	1800–2000	13.00	2000–2200	15.00
22:30		8.13	1575–1800	10.38	1800–2025	12.63	2025–2250	14.88	2250–2475	17.13
25:00	1500–1750	9.25	1750–2000	11.75	2000–2250	14.25	2250–2500	16.75	2500–2750	19.25
27:30		10.38	1925–2200	13.13	2200–2475	15.88	2475–2750	18.63	2750–3025	21.38
30:00	1800–2100	11.50	2100–2400	14.50	2400–2700	17.50	2700–3000	20.50	3000–3300	23.50

* Count only when the left foot hits the floor. Knees must be brought up in front, raising the feet at least 8 inches from the floor.

Stationary Cycling*
(Using a screw-down resistance)

POINT VALUE

Time (min:sec)	15 Mph/ 55 Rpm	17.5 Mph/ 65 Rpm	20 Mph/ 75 Rpm	25 Mph/ 90 Rpm	30 Mph/ 105 Rpm
3:00	—	—	—	—	1
4:00	.5	—	1	—	—
5:00	—	—	1.25	2	2.5
6:00	.75	—	1.5	2.13	2.75
7:00	—	1	1.75	2.25	3
8:00	1	1.25	2	2.5	3.33
9:00	—	1.38	2.25	2.75	3.66
10:00	1.25	—	2.5	3	4
11:00	—	1.5	2.63	3.25	4.25
12:00	1.38	1.63	2.75	3.5	4.5
13:00	1.63	1.88	2.88	3.75	4.75
14:00	1.75	2	3	4	5
15:00	1.88	2.13	3.13	4.25	5.5
16:00	2	2.25	3.25	4.5	6
17:00	2.13	2.38	3.38	4.75	6.5
18:00	2.25	2.63	3.63	5	7
19:00	2.38	2.75	3.75	5.33	7.5
20:00	2.5	2.88	3.88	5.66	8
22:30	3	3.18	4.5	6.63	9
25:00	3.25	3.75	5	7.5	10
27:30	3.5	4.5	5.75	8.5	11.5
30:00	3.75	5	6.5	9.5	12.5
35:00	4.75	6	8	11	14.5
40:00	5.75	7.25	9.5	13	17
45:00	6.75	8.5	11	15	19.5
50:00	7.75	9.75	12.5	17	22.5
55:00	8.75	11	14	19	25
60:00	9.75	12.5	16	22	28

Note: Add enough resistance so that the pulse rate counted for 10 seconds immediately after exercise and multiplied by 6 equals or exceeds 140 beats per minute.

* Stationary cycling is awarded approximately half the points for regular cycling.

Stationary Cycling
(Adjusted for weight and resistance using the Schwinn Calibrated Resistance Ergometer)

Weight (lbs)	Load: 1.0	2.0	3.0	4.0
15:00 Minutes	POINT VALUE			
100	3.20	8.72	18.79	—
120	2.18	5.60	12.03	20.44
140	1.48	4.09	8.18	14.39
160	1.13	3.20	5.94	8.37
180	0.77	2.58	4.54	7.05
200	0.37	2.01	3.76	6.13
220	—	1.56	3.19	4.91
240		1.30	2.67	4.12
30:00 Minutes	POINT VALUE			
100	6.40	17.44	37.58	—
120	4.35	11.19	24.05	40.88
140	2.96	8.18	16.36	28.79
160	2.27	6.40	11.87	16.74
180	1.53	5.15	9.09	14.09
200	0.73	4.01	7.57	12.26
220	—	3.13	6.38	9.82
240	—	2.60	5.34	8.24
45:00 Minutes	POINT VALUE			
100	9.60	26.16	56.36	—
120	6.53	16.79	36.08	61.31
140	4.43	12.26	24.54	43.18
160	3.40	9.60	17.81	25.10
180	2.30	7.73	13.63	21.14
200	1.10	6.02	11.27	18.38
220	—	4.69	9.56	14.72
240	—	3.89	8.01	12.36
60:00 Minutes	POINT VALUE			
100	12.80	34.88	75.15	—
120	8.70	22.38	48.10	81.75
140	5.91	16.35	32.72	57.57
160	4.53	12.80	23.74	33.47
180	3.06	10.30	18.17	28.18
200	1.46	8.02	15.02	24.51
220	—	6.25	12.75	19.63
240	—	5.19	10.68	16.48

Note: Resistance is consistent, regardless of speed.

Stair Climbing
(10 steps; 6"–7" in height; 25°–30° incline)

| Time (min:sec) | Round Trips—Average Number Per Minute | | | | | |
	5	6	7	8	9	10
	POINT VALUE					
3:00	.43	.69	1.00	1.36	1.80	2.33
3:30	.5	.81	1.17	1.59	2.10	2.72
4:00	.57	.92	1.33	1.82	2.40	3.16
4:30	.64	1.04	1.50	2.05	2.70	3.5
5:00	.71	1.15	1.67	2.27	3.00	3.89
5:30	.79	1.27	1.83	2.50	3.30	4.28
6:00	.86	1.38	2.00	2.73	3.60	4.67
6:30	.93	1.50	2.16	2.98	3.90	5.06
7:00	1.00	1.62	2.33	3.18	4.20	5.44
7:30	1.07	1.73	2.50	3.41	4.50	5.83
8:00	1.14	1.85	2.67	3.65	4.80	6.22
8:30	1.21	1.96	2.83	3.86	5.10	6.61
9:00	1.29	2.08	3.00	4.09	5.40	7.00
9:30	1.36	2.19	3.16	4.32	5.70	7.39
10:00	1.43	2.31	3.33	4.55	6.00	7.78
10:30	1.50	2.42	3.50	4.77	6.30	8.17
11:00	1.57	2.54	3.67	5.00	6.60	8.55
11:30	1.64	2.65	3.83	5.23	6.90	8.94
12:00	1.71	2.77	4.00	5.45	7.20	9.33
12:30	1.79	2.88	4.16	5.68	7.50	9.72
13:00	1.86	3.00	4.33	5.91	7.80	10.11
13:30	1.93	3.12	4.50	6.14	8.10	10.5
14:00	2.00	3.23	4.67	6.36	8.40	10.89
14:30	2.07	3.35	4.83	6.59	8.70	11.28
15:00	3.00	3.46	5.00	6.82	9.00	11.67

Point Value For Using a Single Step (approximately 7 inches in height)

Stepping Rate (per min)	Time (min:sec)	Point Value
30	6:30	1.5
	9:45	2.25
	13:00	3.0
35	6:00	2.0
	9:00	3.0
	12:00	4.0
40	5:00	2.5
	7:30	3.75
	10:00	5.0

Rope Skipping

Time (min:sec)	70–90 Steps/Min	90–110 Steps/Min	110–130 Steps/Min
	POINT VALUE		
5:00	1.5	2.0	2.5
7:30	2.25	3.0	3.75
10:00	3.0	4.0	5.0
12:30	4.25	5.5	6.75
15:00	5.5	7.0	8.5
17:30	6.75	8.5	10.25
20:00	8.0	10.0	12.0
22:30	9.25	11.5	13.75
25:00	10.5	13.0	15.5
27:30	11.75	14.5	17.25
30:00	13.0	16.0	19.0

Note: Skip with both feet together, or step over the rope, alternating feet.

Golf

Holes	Point Value
under 4	0
4	0.6
6	1.0
9	1.5
12	2.0
15	2.5
18	3.0
21	3.5
24	4.0
27	4.5
30	5.0
33	5.5
36	6.0

Note: No motorized carts!

Rowing

Time (min)	Point Value
15:00	3.5
30:00	7.0
45:00	10.5
60:00	14.0

Note: 2 oars, 20 strokes a minute, continuous rowing.

Tennis/Badminton/Aerial Tennis
(Doubles)

Time (hr:min:sec)	Point Value
under 14:59	0
15:00	0.38
30:00	0.75
45:00	1.13
1:00:00	1.50
1:15:00	1.88
1:30:00	2.25
1:45:00	2.63
2:00:00	3.00

Note: Points are awarded to players of equal ability.

(Singles)

Time (min:sec)	Point Value
under 4:59	0
5:00	0.33
10:00	0.67
15:00	1.00
20:00	1.33
25:00	1.67
30:00	2.00
35:00	2.33
40:00	2.67
45:00	3.00
50:00	3.33
55:00	3.67
60:00	4.00

Note: Points are awarded to players of equal ability.

Water or Downhill Snow Skiing

Time (hr:min:sec)	Point Value
under 4:59	0
5:00	0.5
10:00	1.0
15:00	1.5
20:00	2.0
25:00	2.5
30:00	3.0
35:00	3.5
40:00	4.0
45:00	4.5
50:00	5.0
55:00	5.5
1:00:00	6.0
1:05:00	6.5
1:10:00	7.0
1:15:00	7.5
1:20:00	8.0
1:25:00	8.5
1:30:00	9.0
1:35:00	9.5
1:40:00	10.0
1:45:00	10.5
1:50:00	11.0
1:55:00	11.5
2:00:00	12.0

Note: Water or downhill snow skiing. Remember, for downhill skiing, it requires 3 hours on the slopes to accumulate 1 hour of actual skiing.

Cross-Country Skiing

Time (min:sec)	Point Value
15:00	4.5
20:00	6.0
25:00	7.5
30:00	9.0
35:00	10.5
40:00	12.0
45:00	13.5
50:00	15.0
55:00	16.5
60:00	18.0

Ice or Roller Skating

Time (hr:min:sec)	Point Value
15:00	1.13
30:00	2.25
45:00	3.38
1:00:00	4.50
1:15:00	5.63
1:30:00	6.75
1:45:00	7.88
2:00:00	9.00

Note: For speed skating, triple the point value.

Volleyball

Time (min:sec)	Point Value
under 4:59	0
5:00	0.33
10:00	0.67
15:00	1.00
20:00	1.33
25:00	1.67
30:00	2.00
35:00	2.33
40:00	2.67
45:00	3.00
50:00	3.33
55:00	3.67
60:00	4.00

Note: For times greater than 1 hour, figure points at a rate of 1 point/15 minutes.

Fencing

Time (hr:min:sec)	Point Value
10:00	1
20:00	2
30:00	3
40:00	4
50:00	5
1:00:00	6
1:10:00	7
1:20:00	8
1:30:00	9
1:40:00	10
1:50:00	11
2:00:00	12

Note: For times greater than 2 hours, figure points at a rate of 1 point/10 minutes.

Football

Time (hr:min:sec)	Point Value
under 4:59	0
5:00	0.5
10:00	1.0
15:00	1.5
20:00	2.0
25:00	2.5
30:00	3.0
35:00	3.5
40:00	4.0
45:00	4.5
50:00	5.0
55:00	5.5
1:00:00	6.0
1:05:00	6.5
1:10:00	7.0
1:15:00	7.5
1:20:00	8.0
1:25:00	8.5
1:30:00	9.0
1:35:00	9.5
1:40:00	10.0
1:45:00	10.5
1:50:00	11.0
1:55:00	11.5
2:00:00	12.0

Note: Count only the time you are actively participating.

Wrestling and Boxing

Time (min:sec)	Point Value
under 4:59	0
5:00	2.0
10:00	4.0
15:00	6.0
20:00	8.0
25:00	10.0
30:00	12.0
35:00	14.0
40:00	16.0
45:00	18.0
50:00	20.0
55:00	22.0
60:00	24.0

Note: For times greater than 1 hour, figure points at a rate of 4 points/10 minutes.

Calisthenics

Time (min)	Point Value
10:00	0.25
20:00	0.50
30:00	0.75
40:00	1.00
50:00	1.25
60:00	1.50

Note: These are continuous, repetitive calisthenics that are more stretching than muscle-strengthening.

Walking or Running on a Motorized Treadmill Set at Various Speeds and Inclines

Speed (mph)	Time (Min)	0%	5%	10%	15%	20%
3 mph	10:00	0.50	0.55	0.70	1.00	1.50
	15:00	0.75	0.82	1.05	1.50	2.25
	20:00	1.00	1.10	1.40	2.00	3.00
	25:00	1.50	1.65	2.10	3.00	4.50
	30:00	2.00	2.20	2.80	4.00	6.00
	45:00	3.50	3.85	4.90	7.00	10.50
	60:00	5.00	5.50	7.00	10.00	15.00
4 mph	10:00	1.32	1.45	1.88	2.64	3.96
	15:00	2.00	2.20	2.80	4.00	6.00
	20:00	2.99	3.29	4.19	5.98	8.97
	25:00	3.98	4.38	5.57	7.96	11.94
	30:00	5.00	5.50	7.00	10.00	15:00
	45:00	8.00	8.80	11.20	16.00	24.00
	60:00	11.00	12.10	15.40	22.00	33.00
5 mph	10:00	2.49	2.74	3.49	4.98	7.74
	15:00	4.00	4.40	5.60	8.00	12.00
	20:00	5.64	6.20	7.90	11.28	16.92
	25:00	7.32	8.05	10.25	14.64	21.96
	30:00	9.00	9.90	12.60	18.00	27.00
	45:00	14.00	15.40	19.60	28.00	42.00
	60:00	19.00	20.90	26.60	38.00	57.00
6 mph	10:00	4.00	4.40	5.60	8.00	
	15:00	6.50	7.15	9.10	13.00	
	20:00	9.00	9.90	12.60	18.00	
	25:00	11.50	12.65	16.10	23.00	
	30:00	14.00	15.40	19.60	28.00	
	45:00	21.50	23.65	30.10	43.00	
	60:00	29.00	31.90	40.60	58.00	
7.5 mph	10:00	6.50	7.15	9.10		
	15:00	10.28	11.31	14.39		
	20:00	14.00	15.40	19.60		
	25:00	17.78	19.56	24.89		
	30:00	21.50	23.65	30.10		
	45:00	32.75	36.02	45.85		
	60:00	44.00	48.40	61.60		

Walking or Running One Mile at Various Altitudes

Time (min:sec)		Point Value			Point Value
Standard	5,000 Feet		8,000 Feet	12,000 Feet	
19:59–14:30	20:29–15:00	1	20:59–15:30	21:29–16:30	1
14:29–12:00	14:59–12:30	2	15:29–13:00	16:29–14:00	2
11:59–10:00	12:29–10:30	3	12:59–11:00	13:59–12:00	3
9:59– 8:00	10:29– 8:30	4	10:59– 9:00	11:59–10:00	4
7:59– 6:30	8:29– 7:00	5	8:59– 7:30	9:59– 8:30	5
under 6:30	under 7:00	6	under 7:30	under 8:30	6

Circuit Weight Training

Time (min:sec)	Point Value
5:00	.84
10:00	1.68
15:00	2.52
20:00	3.36
25:00	4.20
30:00	5.04
35:00	5.88
40:00	6.72
45:00	7.56
50:00	8.40
55:00	9.23
60:00	10.07

Super Circuit Weight Training

Time (min:sec)	Point Value
5:00	1.30
10:00	2.60
15:00	3.90
20:00	5.21
25:00	6.51
30:00	7.82
35:00	9.12
40:00	10.42
45:00	11.72

Minitrampoline

Time (min:sec)	Point Value
5:00	1.25
10:00	2.50
15:00	3.75
20:00	5.00
25:00	6.25
30:00	7.50
35:00	8.75
40:00	10.00
45:00	11.25
50:00	12.50
55:00	13.75
60:00	15.00

Aerobic Dancing and Other Exercise Programs Conducted to Music

Time (min:sec)	Point Value
5:00	1.0
10:00	2.0
15:00	3.0
20:00	4.0
25:00	5.0
30:00	6.0
35:00	7.0
40:00	8.0
45:00	9.0
50:00	10.0
55:00	11.0
60:00	12.0

PHYSIOLOGIC AND PERFORMANCE RESPONSES TO ARM, LEG, AND COMBINED ARM AND LEG WORK ON THE SCHWINN AIR-DYNE ERGOMETER

Oxygen uptake, heart rate, energy expenditure, and performance to arm, leg, and combined arm and leg work on the Schwinn Air-dyne Ergometer was evaluated in 15 men and 15 women by the Institute for Aerobics Research. In both the men and women, maximal exercise values for heart rate, oxygen uptake, and energy expenditure were progressively greater for combined arm and leg work compared to leg work and for leg work compared to arm work. The maximal physiologic values for combined arm and leg work are similar to values on a treadmill test. During submaximal work loads, exercise heart rates and oxygen uptake were higher; and work efficiency was lower for arm work compared to leg work and combined arm and leg work. Our findings indicate that arm and leg work from low to high intensities can be accomplished on the Schwinn Air-dyne Ergometer. Thus, numerous cardiovascular training and conditioning programs can be conducted on this durable and versatile exercise ergometer. (Information provided by Don Hagan, Ph.D., Director of Exercise Physiology, Institute for Aerobics Research.)

Oxygen Uptake and Energy Cost for Work on the Schwinn Air-dyne Ergometer

	For Arm Work		For Leg Work and Arm and Leg Work Combined	
Work Load	Gross vo_2 ml/kg/min	Gross Kcal/min	Gross vo_2 ml/kg/min	Gross Kcal/min
0.5	12.5	4.7	10.5	4.0
1.0	17.0	6.4	14.5	5.5
1.5	21.5	8.1	18.5	7.0
2.0	26.0	9.8	22.5	8.5
2.5	30.5	11.5	26.5	10.0
3.0	35.0	13.2	30.5	11.5
3.5	39.5	14.9	34.5	13.0
4.0	44.0	16.6	38.5	14.5
4.5	48.5	18.3	42.5	16.0
5.0	53.0	20.0	46.5	17.5
5.5	57.5	21.7	50.5	19.0
6.0	62.0	23.4	54.5	20.5
6.5	66.5	25.1	58.5	22.0
7.0	71.0	26.8	62.5	23.5

Aerobics Points for Work with the Legs or Arms and Legs Combined on the Schwinn Air-dyne Ergometer

Work Load	Total Time (Minutes)								
	1	5	10	15	20	25	30	35	40
0.5	0.06	0.3	0.6	0.9	1.2	1.5	1.8	2.1	2.4
1.0	0.10	0.5	1.0	1.5	2.0	2.5	3.0	3.5	4.0
1.5	0.14	0.7	1.4	2.1	2.8	3.5	4.2	4.9	5.6
2.0	0.21	1.0	2.1	3.2	4.2	5.2	6.3	7.4	8.4
2.5	0.29	1.4	2.9	4.4	5.8	7.2	8.7	10.2	11.6
3.0	0.39	1.9	3.9	5.8	7.8	9.8	11.7	13.6	15.6
3.5	0.50	2.5	5.0	7.5	10.0	12.5	15.0	17.5	20.0
4.0	0.63	3.2	6.3	9.4	12.6	15.8	18.9	22.0	25.2
4.5	0.77	3.8	7.7	11.6	15.4	19.2	23.1	27.0	30.8
5.0	0.93	4.6	9.3	14.0	18.6	23.2	27.9	32.6	37.2
5.5	1.10	5.5	11.0	16.5	22.0	27.5	33.0	38.5	44.0
6.0	1.29	6.4	12.9	19.4	25.8	32.2	38.7	45.2	51.6
6.5	1.50	7.5	15.0	22.5	30.0	37.5	45.0	52.5	60.0
7.0	1.72	8.6	17.2	25.8	34.4	43.0	51.6	60.2	68.8

Aerobics Points for Work with the Arms on the Schwinn Air-dyne Ergometer

Work Load	Total Time (Minutes)								
	1	5	10	15	20	25	30	35	40
0.5	0.08	0.4	0.8	1.2	1.6	2.0	2.4	2.8	3.2
1.0	0.12	0.6	1.2	1.8	2.4	3.0	3.6	4.2	4.8
1.5	0.19	1.0	2.0	3.0	4.0	5.0	6.0	7.0	8.0
2.0	0.28	1.4	2.8	4.2	5.6	7.0	8.4	9.8	11.2
2.5	0.39	1.9	3.9	5.8	7.8	9.8	11.7	13.6	15.0
3.0	0.52	2.6	5.2	7.8	10.4	13.0	15.6	18.2	20.8
3.5	0.66	3.3	6.6	9.9	13.2	16.5	19.8	23.1	26.4
4.0	0.83	4.2	8.4	12.6	16.8	21.0	25.2	29.4	33.6
4.5	1.01	5.1	10.2	15.3	20.4	25.5	30.6	35.7	40.8
5.0	1.22	6.1	12.2	18.3	24.4	30.5	36.6	42.7	48.8
5.5	1.44	7.2	14.4	21.6	28.8	36.0	43.2	50.4	57.6
6.0	1.65	8.2	16.4	24.6	32.8	41.0	49.2	57.4	65.6
6.5	1.95	9.8	19.6	29.4	39.2	49.0	58.8	68.6	78.4
7.0	2.23	11.2	22.4	33.6	44.8	56.0	67.2	78.4	89.6

Predicted Maximum Heart Rates Adjusted for Age and Fitness

Age	Very Poor and Poor	Fair	Good and Excellent	Age	Very Poor and Poor	Fair	Good and Excellent
20	201	201	196	45	174	183	183
21	199	200	196	46	173	182	183
22	198	199	195	47	172	181	182
23	197	198	195	48	171	181	182
24	196	198	194	49	170	180	181
25	195	197	194	50	168	179	180
26	194	196	193	51	167	179	180
27	193	196	193	52	166	178	179
28	192	195	192	53	165	177	179
29	191	193	192	54	164	176	178
30	190	193	191	55	163	176	178
31	189	193	191	56	162	175	177
32	188	192	190	57	161	174	177
33	187	191	189	58	160	174	176
34	186	191	189	59	159	173	176
35	184	190	188	60	158	172	175
36	183	189	188	61	157	172	175
37	182	189	187	62	156	171	174
38	181	188	187	63	155	170	174
39	180	187	186	64	154	169	173
40	179	186	186	65	152	169	173
41	178	186	185	66	151	168	172
42	177	185	185	67	150	167	171
43	176	184	184	68	149	167	171
44	175	184	184	69	148	166	170
				70	147	165	170

Note: If the level of fitness is unknown prior to stress testing, use the "Fair" category.

PERCENTILE RANKINGS FOR SIT-UPS

Based upon studies at the Cooper Clinic, these charts for men and women will help you evaluate your exercise progress. They relate fitness categories to the number of sit-ups a person of a particular age can do in a minute.

Percentile Rankings for Sit-Ups per Minute for Men (n = 255) by Decade

Fitness Catalogue	Percentile	TOTAL SIT-UPS PER MINUTE				
Excellent	100	59	58	58	57	57
	95	57	56	55	54	54
	90	55	54	53	50	50
	85	53	52	50	47	47
	80	51	49	47	44	44
Good	75	49	47	45	41	41
	70	47	45	42	38	38
	65	44	43	39	35	35
	60	42	40	37	32	32
Fair	55	40	38	34	29	28
	50	38	36	31	26	25
	45	36	34	29	23	22
	40	34	31	26	20	18
Poor	35	32	29	23	16	15
	30	29	27	21	13	11
	25	27	25	18	10	8
	20	25	22	15	7	4
Very Poor	15	23	20	13	4	3
	10	21	18	10	2	2
	5	19	16	7	1	1
	0	17	13	5	0	0
Decade (Years)		20–29	30–39	40–49	50–59	60–69
n		19	80	81	60	15

Percentile Rankings for Sit-ups per Minute for Women (n = 34) by Decade

Fitness Catalogue	Percentile	TOTAL SIT-UPS PER MINUTE			
Excellent	100	62	52	49	48
	95	60	49	46	45
	90	57	47	44	43
	85	54	45	41	40
	80	52	42	38	37
Good	75	49	40	35	34
	70	46	38	32	31
	65	43	35	30	29
	60	41	33	27	26
Fair	55	38	31	24	23
	50	35	28	21	20
	45	32	26	18	17
	40	30	24	15	14
Poor	35	27	21	13	12
	30	24	19	10	9
	25	22	17	7	8
	20	19	14	6	5
Very Poor	15	16	12	5	4
	10	13	10	4	3
	5	11	7	2	1
	0	8	5	1	0
Decade (Years)		20–29	30–39	40–49	50–60

CORONARY RISK FACTORS

1. Family History
2. Stress, Personality Behavior Patterns
3. Hypertension
4. Cholesterol, Triglycerides
5. Glucose—Diabetes
6. Diet Rich in Fats and Cholesterol
7. Inactivity—Sedentary Living Habits
8. Cigarette Smoking
9. Obesity
10. Abnormal Resting EKG
11. Oral Contraceptives

American Heart Association 1980

Definition of Fitness Categories for Males

Age Group (years)

FITNESS CATEGORY	< 30	30–39	40–49	50–59	60 +
☐ VERY POOR	<14:00	<13:00	<11:30	<9:30	<6:20
☐ POOR	14:00–16:59	13:00–15:29	11:30–13:59	9:30–11:59	6:20– 9:29
☐ FAIR	17:00–20:21	15:30–18:59	14:00–17:14	12:00–15:03	9:30–12:59
☐ GOOD	20:22–22:59	19:00–22:09	17:15–20:36	15:04–18:44	13:00–15:59
☐ EXCELLENT	23:00–26:22	22:10–25:19	20:37–23:30	18:45–21:59	16:00–20:37
☐ SUPERIOR	26:23 +	25:20 +	23:31 +	22:00 +	20:38 +

Based on the Cooper Clinic modified Balke treadmill protocol: 3.3 mph (90m/min), 0% for 1st min, 2% for 2nd min, + 1% for each additional min. to 25%, then + .2 mph until exhaustion.

Definition of Fitness Categories for Females

Age Group (years)

FITNESS CATEGORY	< 30	30–39	40–49	50–59	60 +
☐ VERY POOR	<10:00	<8:30	<7:00	<5:43	<4:02
☐ POOR	10:00–11:59	8:30–10·44	7:00 9:09	5:43– 7:26	4:02– 5:59
☐ FAIR	12:00 14:59	10:45–13:29	9:10–11:59	7:27– 9:59	6:00– 7:59
☐ GOOD	15:00–17:59	13:30–16:17	12:00–14:44	10:00–11:59	8:00–11:18
☐ EXCELLENT	18:00–20:59	16:18–18:55	14:45–16:59	12:00–14:59	11:19 14:39
☐ SUPERIOR	21:00 +	18:56 +	17:00 +	15:00 +	14:40 +

Based on the Cooper Clinic modified Balke treadmill protocol: 3.3 mph (90m/min), 0% for 1st min, 2% for 2nd min, + 1% for each additional min to 25%, then + .2 mph until exhaustion.

CORONARY RISK FACTOR CHARTS

The following coronary risk factor charts are completely new. They have been formulated in view of the latest research we've conducted on what things in your life are most likely to cause you to have future heart trouble.

To use these charts, first choose the one that correlates with your age and sex. Then, go over the chart with your physician and fill in the blanks as you have your medical exam. You can find the number of points to be awarded to each risk factor by looking at the numbers on the left of each column. Then, you should add up the points you've received for each factor and see where that total places you in the "total coronary risk" box on the lower right-hand corner of each page.

NAME:

Males: *40 - 49 Years of Age

PERCENTILE RANKINGS	BALKE TREADMILL TIME (min.)	TOTAL CHOLESTEROL/ HDL RATIO	TRIGLYCERIDE (mg. %)	GLUCOSE (mg. %)	% BODY FAT	RESTING BLOOD PRESSURE SYSTOLIC (mm HG)	DIASTOLIC (mm HG)
YOUR VALUES	13:45 [4]	4.09 [0]	92 [0]	91 [0]	30.7 [3]	118 [0]	80 [0]
99	27:00	2.5	37.0	77.0	6.1	96.0	60.0
97	25:00	2.8	46.0	81.0	9.3	100.0	65.0
95	23:31	3.0	52.0	83.0	10.7	102.0	68.0
90	22:00	3.3	62.0	87.0	13.0	106.0	70.0
85	20:37	3.6	70.0	89.0	14.5	110.0	72.0
80	20:00	3.8	76.0	91.0	15.7	110.0	74.0
75	19:00	4.0	82.0	92.0	16.8	112.0	76.0
70	18:00	4.1	89.0	94.0	17.7	115.0	78.0
65	17:15 [2]	4.3	96.0	95.0	18.5	118.0	78.7
60	17:00	4.5 [1]	102.0	97.0 [1]	19.2	118.0	80.0
55	16:00	4.7	110.0	98.0	20.0	120.0	80.0
50	15:40 [2]	4.9	118.0 [1]	100.0	20.8	120.0	80.0
45	15:00	5.1	126.0	100.0	21.5	120.0	80.0
40	14:30	5.3	136.0	102.0	22.2	124.0	82.0
35	14:00 [4]	5.5 [3]	147.0	104.0	22.9	126.0 [1]	84.0
30	13:30	5.7	160.0	105.0	23.8 [2]	128.0	86.0
25	13:00	6.0 [4]	175.0	108.0	24.7 [1]	130.0	88.0
20	12:00	6.3 [5]	196.0 [2]	110.0	25.9	132.0	90.0 [2]
15	11:30 [5]	6.7	223.0	112.0	27.2 [3]	138.0	90.0
		[6]					
10	10:20 [7]	7.2	259.0	115.0 [1]	28.7 [2]	140.0	95.8
5	9:00	8.2	344.0	121.8	31.8	148.0	100.0 [3]
3	7:40 [9]	8.8	402.3	127.0 [2]	33.8 [3]	152.0	102.0
1	6:00 [10]	10.3	602.9	146.7 [3]	38.1 [4]	162.0 [4]	110.0 [4]
n	5,645	1,711	5,127	5,123	4,292	5,741	5,741

PERSONAL HISTORY OF HEART ATTACK OR BYPASS

0 ■ NONE
2 □ OVER 5 YEARS AGO
4 □ 2-5 YEARS AGO
5 □ 1-<2 YEARS AGO
8 □ 0-<1 YEAR AGO   [0]

FAMILY HISTORY OF HEART ATTACK

0 ■ NONE
2 □ YES, OVER 50 YEARS
4 □ YES, 50 YEARS OR UNDER   [0]

6 □ KNOWN CORONARY HEART DISEASE W/O HEART ATTACK OR BYPASS   [0]

SMOKING HABITS

0 □ NONE
0 ■ PAST 1 YEAR OR MORE
1 □ PAST ONLY LESS THAN 1 YEAR
1 □ PIPE/CIGAR
2 □ 1-10 DAILY
3 □ 11-20 DAILY
4 □ 21-30 DAILY
5 □ 31-40 DAILY
6 □ MORE THAN 40 DAILY   [0]

TENSION - ANXIETY

0 □ NO TENSION, VERY RELAXED
0 □ SLIGHT TENSION
1 ■ MODERATE TENSION
2 □ HIGH TENSION
3 □ VERY TENSE, "HIGH STRUNG"   [1]

3 □ DIABETES   [0]

AGE FACTOR

0 □ UNDER 30 YEARS OF AGE
1 □ 30-39 YEARS OF AGE
2 ■ 40-49 YEARS OF AGE
3 □ 50-59 YEARS OF AGE
4 □ 60 + YEARS OF AGE   [2]

RESTING ECG   EXERCISE ECG

0 ■ NORMAL   ■ 0
1 □ EQUIVOCAL   □ 4
3 □ ABNORMAL   □ 8   [0]

TOTAL CORONARY RISK

□ VERY LOW   (0- 4)
■ LOW   (5-12)
□ MODERATE   (13-21)
□ HIGH   (22-31)
□ VERY HIGH (32 +)   [10]

*Data based on first visit only

© Institute for Aerobics Research - 1982

COOPER CLINIC/ Dallas, Texas

Coronary Risk Profile

NAME: | **Males: *<30 Years of Age**

PERCENTILE RANKINGS	BALKE TREADMILL TIME (min.)	TOTAL CHOLESTEROL/ HDL RATIO	TRIGLYCERIDE (mg. %)	GLUCOSE (mg. %)	% BODY FAT	RESTING BLOOD PRESSURE SYSTOLIC (mm HG)	RESTING BLOOD PRESSURE DIASTOLIC (mm HG)
YOUR VALUES							
99	30:21	2.2	31.0	71.7	2.2	90.0	56.0
97	28:00	2.5	40.0	77.0	4.2	98.0	60.0
95	26.23	2.6	45.0	79.7	5.4	100.0	62.0
90	25:00	2.9	51.0	83.0	7.6	105.0	66.0
85	23:00	3.0	56.0	86.0	8.7	110.0	68.0
80	22:25	3.2	61.0	87.0	9.8	110.0	70.0
75	22:00	3.4	65.0	89.0	11.3	112.0	70.0
70	21:00	3.5	70.0	90.0	12.2	115.0	72.0
65	20:22	3.7	75.0	91.0	13.1	118.0	74.0
60	[2] 20:00	3.8	80.0	93.0	14.1	118.0	76.0
55	19:25	4.0	85.0	94.0	15.0	120.0	78.0
50	19:00	4.1	91.0	95.0	16.0	120.0	78.0
45	18:00	4.2	97.0	96.0	16.9	120.0	80.0
40	18:00	4.4	104.0	98.0	17.6	122.0	80.0
35	17:00	[1] 4.5	114.1	100.0	18.3	124.0	80.0
	[4]		[1]		[1]		
30	16:25	4.7	123.0	100.0	19.7	[1] 127.0	80.0
25	15:40	4.9	133.0	102.0	20.9	130.0	82.0
20	15:00	[2] 5.1	148.0	104.0	[2] 22.1	130.0	84.0
15	[5] 14:00	[3] 5.6	170.0	106.0	23.8	134.0	[1] 88.0
10	13:00	[4] 6.0	196.0	110.0	25.9	[2] 140.0	[2] 90.0
5	11:00	[6] 7.0	[2] 263.8	114.2	29.8	142.0	94.0
3	10:00	7.3	304.9	118.0	32.8	[3] 148.1	96.0
1	7:52	[7] 8.9	437.2	123.5	38.9	165.0	100.0
		[10]		[3]		[4]	[4]
n	1,372	386	1,073	1,074	939	1,397	1,397

PERSONAL HISTORY OF HEART ATTACK OR BYPASS

- 0 ☐ NONE
- 2 ☐ OVER 5 YEARS AGO
- 4 ☐ 2-5 YEARS AGO
- 5 ☐ 1-<2 YEARS AGO
- 8 ☐ 0-<1 YEAR AGO

FAMILY HISTORY OF HEART ATTACK

- 0 ☐ NONE
- 2 ☐ YES, OVER 50 YEARS
- 4 ☐ YES, 50 YEARS OR UNDER

- 6 ☐ KNOWN CORONARY HEART DISEASE W/O HEART ATTACK OR BYPASS

SMOKING HABITS

- 0 ☐ NONE
- 0 ☐ PAST 1 YEAR OR MORE
- 1 ☐ PAST ONLY LESS THAN 1 YEAR
- 1 ☐ PIPE/CIGAR
- 2 ☐ 1-10 DAILY
- 3 ☐ 11-20 DAILY
- 4 ☐ 21-30 DAILY
- 5 ☐ 31-40 DAILY
- 6 ☐ MORE THAN 40 DAILY

TENSION - ANXIETY

- 0 ☐ NO TENSION, VERY RELAXED
- 0 ☐ SLIGHT TENSION
- 1 ☐ MODERATE TENSION
- 2 ☐ HIGH TENSION
- 3 ☐ VERY TENSE, "HIGH STRUNG"

- 3 ☐ DIABETES

AGE FACTOR

- 0 ☐ UNDER 30 YEARS OF AGE
- 1 ☐ 30-39 YEARS OF AGE
- 2 ☐ 40-49 YEARS OF AGE
- 3 ☐ 50-59 YEARS OF AGE
- 4 ☐ 60 + YEARS OF AGE

RESTING ECG   EXERCISE ECG

- 0 ☐ NORMAL ☐ 0
- 1 ☐ EQUIVOCAL ☐ 4
- 3 ☐ ABNORMAL ☐ 8

TOTAL CORONARY RISK

- ☐ VERY LOW (0- 4)
- ☐ LOW (5-12)
- ☐ MODERATE (13-21)
- ☐ HIGH (22-31)
- ☐ VERY HIGH (32 +)

*Data based on first visit only

Coronary Risk Profile

NAME:

Males: *30 - 39 Years of Age

PERCENTILE RANKINGS	BALKE TREADMILL TIME (min.)	TOTAL CHOLESTEROL/ HDL RATIO	TRIGLYCERIDE (mg. %)	GLUCOSE (mg. %)	% BODY FAT	RESTING BLOOD PRESSURE SYSTOLIC (mm HG)	DIASTOLIC (mm HG)
YOUR VALUES							
99	28:30	2.3	35.0	75.0	4.5	94.0	60.0
97	26:25	2.6	42.0	79.0	7.1	100.0	64.0
95	25:20	2.8	46.0	81.0	8.6	100.0	66.0
90	24:00	3.1	55.0	85.0	10.8	106.0	70.0
85	22:10	3.3	62.0	87.0	12.3	110.0	70.0
80	21:10	3.5	68.0	89.0	13.5	110.0	72.0
75	20:40	3.7	74.0	90.0	14.5	112.0	74.0
70	20:00	3.8	80.0	92.0	15.4	114.0	75.0
65	[2] 19:00	4.0	86.0	93.0	16.3	116.0	76.0
60	18:25	4.1	92.0	95.0	17.1	118.0	78.0
55	18:00	4.3	98.0	95.0	17.8	118.0	80.0
50	17:06	[1] 4.5	104.0	97.0	18.5	120.0	80.0
45	17:00	4.7	112.0	99.0	[1] 19.2	120.0	80.0
40	16:00	4.9	[1] 120.0	100.0	20.0	120.0	80.0
35	15:30	[2] 5.1	130.0	101.0	20.8	122.0	80.0
	[4]					124.0	82.0
30	15:00	[3] 5.4	142.0	103.0	21.7	126.0	[1] 84.0
25	14:35	5.6	156.0	104.0	22.6	128.0	85.0
20	14:00	5.9	174.0	106.0	[2] 23.8	[1] 130.0	88.0
15	[5] 13:00	[4] 6.2	197.7	109.0	25.0	132.0	[2] 90.0
		[5]	[2]				
10	12:00	6.7	232.0	111.0	26.9	138.0	90.0
5	10:26	[6] 7.7	303.8	116.0	[3] 29.6	[2] 142.0	96.0
3	9:40	[7] 8.3	366.9	[1] 120.0	31.7	148.0	[3] 100.0
1	7:31	[8] 9.9	582.9	130.0	36.4	[3] 158.0	106.0
		[10]		[3]		[4]	[4]
n	5,623	1,784	4,801	4,801	4,142	5,679	5,679

PERSONAL HISTORY OF HEART ATTACK OR BYPASS

0 ☐ NONE
2 ☐ OVER 5 YEARS AGO
4 ☐ 2-5 YEARS AGO
5 ☐ 1-<2 YEARS AGO
8 ☐ 0-<1 YEAR AGO

FAMILY HISTORY OF HEART ATTACK

0 ☐ NONE
2 ☐ YES, OVER 50 YEARS
4 ☐ YES, 50 YEARS OR UNDER

6 ☐ KNOWN CORONARY HEART DISEASE W/O HEART ATTACK OR BYPASS

SMOKING HABITS

0 ☐ NONE
0 ☐ PAST 1 YEAR OR MORE
1 ☐ PAST ONLY LESS THAN 1 YEAR
1 ☐ PIPE/CIGAR
2 ☐ 1-10 DAILY
3 ☐ 11-20 DAILY
4 ☐ 21-30 DAILY
5 ☐ 31-40 DAILY
6 ☐ MORE THAN 40 DAILY

TENSION - ANXIETY

0 ☐ NO TENSION, VERY RELAXED
0 ☐ SLIGHT TENSION
1 ☐ MODERATE TENSION
2 ☐ HIGH TENSION
3 ☐ VERY TENSE, "HIGH STRUNG"

3 ☐ DIABETES

AGE FACTOR

0 ☐ UNDER 30 YEARS OF AGE
1 ☐ 30-39 YEARS OF AGE
2 ☐ 40-49 YEARS OF AGE
3 ☐ 50-59 YEARS OF AGE
4 ☐ 60 + YEARS OF AGE

RESTING ECG   EXERCISE ECG

0 ☐   NORMAL   ☐ 0
1 ☐   EQUIVOCAL   ☐ 4
3 ☐   ABNORMAL   ☐ 8

TOTAL CORONARY RISK

☐ VERY LOW   (0- 4)
☐ LOW   (5-12)
☐ MODERATE   (13-21)
☐ HIGH   (22-31)
☐ VERY HIGH   (32 +)

*Data based on first visit only

© Institute for Aerobics Research - 1982

COOPER CLINIC/ Dallas, Texas

Coronary Risk Profile

NAME:

Males: *40 - 49 Years of Age

PERCENTILE RANKINGS	BALKE TREADMILL TIME (min.)	TOTAL CHOLESTEROL/ HDL RATIO	TRIGLYCERIDE (mg. %)	GLUCOSE (mg. %)	% BODY FAT	RESTING BLOOD PRESSURE SYSTOLIC (mm HG)	DIASTOLIC (mm HG)
YOUR VALUES							
99	27:00	2.5	37.0	77.0	6.1	96.0	60.0
97	25:00	2.8	46.0	81.0	9.3	100.0	65.0
95	23:31	3.0	52.0	83.0	10.7	102.0	68.0
90	22:00	3.3	62.0	87.0	13.0	106.0	70.0
85	20:37	3.6	70.0	89.0	14.5	110.0	72.0
80	20:00	3.8	76.0	91.0	15.7	110.0	74.0
75	19:00	4.0	82.0	92.0	16.8	112.0	76.0
70	18:00	4.1	89.0	94.0	17.7	115.0	78.0
65	17:15 [2]	4.3	96.0	95.0 [1]	18.5	118.0	78.7
60	17:00	4.5 [1]	102.0	97.0	19.2	118.0	80.0
55	16:00	4.7	110.0	98.0	20.0	120.0	80.0
50	15:40 [2]	4.9	118.0 [1]	100.0	20.8	120.0	80.0
45	15:00	5.1	126.0	100.0	21.5	120.0	80.0
40	14:30	5.3	136.0	102.0	22.2	124.0	82.0
35	14:00 [4]	5.5 [3]	147.0	104.0 [2]	22.9	126.0	84.0 [1]
30	13:30	5.7	160.0	105.0	23.8	128.0 [1]	86.0
25	13:00	6.0 [4]	175.0	108.0	24.7	130.0	88.0
20	12:00	6.3 [5]	196.0 [2]	110.0 [3]	25.9	132.0 [2]	90.0
15	11:30 [5]	6.7	223.0	112.0	27.2	138.0	90.0
		[6]					
10	10:20 [7]	7.2	259.0 [1]	115.0	28.7	140.0 [2]	95.8
5	9:00	8.2	344.0	121.8	31.8	148.0 [3]	100.0 [3]
3	7:40	8.8 [9]	402.3	127.0 [2]	33.8	152.0	102.0
1	6:00	10.3 [10]	602.9	146.7 [3]	38.1	162.0 [4]	110.0 [4]
N	5,645	1,711	5,127	5,123	4,292	5,741	5,741

PERSONAL HISTORY OF HEART ATTACK OR BYPASS

- 0 ☐ NONE
- 2 ☐ OVER 5 YEARS AGO
- 4 ☐ 2-5 YEARS AGO
- 5 ☐ 1-<2 YEARS AGO
- 8 ☐ 0-<1 YEAR AGO

FAMILY HISTORY OF HEART ATTACK

- 0 ☐ NONE
- 2 ☐ YES, OVER 50 YEARS
- 4 ☐ YES, 50 YEARS OR UNDER

- 6 ☐ KNOWN CORONARY HEART DISEASE W/O HEART ATTACK OR BYPASS

SMOKING HABITS

- 0 ☐ NONE
- 0 ☐ PAST 1 YEAR OR MORE
- 1 ☐ PAST ONLY LESS THAN 1 YEAR
- 1 ☐ PIPE/CIGAR
- 2 ☐ 1-10 DAILY
- 3 ☐ 11-20 DAILY
- 4 ☐ 21-30 DAILY
- 5 ☐ 31-40 DAILY
- 6 ☐ MORE THAN 40 DAILY

TENSION - ANXIETY

- 0 ☐ NO TENSION, VERY RELAXED
- 0 ☐ SLIGHT TENSION
- 1 ☐ MODERATE TENSION
- 2 ☐ HIGH TENSION
- 3 ☐ VERY TENSE, "HIGH STRUNG"

- 3 ☐ DIABETES

AGE FACTOR

- 0 ☐ UNDER 30 YEARS OF AGE
- 1 ☐ 30-39 YEARS OF AGE
- 2 ☐ 40-49 YEARS OF AGE
- 3 ☐ 50-59 YEARS OF AGE
- 4 ☐ 60 + YEARS OF AGE

RESTING ECG		EXERCISE ECG
0 ☐	NORMAL	☐ 0
1 ☐	EQUIVOCAL	☐ 4
3 ☐	ABNORMAL	☐ 8

TOTAL CORONARY RISK

- ☐ VERY LOW (0- 4)
- ☐ LOW (5-12)
- ☐ MODERATE (13-21)
- ☐ HIGH (22-31)
- ☐ VERY HIGH (32 +)

*Data based on first visit only

© Institute for Aerobics Research - 1982

COOPER CLINIC/ Dallas, Texas

Coronary Risk Profile

NAME:

Males: *50 - 59 Years of Age

PERCENTILE RANKINGS	BALKE TREADMILL TIME (min.)	TOTAL CHOLESTEROL/ HDL RATIO	TRIGLYCERIDE (mg. %)	GLUCOSE (mg. %)	% BODY FAT	RESTING BLOOD PRESSURE SYSTOLIC (mm HG)	DIASTOLIC (mm HG)
YOUR VALUES							
99	26:00	2.6	38.9	77.0	8.1	96.0	62.0
97	23:27	2.9	47.0	82.0	11.0	100.0	68.0
95	22:00	3.1	53.0	84.0	12.2	104.0	70.0
90	20:00	3.4	63.0	87.0	14.7	110.0	70.0
85	18:45	3.6	73.0	90.0	16.5	110.0	74.0
80	18:00	3.8	80.0	92.0	17.7	114.0	76.0
75	16:45	4.1	87.0	94.0	18.8	116.0	78.0
70	16:00	4.3	93.0	96.0	19.6	120.0	80.0
65	15:04	4.5	100.0	97.3	20.5	120.0	80.0
60	15:00	4.7	106.0	99.0	21.2	120.0	80.0
55	14:00	4.8	113.0	100.0	22.0	122.0	80.0
50	13:30	5.1	122.0	102.0	22.6	125.0	82.0
45	13:00	5.3	131.0	104.0	23.3	128.0	84.0
40	12:25	5.5	141.0	105.0	24.0	130.0	85.0
35	12:00	5.7	152.0	107.0	24.8	130.0	88.0
30	11:30	5.9	164.0	109.0	25.7	134.0	90.0
25	11:00	6.2	180.0	110.0	26.5	138.0	90.0
20	10:00	6.5	197.0	114.0	27.4	140.0	90.0
15	9:30	6.9	225.0	116.0	28.6	142.0	94.0
10	8:15	7.4	268.0	120.0	30.1	150.0	98.0
5	7:00	8.3	347.6	130.0	32.4	158.0	100.0
3	6:00	9.2	406.4	140.0	34.0	162.0	106.0
1	4:00	11.2	651.5	220.9	38.2	180.0	110.0
n	3,111	959	2,891	2,900	2,346	3,259	3,259

PERSONAL HISTORY OF HEART ATTACK OR BYPASS

0 ☐ NONE
2 ☐ OVER 5 YEARS AGO
4 ☐ 2-5 YEARS AGO
5 ☐ 1-<2 YEARS AGO
8 ☐ 0-<1 YEAR AGO

FAMILY HISTORY OF HEART ATTACK

0 ☐ NONE
2 ☐ YES, OVER 50 YEARS
4 ☐ YES, 50 YEARS OR UNDER

6 ☐ KNOWN CORONARY HEART DISEASE W/O HEART ATTACK OR BYPASS

SMOKING HABITS

0 ☐ NONE
0 ☐ PAST 1 YEAR OR MORE
1 ☐ PAST ONLY LESS THAN 1 YEAR
1 ☐ PIPE/CIGAR
2 ☐ 1-10 DAILY
3 ☐ 11-20 DAILY
4 ☐ 21-30 DAILY
5 ☐ 31-40 DAILY
6 ☐ MORE THAN 40 DAILY

TENSION - ANXIETY

0 ☐ NO TENSION, VERY RELAXED
0 ☐ SLIGHT TENSION
1 ☐ MODERATE TENSION
2 ☐ HIGH TENSION
3 ☐ VERY TENSE, "HIGH STRUNG"

3 ☐ DIABETES

AGE FACTOR

0 ☐ UNDER 30 YEARS OF AGE
1 ☐ 30-39 YEARS OF AGE
2 ☐ 40-49 YEARS OF AGE
3 ☐ 50-59 YEARS OF AGE
4 ☐ 60 + YEARS OF AGE

RESTING ECG   EXERCISE ECG

0 ☐   NORMAL   ☐ 0
1 ☐   EQUIVOCAL   ☐ 4
3 ☐   ABNORMAL   ☐ 8

TOTAL CORONARY RISK

☐ VERY LOW   (0- 4)
☐ LOW   (5-12)
☐ MODERATE   (13-21)
☐ HIGH   (22-31)
☐ VERY HIGH   (32 +)

*Data based on first visit only

© Institute for Aerobics Research - 1982

COOPER CLINIC/ Dallas, Texas   Coronary Risk Profile

NAME: Males: *> 60 Years of Age

PERCENTILE RANKINGS	BALKE TREADMILL TIME (min.)	TOTAL CHOLESTEROL/ HDL RATIO	TRIGLYCERIDE (mg. %)	GLUCOSE (mg. %)	% BODY FAT	RESTING BLOOD PRESSURE SYSTOLIC (mm HG)	DIASTOLIC (mm HG)
YOUR VALUES							
99	23:00	2.5	42.0	75.0	6.5	100.0	60.0
97	21:00	3.0	48.0	82.0	10.0	104.0	64.2
95	20:38	3.1	52.6	85.0	11.8	108.0	68.0
90	18:00	3.4	63.0	89.0	14.5	112.0	70.0
85	16:00	3.6	70.0	91.0	16.1	116.0	72.0
80	15:06	3.8	76.4	92.2	17.3	120.0	75.0
75	14:30	4.0	82.0	94.0	18.7	120.0	78.0
70	13:30	4.2	87.0	96.0	19.6 [1]	124.0	80.0
65	13:00	4.4	95.0	98.0	20.5	126.0	80.0
60	12:13 [2]	4.5 [7]	101.0	100.0	21.3	130.0 [1]	80.0
55	11:44	4.7	108.0	101.0	22.1	130.0	80.0
50	11:00	4.9 [2]	118.0 [1]	103.0	22.6	132.0	82.0
45	10:30	5.1	125.0	105.0 [2]	23.6	136.0	84.0 [1]
40	10:00	5.3	135.0	107.0	24.7	140.0 [2]	86.0
35	9:30 [3]	5.5	144.8	109.0	25.6	140.0	88.0
30	9:00 [4]	5.8	156.0	110.0 [3]	26.6	142.0	90.0 [2]
25	8:00	6.0 [4]	170.0	114.0	27.6	146.0	90.0
20	7:15	6.3	188.6 [2]	116.0	28.5	150.0 [3]	92.0
15	6:20 [5]	6.5 [5]	210.0	120.0 [1]	29.7	154.0	95.0
10	5:11 [6]	6.9	245.8 [2]	125.0	31.5	160.0	98.0 [3]
5	3:46 [7]	7.8	304.8	139.0	33.7	170.0 [4]	102.0
3	3:00 [8]	8.2	362.4 [3]	150.2	35.4	180.0	110.0 [4]
1	2:07 [10]	9.1	717.3	175.1	40.2	190.0	112.0
n	835	310	891	890	669	1,039	1,039

PERSONAL HISTORY OF HEART ATTACK OR BYPASS

- 0 ☐ NONE
- 2 ☐ OVER 5 YEARS AGO
- 4 ☐ 2-5 YEARS AGO
- 5 ☐ 1-<2 YEARS AGO
- 8 ☐ 0-<1 YEAR AGO

FAMILY HISTORY OF HEART ATTACK

- 0 ☐ NONE
- 2 ☐ YES, OVER 50 YEARS
- 4 ☐ YES, 50 YEARS OR UNDER

- 6 ☐ KNOWN CORONARY HEART DISEASE W/O HEART ATTACK OR BYPASS

SMOKING HABITS

- 0 ☐ NONE
- 0 ☐ PAST 1 YEAR OR MORE
- 1 ☐ PAST ONLY LESS THAN 1 YEAR
- 1 ☐ PIPE/CIGAR
- 2 ☐ 1-10 DAILY
- 3 ☐ 11-20 DAILY
- 4 ☐ 21-30 DAILY
- 5 ☐ 31-40 DAILY
- 6 ☐ MORE THAN 40 DAILY

TENSION - ANXIETY

- 0 ☐ NO TENSION, VERY RELAXED
- 0 ☐ SLIGHT TENSION
- 1 ☐ MODERATE TENSION
- 2 ☐ HIGH TENSION
- 3 ☐ VERY TENSE, "HIGH STRUNG"

- 3 ☐ DIABETES

AGE FACTOR

- 0 ☐ UNDER 30 YEARS OF AGE
- 1 ☐ 30-39 YEARS OF AGE
- 2 ☐ 40-49 YEARS OF AGE
- 3 ☐ 50-59 YEARS OF AGE
- 4 ☐ 60 + YEARS OF AGE

RESTING ECG   EXERCISE ECG

- 0 ☐   NORMAL   ☐ 0
- 1 ☐   EQUIVOCAL   ☐ 4
- 3 ☐   ABNORMAL   ☐ 8

TOTAL CORONARY RISK

- ☐ VERY LOW   (0- 4)
- ☐ LOW   (5-12)
- ☐ MODERATE   (13-21)
- ☐ HIGH   (22-31)
- ☐ VERY HIGH   (32 +)

*Data based on first visit only

COOPER CLINIC/ Dallas, Texas　　　　　　　　　　　　　　　　**Coronary Risk Profile**

NAME:						**Females: * < 30 Years of Age**

PERCENTILE RANKINGS	BALKE TREADMILL TIME (min.)	TOTAL CHOLESTEROL / HDL RATIO	TRIGLYCERIDE (mg. %)	GLUCOSE (mg. %)	% BODY FAT	RESTING BLOOD PRESSURE SYSTOLIC (mm HG)	DIASTOLIC (mm HG)
YOUR VALUES							
99	25:04	2.0	28.8	65.8	4.2	84.0	54.0
97	23:00	2.2	33.0	72.0	7.7	90.0	58.0
95	21:00	2.3	35.0	75.0	9.2	90.0	58.0
90	19:49	2.4	41.0	78.0	11.1	94.0	60.0
85	18:00	2.5	45.0	80.0	12.9	98.0	62.0
80	17:00	2.6	47.0	81.0	14.9	100.0	64.0
75	16:05	2.7	49.0	83.0	16.0	100.0	66.0
70	15:49	2.8	52.0	84.0	17.1	102.0	68.0
65	15:00	2.8	55.0	85.0	18.0	104.0	68.0
60	14:30 [2]	2.9	58.0	86.0	19.0	106.0	70.0
55	14:00	3.1	61.4	88.0	20.1	108.0	70.0
50	13:30	3.2	65.0	89.0	21.1	110.0	70.0
45	13:00	3.3	71.0	90.0	21.8	110.0	72.0
40	12:13	3.4	76.0	91.0 [1]	22.9	110.0	74.0
35	12:00 [4]	3.5	80.6	92.0	24.2	112.0	75.0
30	11:07	3.6	85.0	94.0	24.7	115.0	76.0
25	11:00	3.7	92.7	95.0	25.9 [2]	116.0	78.0
20	10:30	3.9	104.0	97.0	27.2	118.0	80.0
15	10:00 [5]	4.0 [1]	114.0 [1]	99.0 [3]	29.3	120.0	80.0
10	9:00 [2]	4.2	138.0	101.0	32.4	120.0 [1]	80.0 [1]
5	7:30 [3]	4.7	171.0 [2]	105.0	35.6	130.0	86.0
3	6:30 [4]	5.3	205.3	108.2	39.6	130.0	90.0 [2]
1	5:12 [10]	5.8	277.9	120.0 [1] [3]	42.6	140.0 [2] [4]	90.0 [4]
n	583	190	460	461	364	599	599

PERSONAL HISTORY OF HEART ATTACK OR BYPASS

- 0 ☐ NONE
- 2 ☐ OVER 5 YEARS AGO
- 4 ☐ 2-5 YEARS AGO
- 5 ☐ 1-<2 YEARS AGO
- 8 ☐ 0-<1 YEAR AGO

FAMILY HISTORY OF HEART ATTACK

- 0 ☐ NONE
- 2 ☐ YES, OVER 50 YEARS
- 4 ☐ YES, 50 YEARS OR UNDER

- 6 ☐ KNOWN CORONARY HEART DISEASE W/O HEART ATTACK OR BYPASS

SMOKING HABITS

- 0 ☐ NONE
- 0 ☐ PAST 1 YEAR OR MORE
- 1 ☐ PAST ONLY LESS THAN 1 YEAR
- 1 ☐ PIPE/CIGAR
- 2 ☐ 1-10 DAILY
- 3 ☐ 11-20 DAILY
- 4 ☐ 21-30 DAILY
- 5 ☐ 31-40 DAILY
- 6 ☐ MORE THAN 40 DAILY

TENSION - ANXIETY

- 0 ☐ NO TENSION, VERY RELAXED
- 0 ☐ SLIGHT TENSION
- 1 ☐ MODERATE TENSION
- 2 ☐ HIGH TENSION
- 3 ☐ VERY TENSE, "HIGH STRUNG"
- 3 ☐ DIABETES

AGE FACTOR

- 0 ☐ UNDER 30 YEARS OF AGE
- 1 ☐ 30-39 YEARS OF AGE
- 2 ☐ 40-49 YEARS OF AGE
- 3 ☐ 50-59 YEARS OF AGE
- 4 ☐ 60 + YEARS OF AGE

RESTING ECG　　EXERCISE ECG

- 0 ☐　NORMAL　☐ 0
- 1 ☐　EQUIVOCAL　☐ 4
- 3 ☐　ABNORMAL　☐ 8

TOTAL CORONARY RISK

- ☐ VERY LOW　(0- 4)
- ☐ LOW　(5-12)
- ☐ MODERATE　(13-21)
- ☐ HIGH　(22-31)
- ☐ VERY HIGH　(32 +)

*Data based on first visit only

© Institute for Aerobics Research - 1982

NAME:						**Females: *30 - 39 Years of Age**	

PERCENTILE RANKINGS	BALKE TREADMILL TIME (min.)	TOTAL CHOLESTEROL/ HDL RATIO	TRIGLYCERIDE (mg. %)	GLUCOSE (mg. %)	% BODY FAT	RESTING BLOOD PRESSURE SYSTOLIC (mm HG)	DIASTOLIC (mm HG)
YOUR VALUES							
99	22:00	1.8	23.6	67.7	4.1	85.5	54.0
97	20:00	2.0	30.0	74.0	8.3	90.0	60.0
95	18:56	2.1	34.0	76.0	10.2	90.0	60.0
90	17:30	2.3	39.9	80.0	13.8	96.0	62.0
85	16:18	2.5	43.0	82.0	15.6	98.0	64.0
80	15:21	2.6	47.0	84.0	16.8	100.0	66.0
75	15:00	2.7	50.0	85.0	17.7	100.0	68.0
70	14:04	2.7	53.0	86.0	19.0	104.0	70.0
65	13:30	2.8	56.0	87.0	19.8	104.0	70.0
60	13:00	3.0	59.6	89.0	20.7	108.0	70.0
55	12:35	3.0	62.0	90.0	21.5	108.0	70.0
50	12:00	3.1	66.0	91.0	22.4	110.0	72.0
45	12:00	3.2	69.0	92.0	23.2	110.0	74.0
40	11:07	3.3	73.0	94.0	24.1	112.0	76.0
35	10:45	3.5	78.0	95.0	25.5	114.0	78.0
30	10:00	3.6	82.0	96.0	26.4	116.0	78.0
25	9:45	3.7	87.7	98.0	27.4	118.0	80.0
20	9:00	3.9	95.0	100.0	28.7	120.0	80.0
15	8:30	4.1	102.6	101.0	29.9	120.0	80.0
10	7:45	4.3	120.0	104.0	32.2	124.0	84.0
5	6:30	4.8	150.0	109.0	35.7	130.0	90.0
2	6:00	5.2	167.9	112.8	37.3	140.0	90.0
1	5:00	6.2	235.3	122.1	42.3	150.0	100.0
n	1,514	446	1,068	1,071	842	1,544	1,554

PERSONAL HISTORY OF HEART ATTACK OR BYPASS	SMOKING HABITS	AGE FACTOR
0 ☐ NONE	0 ☐ NONE	0 ☐ UNDER 30 YEARS OF AGE
2 ☐ OVER 5 YEARS AGO	0 ☐ PAST 1 YEAR OR MORE	1 ☐ 30-39 YEARS OF AGE
4 ☐ 2-5 YEARS AGO	1 ☐ PAST ONLY LESS THAN 1 YEAR	2 ☐ 40-49 YEARS OF AGE
5 ☐ 1-<2 YEARS AGO	1 ☐ PIPE/CIGAR	3 ☐ 50-59 YEARS OF AGE
8 ☐ 0-<1 YEAR AGO	2 ☐ 1-10 DAILY	4 ☐ 60 + YEARS OF AGE

SMOKING HABITS:
- 3 ☐ 11-20 DAILY
- 4 ☐ 21-30 DAILY
- 5 ☐ 31-40 DAILY
- 6 ☐ MORE THAN 40 DAILY

FAMILY HISTORY OF HEART ATTACK
- 0 ☐ NONE
- 2 ☐ YES, OVER 50 YEARS
- 4 ☐ YES, 50 YEARS OR UNDER

- 6 ☐ KNOWN CORONARY HEART DISEASE W/O HEART ATTACK OR BYPASS

TENSION - ANXIETY
- 0 ☐ NO TENSION, VERY RELAXED
- 0 ☐ SLIGHT TENSION
- 1 ☐ MODERATE TENSION
- 2 ☐ HIGH TENSION
- 3 ☐ VERY TENSE, "HIGH STRUNG"
- 3 ☐ DIABETES

RESTING ECG   EXERCISE ECG
- 0 ☐ NORMAL ☐ 0
- 1 ☐ EQUIVOCAL ☐ 4
- 3 ☐ ABNORMAL ☐ 8

TOTAL CORONARY RISK
- ☐ VERY LOW (0- 4)
- ☐ LOW (5-12)
- ☐ MODERATE (13-21)
- ☐ HIGH (22-31)
- ☐ VERY HIGH (32 +)

*Data based on first visit only

© Institute for Aerobics Research - 1982

COOPER CLINIC/ Dallas, Texas

Coronary Risk Profile

NAME:

Female: *40 - 49 Years of Age

PERCENTILE RANKINGS	BALKE TREADMILL TIME (min.)	TOTAL CHOLESTEROL/ HDL RATIO	TRIGLYCERIDE (mg. %)	GLUCOSE (mg. %)	% BODY FAT	RESTING BLOOD PRESSURE SYSTOLIC (mm HG)	DIASTOLIC (mm HG)
YOUR VALUES							
99	21:00	1.9	28.0	72.0	7.4	84.9	58.0
97	18:30	2.2	34.0	76.2	12.8	90.0	60.0
95	17:00	2.3	38.1	78.0	14.2	94.0	62.0
90	16:00	2.6	44.0	82.0	17.2	100.0	66.0
85	14:45	2.7	48.4	84.0	18.6	100.0	68.0
80	13:44	2.8	52.6	85.0	20.2	102.0	70.0
75	13:00	2.9	56.0	87.0	[7] 21.3	104.0	70.0
70	12:30	3.0	60.0	88.0	22.5	108.0	70.0
65	[2] 12:00	3.1	63.0	90.0	23.4	110.0	72.0
60	11:30	3.2	67.0	91.0	24.2	110.0	74.0
55	11:00	3.3	71.0	92.0	25.0	110.0	76.0
50	10:37	3.4	75.0	93.0	[2] 25.7	112.0	78.0
45	10:00	3.5	80.0	95.0	26.6	114.0	78.0
40	10:00	3.6	86.0	96.0	27.3	118.0	80.0
35	9:10 [4]	3.8	93.0	97.0	28.2	120.0	80.0
30	9:00	3.9 [1]	100.0	99.0	[3] 29.3	120.0	80.0
25	8:05	4.1	109.2	100.0	30.5	120.0	80.0
20	7:44	4.2	118.0 [1]	102.0	31.5	124.0 [1]	82.0 [1]
15	7:00 [5]	4.4 [2]	132.0	105.0	33.0	130.0	85.0
10	6:30	4.8 [3]	151.0	108.0	34.7	132.0 [2]	90.0
5	5:28	5.3	189.8 [2]	112.0	37.6	140.0	93.4
3	4:45	5.5 [4]	234.4	115.0 [1]	39.4	145.0 [3]	97.2 [3]
1	3:20	7.0 [6] [10]	350.5	125.5 [3]	43.5	158.0 [4]	104.5 [4]
n	1,231	399	1,042	1,040	679	1,345	1,345

PERSONAL HISTORY OF HEART ATTACK OR BYPASS

0 ☐ NONE
2 ☐ OVER 5 YEARS AGO
4 ☐ 2-5 YEARS AGO
5 ☐ 1-<2 YEARS AGO
8 ☐ 0-<1 YEAR AGO

FAMILY HISTORY OF HEART ATTACK

0 ☐ NONE
2 ☐ YES, OVER 50 YEARS
4 ☐ YES, 50 YEARS OR UNDER

6 ☐ KNOWN CORONARY HEART DISEASE W/O HEART ATTACK OR BYPASS

SMOKING HABITS

0 ☐ NONE
0 ☐ PAST 1 YEAR OR MORE
1 ☐ PAST ONLY LESS THAN 1 YEAR
1 ☐ PIPE/CIGAR
2 ☐ 1-10 DAILY
3 ☐ 11-20 DAILY
4 ☐ 21-30 DAILY
5 ☐ 31-40 DAILY
6 ☐ MORE THAN 40 DAILY

TENSION - ANXIETY

0 ☐ NO TENSION, VERY RELAXED
0 ☐ SLIGHT TENSION
1 ☐ MODERATE TENSION
2 ☐ HIGH TENSION
3 ☐ VERY TENSE, "HIGH STRUNG"

3 ☐ DIABETES

AGE FACTOR

0 ☐ UNDER 30 YEARS OF AGE
1 ☐ 30-39 YEARS OF AGE
2 ☐ 40-49 YEARS OF AGE
3 ☐ 50-59 YEARS OF AGE
4 ☐ 60 + YEARS OF AGE

RESTING ECG   EXERCISE ECG

0 ☐   NORMAL   ☐ 0
1 ☐   EQUIVOCAL   ☐ 4
3 ☐   ABNORMAL   ☐ 8

TOTAL CORONARY RISK

☐ VERY LOW   (0- 4)
☐ LOW   (5-12)
☐ MODERATE   (13-21)
☐ HIGH   (22-31)
☐ VERY HIGH.   (32 +)

*Data based on first visit only

COOPER CLINIC/ Dallas, Texas

Coronary Risk Profile

NAME:

Females: *50 - 59 Years of Age

PERCENTILE RANKINGS	BALKE TREADMILL TIME (min.)	TOTAL CHOLESTEROL/ HDL RATIO	TRIGLYCERIDE (mg. %)	GLUCOSE (mg. %)	% BODY FAT	RESTING BLOOD PRESSURE SYSTOLIC (mm HG)	DIASTOLIC (mm HG)
YOUR VALUES							
99	17:04	2.2	34.8	72.8	9.9	90.0	58.5
97	15:44	2.4	40.8	78.0	13.8	96.0	60.0
95	15:00	2.5	46.7	80.0	16.3	98.0	64.0
90	13:27	2.7	54.0	84.0	19.9	102.0	70.0
85	12:00	2.8	60.0	86.0	21.6	108.0	70.0
80	12:00	3.0	66.0	88.0	23.4	110.0	70.0
75	11:00	3.1	70.0	90.0	24.9	110.0	72.2
70	10:30	3.2	74.0	92.0	25.7	114.0	75.0
65	10:00	3.4	80.0	93.0	26.6	116.0	76.0
60	9:30	3.5	86.6	94.0	27.5	120.0	78.0
55	9:21	3.6	93.0	95.0	28.7	120.0	80.0
50	9:00	3.7	100.0	97.0	29.3	120.0	80.0
45	8:30	3.8	106.0	99.0	29.9	123.5	80.0
40	8:00	4.0	113.0	100.0	31.0	126.0	80.0
35	7:27	4.1	122.0	102.0	32.0	130.0	82.0
30	7:00	4.3	128.0	104.0	32.6	130.0	84.0
25	6:34	4.5	140.0	105.0	33.7	134.0	86.0
20	6:00	4.8	158.0	107.0	35.1	140.0	90.0
15	5:43	5.1	170.9	110.0	36.3	142.0	90.0
10	5:00	5.7	191.0	113.1	37.7	150.0	94.0
5	4:00	6.3	230.0	122.1	40.2	160.0	100.0
3	3:21	6.7	260.2	135.0	41.9	166.5	104.2
1	2:30	7.6	368.6	186.9	45.3	180.0	115.0
n	643	237	693	688	386	824	824

PERSONAL HISTORY OF HEART ATTACK OR BYPASS

0 ☐ NONE
2 ☐ OVER 5 YEARS AGO
4 ☐ 2-5 YEARS AGO
5 ☐ 1-<2 YEARS AGO
8 ☐ 0-<1 YEAR AGO

FAMILY HISTORY OF HEART ATTACK

0 ☐ NONE
2 ☐ YES, OVER 50 YEARS
4 ☐ YES, 50 YEARS OR UNDER

6 ☐ KNOWN CORONARY HEART DISEASE W/O HEART ATTACK OR BYPASS

SMOKING HABITS

0 ☐ NONE
0 ☐ PAST 1 YEAR OR MORE
1 ☐ PAST ONLY LESS THAN 1 YEAR
1 ☐ PIPE/CIGAR
2 ☐ 1-10 DAILY
3 ☐ 11-20 DAILY
4 ☐ 21-30 DAILY
5 ☐ 31-40 DAILY
6 ☐ MORE THAN 40 DAILY

TENSION - ANXIETY

0 ☐ NO TENSION, VERY RELAXED
0 ☐ SLIGHT TENSION
1 ☐ MODERATE TENSION
2 ☐ HIGH TENSION
3 ☐ VERY TENSE, "HIGH STRUNG"

3 ☐ DIABETES

AGE FACTOR

0 ☐ UNDER 30 YEARS OF AGE
1 ☐ 30-39 YEARS OF AGE
2 ☐ 40-49 YEARS OF AGE
3 ☐ 50-59 YEARS OF AGE
4 ☐ 60 + YEARS OF AGE

RESTING ECG   EXERCISE ECG

0 ☐   NORMAL   ☐ 0
1 ☐   EQUIVOCAL   ☐ 4
3 ☐   ABNORMAL   ☐ 8

TOTAL CORONARY RISK

☐ VERY LOW   (0- 4)
☐ LOW   (5-12)
☐ MODERATE   (13-21)
☐ HIGH   (22-31)
☐ VERY HIGH   (32 +)

*Data based on first visit only

NAME:

Females: *> 60 Years of Age

PERCENTILE RANKINGS	BALKE TREADMILL TIME (min.)	TOTAL CHOLESTEROL/ HDL RATIO	TRIGLYCERIDE (mg. %)	GLUCOSE (mg. %)	% BODY FAT	RESTING BLOOD PRESSURE SYSTOLIC (mm HG)	DIASTOLIC (mm HG)
YOUR VALUES							
99	19:37	2.0	34.1	75.5	6.2	90.0	58.0
97	15:40	2.2	41.6	79.0	10.7	96.7	60.0
95	14:40	2.6	45.0	83.0	13.2	101.9	64.9
90	12:08	2.7	57.0	85.0	17.1	110.0	70.0
85	11:19	2.9	64.0	87.0 [1]	22.4	114.0	70.0
80	11:00	3.1	71.2	89.0	24.7	118.0	72.0
75	9:17	3.1	78.0	90.7 [2]	26.2	120.0	74.7
70	8:33	3.3	82.0	92.0	26.9	120.0	76.0
65	8:00	3.4	88.0	94.0	27.7	124.0	78.0
60	8:00 [2]	3.5	93.0	95.0	29.1	126.0	78.0
55	7:00	3.7	102.0	96.0	29.8	128.0	80.0
50	6:38	3.8	107.0	98.0	30.0	130.0 [1]	80.0
45	6:30 [1]	4.0	111.8	100.0 [3]	30.7	132.0	80.0
40	6:14	4.3	116.0	101.0	31.3	136.0	82.0
35	6:00 [2]	4.5	128.4 [1]	103.0	32.5	140.0 [2]	84.0 [1]
30	6:00 [4]	4.7	134.2	105.0	33.2	140.0	86.0
25	5:44	4.9	146.0	106.0	35.4	142.0	88.0
20	5:00 [3]	5.1	163.4	108.0	36.3	148.0	90.0 [2]
15	4:02 [5]	5.2	175.0	110.0	38.1	150.0	90.0
10	3:39 [4]	5.9	196.4	114.0	40.3	158.2 [3]	95.1
5	3:00 [5]	6.7	228.4 [2]	122.0 [1]	41.5	172.0 [4]	100.0
3	2:30 [7]	7.8	267.4	136.7 [2]	41.8	180.0	100.0
1	1:40 [10]	13.2	409.6	178.7 [3]	45.9	183.2	105.6 [3] [4]
n	128	91	255	254	101	278	278

PERSONAL HISTORY OF HEART ATTACK OR BYPASS

0 ☐ NONE
2 ☐ OVER 5 YEARS AGO
4 ☐ 2-5 YEARS AGO
5 ☐ 1-<2 YEARS AGO
8 ☐ 0-<1 YEAR AGO

FAMILY HISTORY OF HEART ATTACK

0 ☐ NONE
2 ☐ YES, OVER 50 YEARS
4 ☐ YES, 50 YEARS OR UNDER

6 ☐ KNOWN CORONARY HEART DISEASE W/O HEART ATTACK OR BYPASS

SMOKING HABITS

0 ☐ NONE
0 ☐ PAST 1 YEAR OR MORE
1 ☐ PAST ONLY LESS THAN 1 YEAR
1 ☐ PIPE/CIGAR
2 ☐ 1-10 DAILY
3 ☐ 11-20 DAILY
4 ☐ 21-30 DAILY
5 ☐ 31-40 DAILY
6 ☐ MORE THAN 40 DAILY

TENSION - ANXIETY

0 ☐ NO TENSION, VERY RELAXED
0 ☐ SLIGHT TENSION
1 ☐ MODERATE TENSION
2 ☐ HIGH TENSION
3 ☐ VERY TENSE, "HIGH STRUNG"

3 ☐ DIABETES

AGE FACTOR

0 ☐ UNDER 30 YEARS OF AGE
1 ☐ 30-39 YEARS OF AGE
2 ☐ 40-49 YEARS OF AGE
3 ☐ 50-59 YEARS OF AGE
4 ☐ 60 + YEARS OF AGE

RESTING ECG   EXERCISE ECG

0 ☐   NORMAL   ☐ 0
1 ☐   EQUIVOCAL   ☐ 4
3 ☐   ABNORMAL   ☐ 8

TOTAL CORONARY RISK

☐ VERY LOW   (0- 4)
☐ LOW   (5-12)
☐ MODERATE   (13-21)
☐ HIGH   (22-31)
☐ VERY HIGH   (32 +)

*Data based on first visit only

PHYSICAL PROFILES OF MEN AT DIFFERENT LEVELS OF FITNESS

The following charts are derived from the results of tests conducted on men at different levels of fitness during their first visit to the Cooper Clinic in Dallas. The number of people and their average age are given.

As you can see, there is a direct correlation between levels of fitness and such factors as the ratio of HDL cholesterol to total cholesterol; the percentage of body fat; blood pressure readings; and total body weight. On an average, the men who were classified in the best condition after a treadmill stress test consistently scored in the healthiest categories on the other parts of the exam.

I would suggest that you spend some time studying these charts to see just how important a factor fitness can be in correlating with a well-balanced circulatory system and proper body composition.

Comparable research on women has been done by Dr. Larry Gibbons at the Institute for Aerobics Research in Dallas, and results will be available shortly from the Institute.

Fitness versus Blood Pressure

2998 Males
$\bar{x}$ *Age = 44.5 years*
First visit to Cooper Clinic

Fitness Category	Average Systolic	Diastolic
Very Poor	132.6*	86.3*
Poor	126.8*	83.9*
Fair	124.6*	83.3*
Good	122.5	80.8
Excellent	121.1	79.8

* Significant when compared to Excellent Fitness category.

Fitness versus % Body Fat

2327 Males
$\bar{x}$ *Age = 44.5 years*
First visit to Cooper Clinic

Fitness Category	Average
Very Poor	29.2*
Poor	26.9*
Fair	23.9*
Good	20.8*
Excellent	18.2

* Significant when compared to Excellent Fitness category.

Fitness versus Body Weight (lbs)
2767 Males
x̄ Age = 44.5 years
First visit to Cooper Clinic

Fitness Category	Average
Very Poor	196.0*
Poor	189.6*
Fair	182.5*
Good	174.9*
Excellent	167.9

* Significant when compared to Excellent Fitness category.

Fitness versus Glucose
2539 Males
x̄ Age = 44.5 years
First visit to Cooper Clinic

Fitness Category	Average
Very Poor	112.5*
Poor	107.9*
Fair	105.5*
Good	104.0
Excellent	102.1

* Significant when compared to Excellent Fitness category.

Fitness versus Cholesterol
2587 Males
x̄ Age = 44.5 years
First visit to Cooper Clinic

Fitness Category	Average
Very Poor	237.1*
Poor	238.5*
Fair	228.8*
Good	222.8
Excellent	217.3

* Significant when compared to Excellent Fitness category.

Fitness versus HDL Cholesterol
731 Males
x̄ Age = 44.6 years
First visit to Cooper Clinic

Fitness Category	Average
Very Poor	37.0
Poor	40.0
Fair	41.5
Good	44.5
Excellent	49.3

Fitness versus Total Cholesterol/HDL Ratio
732 Males
x̄ Age = 44.6 years
First visit to Cooper Clinic

Fitness Category	Average
Very Poor	6.06
Poor	5.66
Fair	5.14
Good	4.86
Excellent	4.28

Age versus Cholesterol
2928 Males
x̄ Age = 44.6 years
First visit to Cooper Clinic

Age	< 30	30–39	40–49	50–59	60>
Total Cholesterol	186	200	210	216	216
HDL	44	43	44	44	45
LDL	142	157	166	172	171
Body Weight	176	180	181	179	174
% Body Fat	17%	20%	21%	22%	22%

Fitness versus Triglycerides
2549 Males
x̄ Age = 44.5 years
First visit to Cooper Clinic

Fitness Category	Average
Very Poor	179.4*
Poor	172.4*
Fair	140.2*
Good	114.1*
Excellent	87.6

* Significant when compared to Excellent Fitness category.

STRETCHING

Besides helping you relax mentally and physically, stretching helps prevent injuries and soreness by increasing flexibility. There are two ways to stretch, or elongate, your muscles. Ballistic stretching is an active stretch of bouncing and bobbing. Static stretching is a slow, sustained stretch held for a number of seconds. Both have their place in a good program. The exercises given below should be done as static stretching.

The muscle must be stretched beyond its normal length to be effective. Guard against overstretching, which will probably be painful. Stretch easily at first, letting the tension in the muscles decrease as you hold. If you are new at stretching or if your muscles are very tight, don't hold the stretch longer than 10 to 15 seconds. As flexibility increases, increase the stretch in time and in tension. Relax the muscles slowly and naturally as you stretch. Always remember that stretching should not be painful. While stretching, breathe slowly and naturally to help yourself relax.

Stretching before and after physical activity is important; however, stretching may be done at any time. It helps prepare the muscles for activity, and stretching after activity is also good because your body temperature is raised, which warms the muscles and increases flexibility.

Achilles Tendon and Calf Stretch

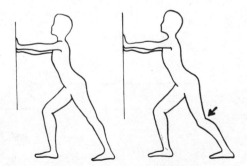

Stand facing wall. Place palms of hands flat against wall. The feet should be about 12 inches apart. Bend the right knee while the left leg is straight behind you. Keep the left heel on the floor, with toes pointing straight ahead. Slowly move your hips forward until you feel a stretch in the calf of the left leg. Hold for 15–30 seconds. Repeat with right leg. The stretch should be felt in the calf and the Achilles tendon.

> **Variation:** Begin in the position described above. Bend the left knee, keeping the heel on the floor. The stretch should be felt in the Achilles tendon.

Hamstring Stretch

Stand in straddle position with toes pointing forward. Turn left foot out and bend the left knee, keeping your body weight over the left leg. Keep right leg straight. Place hands behind back. While holding the chest parallel to the floor, slowly straighten the left knee and hold for 15–30 seconds. Repeat with right leg. The stretch should be felt in the hamstring.

Hamstring Stretch/Leg Up

Stand facing platform or railing which is about waist high. Raise the left leg in front of you and rest foot on railing. Lean upper torso toward the raised leg, bending at the hips. Hold for 15–30 seconds. Repeat with right leg. The stretch should be felt in the hamstring of the raised leg and the lower back.

Hip Flexor Stretch

Place right knee on the floor behind left foot. Move left knee forward so that it is positioned over the toes. Place palms on knee. Without changing position of the right knee, push hips down toward the floor. Make sure knee and toes are pointing forward and not to the side. Hold for 15–30 seconds. Repeat with left leg. The stretch should be felt in front of the hip of the back leg and possibly the groin and hamstrings.

Hamstring Stretch

Sit on the floor with both legs out straight and approximately three to four feet apart with ankles flexed (toes straight up). Lean upper torso toward the left leg bending at the hips. Hold for 15–30 seconds. Repeat with right leg. The stretch should be felt in the hamstring and the lower back.

Gluteal Stretch

Sit with both legs out in front of you. Slip both arms around left leg and raise leg up and toward chest. Hold for 15–30 seconds. Repeat with right leg. The stretch should be felt in the outer thigh and buttocks.

Groin Stretch

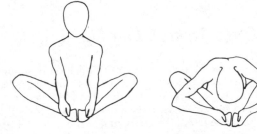

Sit with soles of feet together. Place hands around feet to help stabilize. Sit up straight and push knees to floor. Lean forward with a straight back and hold for 15–30 seconds. The stretch should be felt in lower back and groin.

> **Variation:** Begin in the position described above. Lean forward with rounded back as if to touch the feet with the head. The stretch should be felt in the lower back and groin.

Quadricep Stretch

Lie on stomach with head down. With right hand pull right foot toward the buttocks. Hold for 15–30 seconds. Repeat with left leg. The stretch should be felt in the quadricep (front of the thigh).

Lower Back Stretch

Lie on back and clasp hands around left knee and pull to chest. Do not strain. Hold for 15–30 seconds. Repeat with right leg. The stretch should be felt in the lower back.

Clasp hands around both knees and pull to chest. Hold for 30–45 seconds. The stretch should be felt in the lower back.

SPORTS MEDICINE CLINICS

The following list of sports medicine clinics appeared in the July-August, 1982, issue of *Running & Fitness* and is reprinted with the kind permission of the American Running & Fitness Association, 2420 K Street N.W., Washington, D.C., 20037.

The services offered by sports medicine clinics vary as widely as the needs of the athletes they serve. The following legend has abbreviations for the different services provided by clinics, but for full information it is best to contact the clinic directly. Costs, of course, will also differ.

LEGEND

Services:
ED = Examination and diagnosis
CR = Cardiac rehabilitation
MR = Musculoskeletal rehabilitation
PR = Pulmonary rehabilitation
PT = Physical therapy
SE = Supervised exercise programs
WR = Weight resistance exercise
ST = Stress testing
BO = Bracing & orthotics
SU = Surgical treatment
RE = Research

Staff:
OR = Orthopedist
CA = Cardiologist
MD = Physician
PO = Podiatrist
PH = Physiologist
PT = Physical therapist
CH = Chiropractor
NU = Nutritionist
TR = Trainer
IN = Instructor

Requirements:
@ = Appointment necessary
R = Referral necessary

ALABAMA

U.S. Sports Academy, Sports-medicine & Research Ctr., 124 U. Blvd., Mobile, AL 36608, (205) 343-7700

ARIZONA

Southwest Health Inst., 4602 N. 16th St., Ste. 200, Phoenix, AZ 85016, (602) 264-9806, hours: 8:30 am-5 pm
Services: ED, CR, MR, PR, PT, SE, WR, ST
Staff: CA, MD, PO, PH
@ 1 day in advance

Sports Medicine Clinic, 3100 E. Bell Rd., Phoenix, AZ 85032, (609) 992-3300, hours: 9 am-12 am, 2-5:30 pm
Services: ED, MR, PT, SE, WR, BO, SU
Staff: MD, PO, PT, TR
@ same day

Cardiac Rehabilitation Ctr., St. Joseph's Hosp., 350 N. Wilmot Rd., Tucson, AZ 85711, (602) 296-3211, ext. 2712, hours: Apr.-Oct. 6 am-3 pm, Oct.-Apr. 10 am-6 pm
Services: CR, SE, ST, RE
Staff: CA, PH
@ 3 days in advance, R

Rehabilitation Medicine Sports Clinic, 1500 N. Wilmot Rd., Ste. 140, Tucson, AZ 85712, (602) 886-4141

U. of Arizona Sports Medicine Program, U. of AZ Health Sciences Ctr., Tucson, AZ 85724, (602) 626-7617, hours: 24 hours daily
Services: ED, CR, MR, PR, PT, SE, WR, ST, BO, SU, RE
Staff: OR, CA, PO, PH, PT, NU, TR, IN
@ 1 week in advance

ARKANSAS

Fayetteville Health & Fitness Testing Ctr., Fayetteville Youth Ctr., Calif. Dr., Fayetteville, AR 72701, (501) 442-9242

Human Performance Ctr., Inc., Plaza W., Ste. 880, Little Rock, AR 72205, (501) 664-5750

CVR Clinic, U. of AR, Box 2507, Monticello, AR 71655, (501) 367-6811, ext. 34, hours: 8 am-4:30 pm
Services: CR, SE, ST, RE
Staff: PH
@ 1 week in advance, R

CALIFORNIA

SPORTCARE, 3030 Telegraph Ave., Berkeley, CA 94705, (415) 540-0700
Services: ED, CR, PR, PT, SE, ST
Staff: MD, PH, PT, TR

Ather Sports Injury Clinic, 20664 Santa Maria, Castro Valley, CA 94546, (415) 537-0272, hours: 8:30 am-7 pm
Services: ED, MR, PT, SE, WR, BO, RE
Staff: PH, PT, TR @

PACER Clinic, 2307 Concord Blvd., Concord, CA 94520, (415) 825-1690

St. Helena Hosp. & Health Ctr., Deer Park, CA 94576, (707) 963-3611, ext. 563, hours: 8 am-5 pm
Services: ED, CR, PR, PT, SE, ST, SU
Staff: OR, CA, PO, PH, PT, NU
@

Ather Sports Injury Clinic, 6934 Village Pkwy., Dublin, CA 94566, (415) 828-7212, hours: 8:30 am-7 pm
Services: ED, MR, PT, SE, WR, BO, RE
Staff: PH, PT, TR
@

Foothill Presbyterian Hosp., 250 S. Grand Ave., Glendora, CA 91740, (213) 963-8411, ext. 294

Nat'l. Athletic Health Inst., 575 E. Hardy St., Inglewood, CA 90301, (213) 674-1600, hours: 8 am-5 pm, Sat. 9-11 am
Services: ED, MR, PT, ST, RE
Staff: OR, MD, PH, PT, NU
@

Body Accounting, 17931 Sky Park Cir., Ste. H, Irvine, CA 92714, (714) 751-0522, hours: 8 am-5 pm
Services: ED, ST
Staff: PH
@ 1 week in advance

Scripps Memorial Hosp., Sports Medicine Clinic, 988 Genesse Ave., La Jolla, CA 92038, (714) 457-5584

Memorial Sports Medicine Clinic, 2888 Long Beach Blvd., Ste. 400, Long Beach, CA 90806, (213) 595-5424, hours: 9 am-5 pm
Services: ED, MR, PT, SE, WR, BO, SU, RE
@

Sportsmedicine Clinic, 425 N. Larchmont Blvd., Los Angeles, CA 90004, (213) 462-1491, hours: 9 am-5 pm
Services: ED, PT, RE
Staff: PO
@

Sportsmedicine Clinic, Orthopedic Hosp., 2400 S. Flower, Los Angeles, CA 90007, (213) 742-1300

Marina Sports Medicine & Health Promotion Ctr., Inc., 4640 Admiralty Way, Marina del Rey, CA 90291, (213) 823-6036, hours: 6 am-9 pm, Sat. 7 am-3 pm
Services: ED, CR, MR, PT, SE, WR, ST, BO, SU, RE
Staff: OR, CA, PO, PH, PT, NU
@ 2-5 days in advance

Golden Bear Physical Therapy & Sports Injury Ctr., 1130 Coffee Rd., Ste. 6-B, Modesto, CA 95355, (209) 576-1946, hours: 8 am-5 pm
Services: MR, PT, SE, BO
Staff: PT, NU
@ 1 day in advance, R

Napa Valley Physical Therapy Clinic, 1103 Trancas St., Napa, CA 94558, (707) 224-3131

Laurel Canyon Medical Clinic, 7535 Laurel Canyon Blvd., N. Hollywood, CA 91605, (213) 765-1065, hours: 9 am-5:30 pm

Services: ED, MR, PT, SE, BO, SU, RE
Staff: OR, PO, PH, PT, NU, IN
@

N. Bay Cardiac Treatment Clinic, 205 San Marin Dr., Ste. 5, Novato, CA 94947, (415) 892-0702, hours: 10 am-5 pm
Services: ED, CR, MR, PR, SE, ST, RE
Staff: CA, NU, IN
@, R

SHAPE Ctr., 2935 Telegraph Ave., Oakland, CA 94706, (415) 836-2460, hours: 7 am-6 pm
Services: ED, CR, MR, PT, SE, WR, ST, BO, SU
Staff: OR, CA, PH, PT, TR
@ 2 days in advance, R

Tri-City Orthopedic Surgery, Inc., 3927 Waring Rd., Oceanside, CA 92083, (714) 724-9000, hours: 8:30 am-5 pm
Services: ED, MR, PT, SE, WR, SU, RE
Staff: OR, PT, TR
@ 1 week in advance

Sports Conditioning & Rehabilitation, 871 S. Tustin, Orange, CA 92666, (714) 633-7227, hours: 6 am-8:30 pm, Sat. 8 am-5 pm, Sun. 9 am-3 pm
Services: ED, CR, MR, PR, PT, SE, WR, ST, SU
Staff: OR, PH, PT, IN
@ 1 day in advance

YMCA Cardiac Rehabilitation, 3412 Ross Rd., Palo Alto, CA 94303, (415) 494-1300

Cardiac Rehabilitation Clinic, 3610 McKinley Blvd., Sacramento, CA 95819, (916) 454-5863

Crowl Physical Therapy Ctr., Inc., 5207 Jay St., Sacramento, CA 95819, (916) 452-3788

Human Performance Lab, CSU, 6000 Jay St., Sacramento, CA 95819, (916) 454-6389, hours: 8 am-4:30 pm
Services: SE, WR, ST
Staff: PH, TR
@ 2 weeks in advance

Sports Medicine Clinic, 25 San Anselmo, San Anselmo, CA 94960, (415) 457-3282, hours: Mon., Wed., Fri. 9 am-6 pm, Sat. 9 am-noon
Services: ED, MR, PT, WR
Staff: CH
@ 1-2 days in advance

TREAT Fitness Ctr., 1119 Industrial Rd., San Carlos, CA 94070, (415) 593-8061

Adult Fitness Program, PG 120, SDSU, San Diego, CA 92182, (714) 265-5560

Cardiac Treatment Ctr., Mercy Hosp., 4077 5th Ave., San Diego, CA 92103, (714) 294-8660, hours: 8 am-4 pm
Services: ED, CR, PT, SE, ST
Staff: CA, NU
@ 1-2 weeks in advance

Calif. College of Podiatric Medicine, 1770 Eddy St., San Francisco, CA 94115, (415) 563-3444

Ctr. for Sports Medicine, St. Francis Hosp., 900 Hyde St., San Francisco, CA 94109, (415) 773-4321, ext. 3370

San Jose Medical Clinic, 45 S. 17th St., San Jose, CA 95112, (408) 998-5551

SPRINT—Sports Medicine & Rehabilitation Clinic, 841 Blossom Hill Rd., Ste. 102, San Jose, CA 94404, (408) 224-0262, hours: 8:30 am-5:30 pm, emergency care 9 am-10 pm daily
Services: ED, CR, MR, PR, PT, SE, WR, ST, BO, SU, RE
Staff: OR, CA, PT, TR
@ 1 day in advance, R

Human Performance Ctr., 231 W. Pueblo St., Santa Barbara, CA 93105, (805) 687-8553, hours: 8 am-6 pm
Services: ED, CR, MR, PT, SE, WR, ST, BO, RE
Staff: OR, PH, PT, NU, TR
@ 3 days in advance, R

Ctr. for Sportsmedicine & Fitness, 4835 Van Nuys Blvd, #110, Sherman Oaks, CA 91403, (714) 990-2051

San Joaquin Cardiac Clinic, 4677 Georgetown Pl, Stockton, CA 95209, (209) 951-3405

North Tahoe Orthopedic & Sports Medicine Clinic, Donner Medical Bldg., Truckee, CA 95734, (916) 587-7461, hours: 9 am-5 pm
Services: ED, MR, PT, SU
Staff: OR
@

Colima Internal Medical Group, Inc., 10155 Colima Rd., Whittier, CA 90603, (213) 945-3671, hours: 9 am-6 pm
Services: ED, CR, PR, PT, ST, RE
Staff: CA, MD, PT
@ 2 days in advance

COLORADO

Arvada Foot Clinic, 5727 Allison St., Arvada, CO 80002, (303) 422-6043, hours: 9 am-5 pm
Services: ED, MR, PT, BO, SU, RE
Staff: PO, PT
@ 1 day in advance

Aspen Clinic, 100 Main St., Aspen, CO 81611, (303) 925-5440

Aspen Health Ctr., Box 1092, Aspen Meadows, Aspen, CO 81612, (303) 925-3586, hours: 9 am-7 pm
Services: CR, MR, SE, WR
Staff: TR, IN
@ 1 day in advance

David Greenberg, M.D., 4200 W. Conejos Pl., Denver, CO 80204, (303) 629-7711
Services: ED, MR, PT, BO, SU
Staff: OR, PT
@ 3 days in advance

Denver Sports Medicine, 2005 Franklin, #550, Denver, CO 80220, (303) 839-5383, hours: 8 am-5 pm
Services: ED, MR, PT, SE, WR, BO, SU
Staff: OR, PT, TR
@

Sports Conditioning & Orthopedic Rehabilitation, Inc., 1919 Federal Blvd., Denver, CO 80204, (303) 455-5268, hours: Mon.-Thurs. 9 am-8 pm, Fri. 9 am-6 pm, Sat. 9-11 am

Services: ED, MR, PT, SE, WR, BO, RE
Staff: PT, TR
@ 1 day in advance, R

Sports Conditioning & Orthopedic Rehabilitation, Inc., 4380 S. Syracuse St., Ste. 101, Denver, CO 80237, (303) 455-5268, hours: Mon.-Thurs. 9 am-8 pm, Fri. 9 am-6 pm, Sat. 9-11 am
Services: ED, MR, PT, SE, WR, BO, RE
Staff: PT, TR
@ 1 day in advance, R

Fort Collins Sports Medicine Clinic, 1148 E. Elizabeth, Fort Collins, CO 80524, (303) 484-4879

Hilltop Rehabilitation Ctr., 1100 Patterson Rd., Grand Junction, CO 81501, (303) 242-8980

Steamboat Springs Sports Medicine Rehabilitation & Physical Therapy, Box 5428, 100 Park Ave., Steamboat Village, CO 80499, (303) 879-2655

Community Fitness Ctr., Inst. for Health Ed., 8400 W. 38th Ave., Wheat Ridge, CO 80033, (303) 425-8350

CONNECTICUT

Hartford County Runner's Clinic, 701 Cottage Grove Rd., Bloomfield, CT 06002, (203) 243-1136, hours: Mon.-Fri. 8:30 am-4:30 pm
Services: ED, MR, PT, SE, WR, BO, SU, RE
Staff: OR, PO, PT
@

Orthopedic Module, U. of CT, Health Ctr., Rm. C0200, Farmington, CT 06032, (203) 674-3125, hours: 8 am-5 pm
Services: ED, MR, PT, SE, SU
Staff: OR, PT
@ 2 weeks in advance

Dayton Orthopedic Group, 20 Dayton Ave., Greenwich, CT 06830, (203) 869-1238

Fairfield Cty. Physical Therapy Assn., 20 Dayton Ave., Greenwich, CT 06830, (203) 661-9462

Fitness & Sports Conditioning Ctr. of Greenwich, 20 Dayton Ave., Greenwich, CT 06830, (203) 869-3257, hours: 6 am-9 pm, Sat. 9 am-4 pm, Sun. 11 am-5 pm
Services: ED, MR, PT, SE, WR, BO
Staff: OR, PT, TR, IN
@, R for PT

New Haven Sports Clinic, 17 Hillhouse Ave., New Haven, CT 06520, (203) 436-3470

The Chiropractic Center, 98 East Ave., Norwalk, CT 06851, (203) 838-5544

DELAWARE

Delaware All-Sports Research, 25 Milltown Rd., Wilmington, DE 19808, (302) 998-1070, hours: 9 am-5 pm
Services: ED, MR, PT, SE, WR, BO, SU, RE
Staff: PO, TR, IN
@ 1 week in advance

Delaware Rehabilitation & Sports Medicine Ctr., Foulk & Grubb Rds., Brandywine Plaza, Ste. 133, Wilmington, DE 19810, (302) 475-0680, hours: Mon.-Thurs. 7 am-9 pm, Fri. 7 am-7 pm, Sat. 8 am-1 pm
Services: ED, MR, PR, PT, SE, WR, BO, RE
Staff: MD, PO, PT, TR
@

DISTRICT OF COLUMBIA

Cardiovascular Ctr., 1711 Rhode Island Ave. NW, Washington, DC 20036, (202) 862-9663, hours: 8 am-6 pm
Services: ED, PT, SE, WR, ST
Staff: CA, IN
@ 1 week in advance, R

GWU Cardiac Rehabilitation Program, 22nd & G Sts. NW, Washington, DC 20052, (202) 676-4172, hours: 9 am-4:30 pm
Services: ED, CR, SE, ST, RE
Staff: CA, PH
@ 1 week in advance, R

Runner's Clinic, GWU, 22nd & G Sts. NW, Washington, DC 20052, (202) 676-3997, hours: Thurs. 1-4:30 pm
Services: ED, BO, RE
Staff: OR, PO
@ 1 month in advance

Washington Cardiovascular Evaluation Ctr., 916 19th St. NW, Ste. 815, Washington, DC 20006, (202) 223-5015, hours: 8 am-4 pm
Services: ED, CR, PR, ST
Staff: CA
@ 2 weeks in advance

FLORIDA

LIFE Clinic, 407 Beverly Blvd., Brandon, FL 33511, (813) 681-4634, hours: 6 am-4 pm
Services: ED, CR, MR, PR, PT, SE, WR, ST, RE
Staff: CA, PH, IN
@ 1 day in advance

Tampa Bay Cardiac Program, USF, Tampa, FL 33612, (813) 974-4179

GEORGIA

Athletic Ctr. of Atlanta, 615 Peachtree St. NE, Ste. 1000, Atlanta, GA 30308, (404) 873-2633, hours: 9 am-5 pm
Services: ED, CR, MR, PR, SE, WR, ST, RE
Staff: PH, NU, IN

Northside Sports Medicine Ctr., 993 Johnson Ferry Rd. NE, Ste. 105-C, Atlanta, GA 30342, (404) 255-0770, hours: 8 am-5:30 pm
Services: ED, MR, PT, SE, WR, BO, SU
Staff: OR, PH, PT, NU, TR
@

Preventive Medicine Inst., 300 Boulevard NE, Atlanta, GA 30312, (404) 653-4925, hours: 8 am-4 pm
Services: ED, CR, SE, ST, RE
Staff: CA, PH, PT, NU
@ 1-2 weeks in advance, R

Sports Medicine Clinic, 615 Peachtree St. NE, Ste. 1100, Atlanta, GA 30308, (404) 874-4878, hours: 9 am-5 pm

Services: ED, MR, PT, WR, BO, SU
Staff: OR, PT, NU
@ 1 week in advance

Sports Medicine Education Inst., 20
Linden Ave. NE, Ste. 414, Atlanta,
GA 30308, (404) 892-2544

Atlanta Sports Medicine Clinic,
4600 Memorial Dr., Decatur, GA
30032, (404) 292-5676

HAWAII

Cardiac Rehabilitation Ctr., 401
Atkinson Dr., Honolulu, HI 96814,
(808) 941-3344, ext. 116, hours:
Mon., Wed., Fri. 8 am-6 pm
Services: CR, SE
Staff: CA, IN
R

Honolulu Medical Group, 550 S.
Beretaniz St., Honolulu, HI 96813,
(808) 537-2211

Honolulu Sports Medical Clinic, 932
Ward Ave., #460, Honolulu, HI
96814, (808) 521-6564, hours:
9 am-5 pm
Services: ED, MR, PT, WR, ST, BO,
SU, RE
Staff: OR, CA, MD, PT, NU
@

IDAHO

Idaho Sports Medicine Inst., 125 E.
Idaho, Ste. 204, Boise, ID 83702,
(208) 366-8250, hours:
8 am-5 pm
Services: ED, MR, PT, SE, WR, BO,
SU
Staff: OR, PH, PT, TR
@ 2-3 days in advance

ILLINOIS

Sports Performance &
Rehabilitation Inst., 501 Thornhill
Dr., Carol Stream, IL 60187, (312)
653-7774

Cardiac Rehabilitation & Health
Enhancement Ctr., Swedish
Covenant Hosp., 5145 N. Calif.
Ave., Chicago, IL 60625, (312)
878-8200, ext. 5327

Ctr. for Sportsmedicine, College of
Podiatric Medicine, 1001 N.
Dearborn St., Chicago, IL 60610,
(312) 280-2935,
hours: Wed., Fri. 10 am-6 pm
Services: ED, PT, BO, SU, RE
Staff: PO
@ 1-2 weeks in advance

Edgebrook Running Ctr., 5326 W.
Devon, Chicago, IL 60646, (312)
763-2200,
hours: Sat. 10 am-5 pm
Services: ED, MR, PT, WR, BO, SU,
RE
Staff: OR, PO, PT
@ 1-2 weeks in advance

Physical Therapy Services, Ltd.,
6858 Archer Ave., Chicago, IL
60638, (312) 229-1177
Services: PT, SE
Staff: PT, TR
@ 1 day in advance, R

Physical Therapy Services, Ltd.,
233 E. Erie St., Chicago, IL 60611,
(312) 787-0953
Services: PT, SE
Staff: PT, TR
@ 1 day in advance, R

Physical Therapy Services, Ltd.,
4200 W. Peterson Ave., Chicago,
IL 60646, (312) 545-6885
Services: PT, SE
Staff: PT, TR
@ 1 day in advance, R

Physical Therapy Services, Ltd.,
7447 W. Talcott, Chicago, IL
60631, (312) 763-8440
Services: PT, SE
Staff: PT, TR
@ 1 day in advance, R

Physical Therapy Services, Ltd.,
2510 Dempster, Des Plaines, IL
60016, (312) 296-0100
Services: PT, SE
Staff: PT, TR
@ 1 day in advance, R

Physical Therapy Services, Ltd.,
4343 Grand Ave., Gurnee, IL
60031, (312) 336-7468
Services: PT, SE
Staff: PT, TR
@ 1 day in advance, R

Physical Therapy Services, Ltd.,
695 Roger William, Highland Park,
IL 60035, (312) 433-7016
Services: PT, SE
Staff: PT, TR
@ 1 day in advance, R

Ctr. for Athletic Injury Research,
25 Lakeside, Mahomet, IL 61853,
(217) 586-2118

Leaning Tower YMCA, 6300 W.
Touhy Ave., Niles, IL 60648, (312)
647-8222
Services: CR, SE, WR, ST
Staff: CA, PO, PH, NU, IN
@ 1 week in advance, R

Great Plains Sports Medicine
Fndn., St. Francis Hosp. Medical
Ctr., 624 NE Glen Oak, Peoria, IL
61637, (309) 672-2386, hours:
8 am-4:30 pm
Services: ED, CR, MR, PT, SU, WR,
ST, BO, SU, RE
Staff: OR, CA, PH, PT, NU, TR
@ 1 day in advance, R

Fitness Monitoring, Inc., 4
Continental Tower, 1701 Golf Rd.,
Rolling Meadows, IL 60066, (312)
437-9660, hours:
8:30 am-4:30 pm
Services: ED, PR, SE, ST, RE
Staff: CA, PH, NU, IN
@ 2 weeks in advance

Physical Therapy Services, Ltd.,
1100 Woodfield Rd., Schaumburg,
IL 60195, (312) 490-1140
Services: PT, SE
Staff: PT, TR
@ 1 day in advance, R

Physical Therapy Services, Ltd.,
700 Ogden Ave., Westmont, IL
60569, (312) 655-9393
Services: PT, SE
Staff: PT, TR
@ 1 day in advance, R

Marianjoy Rehabilitation Hosp.,
Roosevelt Rd., Wheaton, Il 60187,
(312) 653-7600

INDIANA

Madison Cty. YMCA, Health Ctr.,
12th & Jackson, Box 231,
Anderson, IN 46015, (317)
644-7796

Indianapolis Physical Therapy & Sports Medicine, 6340 W. 37th St., Indianapolis, IN 46224, (317) 298-9746, hours: 8 am-7 pm, Sat. 8-10 am
Services: MR, PT, SE, BO, RE
Staff: PT, TR
@ 1-2 days, R

Indianapolis Physical Therapy & Sports Medicine, 9302 N. Meridian, Ste. 151, Indianapolis, IN 46260, (317) 846-3531, hours: 8 am-7 pm, Sat. 8-10 am
Services: MR, PT, SE, BO, RE
Staff: PT, TR
@ 1-2 days in advance, R

Adult Physical Fitness Ctr., Human Performance Lab, Ball State U., Muncie, IN 47306, (317) 285-1895
Services: CR, SE, ST, RE
Staff: CA, PH, NU, IN
@ 2 weeks in advance

IOWA

Sports Medicine Ctr., 3716 Ingersoll Ave., Des Moines, IA 80312, (515) 274-9291

KANSAS

U. of KS Fitness Clinic, 122 Robinson Ctr., Lawrence, KS 66045, (913) 864-5049, hours: 1-5 pm
Services: ED, SE, WR, ST, RE
Staff: PH, IN
@

Sports Rehabilitation Assn., Inc., 4510 W. 89th St., Prairie Village, KS 66207, (913) 383-3366

Kansas Cardiology Associates, P.A., 933 N. Topeka, Wichita, KS 67201, (316) 263-5889, (800) 362-2329
Services: ED, CR, PT, SE, ST
Staff: CA, MD, PH

MARYLAND

Union Memorial Hosp., Sports Medicine Ctr., 201 E. Univ. Pkwy., Baltimore, MD 21218, (301) 235-7200, ext. 2538, hours: 9:30 am-6 pm

Services: ED, CR, MR, PR, PT, SE, WR, ST, BO, SU, RE
Staff: OR, CA, PO, PT, NU, TR
@ 3-7 days in advance

Cardiology & Internal Medicine, P.A., 5530 Wisconsin Ave., Chevy Chase, MD 20815, (301) 656-9070, hours: 9 am-4 pm
Services: ED, CR
Staff: CA
@ 2-4 weeks in advance

Sports Medicine Ctr., Inc., 5454 Wisconsin Ave., #1555, Chevy Chase, MD 20815, (301) 986-9252, hours: Mon.-Wed. 9 am-8:30 pm, Thurs., Fri. 9 am-5 pm
Services: ED, CR, MR, PT, SE, WR, BO, SU, RE
Staff: OR, PT, TR
@ 5-7 days in advance

MASSACHUSETTS

Boston U. Ctr., 75 Newton St., Boston, MA 02118, (617) 247-5430

Cardiovascular Health & Exercise Ctr., Northeastern U., 120 Dockser Hall, 360 Huntington Ave., Boston, MA 02115, (617) 437-3144
Services: ED, CR, SE, ST, RE
Staff: CA, PH, PT, IN
@ 2-4 weeks in advance

Div. of Sports Medicine, Children's Hosp., 300 Longwood Ave., Boston, MA 02115, (617) 735-6028, hours: 9 am-5 pm
Services: ED, PT, WR, BO, SU, RE
Staff: OR, PO, PT, TR
@ 1-2 weeks in advance

Health Sciences Fitness Ctr., 36 Cummington St., Boston, MA 02215, (617) 353-2718, hours: 8 am-5 pm
Services: SE, ST, RE
Staff: CA, PH, NU
@ 2 weeks in advance

Medical Care Affiliates, 1 Boylston Plaza, Prudential Ctr., Boston, MA 02199, (617) 262-1500

Braintree Hosp., Sports Medicine Clinic, 250 Pond St., Braintree, MA 02184, (617) 848-5353, ext. 141, hours: 8 am-4:30 pm
Services: ED, MR, PT, WR, BO, RE
Staff: MD, PO, PH, PT, NU, TR
@ same day

Nat'l Athletic Training & Fitness, Inc., 710 West St., Braintree, MA 02184, (617) 848-6474

St. Elizabeth's Hosp. Sports Medicine/Runner's Clinic, 736 Cambridge St., Brighton, MA 02135, (617) 782-7000

Sports Medicine Resource, Inc., 830 Boylston St., Brookline, MA 02167, (617) 739-2003

N. Shore Sports Medical Ctr., 4 State Rd., Danvers, MA 01923, (617) 777-3220, hours: 9 am-9 pm
Services: ED, MR, PT, SE, WR, BO, SU
Staff: OR, PO, PT, TR

START Inc., 91 School St., Springfield, MA 01105, (413) 788-6195, hours: Mon.-Thurs. 7 am-8 pm, Fri. 8 am-5 pm, Sat. 9 am-1 pm
Services: ED, MR, PT, SE, WR, BO, RE
Staff: PT, NU, TR, IN
@ 1 day in advance, R

Berkshire Sports Medicine, Orthopedic Associates of Williamstown, Doctors Park, Adams Rd., Williamstown, MA 01267, (413) 458-8115

MICHIGAN

Cardiac Rehabilitation Inst., 1521 Gull Rd., Borgess Medical Ctr., Kalamazoo, MI 49001, (616) 383-8342

Sportsmedicine Ctr., WMU Health Ctr., Kalamazoo, MI 49008, (616) 383-8138, hours: 8 am-noon, 1-5 pm
Services: ED, MR, PT, SE, WR, ST, BO, SU, RE
Staff: OR, PO, PH, PT, TR
@

Adaptive Rehabilitation Program, LCC, Box 40010, Lansing, MI 48901, (517) 374-5043, hours: 7 am-5 pm
Services: ED, CR, MR, PT, SE, WR, ST
Staff: CA, PH, PT, NU, IN
@, R

Sports Medicine & Orthopedic Surgery, 2410 S. Pennsylvania, Ste. 5, Lansing, MI 48910, (517) 485-2180

Physical Therapy & Sports Medicine, 20002 Farmington Rd., Livonia, MI 48152, (313) 478-7330, hours: 9 am-5:30 pm
Services: ED, CR, MR, PT, SE, WR, BO
Staff: MD, PT, TR, IN
@ 2 days in advance

Ctr. for Medicine & Science in Sport, CMU, Pearce Hall 111, Mt. Pleasant, MI 48859, (517) 774-3580, hours: 10 am-5 pm
Services: ED, CR, MR, PT, SE, WR, ST, BO, SU, RE
Staff: OR, CA, PH, PT, NU, TR, IN
@, R

Oakland Physical Therapy & Rehabilitation, 39595 W. 10 Mile Rd., Novi, MI 48050, (313) 478-6140, hours: 8 am-6 pm
Services: CR, MR, PR, PT, SE, WR, RE
Staff: PT
@ less than 1 day in advance

Don Graham Associates, Inc., 455 Livenois B-14, Rochester, MI 48063, (313) 656-0444

Oakland U. Exercise Physiology Lab, Dept. of Phys. Ed., Oakland U., Rochester, MI 48063, (313) 377-3198

Don Graham Associates, Inc., Provex Office, 22301 Foster Winter Dr., Southfield, MI 48075, (313) 552-8367, hours: 7 am-6 pm
Services: MR, PT, SE, WR
Staff: PT, TR
@ less than 1 day in advance, R

Macomb Heart & Rehabilitation Inst., 42370 Van Dyke, Sterling Heights, MI 48077, (313) 254-1177
Services: ED, CR, MR, PR, PT, SE, WR, ST
Staff: CA, PO, PT, NU, TR
@

Don Graham Associates, Inc., 23700 Van Dyke, Warren, MI 48089, (313) 757-0220, hours: 8:30 am-5 pm, Sat. 9 am-noon
Services: ED, MR, PT, SE, WR, ST, RE
Staff: PT, TR
@ 1-2 days in advance

MINNESOTA

Inst. for Athletic Medicine, 7110 France Ave. S., Edina, MN 55435, (612) 920-8525, hours: 8:30 am-6 pm
Services: MR, PT, SE, WR, BO, RE
Staff: PT, TR
@ 1-2 days in advance, R

Inst. for Athletic Medicine, 606 24th Ave. S., Ste. 708, Minneapolis, MN 55454, (612) 371-6697, hours: 8 am-6 pm
Services: MR, PT, SE, WR, BO, RE
Staff: PT, TR
@ 1-2 days in advance, R

N. Memorial Medical Ctr., 3220 Lowry Ave. N., Minneapolis, MN 55422, (612) 520-5690

Orthopedic Physical Therapy Service, Inc., 393 N. Dunlop, Ste. 733, St. Paul, MN 55104, (612) 646-7827
Services: MR, PT, SE, WR, BO
Staff: PT, TR
@ 1 day in advance, R

St. Croix Orthopedics, 13961 N. 60th St., Stillwater, MN 55082, (617) 439-8807

MISSISSIPPI

Physical Fitness Inst., Box 10024, S. Station, USM, Hattiesburg, MS 39406, (601) 266-5416, hours: 9 am-4 pm
Services: ED, CR, MR, SE, WR, ST, RE

Staff: CA, PH, NU, IN
@ 1 week in advance

MISSOURI

St. Louis Orthopedic Sports Medicine Clinic, 14377 Woodlake Dr., St. Louis, MO 63017, (314) 878-4446
Services: ED, MR, PT, WR, BO, SU
Staff: OR, PT, TR
@ 1 day in advance

MONTANA

Human Performance Lab, U. of MT, Missoula, MT 59812, (406) 243-4211
Services: MR, SE, WR, ST, RE
Staff: MD, PH, PT, NU, TR, IN
@

NEW HAMPSHIRE

Fitness Resource, Rt. 3, Box 198, Concord, NH 03301, (603) 225-6760
Services: ED, CR, MR, PT, SE, WR, ST, RE
Staff: OA, PO, PH, PT, NU, TR, IN
@, R sometimes

NEW JERSEY

Bergen Cty. Heart Assn., Hackensack Hosp., Hackensack, NJ 07601, (201) 487-4000, ext. 383

Sports Medicine Inst., Christ Hosp., 176 Palisade Ave., Jersey City, NJ 07306, (201) 795-8240, hours: 8 am-4 pm
Services: ED, CR, MR, PT, SE, WR, ST, BO, SU
Staff: OR, CA, PO, PT, NU, TR
@ 2-7 days in advance

Hosp. Ctr. at Orange, 188 S. Essex Ave., Orange, NJ 07051, (201) 266-2033

Fitness Inst., Paramus, NJ 07652, (201) 967-0077

Inst. of Health, Exercise, & Athletic Rehabilitation, 160 E. Newman Springs Rd., Red Bank, NJ 07701, (201) 530-0410, hours: 7 am-9 pm, Sat., Sun. 8 am-3 pm
Services: CR, MR, PT, SE, WR, ST, RE
Staff: PH, PT, NU, TR, IN
@, R

CardioRobics, Inc., 673 Morris Ave., Springfield, NJ 07081, (201) 467-3565, hours: 7 am-6 pm
Services: ED, CR, SE, WR, ST
Staff: CA, PH, NU
@ 2-3 weeks in advance

Winslow Sports Medicine Clinic, Rt. 73S, Tansboro, NJ 08009, (609) 767-8400, hours: 9 am-1 pm, 5-10 pm
Services: ED, CR, MR, PR, PT, SE, WR
Staff: PO, PT, NU, TR
@ 2 days in advance

J. F. Kennedy Hosp., Washington Div., Hurfville-Cross Keys Rd., Turnersville, NJ 08012, (609) 589-3300, ext. 126, hours: 1-4:30 pm
Services: ED, MR, PT, SE, WR, ST
Staff: OR, PO, PT
@ for same day

Heartest Inc., 501 Hillcrest Ave., Westfield, NJ 07090, (201) 232-3600, hours: 8 am-5 pm
Services: ED, ST
Staff: CA
@ 1 day in advance

NEW MEXICO

Southwest Sportsmedicine, 5635 Kircher NE, Albuquerque, NM 87109, (505) 345-2683, hours: 9 am-6 pm
Services: ED, CR, MR, PR, PT, SE, WR, ST, BO, SU, RE
Staff: OR, CA, PO, PH, PT, NU, TR, IN
@

Santa Fe Physical Therapy Services, Ltd., 4 Calle Medico, Santa Fe, NM 87501, (505) 988-8097
Services: PT, SE
Staff: PT, TR
@ 1 day in advance, R

NEW YORK

Exercise Lab, Cardiac Rehabilitation, Montefiore Hosp. & Medical Ctr., 111 E. 210th St., Bronx, NY 10467, (212) 920-5046, hours: 8:30 am-5 pm
Services: ED, CR, SE, ST, RE
Staff: OR, CA, PH, PT, NU, IN
@ 1 week in advance, R

Reconditioning Lab, Methodist Hosp., 506 6th St., Brooklyn, NY 11215, (212) 780-3266, hours: 9 am-5 pm
Services: ED, CR, MR, PR, PT, SE, WR, ST, BO, SU, RE
Staff: OR, CA, PO, PH, PT, NU
@ 1-2 days in advance, R

Buffalo Cardiac Work Evaluation Unit, 50 High St., Ste. 1104, Buffalo, NY 14203, (716) 885-2400, hours: 9 am-4:30 pm, closed Thurs.
Services: ED, CR, ST, RE
Staff: CA
@, R

SUNY College at Cortland, Human Performance Lab, Cortland, NY 13045, (607) 753-4944, hours: 1:30-3:30 pm
Services: PT, SE, WR, ST, RE
Staff: PH, TR, IN
@ weeks in advance

Fitness Inst., Hartsdale, NY 10530, (914) 946-4030

Edward G. Hixon, Placid Memorial Hosp., Lake Placid, NY 12946, (518) 891-1610

Rainbow Podiatric Sports Medicine, 566 Broadway, Massapequa, NY 11758, (516) 799-6716

Sports Cardio-Fitness Ctr. of America, 510 Rt. 304, New City, NY 10956, (914) 634-5553, hours: Mon., Wed., Fri. 9 am-6 pm, Tues., Thurs 11 am-7 pm
Services: ED, MR, PT, SE, WR, BO, SU
Staff: OR, PH, PT
@ 1 week in advance

Cardio-Metrics Inst., Inc., 296 Madison Ave., New York, NY 10017, (212) 899-6123

Coronary Disease Prevention & Rehabilitation Ctr., 92nd St., YM-YWHA, 1395 Lexington Ave., New York, NY 10028, (212) 427-6000, hours: 10 am-6 pm
Services: ED, CR, PT, SE, WR, ST
Staff: OR, CA
@ 1-3 weeks in advance

Inst. of Sports Medicine & Trauma, Lenox Hosp., 130 E. 77th St., New York, NY 10021, (212) 794-4627

Sports Medicine, 535 E. 70th St., New York, NY 10021, (212) 535-5500, hours: Mon. noon-5 pm
Services: ED, MR, PT, BO, SU, RE
Staff: OR, CA, PO, PH, IN
@ 1 week in advance

Athletic Medicine, Dept. of Orthopedics, Strong Memorial Hosp., 601 Elmwood Ave., Rochester, NY 14642, (716) 275-5894, hours: 9 am-5 pm
Services: ED, SU, RE
Staff: OR
@

Buffalo Physical Therapy/ SportsCare, 3155 Eggert, Tonawanda, NY 14150, (716) 837-8864
Services: PT, SE
Staff: PT, TR
@ 1 day in advance, R

Buffalo Physical Therapy/ SportsCare, 2900 Ctr. Rd., W. Seneca, NY 14224, (716) 674-0045
Services: PT, SE
Staff: PT, TR
@ 1 day in advance, R

NORTH CAROLINA

The Sports Medicine Clinic, 1822 Brunswick Ave., Charlotte, NC 28207, (704) 375-2383

Human Performance Lab, Wake Forest U., Box 7234, Reynolds Sta., Winston-Salem, NC 27109, (919) 761-5394, hours: 7 am-5 pm
Services: CR, SE, ST, RE
Staff: CA, PH, NY, IN
@ 1 month in advance

OHIO

Cleveland Clinic, 9500 Euclid Ave.,
Cleveland, OH 44106, (216)
444-2601, hours: 9 am-4 pm
Services: ED, MR, PT, SE, WR, ST,
BO, SU, RE
Staff: OR, CA, PO, PT, NU, TR
@ 2-3 weeks in advance

Ohio College of Podiatric Medicine,
10515 Carnegie Ave., Cleveland,
OH 44106, (216) 231-3300,
hours: noon-6 pm
Services: ED, MR, PT, WR, BO, SU,
RE
Staff: PO, PT, TR
@ 3-7 days in advance

Rainbow Sports Medicine Ctr.,
2065 Adelbert, Orthopedic Dept.,
U. Hosp., Cleveland, OH 44106,
(216) 444-3038/368-2863, hours:
9 am-5 pm
Services: ED, MR, PT, SE, WR, BO,
SU, RE
Staff: OR, PT, TR
@

Sports Medicine Associates, 2609
Franklin Blvd., Cleveland, OH
44113, (213) 696-3391

Sports Medicine Clinic, 03U, 337
W. 17th Ave., Columbus, OH
43210, (614) 422-5180, hours:
8 am-3 pm
Services: CR, MR, SE, WR, ST, RE
Staff: CA, PH, TR
@ 2 weeks in advance, R

Midwestern Sports Medicine Clinic,
221 Belmonte Park E., Dayton, OH
45405, (513) 228-2032
Services: ED, MR, PT, SE, WR, ST,
BO, SU
Staff: OR, MD, TR

Rehabilitation Consultants, Inc.,
3187 W. 21 St., Lorain, OH
44053, (216) 282-3341, hours:
7:30 am-6:30 pm, Sat. 9 am-noon
Services: ED, MR, PT, SE, WR, BO
Staff: OR, PT, TR
@ 1-2 days in advance, R

Clinic of Stark City, Inc., 845 8th
St. NE, Massillon, OH 44646,
(216) 833-1397
Services: ED, CR, MR, PT, SE, WR,
ST, BO, SU

Staff: OR, CA, PT
@ 1 week in advance

Tri-Cty. Orthopedic Surgeons, Inc.,
3244 Bailey St. NW, Massillon, OH
44646, (216) 837-8391

**FASCI-Newark Fitness &
Sportsmedicine Ctr., Inc.,** 2040
Cherry Valley Rd., Newark, OH
43055, (614) 344-2149/522-3169,
hours: 6:30 am-9 pm
Services: ED, CR, MR, PT, SE, WR,
ST, SU, RE
Staff: OR, CA, PO, PT, NU, TR, IN
@ 1 week in advance, R

Sportsmedicine Inst., 17 N.
Champion St., Youngstown, OH
44503, (216) 743-8345

OKLAHOMA

Runner's Clinic, U. Family Medicine
Clinic N., 400 NE 50th, Oklahoma
City, OK 73105, (405) 524-2954,
hours: Thurs. 1:30-3:30 pm
Services: ED, MR, PR, PT, ST, BO,
SU, RE
Staff: OR, PH, PT, NU
@ 1-2 weeks in advance

Hillcrest Exercise for Life Program,
1120 S. Utica, Tulsa, OK 74104,
(918) 584-1351, ext. 1626

OREGON

**Ctr. for Sports Medicine & Running
Injuries,** 132 E. Broadway,
Eugene, OR 97401, (503)
683-4703, hours: 8 am-6 pm
Services: ED, MR, PT, SE, WR, BO
Staff: MD, PT, NU, TR
@ 1-2 weeks in advance

PSU Adult Fitness, Box 751,
Portland, OR 97207, (503)
229-4401, hours: 8 am-4 pm
Services: SE, ST
Staff: CA, PH, TR, IN
@ 2 weeks in advance, R

PENNSYLVANIA

Sports Kinetics, 18 Station Ave.,
Berwyn, PA 19312. (215)
647-3299

Braddock General Hosp., 400
Holland Ave., Braddock, PA
15104, (412) 351-3800, ext. 300

**Lower Bucks Hosp. Ctr. for Sports
Medicine & Rehabilitation,** Bath
Rd. & Orchard Ave., Bristol, PA
19007, (215) 785-9443
Services: ED, CR, MR, PR, PT, SE,
WR, ST, BO, SU
Staff: OR, PO, PH, PT, TR
@

Temple U. Ctr. for Sports Medicine,
540 Pennsylvania Ave., Executive
Plaza, Ft. Washington, PA 19034,
(215) 641-0700, hours:
9 am-5 pm
Services: ED, MR, PT, SE, WR, ST,
BO, SU, RE
Staff: OR, CA, PO, PH, NU, TR
@ same day

CGOH Sports Medicine Clinic, 4300
Londonderry Rd., Harrisburg, PA
17109, (717) 657-7415

Penn State Sports Medicine Ctr.,
Milton S. Hershey Medical Ctr.,
Hershey, PA 17033, (717)
534-6007
Services: ED, MR, PT, ST, BO, SU,
RE
Staff: OR, PT, TR
@ 2-3 weeks in advance

La Crest Aerobic Clinic, 626 E.
Main St., Lansdale, PA 19446,
(215) 368-1525, hours:
8 am-9 pm
Services: ED, PR, SE, WR, ST
Staff: OR, MD, TR, IN
@ 2 weeks in advance

**Paoli Sports Medicine &
Rehabilitation Ctr.,** 15 Industrial
Blvd., Paoli, PA 19301, (215)
647-1996, hours: 8 am-6 pm,
Sat. 8 am-noon
Services: ED, CR, MR, PT, SE, WR,
ST, BO, SU
Staff: OR, CA, PT, TR
@ 1 week in advance, R

J. F. Kennedy Hosp., Cardiac
Treatment Ctr., Cheltenham &
Langdon Sts., Philadelphia, PA
19124, (215) 831-7350, hours:
9 am-6 pm
Services: ED, CR, SE, ST

Staff: CA, NU
@ 1-2 weeks in advance, R

Pennsylvania College of Podiatric Medicine, 8th & Race, Philadelphia, PA 19107, (215) 629-0300

Sports Medicine Clinic, U. of PA, 235 S. 33rd St., Weightman Hall E-7, Philadelphia, PA 19104, (215) 662-4090, hours: 9 am-5 pm
Services: ED, MR, PT, WE, WR, BO, SU, RE
Staff: OR, PO, TR, IN
@

Temple U. Ctr. for Sports Medicine, Broad & Tioga Sts., 2nd floor, Philadelphia, PA 19140, (215) 221-2111, hours: 9 am-5 pm
Services: ED, MR, PT, SE, WR, ST, BO, SU, RE
Staff: OR, CA, PO, PH, NU, TR
@ same day

Human Energy Research Lab, 242 Trees Hall, U. of Pitt., Pittsburgh, PA 15269, (412) 624-4387

Orthopedic Specialists of Pottstown, 1603 E. High St., Pottstown, PA 19464, (215) 327-2400, hours: 8:30 a.m-10:30 pm
Services: ED, PT, SE, WR, BO, SU, RE
Staff: OR, PT, TR, IN
@

Human Performance Research, Neil Lab, PSU, U. Park, PA 16802, (814) 865-3453

Bio-Energetiks Rehabilitation & Health Maintenance, 11910 Perry Hwy., Wexford, PA 15090, (412) 935-6110, hours: Mon., Wed., Fri. 8:30 am-8 pm, Tues., Thurs. 10 am-2 pm
Services: ED, CR, MR, PR, PT, SE, WR, ST, RE
Staff: MD, PH, PT, NU, IN
@, R

Pittsburgh Physical Therapy Assn., 11910 Perry Hwy., Wexford, PA 15090, (412) 931-1730

RHODE ISLAND

Earle H. Fulford Fitness Ctr., West St., Barrington, RI 02806, (401) 245-2444, hours: 8:30 am-5 pm
Services: ED, PT, WR, ST, RE
Staff: OR, CA, PO, PH, PT, NU, TR
@

Inst. of Preventive Medicine, 100 Highland Ave., Providence, RI 02906, (401) 331-3391, hours: 8:30 am-4:30 pm
Services: ED, ST, RE
Staff: MD
@ 1 week in advance

SOUTH CAROLINA

USC Sports Medicine Consortium, USC, Columbia, SC 29208, (803) 777-7010, hours: Wed. 1-5 pm
Services: ED, MR, PT, SE, WR, ST, SU, RE
Staff: OR, MD, PH, NU, TR
@, R

Spartanburg YMCA, 266 S. Pine St., Spartanburg, SC 29302, (803) 585-0306

TENNESSEE

St. Mary's Medical Ctr., Oakhill Ave., Knoxville, TN 37917, (615) 971-7765, hours: Mon., Wed., Fri. 10:45 am-12:45 pm
Services: CR, SE, ST
Staff: CA, PT, NU
@ 1 week in advance, R

TEXAS

Hills Medical Sports Complex, 4615 W. Bee Caves Rd., Austin, TX 78746, (512) 327-4881

Cooper Clinic, 12200 Preston Rd., Dallas, TX 75230, (214) 239-7223, hours: 7 am-4:30 pm
Services: ED, CR, SE, WR, ST, RE
Staff: CA, MD, PH, NU, TR, IN
@ 2 weeks in advance

Sports Medicine Clinic of Dallas, 12140 Webb Chapel, #112, Dallas, TX 75234, (214) 241-6243

Sports Medicine Clinic of N. Texas, Inc., 9262 Forest Ln., Dallas, TX 75243, (214) 348-0521

Sports Medicine Clinics of America, 12110 Webb Chapel, #202E, Dallas, TX 75234, (214) 243-2010
Services: ED, MR, PT, SE, WR, BO, SU
Staff: OR, PT, TR
@ 1 week in advance

Highland Park Hosp., 1155 Idaho, El Paso, TX 79902, (915) 544-2900, ext. 275

Houstonian Preventive Medicine Ctr., 11 N. Post Oak Ln., Houston, TX 77024, (713) 680-2611

Sports Medicine & Rehabilitation Clinic, 4330 Medical Dr., Ste. 110, San Antonio, TX 78216, (512) 696-8534, hours: 7:30 am-6 pm, Sat. 8 am-noon
Services: ED, MR, PT, WR, BO, SU
Staff: OR, PO, PT, TR
@ same day

UTAH

Sports Medicine Clinic, 3755 Washington Blvd., Ogden, UT 84403, (801) 393-8800

Human Performance Research Ctr., 116RB, BYU, Provo, UT 84604, (801) 378-3981, hours: 8 am-5 pm
Services: CR, SE, ST, RE
Staff: PH, PT
@ 1 week in advance, R

VERMONT

Neptune Sportsmedicine Clinic, 20 W. Canal St., The Woolen Mill, Winooski, VT 05404, (802) 655-1788, hours: Mon. 8 am-8 pm, Tues. 8 am-5 pm, Wed. 8 am-7 pm, alternating Fri., Sat. 8 am-4 pm
Services: ED, MR, SE, WR
Staff: OR, TR
@

VIRGINIA

Ctr. for Sports Medicine, 2455 Army-Navy Dr., Arlington, VA 22206, (703) 553-2460, hours: 7:30 am-7:30 pm
Services: ED, MR, PT, SE, WR, BO, SU, RE
Staff: OR, CA, PO, PT, NU, TR
@ 2-3 days in advance, R

Hand Surgery & Sports Medicine Div., Dept. of Orthopedics & Rehab., UVA Medical Ctr., Box 159, Charlottesville, VA 22908, (804) 924-2083
Services: ED, CR, MR, PR, PT, SE, WR, ST, BO, SU, RE
Staff: OR, CA, PT, NU, TR
@

Inst. of Human Performance, 9411 Lee Hwy., Fairfax, VA 22031, (703) 591-6200, hours: 9 am-5 pm
Services: ED, CR, SE, WR, ST, RE
Staff: CA, PH, NU
@ 1 week in advance

Northern VA Cardiac Therapy Program, 3300 Gallows Rd., Falls Church, VA 22046, (703) 698-3635, hours: 9 am-4 pm
Services: CR, SE, RE
Staff: CA, PH
R

WASHINGTON

CAPRI, 914 E. Jefferson, Seattle, WA 98122, (206) 323-7550, hours: 9 am-5 pm
Services: CR, SE, ST
Staff: CA, PH
@, R

Sports Medicine Clinic, 1551 NW 54th St., Ste. 200, Seattle, WA 98107 (206) 782-3383, hours: 7:30 am-6 pm, Sat. 8 am-5 pm
Services: ED, CR, MR, PR, PT, SE, WR, ST, BO, SU, RE
Staff: OR, CA, MD, PO, PH, PT, NU, TR, IN
@

Sports Medicine Clinic, 300 Edmundson Pavillion, U. of WA, Seattle, WA 98195, (206) 543-1550, hours: 8 am-5 pm
Services: ED, MR, PT, WR, SU, RE
Staff: OR, MD, NU, TR, IN
@ 1-14 days in advance

Spokane Sportsmedicine, W105 8th St., Ste. 560, S. Ctr. Medical Bldg., Spokane, WA 99204, (509) 456-6560
Services: ED, MR, PT, SE, WR, BO, SU
Staff: OR, PO, PT, NU, TR
@ 1 week in advance, R

WEST VIRGINIA

Sports Medicine Ctr., Wheeling Hosp., Medical Park, Wheeling, WV 26003, (304) 243-3317, hours: 7:30 am-4 pm
Services: ED, CR, MR, PR, PT, SE, WR, ST, BO, SU, RE

Staff: OR, CA, PH, PT, NU, TR, IN
@ 1 day in advance

WISCONSIN

La Crosse Exercise Program, Mitchell Hall, U. of WI, La Crosse, WI 54601, (608) 785-8683, hours: 8 am-4:30 pm
Services: ED, CR, MR, PT, SE, WR, ST, RE
Staff: OR, CA, PO, PH, T, NU, TR, IN
@, R

Fitness Monitoring, Inc., Americana Resort, Hwy. 50, Lake Geneva, WI 53147, (414) 248-8099, hours: 8:30 am-4:30 pm
Services: ED, PR, SE, ST, RE
Staff: CA, PH, NU, IN
@ 2 weeks in advance

Sports Medicine Ctr., U. Hosp., U. of WI, 600 Highland Ave., Madison, WI 53201, (608) 263-1356

Mount Sinai Medical Ctr., 950 N. 12th St., Milwaukee, WI 53201, (414) 289-8134, hours: 7 am-4:30 pm
Services: ED, CR, MR, PR, PT, SE, WR, ST, BO, SU, RE
Staff: OR, CA, PH, PT, NU
@ 3-10 days in advance

FAT-CHOLESTEROL CHART

This chart from the American Heart Association Cookbook has information on the major sources of fat in the diet: dairy and related products; meat, poultry, fish, and related products; and fats and oils. The approximate fat content and cholesterol content of some foods are provided, along with the serving size and calories. Differences between the total fat in a food and the sum of the values listed for the fatty acids occur because some highly polyunsaturated, long-chain fatty acids were not included in the U.S. Department of Agriculture material from which this chart was developed.

Dairy Products and Related Products

	Serving Size	Total Fat (grams)	Saturated Fatty Acids (grams)	Monoun- saturated Fatty Acids (grams)	Polyun- saturated Fatty Acids (grams)	Cholesterol (milligrams)	Food Energy (calories)
MILK							
Fluid Whole	1 cup	9.0	5.0	3.0	trace	34	165
2% (nonfat milk solids added)	1 cup	5.0	3.0	2.0	trace	22	145
1%	1 cup	2.5	1.6	.8	trace	14	103
Skim	1 cup	trace	no data	no data	no data	5	90
Buttermilk (Skim)	1 cup	trace	no data	no data	no data	5	90
CHEESE							
American	1 oz.	9.0	5.0	3.0	trace	25	105
Blue or Roquefort	1 oz.	9.0	5.0	3.0	trace	24	105
Camembert	1⅓ oz.	9.0	5.0	3.0	trace	35	115
Cheddar	1 oz.	9.0	5.0	3.0	trace	28	115
Cottage—Creamed (4% fat)	1 cup	10.0	6.0	3.0	trace	48	260
Cottage—Uncreamed	1 cup	1.0	trace	trace	trace	13	170
Cream	1 tbsp.	6.0	3.0	2.0	trace	16	60
Feta	1 oz.	5.3	3.3	1.9	trace	16	84
Mozzarella (made from partially skimmed milk)	1 oz.	4.7	2.3	2.3	trace	18	70
Muenster	1 oz.	8.5	4.2	4.2	trace	25	105
Parmesan	1 tbsp.	1.8	1.0	.6	trace	5	26
Port du Salut	1 oz.	7.7	4.8	2.6	trace	23	105
Ricotta (part skim)	1 oz.	2.3	1.2	1.1	trace	9	50
Swiss	1 oz.	8.0	4.0	3.0	trace	28	105
Tilsit	1 oz.	7.6	4.7	2.6	trace	23	104
CREAM							
Light	1 tbsp.	3.0	2.0	1.0	trace	10	30
Heavy Whipping (unwhipped)	1 tbsp.	6.0	3.0	2.0	trace	20	55
Sour	1 tbsp.	2.0	1.0	1.0	trace	8	25
Imitation Cream products made with vegetable fat: Liquid	1 tbsp.	2.0	1.0	trace	0	0	20
Powdered	1 tbsp.	1.0	trace	trace	0	0	10
RELATED PRODUCTS							
Ice Milk	1 cup	7.0	4.0	2.0	trace	26	200
Ice Cream—Regular (approx. 10% fat)	1 cup	14.0	8.0	5.0	trace	53	255
Yogurt—Plain made from partially skimmed milk	1 cup	4.0	2.0	1.0	trace	17	125

Cooked Meat, Poultry, Fish and Related Products

	Size Serving	Total Fat (grams)	Saturated Fatty Acids (grams)	Monoun-saturated Fatty Acids (grams)	Polyun-saturated Fatty Acids (grams)	Cholesterol (milligrams)	Food Energy (calories)
Lean Beef, Lamb, Pork & Ham	3 oz.	8.4	3.9	3.5	trace	77	189
Lean Veal	3 oz.	4.8	2.4	2.3	trace	84	177
Poultry	3 oz.	5.1	1.5	2.6	1.0	74	150
Fish[1]	3 oz.	4.5	.9	no data	.3	63	126
SHELLFISH							
Crab	½ cup	2.0	.5	.7	.8	62	85
Clams	6 large	1.0	.3	.3	.4	36	65
Lobster	½ cup	1.0	no data	no data	no data	62	68
Oysters	3 oz. (6 oysters)	1.5	.5	.2	.8	45	53
Scallops	3 oz.	1.3	.4	.1	.8	45	90
Shrimp	½ cup (11 large)	1.0	.2	.3	.5	96	100
CANNED FISH							
Sardines canned in oil; drained solids	3¼ oz. (1 can)	3.0	no data	no data	no data	129	175
Salmon, pink canned[1]	3 oz.	5.0	2.0	1.0	trace	32	120
Tuna packed in oil; drained solids[1]	3 oz.	8.2	3.0	no data	2.0	65	197
RELATED PRODUCTS							
Liver (Beef)	3 oz.	3.4	no data	no data	no data	372	136
Sweetbreads, calf	3 oz.	1.8	no data	no data	no data	396	82
Frankfurters (all beef—30% fat)	8/lb.	17.0	7.1	6.7	trace	34	185
Eggs, chicken, whole	1 large	6.0	2.0	3.0	trace	250[2]	80

[1] Does not account for all of the highly polyunsaturated fatty acids present in fish.
[2] Cholesterol is found only in egg yolks.

Fats and Oils

	Size Serving	Total Fat (grams)	Saturated Fatty Acids (grams)	Monoun-saturated Fatty Acids (grams)	Polyun-saturated Fatty Acids (grams)	Cholesterol (milligrams)	Food Energy (calories)
Peanut Butter	2 tbsp.	16.0	3.2	8.0	4.5	0	190
Bacon, cooked crisp	2 slices	8.0	3.0	4.0	1.0	14	90
Bacon, Canadian (unheated)	3¾ oz.	14.4	5.0	6.0	1.0	75	216
Butter	1 tbsp.	12.0	6.0	4.0	trace	35	100
Lard	1 tbsp.	13.0	5.0	6.0	1.0	13	115
MARGARINES							
Safflower oil, liquid[1,2] STICK	1 tbsp.	11.2	1.5	2.5	6.7	0	100
Corn oil, liquid[1,2] STICK or TUB	1 tbsp.	11.2	2.0	3.6	5.3	0	100
Corn oil, liquid[1,2]	1 tbsp.	11.2	2.1	4.6	4.1	0	100
Partially hydrogenated or hardened fat[1,2]	1 tbsp.	11.2	2.4	6.2	2.0	0	100
Imitation Margarine (Diet)[2]	1 tbsp.	5.5	1.0	1.8	2.5	0	50
Mayonnaise	1 tbsp.	11.0	2.0	2.0	6.0	8	100
Vegetable Shortening (hydrogenated)	1 tbsp.	13.0	3.0	6.0	3.0	0	110
OILS							
POLYUNSATURATED							
Corn Oil	1 tbsp.	14.0	2.0	4.0	8.0	0	125
Cottonseed Oil	1 tbsp.	14.0	4.0	3.5	6.5	0	125
Safflower Oil	1 tbsp.	14.0	1.5	2.0	10.5	0	125
Sesame Oil	1 tbsp.	14.0	2.0	6.0	6.0	0	125
Soybean Oil	1 tbsp.	14.0	2.0	3.5	8.5	0	125
Soybean Oil (lightly hydrogenated)	1 tbsp.	14.0	2.0	7.0	4.8	0	125
Sunflower Oil	1 tbsp.	14.0	1.6	3.9	8.5	0	125
MONOUNSATURATED							
Olive Oil	1 tbsp.	14.0	2.8	7.0	3.9	0	125
Peanut Oil	1 tbsp.	14.0	2.0	10.0	2.0	0	125
SATURATED							
Coconut Oil	1 tbsp.	14.0	13.0	1.0	trace	0	125

[1] First ingredient is listed on label.   [2] Summary of available data. Composition of margarine changes periodically.

CALORIE EQUIVALENTS FOR POPULAR FOODS AND BEVERAGES

Food	Size/Serving	Approximate Calories
Alcohol		
gin, rum, vodka, whiskey		
80 proof	1 1/2 ounces	104
100 proof	1 1/2 ounces	133
Almonds	12 to 15 nuts	90
Apple	1 medium (2 1/2" diameter)	87
Apple juice	3/4 cup	87
Apricots	2 to 3 medium	51
Asparagus	5 or 6 spears	26
Avocado	1/2	185
Bagel, water or egg	1	165
Banana	1 small (6" long)	85
Beans (green, yellow or wax)	1 cup	32
Beans, lima	5/8 cup	111
Beans, red kidney	2/5 cup	118
Beef		
flank steak (lean only)	3 ounces	180
ground, lean	3 ounces	180
roast, lean	3 ounces	180
Beer	12 ounces	151
Blueberries	1 cup	87
Bologna	1 ounce slice	88
Bread		
rye	1 slice	56
white	1 slice	62
wholewheat	1 slice	56
Broccoli	1 stalk (5 1/2" long)	32
Brussels sprouts	9 medium	45
Butter		
sweet	1 tablespoon	108
whipped	1 tablespoon	81
Cabbage	3/5 cup, cooked	14
Cantaloupe	1/4 melon (5" diameter)	30
Carrots	1 large or 2 small	42
Cashews	6 to 8 nuts, roasted	84
Cauliflower	1 cup	27
Celery	1 small stalk (5" long)	3
Cereals		
bran flakes	1 cup	106
corn flakes	1 cup	110
shredded wheat	1 biscuit	89
Cheese		
American	1 ounce	107
Cheddar	1 ounce	112
cottage, uncreamed (1% fat)	1 cup	163

Calorie Equivalents (continued)

Food	Size/Serving	Approximate Calories
Cheese (continued)		
farmer	1 ounce	80
Mozzarella	1 ounce	79
Cherries		
red, sour	1/2 cup	58
sweet	15 large or 20 small	70
Chicken	3 ounces, broiled	180
Cod	4 ounces, broiled	162
Cola	12 ounces	129
Cola, sugar-free	12 ounces	2
Corn	1 medium ear	100
	1/2 cup	70
Crab	3 1/2 ounces, steamed	93
Crackers		
Graham	2 crackers	54
rye wafers	1	24
saltines with unsalted tops	2	26
wholewheat	2	32
Cucumber	1/2 medium	8
Doughnuts, plain	1 average	125
Egg	1 large	80
Flounder	3 1/2 ounces, raw	68
	3 1/2 ounces, baked with oil	202
Frankfurter	1 average	124
Grapefruit	1/2 medium (4″ diameter)	41
Grapefruit juice	2/5 cup	30
Haddock	3 1/2 ounces, broiled	141
Ham, boiled	1-ounce slice	66
Honeydew	1/4 small (5″ diameter)	33
Ice cream	1/2 cup	145
Ice milk	1/2 cup	111
Jams, jellies		
all varieties	1 tablespoon	55
low-calorie	1 tablespoon	29
Lamb	3 ounces, lean	190
Leeks	3 to 4 (5″ long)	52
Lemonade, frozen, from concentrate	1 cup	110
Lentils	2/3 cup, cooked	106
Lettuce	3 1/2 ounces	14
Macaroni and cheese, homemade	1 cup	430
Margarine		
unsalted	1 tablespoon	108
whipped	1 tablespoon	86
Mayonnaise	1 tablespoon	101

Calorie Equivalents (continued)

Food	Size/Serving	Approximate Calories
Milk		
skim	1 cup	89
whole	1 cup	150
Muffins		
blueberry	1 average	112
bran	1 average	104
corn	1 average	141
English	1 whole	138
wholewheat	1 average	103
Mushrooms	10 small or 4 large	28
Nectarines	2 medium	64
Noodles	1/2 cup, cooked	100
Oatmeal/rolled oats	1/2 cup, cooked	148
Oil		
corn	1 tablespoon	126
safflower	1 tablespoon	124
sunflower	1 tablespoon	124
Onions	1 (2 1/4″ diameter)	38
Orange	1 medium (3″ diameter)	73
Orange juice	2/5 cup	48
Peach	1 medium	38
Peanut butter	1 tablespoon	86
Pear	1/2 pear (3″ × 2″)	61
Peas	3/4 cup	84
Pepper, green	1 large shell	22
Pineapple	1/2 cup, diced	52
Plums, Damson	2 medium	66
Popcorn	1 cup, air popped (no oil)	30
Pork loin chop (lean only)	3 1/2 ounces, cooked	250
Potato		
baked	1 (2 1/2″ diameter)	95
	1 (3 1/4″ diameter)	139
fried from raw	1/2 cup	228
mashed with milk and margarine	1/2 cup	94
Raisins	1 tablespoon	29
Rice		
brown, raw	1/4 cup	176
brown, cooked	1 cup	178
white, raw	1/4 cup	178
white, cooked	1 cup	164
wild, raw	1/4 cup	99
wild, cooked	1 cup	220
Roll		
dinner, wholewheat	1 (2″ diameter)	90
hamburger	1 average	89

Calorie Equivalents (continued)

Food	Size/Serving	Approximate Calories
Salad dressing		
French	1 tablespoon	57
French, low-calorie	1 tablespoon	22
Italian	1 tablespoon	77
Italian, low-calorie	1 tablespoon	7
Sauerkraut	2/3 cup, drained	18
Shrimp	3 1/2 ounces	91
Soup		
minestrone	1 cup	115
tomato	1 cup	75
vegetable	1 cup	70
vegetable bean	1 cup	130
Spaghetti	1 cup, cooked	216
Spinach	1/2 cup, cooked	21
Squash, yellow	1 cup	15
Strawberries	1 cup	56
Sugar	1 teaspoon, level	16
Tangerine	1 large or 2 small	46
Tomato	1 large	44
Tomato juice	3/4 cup	34
Tuna		
in oil, drained solids	5/8 cup	197
in water, solids and liquids	1/2 cup	127
Turkey	3 1/2 ounces, roasted	190
Veal chop	3 ounces, broiled	210
Walnuts, English	8 to 15 halves	98
Watermelon	1 slice (6″ diameter × 1 1/2″)	156
Wine, table	3 1/2 ounces	85
Yogurt		
lowfat with nonfat milk solids	1 cup	143
lowfat, vanilla- and coffee-flavored with nonfat milk solids	1 cup	194
Zucchini	1 cup	15

AEROBICS INTERNATIONAL RESEARCH SOCIETY (AIRS)

In an effort to follow a large group of people for several years, correlating their physical activity with their state of health, the Aerobics International Research Society (AIRS) has been established. People from all over the world who are exercising regularly are encouraged to join this society so that the results of regular exercise can be more extensively and objectively evaluated. Members will receive a blank exercise log that they can fill out daily. AIRS will determine the number of points they earn each month, and that information will be stored in the AIRS data bank. Each member will receive a summary of his or her monthly activity for personal files, along with a research report and newsletter from the Aerobics Activity Center. In other words, AIRS can enable you to become a correspondent member of the Aerobics Activities Center. Periodically, you will be asked to complete a health questionnarie, so that the effect of your exercise program can be documented. If you are interested in becoming a member of AIRS (for which there is a nominal yearly fee), write to the Aerobics International Research Society, 12200 Preston Road, Dallas, Texas 75230, and more detailed information will be sent to you. I hope you will join, since it will be motivational for you and will provide our research institute with an invaluable source of data.

SELECTED REFERENCES

CHAPTER ONE

Cooper, K. H. *The Aerobics Way.* New York: M. Evans and Co., 1977, and Bantam Books, 1978.

CHAPTER TWO

Cooper, K. H. *Aerobics.* New York: M. Evans and Co., 1968, and Bantam Books, 1968.

Cooper, K. H., and Cooper, Mildred. *Aerobics for Women.* New York: M. Evans and Co., 1972, and Bantam Books, 1972.

Cooper, K. H. *The New Aerobics.* New York: M. Evans and Co., 1970, and Bantam Books, 1970.

Heart Facts. American Heart Association, Dallas, Texas, 1979.

Richmond, J. B. (Former Surgeon General, U.S. Public Health Service), Statement May 26, 1980, *Dallas Times Herald.*

Whitmer, R. W. *Whitmer's Guide To Total Wellness.* Garden City, N.Y.: Doubleday, 1982.

CHAPTER THREE

Armstrong, S.; Shahbaz, C.; and Singer, G. "Inclusion of meal-reversal in a behaviour modification program for obesity." *Appetite,* Vol. 2, 1981, 1–5.

Bassler, T. J. "Body build and mortality." Letter to the editor. *Journal of the American Medical Association,* Vol. 244, No. 13, 1980.

Blondhein, S. H.; Horne, T.; Kaufmann, N. A.; and Rozen, P. "Comparison of weight loss on low-calorie (800–1200) and very-low-calorie (300–600) diets." *International Journal of Obesity,* Vol. 5, 313–317, 1981.

Bogert, J.; Briggs, G. M.; and Calloway, D. H. *Nutrition and Physical Fitness.* Philadelphia, Pa.: W. B. Saunders.

Ca Bulletin, Vol. 32, No. 4, 1980.

Katahn, M. *The 200-Calorie Solution.* New York: W. W. Norton, 1982.

——*Exchange Lists for Meal Planning.* The American Diabetes Association, Inc., The American Dietetic Association, 1976.

"FDA asks for warning labels on weight control liquid protein." *Journal of the American Medical Association,* Vol. 238, No. 21, 1977.

Freiherr, G. "Pattern of body fat may predict occurrence of diabetes." *Research Resources Reporter,* Vol. 6, No. 1, 1982.

"Carbohydrate-loading may not just be for athletes." *New York Daily News,* March 22, 1982, p. 25.

Hittner, H. M., et al. "Retrolental fibroplasia: Efficacy of Vitamin E in a double-blind clinical study of preterm infants." *The New England Journal of Medicine,* Vol. 305, No. 23, 1981.

"Pritikin vs. AHA diet: No difference for peripheral vascular disease." *Journal of the American Medical Association,* Vol. 246, No. 17, 1981.

Lantigua, R. A., et al. "Cardiac arrhythmias associated with a liquid protein diet for the treatment of obesity." *Boston Medical and Surgical Journal,* Vol. 303, No. 13.

Metropolitan Life's Four Steps to Weight Control, Metropolitan Life Insurance Company, 1966.

Mirkin, G. B., and Shore, R. N. "The Beverly Hills Diet—Dangers of the newest weight loss fad." *Journal of the American Medical Association,* Vol. 246, No. 19, 1981.

Moore, M. "Carbohydrate loading: Eating through the wall." *The Physician and Sportsmedicine,* October, 1981.

Morris, A. "Carbohydrate loading." *The Physician and Sportsmedicine,* December, 1981.

"Nutritional practices in athletics abroad." *The Physician and Sportsmedicine,* January, 1977.

Nutrition and Your Health. Home and Garden Bulletin No. 232. Washington, D.C.: U.S. Department of Agriculture and the U.S. Department of Health and Human Services.

"Obesity may reduce survival, increase risk, in breast cancer." *Journal of the American Medical Association,* Vol. 244, No. 5, 1980.

Shake the Salt Habit. The American Heart Association, Dallas, Texas, 1981.

"At last, the ultimate diet: Total fasting (total foolishness)." *American Medical News,* January 19, 1982, 4.

CHAPTER FOUR

"An update on the cancer–cholesterol connection." *The HMS Health Letter,* October, 1981.

Blair, S. "Changes in coronary heart disease risk factors associated with increased physical fitness in 1546 men." Unpublished report, *The Institute for Aerobics Research,* Dallas, Texas, 1981.

Brown, M. S., and Goldstein, J. L. "Lowering plasma cholesterol by raising LDL receptors." *New England Journal of Medicine*, Vol. 305, No. 9, 1981.

Bruce, R. A. "Primary intervention against coronary atherosclerosis by exercise conditioning?" *New England Journal of Medicine*, Vol. 305, No. 25, 1981.

Ca—A Cancer Journal for Clinicians, Vol. 25, No. 1, 1975. (The American Cancer Society)

"Cholesterol link to cancer is emerging from studies on way to avert coronaries." *The Wall Street Journal*, October 14, 1980.

Cooper, K. H., et al. "Levels of physical fitness versus selected coronary risk factors: A cross-sectional study." *Journal of the American Medical Association*, Vol. 236, No. 2, 1976, 166–169.

Council on Scientific Affairs. "Physician-supervised exercise programs in rehabilitation of patients with coronary heart disease." *Journal of the American Medical Association*, Vol. 245, No. 14, 1981.

"Diet, cholesterol and heart disease." *New England Journal of Medicine*, Vol. 304, No. 19, 1981.

Dehn, M. M., and Mullins, C. B. "Physiologic effects and importance of exercise in patients with coronary artery disease." *Cardiovascular Medicine*, April, 1977.

Falko, J. M.; O'Dorisio, T. M.; and Cataland, S. "Improvement of high-density lipoprotein–cholesterol levels." *Journal of the American Medical Association*, Vol. 247, No. 1, 1982.

Fletcher, G. F. "Exercise and coronary risk factor modification in the management of atherosclerosis." *Heart and Lung*, Vol. 10, No. 5, 1981.

Gotto, A. M., Jr., and Wittels, E. H. "What's new: Arguments for and against the treatment of hyperlipidemia." *Texas Medicine*, Vol. 76, 1980, 38–40.

Hartung, G. H., et al. "Relation of diet to high-density-lipoprotein cholesterol in middle-aged marathon runners, joggers, and inactive men." *New England Journal of Medicine*, Vol. 302, 1980.

"High-density lipoprotein." *The Lancet*, February 28, 1981.

Hjermann, I., et al. "Effect of diet and smoking intervention on the incidence of coronary heart disease." *The Lancet*, December 12, 1981. (The Oslo Study)

Hooper, P. L., et al. "Terbutaline raises high-density-lipoprotein levels." *New England Journal of Medicine*, Vol. 305, No. 24, 1981.

"How bad is cholesterol?" *Newsweek*, June 9, 1980.

Hulley, S. B., et al. "Epidemiology as a guide to clinical decisions: The association between triglyceride and coronary heart disease." *New England Journal of Medicine*, Vol. 302, 1980.

Jones, R. J. "Prevention of coronary heart disease." *Journal of the American Medical Association*, Vol. 245, No. 18, 1981.

Kane, J. P., et al. "Normalization of low-density lipoprotein levels in heterozygous familial hypercholesterolemia with a combined drug regimen." *New England Journal of Medicine*, Vol. 304, 1981, 251–258.

King, W. H.; Brawley, W. L.; and Wick, R. L. "High density lipoprotein (HDL) findings in young airline pilots." American Airlines Medical Department. Paper presented at the 29th International Congress of Aviation and Space Medicine, Nancy, France, September 7, 1981.

Kramsch, D. M., et al. "Reduction of coronary atherosclerosis by moderate conditioning exercise in monkeys on an atherogenic diet." *New England Journal of Medicine*, Vol. 305, No. 25, 1981.

Levy, R. I. "Cholesterol headline criticized." *American Medical News*, July 31, 1981.

Lowenfels, A. B. "Serum cholesterol and colon cancer." *Journal of the American Medical Association*, Vol. 246, No. 3, 1981.

"Low-fat diet, cancer linked." *American Medical News*, May 29, 1981.

Mabuchi, H., et al. "Effects of an inhibitor of 3-hydroxy-3-methylglutaryl coenzyme a-reductase on serum lipoproteins and ubiquinone-10 levels in patients with familial hypercholesterolemia." *New England Journal of Medicine*, Vol. 305, No. 9, 1981.

McBride, G. "A remarkable medicine raises HDL levels." *Journal of the American Medical Association*, Vol. 241, No. 12, 1982, 1686–1687.

Ostrander, L. D., and Lamphiear, D. E. "Coronary risk factors in a community." *Circulation*, Vol. 53, No. 1, 1976.

Peterson, B.; Trell, E.; and Sternby, N. H. "Low cholesterol level as risk factor for noncoronary death in middle-aged men." *Journal of the American Medical Association*, Vol. 245, No. 20, 1981.

Petitti, D. B.; Friedman, G. D.; and Klatsky, A. L. "Association of a history of gallbladder disease with a reduced concentration of high-density-lipoprotein cholesterol." *New England Journal of Medicine*, Vol. 304, No. 23, 1981.

"Regression of atherosclerosis: Preliminary but encouraging news." *Journal of the American Medical Association*, Vol. 246, No. 20, 1981.

Sacks, F. M., et al. "Effect of ingestion of meat on plasma cholesterol of vegetarians." *Journal of the American Medical Association*, Vol. 246, No. 6, 1981.

Shekelle, R. B., et al. "Diet, serum cholesterol, and death from coronary heart disease." *New England Journal of Medicine*, Vol. 304, No. 2, 1981.

Shephard, R. J.; Corey, P.; and Kavanagh, T. "Exercise compliance and the prevention of a recurrence of myocardial infarction." *Medicine and Science in Sports and Exercise*, Vol. 13, No. 1, 1981.

Spodick, D. H. "Normalization of low-density lipoproteins in familial hypercholesterolemia." *New England Journal of Medicine*, Vol. 304, No. 22, 1981.

Storer, T. W., and Ruhling, R. O. "Essential hypertension and exercise." *The Physician and Sportsmedicine*, Vol. 9, No. 6, 1981.

Streja, D., and Mymin, D. "Moderate exercise and high-density lipoprotein cholesterol." *Journal of the American Medical Association*, 1979, 1290–1292.

Traub, Y. M.; McDonald, R. H., Jr.; and Shapiro, A. P. "Attitudes of physicians concerning controversial issues in hypertension." *Archives of Internal Medicine*, Vol. 141, No. 5, 1981.

Ueshima, H., et al. "High density lipoprotein-cholesterol levels in Japan." *Journal of the American Medical Association*, Vol. 274, No. 14, 1982, 1985–1987.

Uhl, G. S., et al. "The relationship between high density lipoprotein cholesterol and coronary artery disease in asymptomatic men." United States Air Force School of Aerospace Medicine, Brooks Air Force Base, Texas.

Verheugt, F. W. A., et al. "Vasectomy and cholesterol." *New England Journal of Medicine*, August 20, 1981.

Vodak, P. A., et al. "HDL-cholesterol and other plasma lipid and lipoprotein concentrations in middle-aged male and female tennis players." *Metabolism*, Vol. 29, 1980 (as seen in *The Physician and Sportsmedicine*, Vol. 9, No. 6, 1981).

"Very low cholesterol may cause cancer." *Journal of the American Medical Association*, January 15, 1981 (as seen in *Medical Self-Care*, Winter, 1981).

Williams, R. R., et al. "Cancer incidence by levels of cholesterol." *Journal of the American Medical Association*, Vol. 245, No. 3, 1981.

Williams, R. S., et al. "Physical conditioning augments the fibrinolytic response to venous occlusion in healthy adults." *New England Journal of Medicine*, 1980, Vol. 302, 987–991.

"Women and exercise." *The New York Times*, November 10, 1981, C2.

CHAPTER FIVE

"C-ing a way to health." *New York Daily News*, November 4, 1981.

"Diets to reduce the risk of cancer—Report of the National Academy of Sciences' two-year study." *Boston Globe*, June 17, 1982.

Florencio, C. A.; Ramos, A.; and Castillo, C. "Effects of iron and Vitamin C supplementation on hemoglobin level and work efficiency." *Abstract Book, The Third Asian Congress of Nutrition*, Jakarta, October 6, 1980, 173–174.

Howald, H., and Segesser, B. "Ascorbic acid and athletic performance." *Roche Information Service*, Pharmaceutical Industries Department.

"The high-fiber diet: Its effect on the bowel." *The Medical Letter*, Vol. 17, No. 23, 1975.

King, J. "Eat more fiber." *Medical Self-Care*, Winter, 1981.

"Nutrition update—New research on vitamin E." *Environmental Nutrition*, Vol. 5, No. 6, 1982.

Gunby, P. "Research on vitamin–cancer relationship getting big boost." *Journal of the American Medical Association*, Vol. 247, No. 13, 1982.

Roberts, H. J. "Perspective on Vitamin E as therapy." *Journal of the American Medical Association*, Vol. 246, No. 2, 1981.

Rosenberg, L., et al. "Selected birth defects in relation to caffeine-containing beverages." *Journal of the American Medical Association*, Vol. 247, No. 10, 1982.

Vitamin Facts. National Dairy Council, 1979.

CHAPTER SIX

Apple, F. "Presence of creatine kinase MB isoenzyme during marathon training." *New England Journal of Medicine*, Vol. 305, No. 13, 1981.

Evenson, L. "Exercise advised for oral contraceptive users." Brief report, *The Physician and Sportsmedicine*. Vol. 10, No. 3, 1982.

Frisch, R. E., et al. "Delayed menarche and amenorrhea of college athletes in relation to age of onset of training." *Journal of the American Medical Association*, Vol. 246, No. 14, 1981.

Hartung, G. H., et al. "Relation of diet to high-density lipoprotein cholesterol in middle-aged marathon runners, joggers and inactive men." *New England Journal of Medicine*, Vol. 302, 1980, 357–361.

"Jogging safe after childbirth." *American Medical News*, December 4, 1981.

Kannel, W. B., et al. "The value of measuring vital capacity for prognosis purposes." *Transactions* of the Association of Life Insurance Medical Directors, Vol. 64, 1980, 66–81.

Killinger, R. Personal letters to Kenneth H. Cooper, M.D.

"Menstrual changes in athletes." *The Physician and Sportsmedicine*, Vol. 9, No. 11, 1981.

O'Herlihy, M. R. "Jogging and suppression of ovulation." Letter to the editor, *New England Journal of Medicine*, 1982.

Pedersen, O.; Beck-Neilsen, H.; and Heding, L. "Increased insulin receptors after exercise in patients with insulin-dependent diabetes mellitus." *New England Journal of Medicine*, Vol. 302, 1980.

Rebar, R. W., and Cumming, D. C. "Reproductive function in women athletes." *Journal of the American Medical Association*, Vol. 246, No. 14, 1981.

Siegel, A. J.; Silverman, L. M.; and Holman, B. L. "Elevated creatine kinase MB isoenzyme levels in marathon runners." *Journal of the American Medical Association*, Vol. 246, No. 18, 1981.

Smith, E. L., Jr.; Reddan, W.; and Smith, P. E. "Physical activity and calcium modalities for bone mineral increase in aged women." *Medicine and Science in Sports and Exercise*, Vol. 13, No. 1, 1981.

"The type-A personality." *Cardiac Alert*, Vol. 3, No. 11, 1981.

Williams, P. T., et al. "The effects of running mileage and duration on plasma lipoprotein levels." *Journal of the American Medical Association*, Vol. 247, 1982, 2674–2679.

Williams, R. S., et al. "Physical conditioning augments the fibrinolytic response to venous occlusion in healthy adults," *New England Journal of Medicine*, Vol. 302, 1980, 987–991.

CHAPTER SEVEN

Aldridge, N. B., et al. "Carotid palpation, coronary heart disease and exercise rehabilitation." *Medicine and Science Sports and Exercise*, Vol. 13, 1981, 608.

"America shapes up." *Time*, November 2, 1981, 94.

Bassler, T. J. "Body build and mortality." *Journal of the American Medical Association*, Vol. 244, No. 13, 1980.

Beaulieu, J. E. "Developing a stretching program." *The Physician and Sportsmedicine*, Vol. 9, No. 11, 1981.

Bhattacharya, A., et al. "Body acceleration distribution and oxygen uptake in humans during running and jumping." *Journal of Applied Physiology*, Vol. 49, No. 5, 1980.

Burfoot, A. "The pulse rate game." *Runner's World*, July, 1981.

Cooper, K. H., et al. "Age-fitness adjusted maximal heart rates," *Medicine in Sport*, Vol. 10, 1977, 78–88. (Basel: Karger) (PMHR = 205 − 1/2 age)

Eames, C., et al. "Results of a required fitness program." *The Physician and Sportsmedicine*, Vol. 9, No. 12, 1981.

Foster, C. "Physiological requirements of aerobic dancing." *Research Quarterly*, Vol. 46, 1975, 120–122.

Gallup, G. "56% of teens include jogging in daily exercise." *The Associated Press*, April, 1979.

Gallup, G. "Half of Americans now exercise daily." *The Gallup Poll*, October 6, 1977.

Gettman, L. R.; Ward, P.; and Hagan, R. D. "A comparison of combined running and weight training with circuit weight training." Institute for Aerobics Research, Dallas, Texas. *Medicine and Science in Sports and Exercise*, Vol. 14, No. 3, 1982, 229–234.

Gettman, L. R., and Pollock, M. L. "Circuit weight training: A critical review of its physiological benefits." *The Physician and Sportsmedicine*, Vol. 9, No. 1, 1981.

Gibbons, L. W., et al. "The acute cardiac risk of strenuous exercise." *Journal of the American Medical Association*, Vol. 244, No. 16, 1980.

Hagan, D. "Inverse relationship between 1.5 mile run time and Texas tennis rankings." Unpublished report. Institute for Aerobics Research, Dallas, Texas, 1982.

Hage, P. "Exercise value 'oversold,' cardiac researcher says." *The Physician and Sportsmedicine*, Vol. 9, No. 7, 1981.

Hart, S., and Patton, R. W. "Cardiovascular training effects of aerobic dance instruction among college age females." *TAHPER Journal*, Spring issue, 1977, 8–9, 34–35.

Igbanugo, V., and Gutin, B. "The energy cost of aerobic dancing." *Research Quarterly*, Vol. 49, 1978, 308–316.

"Jogging is as beneficial to heart as marathon running." *Internal Medicine News*, Vol. 11, No. 14, 1978.

Katch, V. L.; Villanacci, J. F.; and Sady, S. P. "Energy cost of rebound-running." *Research Quarterly for Exercise and Sport*, Vol. 52, No. 2, 1981.

Kattus, A. A. "Exercise conditioning of cardiovascular system—Effects on cardiac patients." Presented June 25, 1966, American Heart Association Meeting, Seattle, Washington.

Legwold, G. "Study says tennis is more than good strokes." *The Physician and Sportsmedicine*, Vol. 9, No. 11, 1981.

Lester, M., et al. "The effect of age and athletic training on maximal heart rate during muscular exercise." *American Heart Journal*, Vol. 76, 1968, 370. (PMHR = 205 − 0.44 [age])

Montgomery, D. L.; Malcolm, V.; and McDonnell, E. "A comparison of the intensity of play in squash and running." *The Physician and Sportsmedicine*, Vol. 9, No. 4, 1981.

Murase, Y., et al. "Longitudinal study of aerobic power in superior junior athletes." *Medicine and Science in Sports and Exercise*, Vol. 13, No. 3, 1981.

Powers, S. K., and Walker, R. "Physiological and anatomical characteristics of outstanding female junior tennis players." *Research Quarterly Exercise Sport*, Vol. 53, 1982, 172–175.

Rockefeller, K. A., and Burke, E. J. "Psycho-physiological analysis of an aerobic dance programme for women." *British Journal Sports Medicine*, Vol. 13, 1979, 77–80.

Selner, A. J., et al. "Roller skating provides good aerobic exercise." (Abstract) *The Physician and Sportsmedicine*, Vol. 9, No. 4, 1981.

Siegel, A. J. "Burn carbohydrates, not hydrocarbons." *The Physician and Sportsmedicine*, Vol. 9, No. 11, 1981.

Sobey, E. "Aerobic weight training." *Runner's World*, August, 1981.

Town, G. P., et al. "The effect of rope skipping on energy expenditures of males and females." *Medicine and Science in Sports and Exercise*, Vol. 12, 1980, 295–298.

Vaccaro, P.; Morris, A. F.; and Clarke, D. H. "Physiological characteristics of masters female distance runners." *The Physician and Sportsmedicine*, Vol. 9, No. 7, 1981.

Weber, H., "The energy cost of aerobic dancing." *Medicine Science Sports*, Vol. 5, 1973, 65–66.

CHAPTER NINE

Aspy, D. N., and Roebuck, F. N. *A Lever Long Enough*. Dallas, Tex.: The National Consortium for Humanizing Education, 1976.

Balanoff, T. "Fire fighters mortality report." International Association of Fire Fighters (1750 New York Avenue, N.W., Washington, D.C. 20006).

Berk, L. S., et al. "Beta-endorphin response to exercise gradation in athletes and non-athletes." Paper presented at Annual Meeting, American College Sports Medicine, Miami Beach, Fla., May 29, 1981.

Bortz, W. M., II, et al. "Catecholamines, dopamine, and endorphin levels during extreme exercise." *New England Journal of Medicine*, Vol. 305, No. 8, 1981.

Carr, D. B., et al. "Physical conditioning facilitates the exercise-induced secretion of beta-endorphin and beta lipoprotein in women." *New England Journal of Medicine*, Vol. 305, No. 10, 1981.

Chernick, V. "Endorphins and ventilatory control." *New England Journal of Medicine*, Vol. 304, No. 20, 1981.

"Endorphins and exercise." *TWA Ambassador*, May, 1979.

"Endorphins through the eye of a needle." *The Lancet*, February 28, 1981.

"Exercise and the endogenous opioids." *New England Journal of Medicine*, Vol. 305, No. 26, 1981.

Fuenning, S. I., et al. *Physical Fitness and Mental Health*, University of Nebraska Foundation, 1981.

Gibbons, L.; Cooper, K. H.; Martin, R. P.; and Pollock, M. L. "Medical examination and electrocardiographic characteristics of elite distance runners." *Annals of the New York Academy of Science*, Vol. 301, 1977, 283–296.

Graboys, T. B. "Celtics Fever: Playoff-induced ventricular arrhythmia." Letter to the editor, *New England Journal of Medicine*, August 20, 1981.

Hartung, H., and Furge. "Personality traits in middle-aged runners and joggers." Baylor College of Medicine, 1977.

Ismail, A. H., and Trachtman, L. E. "Jogging the imagination," *Psychology Today*, March 1973, 79–82.

"Men's hearts failing them for fear . . ." Luke 21:26, Holy Bible (King James Version).

Milesis, C. A., et al. "Effects of different duration of physical training on cardiorespiratory functions, body composition and serum lipids." *Research Quarterly*, Vol. 47, 1976, 716–725.

Moore, M. "Endorphins and exercise: A puzzling relationship." *The Physician and Sportsmedicine*, Vol. 10, No. 2, 1982.

"Nineteen-mile run with fractured leg," *Boston Globe*, April 22, 1982.

"Physical exercise stimulates marked concomitant release of β-endorphin and adrenocorticotrophic hormone (ACTH) in peripheral blood in man." *Experenta 36*, 1980, Basel: Bukhauser Verlag.

"Play 20 questions—Some early-warning signs of burnout." *American Medical News*, July 31, 1981.

Santiago, T. V., et al. "Endorphins and the control of breathing." *New England Journal of Medicine*, Vol. 304, No. 20, 1981.

Stress. Blue Cross Association, Chicago, 1974.

"Two studies trace role of stress in heart disease." *Journal of the American Medical Association,* Vol. 232, No. 7, 1975, 696–700.

CHAPTER TEN

Governor's Commission on Physical Fitness, Austin, Texas.

CHAPTER ELEVEN

"Americans spent $1 in every $10 for health in '80." *United Press International,* October 3, 1980.

". . . as business attacks benefits hikes." *AMA News,* November 28, 1980.

Bjurstrom, L. A., and Alexiou, N. G. "A program of heart disease intervention for public employees." *Journal of Occupational Medicine,* Vol. 20, No. 8, 1978.

Boone, D. W., et al. "Physical fitness programs for industry: Extravagance or wise investment?" Unpublished report, Prudential Insurance Company, Southwestern Home Office, Houston, Texas.

Caldwell, F. "Business invests in employee fitness." *The Physician and Sportsmedicine,* December, 1976.

Cannon, J. G., and Kluger, M. J. "Jogging aid in fighting bacteria." Newspaper synopsis of paper presented at American Societies for Experimental Biology Meeting, New Orleans, April, 1982.

Cardiovascular Primer for the Workplace, NIH Publication No. 81–2210, January, 1981. Washington, D.C.: U.S. Department of Health and Human Services, Public Health Service, National Institutes of Health.

"Checklist for establishing a company wellness plan." *Business Insurance,* September 21, 1981.

"Cost of Canadian absenteeism '10 times greater than strikes.' " *The Vancouver Sun,* October 15, 1980.

Dedmon, R. E., et al. "An industry health management program." *The Physician and Sportsmedicine,* Vol. 7, No. 11, 1979.

Education Employee Fitness, Institute for Aerobics Research, February, 1981.

"Executive fitness: Russian-style." *Executive Fitness,* Vol. 11, No. 12, 1980. (Rodale Press)

Fielding, J. E. "Preventive medicine and the bottom line." *Journal of Occupational Medicine,* Vol. 21, No. 2, 1979.

President's Council on Physical Fitness and Sports. *Fitness in the Workplace.*

"Hospitals enter the 'wellness' business." *AMA News,* June 20, 1980.

"Hospitals join the wellness movement." *Medical Self-Care,* Summer, 1981.

Jennings, C., and Tager, M. J. "Good health is good business." *Medical Self-Care,* Summer, 1981.

LeRoux, M. "Cashing in on wellness." *Business Insurance,* September 21, 1981.

LeRoux, M. "Interest growing in wellness plans." *Business Insurance,* September 21, 1981.

"Ounce of prevention is worth a pound of cure, or so say proponents of the 'wellness' movement." *The Wall Street Journal,* September 15, 1981.

Parkinson, R. S., et al. *Managing Health Promotion in the Workplace.* Palo Alto, Calif.: Mayfield Publishing, 1982.

Peepre, M. "The Canadian employee fitness and lifestyle project." *Athletic Purchasing and Facilities,* December, 1980.

Thomas, D. L. "The high cost of getting well." *Focus,* January 7, 1981.

Tuhy, C. "The new stay-well centers." *Money,* December, 1981.

CHAPTER TWELVE

Anderson, D. E. "Predisposition to breast cancer reviewed." *Newsletter,* The University of Texas System Cancer Center, M.D. Anderson Hospital and Tumor Institute, Vol. 25, No. 2, 1980.

"Annual Pap smears." *American Medical News,* December 26, 1980/January 2, 1981.

"Benign breast lumps may regress with change in diet." *Journal of the American Medical Association,* Vol. 241, No. 12, 1979.

Bolsen, B. "More aggressive treatment urged for patients with prostate cancer." *Journal of the American Medical Association,* Vol. 246, No. 16, 1981.

Bonner, P. "A dental view of stress." *Sky,* June, 1981.

Beahrs, et al. "Irradiation to the head and neck area and thyroid cancer." *Journal of the American Medical Association,* Vol. 244, No. 4, 1980.

Bruce, R. A. "Noninvasive clinical and exercise predictors of sudden cardiac death in men with coronary artery disease." *Texas Medicine,* Vol. 77, 1981.

Delehanty, H. J. "How to keep your teeth." *Medical Self-Care,* Winter, 1981.

Fleshler, B., and Achkar, E. "An aggressive approach to the medical management of peptic ulcer disease." *Archives of Internal Medicine,* Vol. 141, 1981.

Gilbertsen, V. A. "Proctosigmoidoscopy and polypectomy in reducing the incidence of rectal cancer." *Cancer,* Vol. 34, 1974, 936–939.

"High breast cancer rate found in women who took drug to prevent miscarriages." *Los Angeles Times*, December 13, 1977.

Journal of the American Medical Association, Vol. 246, No. 17, 1981, 1873.

Kopens, D. B., et al. "Palpable breast masses: The importance of preoperative mammography." *Journal of the American Medical Association*, Vol. 246, No. 24, 1981.

"Locating malignant polyps." *Journal of the American Medical Association*, Vol. 246, No. 1, 1981.

Margolis, J. R., et al. "Treadmill exercise capacity: Its diagnostic, prognostic and therapeutic implications in the context of coronary artery disease." Paper presented to North Carolina Heart Association, May 27, 1976.

"Mortality for the five leading cancer sites for females by age—1971." *Ca—A Cancer Journal for Clinicians*, Vol. 25, 1975, 2–21. (American Cancer Society)

Podrid, P. J.; Graboys, T. B.; and Lown, B. "Prognosis of medically treated patients with coronary-artery disease with profound ST-segment depression during exercise testing." *New England Journal of Medicine*, Vol. 305, No. 19, 1981.

Pollock, M. L., et al. "A comparative analysis of four protocols for maximal stress testing." *American Heart Journal*, Vol. 92, No. 1, 1976.

Turnbull, K. "Consumer's guide to breast cancer screening." *Medical Self-Care*, Winter, 1981.

Uhl, G. S., et al. "The relationship between high density lipoprotein cholesterol and coronary artery disease in asymptomatic men." United States Air Force School of Aerospace Medicine, Brooks Air Force Base, Texas.

"United States passes annual physical." *American Medical News*, December 26, 1980/January 2, 1981.

"Woman wins $500,000 suit for DES use." *AMA News*, July 27, 1979.

CHAPTER THIRTEEN

"Are spontaneous abortions, tobacco linked?" *Journal of the American Medical Association*, Vol. 239, No. 26, 1978.

"Beta blockers after myocardial infarction." *The Medical Letter*, Vol. 24, No. 608, 1982.

Blair, S., et al. "Associations between coronary risk factors and physical fitness in 3687 adult women." Unpublished report, The Institute for Aerobics Research, Dallas, Texas, 1981.

Blair, S., et al. "Changes in coronary heart disease risk factors associated with increased physical fitness." Unpublished report, The Institute for Aerobics Research, Dallas, Texas.

"Born to drink?" *The Lancet*, January 6, 1979.

"Bypass surgery is often unnecessary, says a Harvard survey of heart patients." *The Wall Street Journal*, November 5, 1981.

Christen, A. G. "The case against smokeless tobacco: Five facts for the health professional to consider." *Journal of the American Dental Association*, Vol. 101, 1980.

Christen, A. G., and Cooper, K. H. *Strategic Withdrawal from Cigarette Smoking*, American Cancer Society, Inc., 1979.

"Cigarette ad outlays up sharply in decade." *AMA News*, September 18, 1981.

"Cigarettes, coronary occlusions, and myocardial infarction." *Journal of the American Medical Association*, Vol. 246, No. 8, 1981.

"Coronary-artery bypass surgery." *Journal of the American Medical Association*, Vol. 246, No. 15, 1981.

"Coronary-artery bypass surgery: Scientific and clinical aspects." *New England Journal of Medicine*, Vol. 304, No. 11, 1981.

"Coronary bypass controversies remain." *AMA News*, December 26, 1980/January 2, 1981.

"Current cardiovascular mortality." *Journal of the American Medical Association*, Vol. 245, No. 6, 1981.

Eckardt, M. J., et al. "Health hazards associated with alcohol consumption." *Journal of the American Medical Association*, Vol. 246, No. 6, 1981.

"Even adequate food intake fails to offset alcohol abuse." *Journal of the American Medical Association*, Vol. 238, No. 21, 1977.

"Fewer women smoke—study." *American Medical News*, May 22, 1981.

Foote, E. "Advertising and tobacco." *Journal of the American Medical Association*, Vol. 245, No. 16, 1981.

Friedman, G. D., et al. "Mortality in cigarette smokers and quitters." *New England Journal of Medicine*, Vol. 304, No. 23, 1981.

Gambrell, R. D., Jr., et al. "Estrogen therapy and breast cancer in postmenopausal women." *Journal of the American Geriatrics Society*, Vol. 28, No. 6, 1980.

Goldman, A. L., et al. "Oral progesterone therapy—oxygen in a pill." *Archives of Internal Medicine*, Vol. 141, 1981.

Hartz, A. J., et al. "Smoking, coronary artery occlusion and nonfatal myocardial infarction." *Journal of the American Medical Association*, Vol. 246, No. 8, 1981.

"Heart attack fatality rates vary worldwide." *American Medical News*, December 5, 1980.

"Heart disease campaign by physicians is urged." *American Medical News*, March 20, 1981.

"Heart-smoking link supported." *American Medical News*, August 21/28, 1981.

Kannel, W. G. "Meaning of the downward trend in cardiovascular mortality." *Journal of the American Medical Association*, Vol. 247, No. 6, 1982, 877–880.

Kozlowski, L. T. "Smokers, non-smokers, and low-tar smoke." *The Lancet*, February 28, 1981.

"Liver ailments—Part 1: Cirrhosis." *The HMS Health Letter*, Vol. 6, No. 3, 1981.

Moore, G. W., and Hutchins, G. M. "Coronary artery bypass grafts in 109 autopsied patients." *Journal of the American Medical Association*, Vol. 246, No. 16, 1981.

"New alcoholism warning issued." *AMA News*, February 6, 1981.

Newell, G. R., and Boutwell, W. B. "Potential for cancer prevention." *The Cancer Bulletin*, Vol. 33, No. 2, 1981.

Noonan, G. "Passive smoking in enclosed public places." *Medical Journal of Australia*, Vol. 2, 1976.

Norris, E. "Risk factors reveal truth about health." *Business Insurance*, September 21, 1981.

"Oral contraceptives and the risk of myocardial infarction." *New England Journal of Medicine*, Vol. 305, No. 25, 1981.

Papoz, L., et al. "Alcohol consumption in a healthy population." *Journal of the American Medical Association*, Vol. 245, No. 17, 1981.

"The 'pill' receives mixed reviews in latest report of Walnut Creek study." *Journal of the American Medical Association*, Vol. 246, No. 10, 1981.

"Pregnant women and alcohol." *AMA News*, 1981.

Rahimtoola, S. H., et al. "Changes in coronary bypass surgery leading to improved survival." *Journal of the American Medical Association*, Vol. 246, No. 17, 1981.

"The risk factor update project." Centers for Disease Control, Public Health Service, U.S. Department of Health and Human Services, Atlanta, Ga., May, 1981.

Ross, R. K., et al. "A case-control study of menopausal estrogen therapy and breast cancer." *Journal of the American Medical Association*, Vol. 243, No. 16, 1980.

Slone, D., et al. "Risk of myocardial infarction in relation to current and discontinued use of oral contraceptives." *New England Journal of Medicine*, Vol. 305, No. 8, 1981.

Smoking: Facts You Should Know. American Medical Association, Chicago, 1971.

Stadel, B. V. "Oral contraceptives and cardiovascular disease (Part One)." *New England Journal of Medicine*, Vol. 305, No. 11, 1981.

Stadel, B. V. "Oral contraceptives and cardiovascular disease (Part One and Part Two)." *New England Journal of Medicine*, Vol. 305, No. 11 and No. 12, 1981.

Unless you decide to quit, your problem isn't going to be smoking; your problem's going to be staying alive. Washington, D.C.: U.S. Government Printing Office, 1972.

White, J. R., and Froeb, H. F. "Small-airways dysfunction in nonsmokers chronically exposed to tobacco smoke." *New England Journal of Medicine*, Vol. 302, 1980.

INDEX